Delaying the Dream

MAKING THE MODERN SOUTH

David Goldfield, Series Editor

KEITH M. FINLEY

Delaying the Dream

Southern Senators and the
Fight against Civil Rights,
1938–1965

Louisiana State University Press ✠ Baton Rouge

Published by Louisiana State University Press
Copyright © 2008 by Louisiana State University Press
All rights reserved
Manufactured in the United States of America
Louisiana Paperback Edition, 2010

DESIGNER: Barbara Neely Bourgoyne
TYPEFACE: Modern No. 20, display; Whitman, text

Library of Congress Cataloging-in-Publication Data

Finley, Keith M., 1973–
  Delaying the dream : southern senators and the fight against civil rights, 1938–1965 /
Keith M. Finley.
    p. cm. — (Making the modern South)
  Includes bibliographical references and index.
  ISBN 978-0-8071-3345-3 (cloth : alk. paper) 1. Civil rights movements—United States—
History—20th century. 2. African Americans—Civil rights—History—20th century. 3. United
States—Congress—Senate—History—20th century. 4. Legislators—United States—History—
20th century. 5. Legislators—Southern States—History—20th century. 6. United States—
Race relations—Political aspects—History—20th century. 7. Southern States—Race relations—
Political aspects—History—20th century. I. Title.
  E185.61.F485 2008
  323.1196'073—dc22

                                                                                    2008002564
  ISBN 978-0-8071-3711-6 (paper : alk. paper)

The paper in this book meets the guidelines for permanence and durability of the Committee
on Production Guidelines for Book Longevity of the Council on Library Resources. ♾

For my parents

Contents

Acknowledgments

LIKE ANY AUTHOR, I am indebted to many individuals who either directly or indirectly offered assistance at various points in the development of this project. Archivists and librarians across the American South and beyond have made my sojourns at their institutions both productive and enjoyable. Where would we historians be without them?

Several scholars have freely given of their time to assess this manuscript. Thanks to them, this is a much better book. William Cooper, Charles Royster, Charles Shindo, and Wayne Parent all read and commented on its contents. Gaines Foster worked with me on all phases of this project's development and selflessly gave of his time to ensure that I produced the best possible book that I could. All history students would be fortunate to have a mentor like him. Samuel C. Hyde, Jr., has provided guidance at every stage of my professional development from my days as a Master's student to the present. He remains a good friend and a trusted advisor.

The great folks at LSU Press, especially Rand Dotson, have made work on this project a thorough enjoyment. Their commitment to their authors is exemplary.

To my family who have anxiously anticipated this book's publication, I hope you find it worth the wait. Your contributions to its completion are immeasurable.

Last and certainly not least, I would like to thank my best friend and soon-to-be-wife Jessica and her boys, Joseph and Joshua, for helping me discover that there are a few things in life more important than history. Thank you for that and for everything else.

Delaying the Dream

Introduction

MOST HISTORICAL ASSESSMENTS of America's civil rights struggle focus on either the fight by the African American community or the leaders who directed the political coalition that championed black legal and political equality. Many approach the civil rights movement from the top down by studying figures such as Martin Luther King Jr. and Lyndon Johnson, both considered central actors in the civil rights drama. Other historians focus on the movement from the bottom up, often by replicating the theoretical foundation of slave studies with their emphasis on community consciousness. Still others explore specific facets of the struggle, such as particular events or places, judicial and legal developments, presidential policies, or civil rights organizations. Despite an enormous amount of literature devoted to civil rights, only a limited number of works analyze white opposition in significant detail. Several historians have addressed the subject at the regional level, and a handful of scholars have explored the topic in specific monographs, such as biographies of southern politicians. These studies demonstrate the value of examining the white southern perspective of the civil rights struggle, just as they point to the need for still further research. In a recent essay, Charles Eagles noted that civil rights historiography tended toward an "asymmetrical" emphasis on the advocates of black equality. Greater attention to the interests that championed segregation, he argues, would provide a more complete picture of America's civil rights movement.[1]

1. See Note on Sources. Charles W. Eagles, "Toward New Histories of the Civil Rights Era," *Journal of Southern History* 66 (November 2000): 815–848.

In depicting the heroic struggle for black equality, historians and journalists often emphasize episodes that illustrate a central theme in many of their narratives—the ferocity of white opposition. Evidence of southern extremism, of course, is not hard to find. From the "Ole Miss" riots to the depredations of Eugene "Bull" Conner's Birmingham police force, violent episodes in the Jim Crow South frequently occurred. Studies of these events reveal much about the region, especially the oppression faced by African Americans. However, caricaturing white opposition solely in terms of its most egregious actions obfuscates less dramatic but arguably more important facets of the southern fight. Few historical events lend themselves to such a sharp delineation between right and wrong as does the civil rights struggle. Moral righteousness clearly rested with those arrayed against Jim Crow. The self-evident justness of the civil rights crusade, however, should not blind the historian to his or her obligation to understand all actors and sides in a social confrontation. This study does not seek to downplay the excesses of the white South; they remain an integral part of the story. It explores gradations in white opposition by examining how the region's principal national spokesmen—its U.S. senators—addressed themselves to the civil rights question and how their rhetoric and legislative tactics exhibited characteristics that both mirrored and differed from those of the region's more incendiary leaders.[2]

A relatively small number of historians and journalists have explored the fight for civil rights in the U.S. Senate in great depth. Robert Mann's study of the legislative push for black equality in the Senate from 1949 to 1965, *The Walls of Jericho,* has received considerable praise for its careful treatment of the three major figures in the struggle—Richard Russell, Hubert Humphrey, and Lyndon Johnson—in addition to other significant participants in the nation's twentieth-century debate over civil rights. It remains an important work in the field. Mann sought to capture the high drama of the legislative struggle for racial equality by exploring the interaction of that fight's key players with one another, with colleagues, and with the rules governing the U.S. Senate. In pursuit of this objective, his astute observations regarding the legislative process proved pathbreaking when written and ring true today. *The Walls of Jericho* offers a synopsis of the major principles that informed southern resistance to civil rights on the national level. This work explores

2. See Note on Sources for a sampling of the literature that tends to define all white southerners by the actions of the region's most intransigent leaders.

those principles in greater detail to offer deeper insight into the forces guiding southern resistance. The time frame of Mann's study, although suitable for the biographical approach he employs, tends to downplay the significance of the pivotal years before 1948, when southerners in Washington began formulating the strategy and the rhetoric they would employ for the remainder of the civil rights fight. By time Johnson, Humphrey, and Russell crossed paths, the pattern of southern resistance, in terms of both strategy and rhetoric, had already taken shape. Outwardly, resistance efforts altered in the 1950s and 1960s, but these changes all stemmed from a conceptualization of the civil rights fight as one that would increasingly go against the South that appeared in the 1930s and 1940s.[3]

Many scholars paint a stagnant portrait of southern resistance in which there existed no ideology behind the defense of Jim Crow. Instances that disprove this preconception are often dismissed as a veneer concealing racial prejudice. A more detailed analysis of the Senate's Dixie bloc reveals that its members conducted a multifaceted rearguard battle that ultimately postponed the achievement of black legal and political equality until the 1960s. Long before the emergence of the grass-roots protest movement that toppled Jim Crow, southern senators recognized that the forces advocating social equality would grow until de jure segregation fell. This perception did not emerge in the wake of the 1954 *Brown v. Board of Education* decision or even in the face of growing black protest as illustrated by the Baton Rouge

3. Several biographies of southern senators exist, including Thomas A. Becnel, *Senator Allen Ellender of Louisiana: A Biography* (Baton Rouge: Louisiana State University Press, 1995); Nadine Cohodas, *Strom Thurmond and the Politics of Southern Change* (New York: Simon and Schuster, 1993); Gilbert C. Fite, *Richard B. Russell, Jr., Senator from Georgia* (Chapel Hill: University of North Carolina Press, 1996); Virginia Van der Veer Hamilton, *Lister Hill: Statesman from the South* (Chapel Hill: University of North Carolina Press, 1987); Ronald L. Heinemann, *Harry Byrd of Virginia* (Charlottesville: University Press of Virginia, 1996); and Robert Mann, *Legacy to Power: Senator Russell Long of Louisiana* (New York: Paragon House, 1992). For some of the works that address the legislative fight in Washington, see Note on Sources; Robert Caro, *The Years of Lyndon Johnson: Master of the Senate* (New York: Knopf, 2002); John A. Goldsmith, *Colleagues: Richard B. Russell and His Apprentice Lyndon B. Johnson* (Washington, D.C.: Seven Locks Press, 1993); Robert D. Loevy, ed., *The Civil Rights Act of 1964: The Passage of the Law that Ended Racial Segregation* (Albany: State University of New York Press, 1997); Whalen and Whalen, *The Longest Debate: A Legislative History of the 1964 Civil Rights Act* (Cabin John, Md.: Seven Locks Press, 1985); and Robert Mann, *The Walls of Jericho: Lyndon Johnson, Hubert Humphrey, Richard Russell, and the Struggle for Civil Rights* (New York: Harcourt Brace, 1996).

and Montgomery Bus Boycotts in the 1950s, but much earlier during the presidency of Franklin D. Roosevelt. Seeking to lessen the pressure against them, they altered both their strategy and the nature of their arguments with an eye on convincing their Senate colleagues, and white Americans in general, that the legislators from Dixie were not mere obstructionists but defenders of constitutional principles. As many have chronicled, the Rules of the Senate played a central role in southern resistance efforts. Nonetheless, southern senators could not have blocked significant civil rights advances without the support of their northern colleagues. Southerners successfully courted nonsouthern senators for decades by nationalizing their defense of sectional interests. In order to understand why the nation took so long to enact black legal and political equality, one must first understand the nature of southern opposition in the U.S. Senate. This work explores the broad tactical and ideological considerations upon which all southern caucus members agreed as well as the ways individual senators chose, within the context of this consensus, to define their opposition to civil rights.

The U.S. Senate served as the preeminent legislative battleground in the southern fight to preserve Jim Crow. Throughout the twentieth century, bills designed to protect the rights of black Americans routinely passed in the House of Representatives only to meet defeat or emasculation in the Senate. Southern senators themselves acknowledged the primacy of their role in defending segregation, labeling the upper house the place "where the battle would be won or lost." Institutional factors unique to the Senate, in part, accounted for the longevity of the civil rights fight. Senate Rules permitted almost unlimited debate, a fact that enabled a relatively small number of individuals to prevent action on legislation objectionable to them by filibustering. Seniority also figured prominently in thwarting civil rights advances. Representing one-party states, southern senators faced little opposition on election day and thus could expect, barring personal indiscretions, lengthy tenures in office. As a result, they controlled many of the Senate's standing committees, granting them considerable influence over much of the legislation discussed in the chamber. Southern senators routinely traded favors on policy issues of little relevance to their region in exchange for support on the all important civil rights question. Southern senators, in effect, transformed the chamber into a citadel of their interests, and from its ramparts they obstructed substantive civil rights advances for decades. Throughout the civil rights battle, they knew that support for black equality outside the South remained anything but solid and that they, within limits, could stall the formation of a broad legislative coalition capable of destroying "the southern way of life."

In the late New Deal era, southern senators better organized their ranks owing to the emergence of a bipartisan consensus supporting antilynching legislation. Never before in the twentieth century had they faced such pressure aimed at changing an aspect of the southern racial order. The emerging crisis transformed the once loosely knit legislative group into the southern caucus, or what Illinois Democrat Paul Douglas called the "battalion of death" for its success in thwarting substantive civil rights advances. During debate over the Wagner–Van Nuys antilynching bill in 1938, southern senators outlined a framework from which they conceptualized the battle against civil rights through the 1960s. Foremost, they believed that politicians above the Mason-Dixon line supported civil rights solely for political gain. Southern senators argued that northern politicians with a large number of African American constituents attempted to curry favor with black voters, who held the balance of power in statewide elections, by advocating legislation supported by the minority group. To remain in office, these northern statesmen had to satisfy the demands of their pivotal black electorates or risk losing their next election.[4]

4. Paul H. Douglas, *In the Fullness of Time: The Memoirs of Paul H. Douglas* (New York: Harcourt Brace Jovanovich, 1971), 217 ("battalion of death"). A major debate in civil rights historiography centers on defining when the civil rights movement began. Some historians label the New Deal as the foundation of the civil rights crusade. See Anthony J. Badger, *Prosperity Road: The New Deal, Tobacco, and North Carolina* (Chapel Hill: University of North Carolina Press, 1980); Adam Fairclough, *Race and Democracy: The Civil Rights Struggle in Louisiana, 1915–1972* (Athens: University of Georgia Press, 1995); John B. Kirby, *Black Americans in the Roosevelt Era: Liberalism and Race* (Knoxville: University of Tennessee Press, 1980); Robert J. Norrell, *Reaping the Whirlwind: The Civil Rights Movement in Tuskegee* (Chapel Hill: University of North Carolina Press, 1998); Doug McAdam, *Political Process and the Development of Black Insurgency, 1930–1970* (Chicago: University of Chicago Press, 1982); Harvard Sitkoff, *A New Deal for Blacks: The Emergence of Civil Rights as a National Issue* (New York: Oxford University Press, 1978); Nancy Weiss, *Farewell to the Party of Lincoln: Black Politics in the Age of FDR* (Princeton, N.J.: Princeton University Press, 1983); and Raymond Wolters, *Negroes and the Great Depression: The Problem of Economic Recovery* (Westport, Conn.: Greenwood Press, 1970). Others consider World War II as the catalyst for the civil rights movement. See John M. Blum, *V was for Victory: Politics and American Culture During World War II* (New York: Harcourt Brace Jovanovich, 1976); Richard M. Dalfiume, "The 'Forgotten Years' of the Negro Revolution," *Journal of American*

Not surprising, southern senators also held northern black communities in low regard. According to caucus participants, blacks voted in blocs at the urging of a handful of African American activists. Southerners considered the National Association for the Advancement of Colored People (NAACP), the nation's preeminent civil rights organization in the 1930s, the chief formulator of black opinion in the North. Like any lobbying group, the NAACP, southerners believed, would have to continually broaden its agenda or risk legislating itself into obsolescence. Southern senators looked beyond the limited antilynching agenda advocated by the NAACP in the 1930s and believed that if a bill to curb lynching passed, the organization would demand further concessions until one day it would request an end of segregation. And if the NAACP broadened its legislative wish list, then the black community that it controlled would pressure its elected officials into supporting the new objectives. Northern politicians, in turn, would champion all of their constituents' future requests, if for no other reason then to ensure that they remained in office. Based on this outlook, it comes as no surprise that southern senators considered the limited antilynching crusade of the 1930s as the initial act in a play that might culminate in the demise of Jim Crow. A similar perception informed the southern view of all subsequent civil rights pressure groups. Despite their grim outlook, caucus members held out hope that they could arrest the expansion of civil rights activism.

In the 1930s, southern senators believed that by defeating bills that threatened only the periphery of the Jim Crow edifice, such as antilynching legislation, they could halt a broadening of the civil rights agenda by preventing the formation of an "opening wedge" through which more sweeping

History 55 (June 1968): 90–106; Lee Finkle, "The Conservative Aims of Militant Rhetoric: Black Protest During World War II," *Journal of American History* 60 (December 1973): 692–713; and Merl E. Reed, *Seedtime for the Modern Civil Rights Movement: The President's Committee on Fair Employment Practice, 1941–1946* (Baton Rouge: Louisiana State University Press, 1991). Still others consider the period following the Supreme Court's *Brown v. Board* ruling as the origins of the civil rights movement. See Rhoda L. Blumberg, *Civil Rights: The 1960s Freedom Struggle* (Boston: Twayne, 1984); Taylor Branch, *Parting the Waters: America in the King Years, 1954–1963* (New York: Simon and Schuster, 1988); John A. Salmond, *"My Mind Set on Freedom": A History of the Civil Rights Movement, 1954–1968* (Chicago: Ivan R. Dee, 1997); Juan Williams, *Eyes on the Prize: America's Civil Rights Years, 1954–1965* (New York: Viking Press, 1987); and Raymond Wolters, *The Burden of Brown: Thirty Years of School Desegregation* (Knoxville: University of Tennessee Press, 1984).

proposals would flow. Despite stopping the antilynching crusade, they discovered in the 1940s that the forces championing civil rights did not view legislative setbacks as a suitable reason to limit their demands. During World War II, southern senators faced bills that transcended the scope of antilynching legislation. In spite of their earlier successes, caucus participants discovered that the drive against Jim Crow had already begun. From that point forward, they realized that defeat represented the only possible outcome of their resistance. No matter how many legislative victories they secured, they steadily lost confidence in their ability to hold the line. Their long-term tactical objective thus shifted from preventing to postponing the assault against segregation. To accomplish that, they adopted a strategy that centered on strategic delay. Under it, they took a holistic view of the legislative situation that required them to adjust their former exclusive reliance on the filibuster.

In formulating their opposition to civil rights from the 1940s forward, southern senators assessed several factors, including the type of legislation they confronted, the level of public support for a particular measure, the president's commitment to it, and, most important, the sentiments of their Senate colleagues. Taking all of these factors into consideration, the caucus allowed northern opinion to guide its opposition. On some occasions, southern senators permitted bills only loosely connected to the hegemonic white power structure in the South to come to a vote without a filibuster. Such legislation invariably passed in the absence of southern obstructions. Other times, they weakened more substantive bills through amendments and then allowed a vote. When limited support for a measure existed, caucus members returned to the filibuster. The approach they adopted depended largely on what they felt Americans outside of Dixie would accept. Regardless of strategy, southern forces assiduously courted those beyond the Mason-Dixon line. They believed, quite rightly as it turned out, that by appearing as something other than total obstructionists they could win the goodwill of northern senators. Southern senators hoped their efforts to sway their colleagues would pay dividends when broader civil rights proposals reached the chamber. All caucus actions thus had the singular objective of extending the life of Jim Crow by recruiting northern assistance in the southern drive to stymie substantive civil rights advances.

The adoption of more flexible tactics coincided with alterations in how southerners addressed the civil rights question. An analysis of southern rhetoric provides valuable insight into changes in the region's defense of Jim Crow over time. Southern senators, who represented statewide constituencies, often reflected and, at times, influenced mainstream segregationist thought in their respective states. In many ways, southern senators served as the South's primary spokesmen as well as its principal philosophers. They, more so than the region's House delegation, who represented smaller electorates, spoke for the white southern majority and, because of rules governing unlimited debate, had the opportunity to enunciate fully the racial policy belief that allegedly necessitated Jim Crow. Although southern demagogues, such as George Wallace and Orval Faubus, receive the most scholarly attention, they were far less effective in safeguarding segregation and far less indicative of the thinking of most white southerners than were Dixie's senators. Southern senators operated in a world in which the passions that often inflamed politics on the state level were best left muted. Distilling and shaping the southern defense of segregation in a manner that reflected the desires of their constituents without alienating their Washington colleagues represented their most important service to the white South. They spoke for the silent southern majority who did not participate in violence, but who nonetheless believed in the sanctity of Jim Crow. By understanding what the region's senators argued, it therefore becomes possible to discern the relationship of white southerners in general to segregation. Just as all southerners did not partake in racial violence, so too did they not necessarily view the racial etiquette of the region in the same way. How these differing conceptions of the issue found expression in southern rhetoric on the Senate floor is a major focus of this work.

Before the late 1930s, Jim Crow required little validation because it faced few serious challenges. At that time, southern senators routinely depicted blacks as inferiors with none of the attributes thought essential for success in American society. Southern senators considered African Americans child-like in their mental abilities but savage in an alleged innate predisposition to violence. As the civil rights movement strengthened, southern senators changed their rhetoric. Caucus members could no longer rely on racial stereotypes as their primary validation for segregation. With interest in civil rights increasing, they focused their energies on convincing those they believed not hopelessly beholden to black voting blocs, especially Republicans and western Democrats, that the Constitution, if not morality, rested with southerners. Alterations in how Washington statesmen defended segregation coincided with a similar move throughout the South to construct a unified, although not always logical, segregationist ideology that represented the distillation of preexisting legal, social, and cultural arguments defending racial separation. Overt racist appeals thus dwindled as the caucus redirected its attention to strengthening its basis for opposing civil rights legislation.

Continued northern acceptance of the South's constitutional arguments hinged on the ability of Dixie's senators to keep legal concerns at the forefront of their public fight. Caucus members had two objectives when fashioning their rhetoric. First, they knew that excessive race baiting would alienate northern public opinion and thus impede their ability to prolong the life of Jim Crow. Fierce denunciations of African Americans could only weaken the southern contention that more than mere racism informed their opposition to civil rights. Second, they recognized that their constituents expected at least a rudimentary airing of the prevailing white southern attitude regarding the necessity of Jim Crow. For consumption on the home front, they touted the beneficence of segregation, all the while appealing to a storyline that all southerners knew. Seminal episodes in the region's history such as Reconstruction and the Civil War were routinely mentioned in their arguments, but they received far less attention than one would expect. Indeed, the mythology of the Old South did not necessarily aid individuals formulating arguments in support of a new and different mythology, a mythology based not on chattel slavery but on the constitutionality of de jure segregation. Although race informed both myths, the latter's defenders worked within the political system and thus could not dwell indefinitely on matters of race or region. Caucus members balanced their rhetoric between placating constituents and winning over nonsoutherners with the latter objective given first priority. At the same time, they realized that many northerners shared the same racial sensitivities found below the Mason-Dixon line. Southern senators thus played to northern prejudices, especially the fear of amalgamation, without bitterly denouncing the black race. Long before George Wallace and Richard Nixon tapped into American prejudices through the use of racial euphemisms in their presidential campaigns, southern senators had employed code words and phrases that touched on race-centered themes, but that remained vague enough to allow northern statesmen the freedom to adopt the caucus' arguments with little fear that they too would be considered racists.

Many northern politicians might have privately agreed with the prejudices that dictated southern opposition; however, they would unlikely make race a cornerstone of their own validation for voting against civil rights.

Southern senators rarely wanted for explanations of why others should oppose "anti-South" legislation. Most caucus participants focused their attacks on how individual civil rights bills threatened the entire American political system. To appeal to chamber moderates and conservatives, they deliberately depicted their fight as one in which they defended state and individual autonomy against a ravenous federal government bent on centralizing power in Washington. Southern senators thus transformed their defense of Jim Crow from a fight to safeguard an antiquated regional custom into a larger battle to stem the erosion of local authority and individual liberty. The American Revolution took on great significance during the civil rights debates, eclipsing both the Civil War and the Reconstruction era in its manifold usage. Inheritors of a classical republican ideology, southern senators, like the founding fathers, viewed politics as fraught with intrigue. At its heart, strategic delay was built upon a conspiracy view that saw concentrations of power, either in the form of special interest activism or in the designs of the federal government, as geared toward stripping southern states of their political autonomy. Rather than emphasize the racial issue at the heart of the civil rights debate, they routinely depicted their opposition in lofty terms as a defense of constitutional principles as wrought by the founders. Not surprisingly, many northerners found arguments urging the limitation of federal power convincing. By trying to expand their opposition into a national, rather than a sectional, battle, southern senators hoped to obfuscate the true issue at stake in the debate—the inherent inequality and repression of the system of white supremacy that they championed. Southerners, of course, made every effort to steer Senate discussion away from what would surely have been a less convincing defense of the Jim Crow system as it existed on the ground. Keeping the scope of civil rights debate limited to arcane legal arguments and the constitutional shortfalls of a particular measure, along with skillful employment of the rules safeguarding minorities embedded in Senate precedent, enabled caucus members to prevent the passage of substantive civil rights legislation for thirty years.

Despite major alterations in how they critiqued civil rights proposals, southern speeches continued to reassure constituents of their fealty to regional interests in their presentation of segregation and white supremacy. When southern senators addressed segregation directly, more often than not they focused on the alleged racial tranquility created by Jim Crow. Caucus members argued, frequently in spite of significant evidence to the contrary, that all southerners preferred to live under segregation. Blacks and whites were comfortable under its code of etiquette and desired its maintenance because both had access to the same social, economic, and political opportunities. Whites, according to southern senators, did not transgress the rights of blacks, and the latter, with a few exceptions, found little to fault with the system. When evidence of black unrest emerged, southerners sought an external cause. Outsiders, who varied in southern lexicon from northern agitators to communist fellow travelers, inspired African American protests in an effort to destroy the organic laws of the region. No racial problem existed below the Mason-Dixon line, southerners contended, and none should be sought. In the eyes of southern senators, the South should remain segregated because the Jim Crow system represented the only viable mechanism for producing social harmony in a region with a biracial population. Southern senators, of course, believed in the legality and justness of the racial institutions that they defended. They did not address shortfalls in the system because, for the most part, they did not believe that any shortfalls existed. Blind to the inadequacies of segregation and convinced of the constitutionality of their "way of life," white southerners found the status quo worth preserving. Many northerners, in turn, unwittingly became tacit conspirators in prolonging Jim Crow by accepting southern claims of the region's racial tranquility.

Southern senators, of course, could never completely divorce the question of racial distinctions from their critique of "anti-South" legislation. At some point in most civil rights debates, it became necessary for them to explain why segregation existed in the first place. Contrary to many historical treatments of the subject that reduce southern racial views to a monolith, Dixie's Senate delegation varied considerably in how its members addressed segregation. All caucus participants, at least publically, agreed that blacks and whites preferred living apart and that segregation was a deeply rooted cultural tradition best left undisturbed. Individual southern senators, however, employed different portions of the segregationist ideology to validate Jim Crow. In general, the caucus divided into two camps. The majority of its participants stressed the "many, many" perceived differences between the races that they believed necessitated a race-based social order. Within this group, there existed an array of explanations for Jim Crow that ranged from fears of black violence to claims that God willed racial separation. Few senators remained wedded to any one explanation, and many of them fluctuated between several throughout their careers. On the other hand, a much smaller number of southern senators downplayed racial distinctions by focusing their attention more specifically on cultural concerns. Using this approach, caucus moderates stressed the longstanding southern tradition of segregation that emerged after years of trial and error experimentation. In some form, racial separation had always influenced life below the Mason-Dixon line and was thus a cultural norm in the hearts and minds of all southerners. Change might occur in the region, they noted, but if it did, it should only come slowly over time at the urging of southerners themselves. From their perspective, if northerners wanted to help southern blacks, they should work to eradicate the discriminatory economic policies practiced by northern financiers and ensure that the South received its fair share of federal funding. Economic advances in the region, in turn, would assist all southerners regardless of race. Although they often privately criticized white violence, the members of the more moderate wing of the caucus nonetheless worked in concert with the group's hardliners for the duration of the civil rights fight. Unanimous consent governed caucus actions, and southern racial moderates went lock-step into battle with the extremists. Rather than challenge the excesses of Jim Crow that they privately lamented, racial moderates stayed silent, fearing the possibility of a white backlash against them.

In a larger sense, all caucus members, regardless of rhetoric, failed to provide the South with the moderate leadership they so effectively employed in Washington to sway their Senate colleagues. These same legislators, who skillfully stewarded segregation through many legislative challenges, neither encouraged their constituents to turn against the sway of the demagogue nor urged them to refrain from violence as the protest movement expanded. Southern senators ultimately suffered from self-imposed restraints. Ever mindful of federal incursions against state autonomy, they, as Washington officials, felt uneasy about meddling in politics below the Mason-Dixon line. State affairs were largely left to state officials, who only answered to like-minded white southerners and thus had less concern for national opinion. Without a countervailing force, local politics veered toward extremism, a fact that undermined the resistance of the region's national statesmen, who could only succeed by courting nonsoutherners. By allowing more radical state politicians, who suffered few consequences for their actions due to mass black disfranchisement, to dictate the situation on the ground, Dixie's Senate delegation ultimately hastened the type of federal intervention it had long sought to postpone.

Southern senators profoundly influenced the course of the civil rights struggle in America. Early in the twentieth-century battle for social equality, they settled on a policy of delay that had as its principal objective slowing what they perceived as an inexorable drive to destroy segregation. Their ability to stall civil rights advances in the U.S. Senate from the 1930s through the 1960s occurred because of their flexible tactics, along with their adoption of more edifying arguments in defense of segregation. The caucus could never have succeeded without the support of northern politicians, who utilized the constitutional arguments of southerners to validate their own lack of interest in Dixie's black citizens. In an article on the fight against antilynching legislation from 1920 to 1940, George Rable observed that southerners were caught completely off guard by the intensity of black protest in the 1950s and 1960s. Rable overlooked the significance of the growing acceptance of strategic delay as an ordering mechanism for the southern fight in Washington. Irrational fears played no part in the construction of strategic delay as attested to by later civil rights developments that demonstrated the sound foundation on which southern senators staked their fight. They foresaw growing pressure against the region all along. These statesmen, however, misjudged the impact of legislative foot dragging on the nonviolent resistance movement. By preventing substantive civil rights advances through strategic delay and by failing to challenge the demagogues on the local level, southern senators unintentionally provided a catalyst for grass-roots activism. Once it became evident that Washington politicians would not act on civil rights legislation, black activists took the drive for social equality into the streets across the South. After a series of nonviolent protests culminated in violent white responses, northern legislators could no longer accept southern claims of the racial tranquility created by Jim Crow. Not until the extreme and widely reported turmoil surrounding the Birmingham civil rights protests in 1963 did many northern senators begin to seriously challenge the mythological portrait of the South described by southern senators. With southern prejudices exposed, the claims of the region's senators lost much of their credibility, and with that the South lost segregation. The southern caucus had engaged in a successful rearguard battle for decades, but it could not outlast the impact of the grass-roots protest movement that its skillful delaying tactics helped to produce.[5]

When the 1964 Civil Rights Act, which largely destroyed de jure segregation, and the 1965 Voting Rights Act, which undermined the South's discriminatory voter registration laws, passed, most southern senators had spent the previous fifteen years informing their constituents about the growing likelihood of defeat in the civil rights fight. Their lamentations regarding the worsening political situation tapped directly into the memory of the Lost Cause. The end result of the Confederate effort proved to be defeat, and under the doctrine of strategic delay, the same end, caucus members alerted their constituents, would again likely befall the region. After their failure, southern senators and their electorates in general could claim that they had fought a principled battle that they lost only through force of numbers. With the legislative conflict decided, the region began the process of adapting. The ideas that undergirded strategic delay softened the defeat, helping to ensure that southerners did not take the same drastic actions as their forefathers did a century before. Despite their earlier failure to provide the region with moderate leadership, southern senators, to their credit, played a pivotal role in ensuring that the end of Jim Crow did not culminate in widespread racial turmoil. The moderation that had long guided their actions in Washington finally found expression on the state level as caucus members urged their constituents to accept the collapse of Jim Crow without violence. If they had played as prominent a role in the 1950s and early 1960s as they did after segregation fell, they would have undoubtedly lessened the severity of the white response to threats against segregation.

5. George C. Rable, "The South and the Politics of Anti-Lynching Legislation, 1920–1940," *Journal of Southern History* 51 (May 1985): 220.

1. Opening Pandora's Box

ON 13 APRIL 1937, African American defendants "Bootjack" McDaniels and Roosevelt Townes entered a not guilty plea for the murder of white grocer, George Windham. Following the arraignment of the two detainees at the Winona County, Mississippi, courthouse that afternoon, a mob abducted them in plain view of their police escort and drove them to the nearby town of Duck Hill. In a wooded lot, nearly five hundred spectators watched as the abductors fastened McDaniels and Townes to adjacent trees. One member of the mob, burnishing a lit blow torch, demanded a confession from McDaniels. After repeated applications of the flame to his legs and torso, McDaniels admitted his role in the crime and fingered Townes as his accomplice. Satisfied with the confession, members of the mob shot McDaniels before turning their attention to the other captive. Townes too initially denied his involvement, only to announce his guilt after suffering repeated burns from the blow torch. An even worse fate met Townes as the lynchers kindled a fire at his feet, burning him alive. The gruesome murder witnessed by hundreds of Mississippians, none of whom made an effort to stop the carnage, received national media attention. Despite witnessing the initial abduction in broad day light, the police officers charged with guarding the black defendants claimed not to have recognized a single member of the mob. Without a suspect, the lynching at Duck Hill went unsolved and unpunished. For many, the miscarriage of justice in Mississippi underscored the necessity of federal legislation aimed at curtailing this heinous crime. Duck Hill became a powerful propaganda tool in the decades-long fight for antilynching legislation.[1]

1. *Time,* 26 April 1937, 16–17. The *Newsweek* account of the lynching erroneously reverses events, placing the death of Townes before that of McDaniels. *Newsweek,* 24 April 1937, 12;

Following World War I, the number of lynchings rose significantly after two decades of steady decline. According to Tuskegee Institute statistics, eighty-three lynchings occurred in 1919, up from sixty-four in 1918 and the record low of thirty-eight in 1917. In 1922, Republican congressman Leonidas C. Dyer of Missouri responded to the increase by introducing legislation that would make lynching a federal crime. His bill contained punishment clauses that covered both the participants in the murder and the local law enforcement officials responsible for protecting the victims. A final section of the measure made counties in which a lynching took place culpable for indemnity payments of up to ten thousand dollars to a victim's family. Partisan divisions marked legislative action on the Dyer bill. With President Warren G. Harding endorsing the legislation, Republican members of the House of Representatives rallied behind it. By comparison, the Democratic response proved cool. A near-straight party-line vote led to the 231 to 119 passage of the Dyer proposal, an event that witnessed only eight Democrats supporting the antilynching measure. Stiff southern opposition to the bill in the U.S. Senate led to its abandonment after twenty-one days of debate.[2]

Awakened to the politicization of lynching that accompanied the Dyer bill, southern states increased their efforts to prevent the crime. Immediate results met this offensive. Whereas fifty-one lynchings occurred in 1922, only seven took place in 1929. During the Great Depression, the number of lynchings again rose, reaching a peak of twenty-four in 1933. Renewed pressure in the 1930s for a federal antilynching law resulted, prompting Democratic senators Robert F. Wagner of New York and Edward P. Costigan of Colorado to introduce new legislation. Their proposal reduced the Dyer bill's definition of a lynch mob from five individuals to three but maintained the punishment clause for law enforcement officials and the indemnity clause for counties in which the crime occurred. Costigan and Wagner further narrowed the scope of their bill by not providing for punitive action against the actual partici-

Philip Dray, *At the Hands of Persons Unknown: The Lynching of Black America* (New York: Random House, 2002), 359–360.

2. All lynching statistics from Monroe N. Work, ed., *Negro Year Book: An Annual Encyclopedia of the Negro, 1937–1938* (Tuskegee, Ala.: Negro Yearbook, 1937), 156. For the House vote on the Dyer bill, see *Congressional Record* (hereafter cited as *CR*), 67th Cong., 2nd sess., 26 January 1922, 1795–1796. For background, see Franklin L. Burdette, *Filibustering in the Senate* (Princeton, N.J.: Princeton University Press, 1940), 133–137.

pants in a lynching. In 1935, debate on the Costigan-Wagner bill began and ended in the U.S. Senate. As in 1922, a handful of southern senators brought legislative action to a halt through a series of lengthy speeches that hinted at a much larger filibuster to come. After a week of debate, the chamber abandoned the measure. Despite the southern success, an important political development emerged from the 1935 fight. Unlike the straight party-line battle over the Dyer bill, the Costigan-Wagner proposal enjoyed greater bipartisan support. For many southerners, the fact that two prominent Democrats led the crusade for a federal antilynching law meant a substantive change had occurred in the civil rights fight. Long the bastion of white supremacy, the national Democratic Party appeared on the verge of abandoning the interests of its southern wing.[3]

Certain northern politicians gravitated toward the antilynching campaign in response to demands from segments of the coalition of groups that formed the foundation of the New Deal consensus. Farmers, urban workers, and ethnic minorities, sometimes neglected by the Republican administrations of the 1920s, found their interests supported by Franklin D. Roosevelt and the overwhelming Democratic majority in both houses of Congress. Attempting to capitalize on the changing allegiance of the electorate, many northern statesmen sought to keep interest groups that benefitted from New Deal programs in the Democratic column. African Americans were one segment of the population that gained an increased voice in the 1930s, albeit more at the urging of Eleanor Roosevelt than the president. Eleanor often served as the administration's moral compass, urging the president and his advisors to equitably handle the dispensation of New Deal programming so that black communities were not overlooked. She invited African Americans to the White House just as she championed their causes, like antilynching, at a

3. Burdette, *Filibustering in the Senate*, 179–181; Jacquelyn Dowd Hall, *Revolt Against Chivalry: Jessie Daniel Ames and the Women's Campaign Against Lynching* (New York: Columbia University Press, 1979); J. Joseph Huthmacher, *Senator Robert F. Wagner and the Rise of Urban Liberalism* (Cambridge: Harvard University Press, 1968); Rable, "South and the Politics of Anti-Lynching Legislation," 201–220; George B. Tindall, *The Emergence of the New South, 1913–1945*, vol. 10 of *A History of the South* (Baton Rouge: Louisiana State University Press, 1967), 550–555; Joel Williamson, "Wounds Not Scars: Lynching the National Conscience and the American Historian," *Journal of American History* 83 (March 1997): 1221–1253; Zangrando, *The NAACP Crusade Against Lynching, 1909–1950* (Philadelphia: Temple University Press, 1980).

time when her husband opted for expediency and the nation for indifference. For Franklin Roosevelt, politics remained the art of the possible. Pushing civil rights programs would precipitate the withdrawal of southern support for his other programs. Without that support, legislation that would benefit all Americans regardless of race would remain unpassed. Furthermore, beginning during World War I, thousands of black Americans began leaving the South in search of greater opportunity. Although many communities did not welcome the migrants, participants in the black diaspora enjoyed greater freedom in the North than afforded to them in the land of Jim Crow. Looser suffrage requirements beyond Dixie's borders also granted many blacks a political voice they had not possessed below the Mason-Dixon line. Since the majority of the migrants settled in urban centers, they magnified their political clout by forming powerful voting blocs. Northern politicians recognized that in part their continued electoral success required winning the confidence of these newly established black communities. Championing civil rights legislation became the principal mechanism for capturing the allegiance of black voters—or at least that was how some southern politicians began perceiving the situation thanks in part to the propaganda of a particular civil rights pressure group.[4]

A major catalyst for this shift in southern thinking was the NAACP, established in 1909. The organization placed itself in direct opposition to Booker T. Washington's Tuskegee machine, which focused on black economic advancement, while following a cooperationist stance toward segregationists. From the outset, the NAACP made full black equality its stated goal, although securing the franchise remained its foremost long-term objective. The organi-

---

4. Anthony J. Badger, *The New Deal: The Depression Years, 1933–1940* (New York: Hill and Wang, 1988); Alan Brinkley, *The End of Reform: New Deal Liberalism in Depression and War* (New York: Knopf, 1995); Lizabeth Cohen, *Making a New Deal: Industrial Workers in Chicago, 1919–1939* (New York: Cambridge University Press, 1990); Alan Dawley, *Struggles for Justice: Moral Responsibility and the Liberal State* (Cambridge: Harvard University Press, 1991); Doris Kearns Goodwin, *No Ordinary Time: Franklin and Eleanor Roosevelt: The Home Front in World War II* (New York: Touchstone , 1994), 161–172; James Grossman, *Land of Hope: Chicago, Black Southerners, and the Great Migration* (Chicago: University of Chicago Press, 1989); Kirby, *Black Americans in the Roosevelt Era*; Nicholas Lemann, *The Promised Land: The Great Black Migration and How It Changed America* (New York: Knopf, 1991); William E. Leuchtenberg, *Franklin D. Roosevelt and the New Deal, 1932–1940* (New York: Harper and Row, 1963); Sitkoff, *New Deal for Blacks*; Weiss, *Farewell to the Party of Lincoln*.

zation in the short-term put its support behind the drive to make lynching a federal crime. Many activists, especially in the 1910s, 1920s, and early 1930s, doubted an antilynching bill would ever pass or even could bring tangible improvements in the daily life of black southerners if it did. Nonetheless, the NAACP viewed the publicity surrounding Capitol Hill fights on civil rights as valuable publicity, as a means of getting its message of equality on the national agenda and before as many Americans—especially those who would ordinarily not consider the plight of African Americans—as possible. When need be, the NAACP flexed its political muscle by inflating both its hold over northern blacks and the actual numbers of blacks casting ballots in any given election. These scare tactics were meant to pressure northern politicians from states with sizable black constituencies to vote "right" on civil rights proposals. Careful examination of the NAACP's statistics reveal their exaggerated nature, prompting serious doubts regarding the group's dubious claims that the black population held the balance of power in many northern states. Regardless of the actual strength behind the NAACP, southern senators took seriously the organization's threats. Southern critiques of civil rights legislation now included condemnation of a group dominated by black voters that compelled northern politicians to do its bidding. Repeated failure met the NAACP's antilynching campaign, yet the organization never ceased its agitation, a fact that made southerners even more defensive. For the NAACP, all efforts, even unsuccessful ones, meant that the harsh light of public scrutiny would fall on the South, and when that happened the organization's leaders knew their cause would gain strength. Pressure, constant and searching, was to be applied until political equality was attained. It was a long-term vision, one that would unfold slowly, but it was one the NAACP believed worthy of pursuing. Justice would one day prevail. As subsequent Senate debates would illustrate, southerners imbued the antilynching fight with incredible significance. They had good reason for their concern.[5]

Despite the defeat of the Costigan-Wagner bill in 1935, interest in a federal antilynching law remained. With local southern officials seemingly unwilling or unable to thwart the crime, some national legislators renewed their

5. Manfred Berg, *The Ticket to Freedom: The NAACP and the Struggle for Black Political Integration* (Gainesville: University Press of Florida, 2005), 4, 10–21, 25, 27, 40–43, 51–56; Tushnet, *NAACP's Legal Strategy;* Walter F. White, *A Man Called White: The Autobiography of Walter White* (New York: Viking Press, 1948); Zangrando, *NAACP Crusade Against Lynching.*

drive for a federal antilynching statute to end law enforcement lapses such as occurred at Duck Hill. At the very moment of the Duck Hill murders, discussion in Washington focused on a federal antilynching law authored by Joseph A. Gavagan, a Democrat from the overwhelmingly black New York district of Harlem. After the Mississippi slayings, enthusiasm for the then-stalled Gavagan bill increased, culminating in its passage in the House of Representatives, 277 to 119. Victory in the House represented a small but significant hurdle for antilynching advocates. Final success hinged on pushing the measure through the U.S. Senate. Upon this last and most difficult barrier rested the fate of antilynching legislation.[6]

Senate rules held the potential of preventing passage of Gavagan's proposal. In theory the U.S. Senate permitted almost unlimited debate, a fact that enabled a senator to address himself on a particular subject for as long and as often as his physical capabilities permitted. In practice, Senate Rule 22 established guidelines for cloture, or what southerners called the "gag rule." Adopted in 1917 in response to a controversial filibuster against President Woodrow Wilson's plan to arm American merchant vessels for protection against German U-boat assaults, the rule stipulated that the curtailment of debate, or cloture, could occur only if two-thirds of those senators present and voting agreed to the action. With such stringent guidelines, successful cloture votes proved rare. Despite the rule, therefore, the Senate maintained its reputation as the "worlds greatest deliberative body." When several senators similarly inclined worked together, they could bring legislative action in the chamber to a halt. By engaging in a filibuster, southerners defended the interests of their region by talking in relays until they forced the removal of an objectionable bill from consideration. Filibusters occurred infrequently, and in the twentieth century southerners most often employed the technique when faced with what they considered grave threats to the region's racial system. As V. O. Key demonstrated in *Southern Politics*, the South's congressional and senatorial delegations exhibited little uniformity in their voting behavior. Only regarding civil rights did legislators from the region act in concert. Race-related legislation unified southern statesmen and race-based initiatives served as the catalyst for their filibusters. Southerners met

6. For the House vote on the bill, see *CR*, 75th Cong., 1st sess. (subsequent *CR* citations refer to the 75th Cong., 1st sess. until noted otherwise), 15 April 1937, 2563–64; *Time*, 19 April 1937, 14; *Time*, 26 April 1937, 17.

the Dyer and Costigan-Wagner bills with filibusters that forced antilynching advocates to remove their legislation.[7]

Successful filibusters often relied on more than just the cloture guidelines established by Senate Rule 22. In the 1922 fight over the Dyer bill, for example, southerners utilized Senate Rule 3, which made the reading and correcting of the previous day's *Senate Journal,* or minutes, privileged business. Under usual circumstances, the chamber customarily approved the Journal without debate by unanimous consent. By voicing their objection, southerners made the correction of the Journal the body's pending business, thereby creating a parliamentary situation that thwarted any other legislative action. Until the Senate approved the *Journal,* no other business could be transacted. More important for southern interests, debate on the *Journal* fell beyond the jurisdiction of Rule 22 and thus beyond the guidelines governing cloture. Antilynching advocates soon relented, recognizing the impossibility of shutting off debate on the *Journal* discussion that undermined consideration of the Dyer bill.

Along with Senate Rules 3 and 22, southern dominance of the committee system would in later years serve as a valuable weapon in the fight against civil rights. In 1937, the Senate Judiciary Committee that held jurisdiction over antilynching legislation contained few southern members, none of whom had a realistic chance of ascending to the chairman's post in the foreseeable future. With civil rights growing in importance, southern senators focused their attention on stacking the committee with reliable members, an effort that eventually culminated in one of their own serving as chairman. But like all things in the Senate, that would take time. Indeed, not until James Eastland of Mississippi attained the chairman's seat in 1956 would a southerner control the Judiciary Committee. To meet the threat in the 1930s, southerners employed other delaying tools. For example, Indiana Democrat Frederick Van Nuys followed the defeat of the Costigan-Wagner bill in 1936 with a request for funding to conduct an investigation of southern lynching. The decision to fund such an investigation rested with the Audit and Control Committee chaired by James Byrnes of South Carolina. Throughout 1936, Byrnes refused to convene his committee, an action that killed Van Nuys's request. Southern senators oversaw other committees of vital interest to their

---

7. V. O. Key, *Southern Politics in State and Nation* (New York: Knopf, 1950), 345–368.

colleagues. By tradition, Senate committee chairmanships fell to members of the majority party who had accrued the most seniority on a particular committee. Time in office determined committee assignments. Representing one-party states, southerners frequently faced only limited opposition on election day. As a result, most of them experienced lengthy tenures in office that enabled them to accumulate considerable seniority privileges. A disproportionate number of the Senate's standing committees thus fell under the direction of southern chairmen. During the Seventy-fifth Congress in 1937, southerners chaired the Finance, Appropriations, Agriculture, and Post Office Committees, all of which held jurisdiction over bills that affected the entire Senate membership. Even committees not run by southerners had chairs sympathetic to the region's interests. Using the leverage these committees granted them, southerners could subtly pressure their colleagues throughout the voting process. A Wyoming senator, for example, would find funding for a rural post office infinitely more important than a civil rights bill. As a result, he would likely curry favor with southern leaders by voting against cloture on an antilynching bill in exchange for an expeditious hearing on a measure critical in his bailiwick. When the Gavagan antilynching proposal reached the Senate, southern legislative leaders planned their defense with considerable power in their hands. They would need all of the parliamentary devices at their disposal when they faced the first civil rights proposal in the twentieth century with widespread bipartisan support.[8]

Prior to the late 1930s, the legislative situation did not warrant a significant organization of the Senate's southern ranks. In both 1922 and

8. For studies that address southern use of Senate rules, see Hugh A. Bone, *Party Committees and National Politics* (Seattle: University of Washington Press, 1960); Burdette, *Filibustering in the Senate,* 133–137, 179–181; Robert C. Byrd, *The Senate, 1789–1989: Addresses on the History of the United States Senate* (Washington, D.C.: Government Printing Office, 1988); Caro, *Master of the Senate,* 78–105; George H. Haynes, *The Senate of the United States: Its History and Practice* (New York: Russell and Russell, 1960); Key, *Southern Politics;* Donald R. Matthews, *U.S. Senators and Their World* (New York: Knopf, 1960); Floyd M. Riddick, *Senate Procedure: Precedents and Practices* (Washington, D.C.: Government Printing Office, 1981); and William S. White, *Citadel: The Story of the United States Senate* (New York: Harper Collins, 1956). For Senator Byrnes's actions as chair of the Audit and Control Committee, see James Byrnes (hereafter cited as JB) to Wingate Waring, 23 April 1936, Box 42, "Legislation, 1933–1941—Antilynching, 1937" Folder, James F. Byrnes Collection, Manuscripts and Special Collections, Strom Thurmond Institute, Clemson University, Clemson, South Carolina. (hereafter cited as Byrnes MSS).

1935, fewer than ten senators from states of the former Confederacy actively engaged in the filibusters that blocked antilynching legislation. Although most of the region's senators opposed these measures, the majority of them recognized that the bills stood little chance of success and thus they left the task of defeating the proposals to the region's more demagogic statesmen, who made race a centerpiece of their election campaigns. Despite its defeat in 1935, the Costigan-Wagner bill concerned southern senators because of its bipartisan appeal. The boost given the antilynching crusade by the Duck Hill incident heightened that concern and pointed to the need for greater cohesion in the southern ranks to meet the threat posed by civil rights legislation. The freedom to remain on the sidelines during civil rights battles increasingly became a luxury that southern senators could ill afford to indulge.

Concurrent with the development of greater southern unity in the Senate emerged the need for a command structure to organize the region's statesmen. Texas senator Thomas Connally's southern peers selected him to lead the fight against any proposal that "was a sectional bill aimed against the South." Born on 19 August 1877, Connally spent his boyhood on the plains of central Texas as the son of a Confederate veteran turned farmer. Although his youth encompassed two distinct historical worlds, one associated with the Old South and the other with the Wild West, his fidelity to southern interests brooked no compromises. He won election to the U.S. Senate in 1928 and quickly gained recognition for his knowledge of foreign affairs, a skill he honed during his tenure in the House of Representatives from 1917 to March 1929, when he took his seat in the upper chamber. To many observers, Connally seemed a caricature from another generation. Throughout his career, he wore an anachronistic black string tie and long black coat in a manner reminiscent of a nineteenth-century statesman. Tall and lean with a gray mane that curled over his collar, the Texan, according to North Carolina Senator Josiah Bailey, was "the only man in the United States Senate who could wear a Roman Toga and not look like a fat man in a nightgown." In addition to his imposing physical presence, Connally proved an effective orator. Delighting spectators and senators alike, a Connally speech came "complete with facial expressions, gestures, and even pantomime," as the Texan paced the row of seats adjacent to his desk. Despite his senatorial appearance, he possessed an acid tongue that he often turned on opponents without regard for chamber protocol governing verbal exchanges. Journalist

William S. White, who wrote fondly of the Senate's southern members, considered Connally as "unpredictable as an undischarged Roman candle," a fact that caused other senators to walk "warily but still fondly about him."[9]

More than his dynamic personal traits raised Connally to the leadership of the southern Senate group at the time of its greatest twentieth-century crisis. Compared to many of the region's senators, he possessed the least political baggage in so much as he was not noted for demagoguery and remained a solid supporter of the New Deal. As a result he remained popular with nonsoutherners for his apparent moderation, at least in comparison to the excesses of many of his regional cohorts. Extreme southern racists such as South Carolina's "Cotton Ed" Smith and Mississippi's Theodore Bilbo proved too controversial to hold the leadership post. Others, such as Josiah Bailey, Harry Byrd of Virginia, and later Walter George of Georgia, developed reputations as fierce opponents of the New Deal, making them something less than favorites of the Senate's overwhelming Democratic majority. Throughout the 1930s, Tom Connally had remained loyal to the New Deal. Not until the 1937 effort to pack the Supreme Court with more liberal justices did Connally finally abandon his support for the Roosevelt administration, making him the one southerner with a voting record consistent with that of nonsouthern Democrats. If a northern senator needed a reason not to vote for cloture, Connally was the man best suited to do the convincing. His physical presence, oratorical skills, and moderate policy preferences, along with his desire for the post, made him a formidable commander of the southern opposition. The Texan would soon need all of his personal and political attributes as Senate debate on the 1937 Gavagan antilynching bill neared.[10]

Following House action, the Senate Judiciary Committee received the Gavagan bill. In the committee, Democrats Robert Wagner of New York and

9. John Bankhead to Knox Gilmore, 7 July 1943, Box 126, "Anti-Lynching Bill—78th Congress" Folder, Thomas Connally Papers, Library of Congress, Washington, D.C. (hereafter cited as Connally MSS) ("was a sectional . . ."); Tom Connally, *My Name Is Tom Connally* (New York: Thomas Y. Crowell, 1952), 9–76; J. T. Salter, ed., *Public Men: In and Out of Office* (Chapel Hill: University of North Carolina Press, 1946), 311 ("the only man . . ."). For a description of Connally pacing the chamber, see Allen Drury, *A Senate Journal, 1943–1945* (New York: McGraw-Hill, 1963), 164 ("complete with facial . . ."); White, *Citadel,* 5 (unpredictable as a . . .") and ("warily but still . . .").

10. For the southern reaction to the New Deal, see James C. Cobb and Michael V. Namorato, eds., *The New Deal and the South: Essays* (Jackson: University Press of Mississippi, 1984);

Frederick Van Nuys of Indiana championed their own antilynching bill that closely followed the 1935 Costigan-Wagner proposal. The measure provided for a maximum penalty of a five-year jail term and a five-thousand-dollar fine for any state official who failed to protect a prisoner from a mob, defined by the bill as two or more persons. Under the legislation, counties where a lynching occurred would be held liable to the victims' families for as much as ten thousand dollars. In a decision that would later haunt civil rights advocates, they permitted Illinois Democrat William Dieterich to insert a rider to their bill that exempted mob and labor related murders from the proposed federal antilynching statute. Dieterich argued that the Wagner–Van Nuys bill, as originally drafted, employed too broad a definition of lynching. He wanted to remove certain kinds of violence from the definition, not because he sanctioned such actions, but because he believed the indemnity clause of the bill would force local communities to pay for murders committed between groups of lawbreakers such as gangsters. No other motives, according to the senator, rested behind his actions.[11]

On 22 June 1937, the Judiciary Committee reported both the Gavagan and the Wagner–Van Nuys measures, with the latter given preference by the committee's membership. Both bills remained on the Senate calendar for over a month as the chamber focused on funding New Deal relief programs. Then, on 11 August 1937, Robert F. Wagner motioned for the Senate to proceed to the consideration of House Resolution 1507, his antilynching bill. Following Wagner's unexpected motion, Senate Democratic leader Alben Barkley of Kentucky scrambled to evade a contentious floor debate since he wanted to bypass the issue in that session. Indeed, Barkley had informed Vice President John Nance Garner, who presided over the Senate, to avoid recognizing Wagner. When Garner looked around the chamber on 11 August, none of the senators Barkley had appointed to present legislation had appeared. With no other option, Garner, according to Senate Rules, had to recognize the senator from New York. Barkley pushed to adjourn the Senate, which would have

---

Frank Freidel, *F. D. R. and the South* (Baton Rouge: Louisiana State University Press, 1965); James T. Patterson, *Congressional Conservatism and the New Deal: The Growth of the Conservative Coalition in Congress, 1933–1939* (Lexington: University Press of Kentucky, 1967); and Tindall, *Emergence of the New South,* 473–649.

11. For the referral of the bill to the Judiciary Committee, see *CR,* 19 April 1937, 2575; *Time,* 26 April 1937, 17.

superceded the motion made by Wagner. This maneuver failed, twenty-seven to thirty-five. A subsequent motion to recess succeeded, thirty-six to twenty-three. The recess enabled the Senate leadership to work out an agreement that returned the antilynching measure to the calender with an assurance that action on the bill would commence in the special session scheduled for later that year. Barkley offered one caveat to the agreement; discussion on House Resolution 1507 would begin after action on an important farm subsidy measure. Before resolution of the controversy, Tom Connally delivered an important address that set the foundation for the southern opposition to federal antilynching laws, foreshadowing the rhetoric employed by others during the subsequent fight.[12]

Connally observed on 11 August 1937 that political expediency led to the "seemingly mad contest" between Wagner and others concerning who could "speak more oftener and more loudly on this bill." The next day he sharpened his attack on the legislation, but before proceeding he described his personal feelings about lynching. He, like all the southerners who would later speak, noted his opposition to any form of murder or lawlessness. However, he argued that federal antilynching statutes rested on unconstitutional use of the Fourteenth Amendment. Advocates for the legislation claimed that lynching occurred because state appointed law enforcement officials willingly permitted mobs to abduct their detainees and thus imparted a quasi–state sponsored legitimacy to the crime. As a result, the transgression fell under the jurisdiction of the equal protection clause of the Fourteenth Amendment. A policeman, civil rights advocates argued, as an officer of the state, was the embodiment of the state in the area he patrolled. His tacit acceptance of the abduction of someone under his care therefore constituted state complicity in denying the victim his or her Fourteenth Amendment rights. Ultimate responsibility rested with the state since it provided not only no mechanism for stopping this violation but also no apparent desire to prosecute it. A major consideration behind the decision to drop punishment clauses for the participants in a lynch mob was the Fourteenth Amendment. During the 1922 Dyer bill fight, southerners questioned the constitutionality of defining the

12. For the Judiciary report of the bill, see *CR*, 22 June 1937, 6113. Wagner's motion can be found in *CR*, 11 August 1937, 8694–8695. The votes on adjournment and recess appear in *CR*, 11 August 1937, 8696–8697. Barkley's agreement appears in *CR*, 12 August 1937, 8759; *Newsweek*, 21 August 1937, 10.

actions of a lynch mob as a state-sponsored undertaking. Recognizing that
the southern interpretation of the Fourteenth Amendment proved consistent
with several Supreme Court rulings, supporters of a federal antilynching law
abandoned the clause to make it more compatible with the prevailing legal
consensus. Advocates of the legislation now believed that their bill would
meet any court challenge. Connally offered a very different interpretation of
the Amendment that questioned even the revised antilynching proposal. He
maintained it applied solely to "state action and state action alone." No state,
he observed, possessed a law that sanctioned lynching. Therefore, the crime
did not fall under the jurisdiction of the Fourteenth Amendment because
only individuals, not the state, allowed lynchings to take place. Final guilt did
not extend to the state; it remained with the negligent officer. States already
provided legal punishment for all forms of murder, including lynching, thus
fulfilling their constitutional obligations. For this reason, the foundation of
all antilynching bills, the Fourteenth Amendment, did not apply to the issue
under discussion. A vote for the bill, the Texan liked to note, would violate a
senator's oath to uphold the law since it proved so clearly unconstitutional.[13]

In denouncing the bill, Connally turned to the historical legacy of Reconstruction. "I invoke the shade of Thaddeus Stevens, bitter partisan that he
was, hater of the section from which I come, frenzied by passion," he stated.
"I invoke his spirit to come back now and speak a word of caution on this
floor." Even Thaddeus Stevens, Connally explained, would not have dreamed
of distorting the Fourteenth Amendment in the manner that antilynching
advocates proposed. Further delving into southern history, the Texan pointed
to the great progress made by the South in the area of race relations, despite
the ravages inflicted on it during the Civil War. Both of his forays into the
region's past proved direct but were limited to a few sentences within his
multipage oration. He apparently added his cursory analysis of these episodes in southern history largely for the benefit of constituents. Connally did
not need to go much further than mentioning Thaddeus Stevens; his name
carried with it the odium of treachery for many southerners. By appealing
to traditional southern interpretations of history that emphasized northern
transgressions, Connally demonstrated his fealty to regional racial norms.
On the other hand, limited reference to that historical legacy in his address

13. *CR*, 11 August 1937, 8695 ("seemingly mad . . .") ("speak more oftener . . ."); *CR*, Connally, 12 August 1936, 8738 ("state action . . .").

alerted his Senate colleagues that his opposition to the bill rested on solid constitutional footing. Had he waxed long on northern depredations instead of on the shortfalls of the bill, he would have done little to advance the southern fight.[14]

At the same time in which he sought to downplay the sectional nature of the southern opposition, Connally ultimately attempted to illustrate northern sectionalism. He aimed to recast the antilynching fight from a moral crusade against a barbarous crime to a political ruse designed to gain votes at the expense of the Constitution. Civil rights advocates, according to the Texan, did not wish to right a historic wrong against African Americans, but only to procure personal political gain. In stripping the veneer of morality from the antilynching advocates, he provided nonsouthern senators a legitimate rationale for opposing the bill that did not make them appear as tacit supporters of the crime. By Connally's logic, he and his southern cohorts served as the true defenders of principle in the fight since it fell on them to preserve the sanctity of the Constitution by checking a temporary gust of political passion. Moreover, Connally contended, if northerners left the South alone it would solve its own problems. "We are trying to solve them and we have done pretty well with them. In the matter of lynching, we are opposed to lynchings. I am opposed to lynchings, and over the years the problem has been largely solved." Why, he wondered, create a federal law to curtail a crime that had all but disappeared? Next, Connally lambasted mob exemption from the bill because gang related activities most often occurred in the nation's large northern cities. The charge of sectional bias proved particularly telling in light of the amendment championed in committee by Illinois Democrat William Dieterich, who hailed from the state containing Al Capone's Chicago. Despite Dieterich's explanation for his amendment, Connally condemned the Illinoisan's attempt to define a murder committed by a group of northerners as a gang-related incident and a similar crime committed by a group of southerners as a lynching. In both instances, a mob murder took place, but under the Wagner–Van Nuys bill only southerners would receive punishment. If this was not a sectional bill, Connally speculated, then why were gang killings removed from its jurisdiction? The Texan demanded an answer, but one was not forthcoming.[15]

14. *CR*, 12 August 1937, 8739 ("I invoke . . .").
15. *CR*, Connally, 12 August 1937, 8744 ("We are trying . . ."), 8745–8747 (gangsters).

Connally's address symbolized a significant change in southern rhetoric. Where once many southerners defined their opposition to antilynching legislation in the context of defending white womanhood, some, in the 1930s, began portraying the issue as a vote-grabbing scheme by northern senators with large black constituencies. In addition, they attempted to depict the North as simmering with social unrest as seen by the prevalence of labor, gang, and racial violence. The South, as described by the region's senators, bordered on the idyllic, with peace and good order the standard. With another showdown on the lynching question pending, southerners now more than ever contrasted the glories of the South with the disorders of the North.

Three months after Connally's oration, the special session began without the Farm bill ready for debate. Civil rights advocates refused to allow their pet initiative to die without action before the holiday season. In the absence of the Farm bill, Robert Wagner took matters into his own hands by moving for the Senate to consider his antilynching measure. As in August, Connally responded with a denunciation of the New Yorker that echoed his earlier speech. "The President wants the Congress to address itself first to farm legislation," he remarked, while Wagner "wants to go on a vote-catching expedition in Harlem." He again reminded the chamber of the sectional nature of the proposal, especially the amendment that excluded communities from the indemnity portion of the bill in cases involving gangsters and racketeers. Summing up his views, he exclaimed, "it is aimed at the South. This is a bill to brand us as barbarians. This is a bill to brand us as backwards. This is a bill to cover all of us with odium, without keeping any on their hands if they can help it." Connally did not deny that some level of racial tension existed in the South, but he contended that Dixie's social ills paled in comparison to those found in the North. Statesmen beyond the Mason Dixon line should first rid their communities of mob and labor violence, as southerners largely accomplished with the lynching problem, before casting judgement on other regions. With these words, Connally set the tone for the next speaker, who had his own reasons for condemning the bill.[16]

North Carolina senator Josiah Bailey followed the Texan on the floor. To observers, the sixty-five-year-old Bailey appeared cold and aloof. A man in

16. Wagner's motion can be found in CR, 16 November 1937, 75th Cong., 2nd sess. (until otherwise noted, subsequent CR citations refer to the 75th Cong., 2nd sess.), 38; CR, 16 November 1937, 39 ("The President wants . . ."); CR, 17 November 1937, 70 ("it is aimed . . .").

poor health, he suffered from frequent, persistent migraines. Despite his personal reserve and physical frailty, on those rare occasions the reclusive North Carolinian addressed the chamber, his colleagues could expect a notable performance complete with desk pounding and impassioned rhetoric. On this one, Bailey became the first southern senator to outline what he perceived as a dangerous aspect of the antilynching fight that had received only limited attention in the past. Of course, Bailey observed, he believed the Wagner–Van Nuys proposal lacked constitutional foundation, but that represented its least worrisome characteristic. According to him, the measure was far more than a mild antilynching bill; it represented the vanguard of a much larger movement aimed at dismantling southern society. "It is merely the opening of Pandora's box," he warned. "Senators should know that. They are taking a step from which there is no retreat." To further dramatize his case, he continued, "I fear it, I dread it, I fight it, I argue against it because I know it is wrong and because I know the moment it goes through here the very men who put it forward will be almost compelled to go ahead with the old Civil Rights Act [of 1875]. Then we will have the battle of Reconstruction all over again in America. That will destroy the South." If anyone failed to see the true implication of the antilynching crusade, he described a possible scenario that went beyond even Connally's critique of the bill. In Bailey's eyes, the Wagner–Van Nuys initiative was bad enough, but only eight lynchings had occurred in 1936 according to Tuskegee Institute statistics. Because of this low number, the legislation would produce little hardship in the South. Nonetheless, if this particular bill passed, it would set a precedent for still further civil rights advances. Like Connally, Bailey considered antilynching advocates the pawns of black voting blocs. Should Wagner–Van Nuys pass, minority interests would seek greater advances—advances that would one day lead to an assault against segregation. "I would go to almost any limit to prevent it not because of just what we have before us in the bill—we can stand it—but I can foresee the same gentleman coming up here in a little while with another civil rights bill." If this occurred, Bailey concluded, "I hope we shall have enough Senators here to filibuster until the crack of dawn and back again."[17]

17. Caro, *Master of the Senate*, 62; Drury, *Senate Journal*, 17; John R. Moore, *Senator Josiah Bailey of North Carolina: A Political Biography* (Durham, N.C.: Duke University Press, 1968), 3–6; *Newsweek*, 4 May 1935, 10; *CR*, 18 November 1937, 113 ("it is merely . . .") and ("I fear it . . ."), 114, and ("I would go . . .") and ("I hope we . . ."); Work, *Negro Year Book*, 156.

Not all of the southern speakers in the 1937 special session couched their arguments in a manner that deemphasized racial prejudices. Charles O. Andrews of Florida, for example, found the subject of rape inextricably linked with the crime of lynching. Since the former begets the latter, the Senate should pass "an anti-rape bill," which according to his logic would eliminate the central cause of lynchings—rape—and as a bonus extirpate lynching as well. The myth of the black mammy and her love for her "charges" also found its way into his oration. Andrews illustrated what he considered the positive nature of race relations in the South by telling a story that emphasized the protection against the depredations of Yankee forces during the Civil War that black mammies gave their white mistresses. To wit, he concluded, "there is nothing more beautiful in history than the relation which then existed, and to a large extent now exists, between the old black mammy and her charges." Andrews's address touched upon many of the themes that would become increasingly rare as the civil rights fight grew in intensity in subsequent decades. Imagery of the black mammy and black rapist appeared in different permutations as the legislative battle for racial equality ensued, but the particular poignancy of the examples employed by Andrews grew infrequent as southerners shifted their strategic goals from wasting time as they did in 1922 and 1935 to swaying the opinions of those senators not immediately predisposed toward the southern viewpoint.[18]

Born in 1877, the Floridian grew up in the post-Reconstruction South at a time when the region was in the process of "sanitizing" its memory of the Civil War and defining the meaning of the Lost Cause. As such, he integrated into his political vocabulary all of the myths regarding the region's history that helped the Old South transform itself into the New. In many ways, Andrews stood on the precipice of a generational divide at the time he delivered his denunciation of the Wagner–Van Nuys bill. Now numbered among his southern colleagues were five senators born after 1885 who had less of a direct connection to either the Civil War or Reconstruction. Four of those southerners would remain in the Senate long enough to witness the destruction of Jim Crow that the region's statesmen so feared in the late New Deal. For these younger politicians, Andrews's conceptualization of southern race relations proved less salient since they spent their formative years in a South where the social upheaval that resulted in the transition from slavery to Jim

18. *CR*, 22 November 1937, 208 ("an anti-rape . . ."), 212 ("there is nothing . . .").

Crow had ended. Future southern Senate leaders viewed segregation as a fact of life, they grew up under the system and accepted it as a matter of course. Racial prejudice still remained a consistent feature of southern opposition into the 1960s, but its tone changed. Overt references to black inferiority grew less frequent as a new generation of southerners adopted the logic of segregation as the cornerstone of their racial worldview. No longer harping on black faults, they chose instead to emphasize that southern whites were not better, but only different from southern blacks. Because of these differences, the two races preferred to live apart. Both groups respected the interests of their opposite and neither race transgressed the rights of the other. More revealing, references to the white race uplifting and improving the black race largely disappeared. White southerners before the advent of segregation lived and worked in close proximity to African Americans, just as they relied on them for labor. They believed that they had a vested interest in "improving" their black neighbors. Southerners born after the advent of Jim Crow experienced a spatial separation from the region's black citizenry that created a physical as well as a mental distance between the races. Whites no longer intimately knew blacks and, in turn, lost interest in "uplifting" their opposite. They accepted blacks for who they were and left them to fend for themselves without even the pretext of paternalism expressed by their forebears. Stripped of legal and political rights under Jim Crow, southern blacks were cast adrift. Although repeatedly stressing the equality portion of the "separate but equal" doctrine, the white South abandoned its black counterpart and the rhetoric of the region's statesmen reflected this indifference. The southern defense of the region's racial system also changed because the nature of the political landscape changed. Southern senators who led the fight against civil rights after World War II did so under different circumstances than those facing individuals like Charles Andrews in the late New Deal. The prospects for successful civil rights action increased each year and with it came the need for a more dignified southern defense that focused less on race baiting and more on constitutional arguments. During the antilynching fight in 1938, Old South paternalism still remained very much evident.[19]

19. Gaines M. Foster, *Ghosts of the Confederacy: Defeat the Lost Cause and the Emergence of the New South* (New York: Oxford University Press, 1987), 196 ("sanitizing"); Paul Gaston, *The New South Creed: A Study in Southern Myth-Making* (New York: Knopf, 1970).

Born in 1866, "Cotton Ed" Ellison D. Smith of South Carolina, who had the dubious distinction of being the "sloppiest man" on Capitol Hill, used his Senate office both as a place of work and as his official domicile when in Washington. The Senate's maid staff refused to clean his office after he began using the entire room as one large cuspidor, trifling not with expelling tobacco juice in a spittoon. In accordance with his lack of refinement, he chose not the paternalism of Andrews but the race-baiting politics common in the South after Reconstruction. For Smith, the Yankee invasion during the Civil War unleashed on the region a race unprepared for life outside of bondage. The hostile black enemy in the midst of the white South, Smith believed, required constant supervision lest they retrogress to their innate state of barbarism. Instilling fear in the hearts of southern blacks, according to the South Carolinian, served as the only means of checking the baser instincts of African Americans. In *The Mind of the South*, Wilbur Cash speculated that demagogues such as Smith incited lynchings through their bitter condemnations of blacks. When Cotton Ed took the floor in November 1937, he shared with senators his version of southern race relations. Smith's oration provided a rationale for a segregated social system that joined overt racism, stripped of the marginally edifying black mammy plot line, with the emerging southern consensus regarding the alleged political forces behind the antilynching fight. "We do not take them [blacks] into fellowship with us in the home or in the school," Smith opined, "because it is dangerous." He noted that provide the African American community with its own separate institutions and it would not challenge the existing racial order. By nature, he claimed, blacks preferred segregation, only outside agitators could alter their instinctive predilection for separation. Disrupt the social equilibrium as the antilynching crusaders desired and risk facing serious "consequences." Smith never elaborated what deleterious consequences he so feared, but to his southern constituents he did not have to. They knew precisely what he meant because he spoke to them in the common idiom of southern race relations at that time, in which no crime fell beyond the believed depravity of the region's black citizenry. More important, Smith also pointed to the vanguard nature of the antilynching bill. Like Bailey, he did not fear the legislation per se—he feared what passage of that bill might provoke in southern black communities. His statement illuminates an important aspect of the Jim Crow system: its precarious stability. Even minor affronts to the system, if Cotton

Ed was to be believed, could undermine the entire structure. By carrying Bailey's arguments even further, Smith saw the antilynching bill as not only a spur for black activism in the North but also a potential catalyst for black activism in the South. Despite frequent southern assurances that the region's blacks were happy under Jim Crow, Cotton Ed saw the limitations of their contentedness. An incentive to challenge the existing system, even a small one such as the Wagner–Van Nuys bill, could cause a wave of opposition against southern racial etiquette that would crest only after it destroyed the Jim Crow system.[20]

Before long, the anticipated farm legislation was ready for consideration. Not willing to continue the fight at that time, Robert Wagner withdrew his motion to consider his bill. Wagner–Van Nuys, however, did not disappear. On 20 December 1937, at the close of the special session that witnessed initial skirmishes over the antilynching bill, Senate leaders announced their intention of making the measure the first order of business on the 6 January 1938 opening of the third session of the Seventy-fifth Congress. For Tom Connally and his southern forces, the situation looked bleak. Not only did the bill hold priority—no more farm bills to divert attention—but media outlets and the NAACP claimed that seventy senators had already pledged for the bill, a number that exceeded the prerequisite two-thirds majority needed to invoke cloture. Some observers believed that southerners would eschew a filibuster that would surely fail, rather than risk setting a dangerous precedent regarding civil rights. If a cloture vote succeeded, it was believed that senators would prove more likely to follow a similar course should civil rights again become a major issue. By allowing the antilynching bill to pass, southerners could rely on the judicial system to rule the measure unconstitutional, as all of the region's spokesmen contended that it was. Such speculation overlooked the importance of Bailey's November speech that heralded the emergence of a strategic vision that soon gained almost universal acceptance among southern senators. Failure to thwart the antilynching measure increased the risk of opening a wedge through which more far-reaching proposals would come. Any concession would hasten the destruction of segregation. Southerners had to take a stand.

20. William Miller, *Fishbait: The Memoirs of the Congressional Doorkeeper* (Englewood Cliffs, N.J.: Prentice-Hall, 1977), 158–159 ("sloppiest man"); Cash, *Mind of the South*, 301–302; *CR*, 19 November 1937, 177 ("we do not . . .") and ("consequences").

Implicit in their arguments was recognition that some northern statesmen supported civil rights to strengthen their hold on black voters. In order
to remain in office, many politicians above the Mason-Dixon line, southerners speculated, would adopt a ceaseless crusade on behalf of their black
constituents. Southerners believed that minority voting blocs, no matter
what their stated intentions in the late New Deal, really desired full social
equality. The NAACP had made that point crystal clear. It stood to reason
thus from the southern viewpoint that if black pressure groups ultimately
desired the end of segregation, northern politicians would one day advocate
the same goal once the voting bloc to which they were beholden demanded
it. At least in 1938, southerners still believed that by winning battles against
legislation aimed only at the periphery of the Jim Crow system, such as antilynching proposals, they would halt black demands for more inclusive civil
rights bills and especially measures threatening the end of segregation. Their
belief that success on the outskirts of the Jim Crow citadel would stymie
legislative forays closer to the system's core later changed as events indicated
that the slow push against the region's fortress of white supremacy would
continue unabated no matter how many victories they secured. In their immediate present, they fought the Wagner–Van Nuys bill fully believing that
their triumph would dampen pressure in the black community for broader
civil rights legislation. Many southern senators did not address themselves
to this new southern conceptualization of the political landscape that Bailey
unveiled before Wagner withdrew his bill, but circumstances indicated that
they would soon get that opportunity.[21]

Acting in his capacity as head of the Senate's southern bloc, Tom Connally
sent a letter at the end of December, marked "personal and confidential," to
opponents of the antilynching bill, suggesting that they convene a tactical
discussion "so that there may be uniformity of action among our group when
the bill is taken up." With the odds against them, the southerners met, knowing the importance of convincing those who already promised to vote in fa-

21. *Time*, 24 January 1938, 8. For Wagner's withdrawal, see *CR*, 23 November 1937, 266. For
the agreement to take up the bill in 1938, see *CR*, 20 December 1937, 1934; *Washington Post*, 9
January 1938, 9; *Newsweek*, 17 January 1938, 12; Zangrando, *NAACP Crusade Against Lynching*,
146. According to the *New York Times*, 22 June 37, 1, Connally claimed that the southern group
would likely not filibuster. The *Atlanta Constitution*, 3 January 1938, 1, 5, notes the likelihood of
southern failure.

vor of the bill to alter their decisions. Doing so required a partial break from their usual filibuster techniques, eliminating heavy doses of nongermane material in exchange for more focused arguments on the unconstitutionality of the proposal. Success in what they labeled an "educational campaign" rather than what they considered the pejorative term filibuster required that they thwart legislative action on other important bills to create a groundswell of opinion in favor of withdrawing the antilynching proposal. Also important, southern senators had to avoid increasing animosity against themselves. Accomplishing this goal necessitated that some southerners, who generally avoided filibusters, deliver speeches against the measure in order to lend credence to the arguments of the region's more vocal advocates of white supremacy. At the same time, members of the group given to racial demagoguery demanded the opportunity to air their grievances, a prospect not fully in accordance with the larger southern scheme of swaying, not alienating, their colleagues. Everyone in the chamber expected the region's incorrigible racists to speak, and Connally knew that he could not silence them. He needed their support and, more important, their voices if the filibuster extended any length of time. The key became convincing the unabashed defenders of white supremacy to hold off on their orations until after the moderate senators had spoken. By that time, the filibuster would be into its second week and, at that point, attendance in the chamber would likely be sparse. A rabid speech delivered to an empty room would produce little damage, while proving beneficial in extending the "educational campaign."[22]

As the Senate had agreed during the special session, it met in early 1938 and promptly took up the antilynching bill. Southern forces began their most important filibuster up to that point on what would increasingly become their most daunting challenge: civil rights. Early in the "educational campaign," southern speakers made clear that they would address themselves to certain key items raised during the preliminary skirmishes the previous year. They emphasized that political expediency dictated the introduction of the bill. Northern senators from states with large urban centers, and therefore large black populations, seemed disproportionately in favor of antilynch-

22. Tom Connally (hereafter cited as TC) to Richard B. Russell (hereafter cited as RR), 23 December 1937, Box 1, Folder 4, Richard B. Russell Collection, Richard B. Russell Library, University of Georgia, Athens (hereafter cited as Russell MSS) ("so that there . . .").

ing legislation. From their perspective, this could only mean that northern politicians, recognizing the balance of power inherent in black voting blocs, sought civil rights advances more for electoral advantage than for the stated purpose of stopping lynching. A different, but interrelated theme, was the sectional nature of the bill. Often drawing parallels to the excesses of Reconstruction, southern senators stressed that feature of the legislation that best illustrated northern sectionalism—the proviso excluding gang related slayings from the punishment clauses of the measure. Throughout the debate, they refused to vote on an amendment to strike the controversial section. To do so would obfuscate the designs of the bill's drafters—the punishment of the South. Dieterich's amendment represented irrefutable proof, more proof than any statesman should need, according to the southerners, of the sectional nature of the proposal.[23]

Southern acceptance of the bill as part of a long-term process aimed at undermining the South's racial system went hand-in-hand with their denunciation of northern politicians who courted the black vote. Political expediency coupled with the pressure of black activists could only lead to one result: the end of segregation. The NAACP and other groups, southerners argued, would not stop their agitation with the passage of the Wagner–Van Nuys bill. Indeed, in order to survive, these organizations had to press an ever-broadening civil rights agenda or risk legislating themselves into obsolescence. In turn, politicians outside the South would have to support additional civil rights initiatives or risk losing the black vote. Mississippi's Pat Harrison warned fellow Democrats regarding this scenario, "You may win their favor for a short period, but paid lobbyists . . . are never quiet; they must remain active . . . and when they shall have accomplished the passage of this measure through your generous but dangerous votes, they must then get busy upon something else." Allen Ellender of Louisiana proved more direct in his threats, noting that "if this anti-lynching bill goes through . . . the next thing we shall find is that an effort to obtain social equality will be made by the same small group of Negro politicians." Because of this fear, the south-

23. For examples of the southern critique of political expediency, see *CR*, 75th Cong., 3rd sess. (subsequent *CR* citations are from the 3rd sess. of the 75th Cong. until otherwise noted), 7 January 1938, 158–159 (McKellar); *CR*, 10 January 1938, 253 (Harrison); *CR*, 12 January 1938, 381 (Bailey). For condemnation of the bill's sectional nature, see *CR*, 8 January 1938, 228 (Smith); *CR*, 12 January 1938, 379 (Bailey).

ern Senate delegation began viewing its fight against civil rights in broader terms. Over time, southern senators grew increasingly aware of the importance of slowing the drive for black equality that they now recognized as the ultimate goal of civil rights activists. Many southerners who participated in the 1938 filibuster later became the leaders of the group in the 1950s, when the pressure for civil rights far eclipsed that of the late New Deal. These junior senators from the South took the rhetoric of the 1930s seriously, using it to explain Washington developments to their constituents and employing it as a framework for guiding their individual actions. When the old guard such as Tom Connally and Josiah Bailey handed the task of protecting the racial system of the South to younger men, they did so knowing that their conception of the civil rights fight, as a battle against a vast but hidden effort to destroy segregation, would persist. From the fear that civil rights activism would not abate until Jim Crow fell expressed in the 1930s later emerged the strategy that would guide the southern defensive into the 1960s.[24]

Although the majority of the southerners who participated in the filibuster focused on the same major flaws of the bill, they often differed in the manner in which they conveyed their opposition to it. Like their slave-holding forebears, many southern senators took a paternalistic tone, considering it the responsibility of the white South to uplift their black neighbors. Individual southern senators varied, however, in how they viewed the overall ability of the black community to function without white guidance. Just as many slaveholders in the antebellum era adopted a fatherly relationship with their chattel, southerners in the 1930s considered the Jim Crow system a school of civilization, a continuation of the slave system made necessary by the Thirteenth Amendment that gave freedom to a still "uncivilized" race. Under the complex code of racial etiquette below the Mason-Dixon line, according to white southerners, black Americans were content with their social standing. Evidence to the contrary resulted from the provocation of those beyond Dixie's borders. Homegrown discontent simply did not exist in the worldview enunciated by southern senators. Speech after speech on the Senate floor touted the amicable and symbiotic nature of southern race relations. Despite differences in their views of the black community that ranged

24. *CR*, Harrison, 10 January 1938, 257 ("you may win . . ."); *CR*, Ellender, 15 January 1938, 580 ("if this . . .").

from open disdain to fatherly regard, the group, almost to a man, viewed the existing racial order in the South as the most effective given the tensions inherent in a biracial society. A white southerner, they theorized, could intuit the desires of African Americans because of his proximity to them throughout his life. Northern politicians knew nothing of the black community and sought its favor only for electoral advantage. In order to understand their use of race as well as the differences in their approach to the issue, it is useful to examine in greater detail how select but representative southern senators couched their opposition.[25]

South Carolina senator James F. Byrnes, who later served as secretary of state under Harry S. Truman and as a Supreme Court justice, spoke early in the debate. Since he generally eschewed filibusters, his address lent an air of respectability to the southern effort. Although the fifty-six-year-old Byrnes described himself as a simple man content with "three meals a day, two suits a year, and a reasonable amount of bourbon," he possessed a fierce demeanor when riled, something he demonstrated before he concluded his remarks against the Wagner–Van Nuys bill. Byrnes considered lynching a form of murder that fell under the auspices of local statutes governing the transgression. He warned that a federal antilynching law "may cause the people of the states who are striving to promote the cause of law and order to lose their interest or resent efforts to interfere with the States in their jurisdiction of murder cases." Only "by the education of our people," he observed, would lynching end. When he took the Senate floor to deliver his remarks on 11 January 1938, his oration exhibited paternalism in its emphasis on the interconnectedness of the South's black and white citizens. The relationship proved anything but that between equals. Whites provided benign guidance; blacks demonstrated their appreciation by following orders. According to Byrnes, the number of lynchings fell each year because the region's black population now committed fewer assaults against white women. "That," he argued, "has been due to the moral improvement of the Southern Negro." Their moral uplift stemmed, in his eyes, from greater educational opportunities granted to them by white southerners. As he indicated before the

25. For typical southern views on race, see CR, 7 January 1938, 144, 147 (McKellar); CR, 8 January 1938, 228–229 (Smith); CR, 10 January 1938, 257 (Harrison); CR, 14 January 1938, 503–504 (Ellender); CR, 15 January 1938, 578 (Ellender); CR, 9 February 1938, 1685, 1703 (Ellender).

Wagner–Van Nuys fight, he believed that southern officials might abrogate their responsibility for African Americans—a burden placed on them since the Civil War—if outside agitators succeeded in changing the existing order. Anything but gradual improvement initiated from within would undermine the fragile social structure established by the region in the years following Reconstruction.[26]

After defending southern race relations, Byrnes focused on what most of his regional colleagues considered the true intent of the bill, procuring black votes. Like Tom Connally in 1937, the South Carolinian likened Senator Robert Wagner of New York to Thaddeus Stevens. Unlike Stevens, who was driven by "hatred," Byrnes opined that Wagner was "prompted by hope—the hope of securing votes from the Negroes of New York City." Some of the zeal on the part of antilynching advocates, Byrnes believed, derived from NAACP pressure. Throughout the filibuster, NAACP director Walter White sat in the Senate gallery listening to the debate. White's presence did not go unnoticed. When Byrnes turned his attention to the gallery spectators, he had a special message for White, for the media, and for his colleagues. Pointing directly at White, Byrnes bitterly remarked that "one Negro . . . Walter White . . . has ordered this bill passed. If a majority can bring about a vote this bill will pass." Driving home the theme of political expediency among some politicos, he commented that if White permitted the withdrawal of the bill, "its advocates would desert it as quickly as football players unscramble when the whistle of the referee is heard." But as a lobbyist White would never make such a request. Instead, he would seek further and deeper concessions from Washington. "What legislation will he next demand of the Congress of the Unites States?" Byrnes asked. Answering his own question, he continued, "I do not know; but I know he will make other demands, and that those who are willing to vote for this bill because he demands it will acquiesce in his subsequent demands." Here Byrnes defined the nexus of forces that might

26. In his autobiography, Byrnes devoted little attention to civil rights. James F. Byrnes, *All in One Lifetime* (New York: Harper, 1958); Walter J. Brown, *James F. Byrnes of South Carolina: A Remembrance* (Macon, Ga.: Mercer University, 1992), 36 ("three meals . . ."); JB to Frank H. Hallion, 12 March 1937, Box 42, "Legislation 1922–1944, Anti-Lynching 1937," Byrnes MSS ("may cause people . . ."); JB to K. G. Finley, 23 March 1936, Box 42, "Legislation 1922–1944, Anti-lynching 1937" Folder, Byrnes MSS ("by the education . . ."); *CR*, 11 January 1938, 306 ("That has been . . .").

destroy Jim Crow. If enough statesmen bowed to the NAACP's agenda, the end of segregation would be the result. Byrnes announced that he and his southern colleagues decided on taking principled action to thwart such interest group influence. He left it up to his nonsouthern colleagues whether they too would join the fight against outside intervention in Washington politics.[27]

On 10 January 1938, forty-one-year-old Richard Brevard Russell of Georgia alerted the Senate that he intended to deliver an address against the antilynching bill. Tom Connally, along with many others in the chamber, recognized the talents of the young Georgian. In part, Russell's commanding physical presence highlighted by his rigid posture and aristocratic mien set him apart from his colleagues. But his greatest attribute, one that made him indispensable to Connally, was his knowledge of the Senate Rules. From the moment, he arrived in Washington, Russell began memorizing the body's twenty-two standing rules, before turning to the chamber parliamentarian for additional tutoring in Senate precedents. When Richard Russell completed his self-imposed education, he knew more about the history and operation of the Senate than most of his colleagues. Armed with this knowledge, he became an asset to Connally, who made the Georgian his principal lieutenant in the fight against the Wagner–Van Nuys bill. Although Russell employed his parliamentary skills in many legislative fields, he considered defending southern racial norms most important. His lineage as the descendant of a prosperous slaveholding family ruined by the Civil War and his avid interest in the very same conflict that destroyed his ancestors' fortunes, only heightened his passion for the southern cause. And when Richard Russell focused his energies on an issue, victory often followed. An opponent of Russell on the civil rights question once noted that Russell's prominent Roman nose proved an effective barometer of the Georgian's mood. If his nose was "tilted haughtily in the air" before an oration, the civil rights advocate remarked, "we knew we were in for trouble." When Russell entered the chamber on 11 January 1938 to deliver the promised speech, his prominent nose jutted in the air.[28]

Only in his fifth year of Senate service, Russell's brief career encompassed

27. CR, 11 January 1938, 306 ("prompted by hope . . ."). All other Byrnes quotations can be found in CR, 11 January 1938, 310. Time, 24 January 1938, 9.

28. Caro, Master of the Senate, 164–202; Fite, Richard B. Russell, Jr., xi–167; Mann, Walls of Jericho, 22–46; Time, 12 August 1957, 13–16; Douglas, In the Fullness of Time, 227 ("tilted haughtily . . .").

the 1935 Costigan-Wagner filibuster, during which the Georgian largely remained silent. In 1938, he broke his silence by delivering his first major civil rights address. Russell began his presentation by emphasizing the connection between the antilynching campaign and the desire to procure black votes. He also turned to a tactic he would employ frequently in all subsequent civil rights fights—pointing out the hypocrisy of many northern statesmen. How could they in good conscious condemn the South for a crime that occurred with great infrequency, without also addressing the growing murder rates in large urban centers above the Mason-Dixon line? In the end, Russell accused antilynching advocates of false advertising. They were attempting to take a "dead pole cat," dress it up, and pass it off as "hickory smoke cured ham," he argued. His analogy referred to that, despite its antilynching label, the bill did not punish those who committed the actual murder. Instead, Wagner–Van Nuys would punish officers of the peace, who may or may not have had anything to do with the crime, and innocent taxpayers, whose only transgression was their misfortune of residing in a county where a lynching occurred. With this and with all of the other shortfalls of the proposal that he outlined, the Georgian hoped some of his colleagues would recognize that this bill was not "hickory smoke cured ham."[29]

Sometime after his first speech, Russell discovered a communist pamphlet, titled, "The Road to Liberation for the Negro People," with direct relevance to the pending legislation. He found the booklet so disturbing that he began drafting a second address. The tract illustrated that the antilynching bill represented the first step of a larger plan to create an independent "Negro Soviet Republic" in the South. Russell seized the opportunity to link the communist propaganda with the growing civil rights movement. In addition, the pamphlet bolstered southern contentions regarding the vanguard nature of the antilynching bill. Before embarking on his second speech, the Georgian reassured the senators present of his paternalistic regard for African Americans. "I have no prejudice against the Negroes," he remarked, and "I am glad that the Negroes with whom I have come in contact have called me their friend." He praised the South's success in aiding its black citizens, in carrying a "race that had known only savagery and slavery" to a "new day of civilization." After dispensing hosannas on the southern racial order, he

29. *CR*, 11 January 1938, 312 and 314 (desire for black votes), 317 (northern murder rates), 311 ("dead polecat . . ."), 362 (summation of the bill's shortfalls).

addressed the importance of holding the line against the push to eradicate the Jim Crow system.[30]

Russell outlined a four-step process contained in the Communist pamphlet, remarkably prescient as it turned out. Even more important, the speech illuminated the strategic vision that informed Russell's own leadership when he eclipsed Tom Connally as head of the southern bloc. A federal antilynching law, he began, represented the first step in a program meant to polarize public opinion against the South. Initiatives stripping the right of states to fix suffrage requirements would follow, swelling the voting rolls with blacks bent on gaining restitution from the white South. With suffrage and the strength of black voting blocs expanded, bills aimed at dismantling the Jim Crow system would emerge before a final push to remove state laws prohibiting interracial marriage. Next, and the least plausible of the scenarios outlined in the pamphlet, would be the creation of an independent African American nation in the southern black belt. This agenda, supported by the Communist Party, which published the pamphlet to which Russell referred, proved identical to the objectives of the NAACP and certain northern liberals, minus, of course, the goal of an American "Negro Soviet Republic." If senators could not accept arguments concerning the dubious constitutionality or sectional nature of the bill, Russell opined, then surely they could see that proponents of the measure were mere communist handmaidens. Of all the speeches during the 1938 filibuster, both of Russell's proved of paramount importance, not so much for how they influenced the chamber, although they did do that, but for what they foretold of future southern strategy when Russell led the southern opposition. Allowing the antilynching bill to pass would set in motion an inexorable chain of events. The Georgian thought that each time the South retreated on a civil rights question the enemy would push a little closer to the Jim Crow citadel. As Russell himself noted to a constituent, "if we are finally exhausted and permit the passage of the anti-lynch bill, it would be followed by legislation to break down segregation of the races in schools, hospitals, churches, restaurants, hotels, bath houses, and all other public places, as well as by bills giving the ballot to every negro, and striking down State statutes preventing intermarriage of the races."

30. RR to John Boykin, 21 January 1938, Box 2, Folder 3, Russell MSS (Russell discovers communist threat); CR, 26 January 1938, 1098–1111 (discussion of the pamphlet), 1100 ("I have no . . ."), 1101 ("race that had . . .").

Failure in 1938, or at any future point, would prove disastrous. Later, Russell, who fully recognized the implications of capitulating on any civil rights proposal, became instrumental in adjusting the southern strategy to more accurately reflect the political situation by permitting the passage of minor initiatives to delay a major assault on Jim Crow. When he orchestrated the shift in southern strategy, he employed the same conceptual framework that guided his actions during the Wagner–Van Nuys fight, a framework that held that ceaseless civil rights activism brought about by vote-hungry northern politicians and pressure groups bent on forcing black social equality would lead to a persistent legislative crusade against segregation. To Richard Russell would eventually fall the task of defusing the civil rights juggernaut. He would meet future challenges by conceptualizing those battles in the same framework employed by southern senators prior to World War II.[31]

If Richard Russell sprang from the South's native aristocracy, then Mississippi's Theodore Bilbo reflected the region's poorer citizenry, its plain folk. Bilbo staked his electoral success on projecting an image of his humble origins. Until the end of his career, he reminded constituents, "I am one of you." His identification with the common man extended beyond the rhetorical as evidenced by the rumors of womanizing and financial difficulty that plagued him until his death. Although he compiled a liberal voting record on many of the major social issues of the day, he remained notorious for his racial demagoguery, which grew in proportion to the civil rights threat. As his defense of white supremacy increased in virulence later in his career, so too did his ego, a fact that led him to dub himself "The Man." Those less fond of the Mississippian referred to him as the "Bilbonic Plague." During his Senate orations in 1938, Bilbo adopted many of the themes broached by others, but unlike many of them, he injected overt racist appeals and imagery clearly on the wane among southerners, who found their leverage in the Senate diminishing. In order to win over their colleagues, the southern bloc needed to rely less on racial invective and more on constitutional arguments. Bilbo only partially recognized this. His comment to a constituent that "we are trying to preserve states' rights and protect the virtue of Southern White women," captures his ambiguous position. As if uncertain of the correct path, Bilbo opted

31. *CR*, 26 January 1938, 1101–1102 (outline of the process); RR to W. T. Duncan, 29 January 1938, Box 2, Folder 4, Russell MSS ("if we are . . .").

for the best of both worlds. He embraced constitutional arguments when the mood struck him, without closing the door on oratory still common among politicians from the region as seen in his defense of white womanhood. The Mississippian straddled the border between the rhetorical approach of the old and the new southern statesman.[32]

Many southerners limited their antiblack rhetoric during the 1938 filibuster. For Theodore Bilbo the time to denude his message had yet to arrive, and indeed, it never would. Describing the black race in America, Bilbo argued, "He is an obstacle, he is in the way; he retards progress; and as more and more Negroes multiply they drag down our progress and our civilization to lower levels." During another speech, he observed that "as a slave we have set him free; and we are now engaged in a vain and foolish attempt, despite his admitted racial inferiority, lack of creative and inventive genius, to make him an equal to the white man socially and politically." Considering his harsh view of African Americans, it comes as no surprise that he took the myth of the black rapist to heart. On the floor of the U.S. Senate, he noted that he fought the antilynching bill for the "protection of the wives, mothers, daughters, and sweethearts of Dixie." In a letter to a constituent written about the same time, the Mississippian went even further, observing that "it is through fear of the White Man that the negro has refrained from committing so many atrocious crimes." Although it happened rarely in the late 1930s, lynching, in Bilbo's mind, still had a residual influence on southern blacks in preventing them from indulging in what he considered their innate depravity.[33]

Like other southerners, Bilbo contended that the demands of the black

32. Chester M. Morgan, *Redneck Liberal: Theodore G. Bilbo and the New Deal* (Baton Rouge: Louisiana State University Press, 1985); A. Wigfall Green, *The Man: Bilbo* (Baton Rouge: Louisiana State University Press, 1963); Salter, *Public Men*, 278. The sobriquet "The Man" originally represented an abbreviated version of the phrase "the man of the people." Because of Bilbo's racism, the nickname increasingly became associated with the term employed by African Americans to describe any white person. "The man" in such a context not only defined an individual in a position of authority but also emphasized that person's role in the oppression of the black community. Theodore G. Bilbo (hereafter cited as TB) to W. M. Paige, 22 January 1940, Box 1076, Folder 9, Bilbo Collection, McCain Library, University of Southern Mississippi, Hattiesburg (hereafter cited as Bilbo MSS) ("I am one . . ."); TB to John R. Webster, 2 February 1938, Box 334, "2 February 1938" Folder, Bilbo MSS ("we are trying . . .").

33. *CR*, Bilbo, 1 February 1938, 1345 ("he is an . . ."); *CR*, 21 January 1938, 887 ("as a slave . . ."); *CR*, 21 January 1938, 873 ("protection of the . . ."); TB to Quincy Ewing, 18 January 1938, Box

population would not cease with the passage of the antilynching bill. "Give him this law and then he will demand something else," Bilbo claimed. But unlike some southerners who advocated a cordon defense against future civil rights thrusts, the Mississippian opted for the offensive. During the 1938 filibuster, he advocated legislation that would repatriate the black population to Africa. He did not consider the scheme farfetched, arguing that the forcible removal of the Indians to the western frontier served as a successful precedent for his own initiative. Although, the logistics of the plan needed to be perfected, he intended emigration to be voluntary and clearly viewed it as something more than a ruse to sustain the southern filibuster. In Bilbo's eyes, a symbiotic relationship between black and white citizens could not exist, even within the structure of the Jim Crow system, without the eventual amalgamation of the races. Once that occurred, the extinction of the American republic would follow. Near the end of a speech on 21 January 1938, he summarized his racial animosity: "I hold that the presence of the Negro race has been the greatest curse that has ever visited upon the South. . . . He has caused privation, suffering, and shame beyond the power of omnipotence to measure." Like Russell, Bilbo believed that something needed to be done, but he felt that no form of delay could preserve a completely segregated social order. Amalgamation, mongrelization, and extinction proved the only possible outcome for the South and the nation if his colleagues chose not to enact his plan. His concerns, like those of Russell, stemmed from the belief that the desegregation of public schools, which all southerners viewed as a long-term objective of civil rights advocates, would encourage white children to abandon their natural aversion to their black counterparts. A generation raised in desegregated schools and force-fed a message of racial equality would invariably lead to amalgamation and, according to the prevailing racist logic of the era, the destruction of American society.[34]

332, "18 January 1938 B" Folder, Bilbo MSS ("it is through . . ."). For additional insight into Bilbo's views on race, see Theodore G. Bilbo, *Take Your Choice: Separation or Mongrelization* (Poplarville, Miss.: Dream House, 1947).

34. *CR*, 21 January 1938, 88 ("Give him this . . ."). Ironically, the Universal Negro Improvement Association's head, the colorful and controversial black activist Marcus Garvey, who had long advocated black resettlement to Africa, announced his support for the plan. Bilbo wrote to Garvey upon receipt of his letter offering assistance, "I am happy to know your organization will give me the fullest cooperation in the program that I am trying to project for the benefit

Many southerners not accustomed to joining the likes of Theodore Bilbo nonetheless prepared orations when it became clear that a protracted filibuster would take place. In 1938, southern constituencies expected all elected officials to do their part in preserving the region's "way of life." Florida's Claude Denson Pepper knew that he could not remain on the sidelines. Born in Alabama at the turn of the twentieth century, Pepper eventually settled in Florida in his midtwenties to pursue a legal career. Following the commencement of his Senate tenure in 1936, he developed a reputation as an ardent New Dealer, even winning unrestricted access to President Franklin D. Roosevelt. His diary entries from the period indicate a man with different plans for himself and for the South, plans not wholly consonant with political reality. On 17 November 1937, for example, Pepper recorded that Senator Joseph A. Guffey of Pennsylvania told him that "in talking on the anti-lynching bill not to be too severe on the negroes because" he "had a future in the National picture." The entry indicates that even at this early stage in his career, some considered Pepper something other than the usual southern partisan. In December 1937, Pepper lunched with a constituent in Jacksonville, Florida, where he learned of the support given the antilynching fight by some women, several churches, and assorted civic organizations below the Mason-Dixon line. Summarizing his impression of the encounter, he wrote, "just indicates the South is changing and I am glad to see it." This passage underscores that the Floridian was, at best, a lukewarm defender of regional racial interests. He wanted the South to change and to do so it would have to abandon its anachronistic system of racial segregation. Later in his career, he would completely break with other southern senators. For Claude Pepper in 1938, however, pragmatism got the better of principle. Pressure to enact antilynching legislation forced him to make a decision concerning his willingness to assist his southern colleagues. Electoral success proved the deciding influence. Pepper's Senate mandate stretched only two years since his initial election filled a vacancy left by the death of Duncan Fletcher. In November 1938, he faced reelection. Abandoning his colleagues in the antilynching fight might jeopardize his chances for victory. Putting aside his reservations about the filibuster, the Floridian drafted a lengthy address. Pep-

---

of the Negroes of the United States." TB to Marcus Garvey, 24 August 1938, Box 1091, Folder 9, Bilbo MSS. *CR*, 21 January 1938, 893 ("I hold that . . .").

per had no intention of matching the racist demagoguery of Bilbo, nor did he aim to outdo Richard Russell in his passionate denunciation of northern hypocrisy. But, he would participate.[35]

On 24 January, Pepper took the Senate floor, delivering a speech that highlighted the central points in the southern fight against the antilynching bill. In it he applauded the amicable race relations in his home state of Florida and touted the great strides made by the South in stopping the crime of lynching. According to Pepper, lynching had an economic component in that poor whites, who usually committed the infraction, sought to maintain their social status by becoming the strongest defenders of white supremacy. So long as economic conditions in the South limited the social mobility of the region's poor, economically depressed whites would seek to maintain their feelings of superiority over the black man, who often served as employment competition, through violence. If northerners abandoned discriminatory freight rates and other prejudicial economic policies, the South would flourish and lynching would cease. He noted further that "southerners are not Negro haters and Negro killers. They are in their hearts constitutional Democrats, the cardinal principle of whose philosophy is a due respect for and observance of local self-government." After following the script established by others, Pepper turned to a legalistic analysis of the loopholes and absence of clarity that he believed marked the Wagner–Van Nuys bill. Pepper went through the motions in 1938, delivering a pro-forma address on the South's ability to govern itself. In the short term, the speech fulfilled his immediate objective of a November electoral triumph. Looking back in the twilight of his life after decades of public service marked by support for liberal social programs and advocacy of civil rights, Pepper could not forget the 1938 filibuster. "I wish this sorry chapter could be expunged from my record and more importantly from my memory," he wrote in his 1987 autobiography. Much as he might have hoped to avoid the civil right issue in 1938, political pressure forced him in line with the solid South.[36]

35. Claude D. Pepper, *Pepper: Eyewitness to a Century* (New York: Harcourt, Brace, Jovanovich, 1987), vii–60; Claude Pepper (hereafter cited as CP) Diary, 17 November 1937, Series 439, Box 1, Folder 1, Claude Pepper Collection, Claude Pepper Library, Florida State University, Tallahassee (hereafter cited as Pepper MSS) ("that in talking . . ."); CP Diary, 9 December 1937, Series 439, Box 1, Folder 1, Pepper MSS ("just indicates that . . .").

36. *CR*, Pepper, 24 January 1938, 976 (Florida race relations), 975–976 (economic issues), 981 ("southerners are not . . ."); Pepper, *Pepper*, 66 ("I wish this . . .").

At the start of the third session of the Seventy-fifth Congress, southern senators held one objective, killing the antilynching bill. Based on the odds against them, many doubted that they could achieve their goal. Early in 1938, for example, Theodore Bilbo echoed Tom Connally's forecast of the previous year by noting the possibility of defeat. He commented that despite the filibuster, "I am afraid it is going to pass regardless of what we say or do." In particular, southerners feared that a cloture petition would prove successful if all senators who committed themselves in advance followed their initial convictions. If that occurred, a simple majority would then easily pass the bill. Southerners also recognized that many of their Republican colleagues, who represented a decided minority in the chamber, would prove reluctant to support cloture, if given suitable reasons, lest the same device one day be used against them. As things turned out, southerners had little to fear. On 27 January 1938, the cloture showdown occurred. Victory for the South proved total. Not only did they stave off the dreaded two-thirds margin governing cloture, but more than half of the chamber sided with them in a lopsided vote (thirty-seven to fifty-one) that saw all but one of the Republican Party's thirteen senators and fifteen nonsouthern Democrats siding with Connally's forces. Success changed the tenor of the southern outlook. By the end of January, most of them saw victory within reach. Their attempt to win votes on the merits of their arguments had paid dividends. Describing the southern efforts, Richard Russell observed that "the fight we have made has crystallized public opinion in our favor, even in the Northern and Western states." Bilbo too recognized the gradual erosion of antilynching support. In his inimitable way, "The Man" described the changing legislative situation in more colorful terms than the reserved Russell. "I think we have these damn Yankees whipped to a frazzle," he commented.[37]

The cloture vote reveals much regarding the perceived importance of racial equality outside of the South. Members of both political parties demonstrated a marked disinterest in civil rights. At least for the moment, south-

---

37. TB to J. D. Roberts, 11 January 1938, Box 331, "11 January 1938 B" Folder, Bilbo MSS ("I am afraid . . ."); New York Times, 16 January 1938, 6, announces the filibuster would not be broken; Washington Post, 20 January 1938, 1, notes that westerners such as Nebraska's George Norris have altered their once positive assessments of the bill. For the cloture vote, see CR, 27 January 1938, 1166; RR to John A. Boykin, 29 January 1938, Box 2, Folder 3, Russell MSS ("the fight we . . ."); TB to W. H. Walker, 29 January 1938, Box 334, "29 January 1938 B" Folder, Bilbo MSS ("I think we . . .").

ern senators had the votes with plenty to spare. Initial prognostications that the antilynching proposal would easily sail through Congress in 1938 proved excessively sanguine once it became evident that many nonsoutherners saw little to gain from pushing the antilynching question. In fact, the debate's pivotal speech came not from southern mouths but from that of one of the Senate's most respected members, Idaho Republican William Borah, who added credence to southern claims by echoing arguments that the bill was hopelessly unconstitutional. Borah, like many of his colleagues, found the overarching conservatism that informed the southern position fully consistent with his own ideological outlook.

Uniform Republican voting behavior indicated the formation of a new conservative coalition born of political necessity. The coalition emerged from the ashes of Franklin Roosevelt's failed 1937 Court Packing Plan. Until then, congressional opposition to Roosevelt's New Deal initiatives were limited and disorganized. As the economy stabilized, partisan sniping commenced. Alone, the handful of Republicans on Capitol Hill lacked the power to halt what they considered the unnecessary expansion of the federal government. To make a difference, the GOP needed friends if it hoped to mount a meaningful opposition. But who among the Democratic ranks shared the same ideological predispositions? Who also shared the same reservations regarding the expansion of national over state prerogatives? One constituent part of the Democratic ranks suited the need. Fortuitously, a regional bloc of Democrats was also in search of new allies.[38]

The Democratic Party had reached a crossroads by the late 1930s, torn between those committed to the expansion of the welfare state created by the New Deal and the continuation of government management of the economy, and those convinced that federal power posed a threat to free enterprise and local governing institutions. Democratic factions generally cleaved along regional lines with southerners, leaning toward a narrower, or more Republican, view of governmental responsibility. Politicians from industrialized northern states gravitated toward the expansion of the government's role, whereas many from the South and portions of the nonindustrialized West harbored reservations regarding this trend. In the end more than intra- and intermural squabbles forged the conservative coalition. Ultimately, it was an

38. Brinkley, *End of Reform;* Patterson, *Congressional Conservatism.*

issue as old as the republic and one that southern senators defended with the utmost of vigor that brought them in union with the Party of Lincoln.[39]

Once members of the Democratic Party began pushing for antilynching legislation, it did not take much imagination to connect the dots, to see that the broadening of federal power associated with the New Deal had direct implications on segregation, especially in light of the formation of activist organizations such as the NAACP that promised election-day retribution for those politicians who opposed the civil rights agenda. For southerners it was easy to envision a day when the northern wing of the party would attempt to dismantle Jim Crow by using the precedent of federal preeminence ensconced during the New Deal. Southerners, like Republicans, had independently reached a critical juncture in the late 1930s; each needed and each found a perfect match in the other. Southerners had located votes to fight civil rights, whereas Republicans had forged a coalition that ensured their agenda would not be subsumed by that of the overwhelming Democratic majority. In short, the ideological distance between a southern Democrat and a moderate or conservative Republican was much shorter than it was between southerners and liberal northern Democrats. This conservative coalition would profoundly impact future political discourse in the United States, ultimately delimiting the scope of the nation's political agenda for much of the twentieth century.[40]

Now, time became the enemy of antilynching advocates. The filibuster stalled legislative action in the chamber, and by February a significant number of important administration bills lay dormant as the southern forces continued their "educational campaign." At times, it appeared the southerners were only just getting started. Theodore Bilbo, for example, threatened to unveil a thirty-day speech, indicating that if pressed, the South would not capitulate. Louisiana's forty-eight-year-old junior senator, Allen J. Ellender, also had grand intentions. On 14 January 1938, he obtained the floor to begin an address that he completed six days later. Chamber rules sanctioned such dil-

39. Theodore Rosenof, *Patterns of Political Economy in America: The Failure to Develop a Democratic Left Synthesis, 1933–1950* (New York: Taylor and Francis, 1983).

40. Cobb and Namorato, *New Deal and the South*, 97–116; Douglas C. Abrams, *Conservative Constraints: North Carolina and the New Deal* (Jackson: University Press of Mississippi, 1992); Freidel, *F. D. R. and the South*; Morgan, *Redneck Liberal*; Tindall, *Emergence of the New South*; Weiss, *Farewell to the Party of Lincoln*.

atory practices by permitting a unanimous consent agreement to recess the chamber until the next calendar day with the senator who made the request still holding the floor. Senate rules also held that a senator could deliver only one speech on the same matter each legislative day. By calling for recesses and by never relinquishing the floor, Ellender, although speaking for a series of days on the same subject—the antilynching bill—never ran afoul of chamber protocol. In the Senate, an institution governed by precedent and professional courtesy, a request by a member to recess for the day customarily met approval. Voicing an objection served as a most unsenatorial action, one that would surely lead to retribution from friend and foe alike. "To get along you needed to go along" remained a nostrum all senators knew. Ellender thus in 1938 could deliver a rambling oration over the course of a week, stopping each day when he had had enough merely by asking his colleagues for a recess. The legislative day would not end and thus Ellender could commence his remarks the next day. Calendar days might pass, but without an adjournment a legislative day remained constant. For all practical purposes, senators, at least in their world, controlled time. Unanimous consent agreements were entered into for an array of purposes, even to suspend time so that individual senators did not unduly tax themselves or when strict adherence to parliamentary procedure proved inconvenient. Precedents governing recesses and adjournments aided southern senators and their filibuster efforts. Frequent quorum calls and lengthy questions posed by his regional peers during his remarks further spelled the Louisianan. At least in the first half of the twentieth century, there proved a general unwillingness among senators to put southern feet to the fire, to keep them talking and talking without adjournment. As such, southern filibusterers faced obstacles in their resistance efforts, but not nearly as many as they would face when advocates of racial change challenged the status quo and used the Senate rules against southerners. That point, however, was along way off.

Over the course of the week, the five-foot four-inch Louisianan with a penchant for vigorous physical exercise in the Senate gymnasium ranged over the race question, focusing particular attention on reading into the *Congressional Record* excerpts from works that linked race mixing to the collapse of history's great empires. Ellender's endurance knew no boundaries. Even during his record-setting six-day filibuster, totaling twenty-seven hours and forty-five minutes, he often played a full eighteen holes of golf in the morning before arriving on Capitol Hill to continue his address. Because of his vitality, Senate liberals dubbed him the "Little Bull" and the "Minotaur." Furthermore, the Louisianan threatened to force his Senate colleagues to vote on amendments that would put them on record regarding interracial marriage. If the Senate voted cloture, Ellender would push for the chamber to pass judgement on amendments making interracial coupling a federal offense. The Senate responded with howls of protest, but the chorus of complaints could not hide the fact that most Americans in the 1930s, including those in the North, held considerable racial animosity. Few legislators possessed the courage to risk a vote on Ellender's proposals, a fact that undoubtedly influenced the cloture decision. Little wonder that with "The Man" and the "Minotaur" vowing to speak until Christmas and threatening to force their colleagues into compromising situations, many senators began losing interest in the Wagner–Van Nuys fight.[41]

More important than the bluster of Bilbo and Ellender proved the moderate addresses of men such as Byrnes, Russell, and Pepper; they provided those beyond the Mason-Dixon line a rationale for voting against the bill that transcended race. The 1938 debate taught future southern Senate leaders a valuable lesson. By raising constitutional objections to the bill, they found that their northern and western colleagues waffled in their convictions. Although they paid lip service to civil rights, nonsoutherners as yet lacked a firm commitment to the cause. In a final effort to shut off debate, Wagner forwarded a second cloture petition. On 16 February, it too failed, this time forty-two to forty-six. The second cloture vote closely followed the earlier Senate division on the same question. A handful of senators altered their decision in a meaningless gesture of support for a bill without a chance of coming to a vote, let alone of passing. Southerners exalted in their complete and total victory. With that vote, the antilynching fight ended in the Seventy-fifth Congress. On February 21, Wagner removed his bill from consideration; House Joint Resolution 596, a bill to make "an additional appropriation for

41. For Bilbo's thirty-day speech threats, see TB to Lloyd T. Benford, 27 January 1938, Box 333, "27 January 1938 B" Folder, Bilbo MSS; TB to W. H. Walker, 29 January 1938, Box 334, "29 January 1938 B" Folder, Bilbo MSS; Becnel, *Senator Allen Ellender*, 3–79. For examples of Ellender's tactics, see CR, 17 January 1938, 624 and CR, 19 January 1938, 754. For Ellender's threat regarding miscegenation, see CR, 14 January 1938, 506–507; *Newsweek*, 31 January 1938. For the origins of Ellender's nicknames, see Douglas, *In the Fullness of Time*, 217.

relief purposes," replaced it. Combating the ongoing economic depression had superceded the civil rights crusade.[42]

Although victory in this case came more easily than expected, future vigilance became essential for the southern forces lest additional assaults against the region prove successful. Tom Connally, for example, recognized that the most effective weapon in the antilynching fight remained the South's ability to curtail the crime. In a letter to the head of the Association of Southern Women for the Prevention of Lynching, Connally expressed his hope that the organization "may be able to bring vividly to the Governors and other officials the imperative desirability of preventing lynching through the regular state action and legal processes." This statement underscored the connection he saw between controlling the crime in the South and his ability to array the region's senators in winning the legislative battle in Washington. Should a resurgence in the crime occur, future antilynching fights might result in a different outcome. Despite their victory, the southern forces still had cause for concern. During the filibuster, Claude Pepper noted in his diary following a meeting with the leader of the NAACP that Walter White considered the bill "good propaganda against lynchings" even if it eventually fell short of passage. Pepper's observation indicated that the leadership of the NAACP did not view the defeat of the Wagner–Van Nuys bill as the end of their antilynching campaign. They would try again. Beyond increased political pressure from the black community, some noted growing opposition against the South in Washington. Senator Jimmy Byrnes, for example, remarked to a constituent, "It is difficult for one not a member of Congress to realize the sectional feeling now existing against the South." Such tension emanating from Capitol Hill and increasingly from northern black communities portended a difficult future. As yet, few southern senators addressed what Cotton Ed Smith considered the susceptibility of southern blacks to outside agitators. Later, it would become the subject of much analysis. At some point, however, all of these trends would coalesce into a single powerful lobby capable of forcing the South to capitulate. Speaking on behalf of his regional cohorts at the end of 1938, Thomas Connally still felt optimistic. In spite of continued pressure for antilynching legislation, he said, "I feel that the public opinion of the nation is opposed to such a purely political proposal." How

42. The second cloture vote can be found in *CR*, 16 February 1938, 2007. Introduction of the relief appropriation appears in *CR*, 21 February 1938, 2210.

long national public opinion would remain ambivalent to the civil rights crusade remained the larger and as-yet-unanswered question. So long as the majority of Americans demonstrated reluctance to embrace the cause of civil rights, southerners knew they could defend the Jim Crow system. If that popular indifference changed, they would, in turn, lose the ability to sway their colleagues less committed to civil rights as they had succeeded in do-ing against Wagner–Van Nuys. Once that happened, the end would quickly come. For now, the southern group and their Senate colleagues turned their sights on Europe where events there spiraled toward another world war.[43]

The 1938 fight marked southern recognition that the antilynching cam-paign represented one phase of a larger effort aimed at destroying Jim Crow segregation. By stopping the Wagner–Van Nuys bill, they hoped to arrest fur-ther efforts to undermine southern racial norms. Although victory met their actions, their success did not come without disappointment. With the national Democratic Party contesting the Republican hold over African American vot-ers, in conjunction with what southerners considered the NAACP's dominance over both the black population and northern politicians, the mild civil rights pressure of the 1930s was fast becoming an unceasing campaign against the South. Recognizing that civil rights activists aimed at dismantling segregation, southern senators believed that by winning victories against legislation that only tangentially threatened the region's racial order, such as antilynching proposals, they would keep their opponents from advancing bills that more directly threatened Jim Crow. Southern logic during the New Deal held that civil rights advocates would not push for social equality if they could not even muster sufficient support to carry an antilynching proposal. Circumstances in the late 1930s also forced southern senators to alter their traditional pat-terns of obstruction in exchange for a more dignified line of argumentation. The future would require further adaptations in both their strategy and their rhetoric that drew heavily on the lessons learned in the antilynching battle.

43. TC to Jessie D. Ames, 7 February 1938, Box 127, "Anti-Lynching File" Folder, Connally MSS ("may be able . . ."). Not everyone agreed with Connally's assessment. Liberal mouth-piece *New Republic* on 9 March 1938, 114 contended just the opposite, that all Americans, even southerners, favored an antilynching bill. CP Diary, 12 February 1938, Series 439, Box 1, Folder 2, Pepper MSS ("good propaganda . . ."); JB to S. W. Copeland, 8 November 1938, Box 12, "Miscellaneous 1938-C" Folder, Byrnes MSS ("it is difficult . . ."); transcript, press pelease, 30 December 1938, Box 554, "Press Release, 1938" Folder, Connally MSS ("I feel that . . .").

2. The Origins of Strategic Delay

IN SEPTEMBER 1939, Nazi Germany invaded Poland and World War II began. At first, the United States remained neutral, but following the Japanese attack on Pearl Harbor in December 1941, it entered the conflagration against the Axis powers. Washington statesmen met the crisis by orchestrating an enormous mobilization that pulled the country out of the economic depression that had lingered for over a decade. Involvement in a war to crush totalitarianism abroad triggered important questions concerning injustices at home. During the war, a growing sense of discontent and solidarity grew among African Americans. Many challenged the inherent contradiction of the nation's war aims, which touted a fight for freedom at the same time it maintained a segregated society. Black soldiers fought with distinction in a segregated U.S. military, despite suppositions to the contrary raised by staunch segregationists. If these soldiers were good enough to fight and die for their country, many reasoned, certainly they deserved equality before the law. But African Americans, especially those in the South, lived under a two-tiered social system in which they enjoyed few of the economic opportunities afforded their white neighbors and almost none of the political advantages. Attempting to rectify the dichotomy between the country's foreign and domestic policies, several national legislators increased their agitation for civil rights. While some renewed their efforts on behalf of the antilynching crusade, others viewed the elimination of the poll tax as a modest way of demonstrating the nation's adherence to the principle of liberty. Going even further, numerous politicians pushed for the creation of a permanent Fair Employment Practices Commission (FEPC) to eliminate discriminatory hiring practices. Southern senators thus faced an ever-widening assault on their region's racial system. As a result, they prepared a spirited defense against civil rights legislation that reflected the continued relevance of the ideas expressed during the 1938 antilynching fight. A small step down the path toward racial equality, they believed, would only encourage further incursions against the Jim Crow system. Unlike in 1938, they began to doubt their ability to contain the advance. Where once they believed they could stop the push for social equality by thwarting the antilynching crusade, they increasingly realized that regardless of their efforts, the push for civil rights would continue. The drive to abolish the poll tax and the clamor for a permanent FEPC debunked their belief that they could keep the battle on the periphery of the Jim Crow system. They concluded that they would have to alter their strategy or risk losing everything. Too much was at stake for them to do otherwise.[1]

Before the United States entered the war, southern senators faced a familiar controversy. In 1940, antilynching legislation reappeared, prompting southern leader Tom Connally to muse that "the states are doing a most excellent job in preventing lynching and it's my view that it will entirely disappear." Tuskegee Institute statistics regarding the crime reveal the truth behind the Texan's remarks. The crime still occurred, but its frequency had dwindled to fewer than ten a year—too many for any law abiding citizenry to sanction, but far fewer than in the past. For Connally and his cohorts, the evidence bore out their claims that attitudes regarding the crime were altering. As in 1938, he emphasized that political expediency dictated the bill's introduction. He observed to a constituent, "I have no prejudice whatever against the colored race, but I do not believe in passing legislation based on race purely for political effect." Commenting about the prospect of antilynching legislation, he offered, "I do not believe it has any chance of passing at this Session of Congress." More important, he stressed that the South could solve its internal problems without federal intervention. To Jessie Daniel Ames, founder of the Association of Southern Women for the Prevention

1. For background, see Blum, *V Was for Victory*; Dalfiume, "'Forgotten Years' of the Negro Revolution," 90–106; Finkle, "Conservative Aims," 692–713; Goodwin, *No Ordinary Time*; Kirby, *Black Americans in the Roosevelt Era*; Steven F. Lawson, *Black Ballots: Voting Rights in the South, 1944–1969* (New York: Columbia University Press, 1976); Steven F. Lawson, *In Pursuit of Power: Civil Rights and Black Politics in America Since 1941* (Philadelphia: Temple University Press, 1991); Reed, *Seedtime for the Modern Civil Rights Movement*; Sitkoff, *New Deal for Blacks*.

of Lynching, Connally claimed, "We want to demonstrate to the world that the southern people are making a heroic effort to control this situation and that they are succeeding." Although he defined the issue in narrow terms as a sectional bill designed to eradicate a crime that infrequently occurred, the Texan nonetheless fought for a cultural system predicated on black inferiority. When asked if he would defend white supremacy, he succinctly remarked, "We shall stand fast." Although he optimistically heralded the death of the antilynching crusade, the southern leader grew less sanguine regarding the long-term future of Jim Crow.[2]

Connally's correspondence in the early 1940s depicted the civil rights fight in national political terms as a battle in which the South, even in the Democratic Party, was steadily losing ground. Northern Democrats, he claimed, "are in many cases harder on us than the Republicans of other days." His allusion to the Reconstruction era pointed to the larger framework that informed his belief in the existence of antisouthern discrimination of "a political as well as a business and commercial character." Even worse, he saw no end to the sectional antipathy. "We are doing the best we can but being in a decided minority we don't get very far," he noted regarding the southern position in Washington. Because they could not mount their own offensive, southerners utilized the protections granted minority interests in the U.S. Senate such as the filibuster. They also used the privileges seniority afforded them to ensure that congressional actions neither challenged segregation nor provided much if any assistance to African Americans. In short, they guaranteed that national legislation aided as few blacks as possible, while making sure that the dispensation of federal programs remained in state hands so that local norms, such as those that created Jim Crow, determined the allocation of assistance.[3]

2. TC to J. F. Lane, 16 February 1940, Box 126, "Hearings—Anti-Lynching" Folder, Connally MSS ("the states are . . ."); TC to George L. Allen, 23 May 1940, Box 126, "Hearings—Anti-Lynching" Folder, Connally MSS ("I have no . . .") and ("I do not . . ."); TC to Jessie Daniel Ames, 27 January 1940, Box 126, "Hearings—Anti-Lynching" Folder, Connally MSS ("we want to . . ."); telegram, TC to F. E. Wilkerson, 15 January 1940, Box 126, "Newspaper Clipping and Articles—Anti-Lynching" Folder, Connally MSS ("we shall stand . . .").

3. TC to W. B. Washington, 30 March 1940, Box 127, "Anti-Lynching—Correspondence Regarding 1930–1941" Folder, Connally MSS ("are in many. . ."); TC to D. Harold Byrd, 2 February 1940, Box 126, "Hearings—Anti-Lynching" Folder, Connally MSS ("a political as . . .")

Tom Connally's concerns for the future also revealed an important development in the philosophy of southern senators. As a group, they began to
realize the necessity of thinking in broader terms than merely defeating all
civil rights bills, a philosophy that had once dominated their strategy. The
immediate as well as the future implications of their actions required more
careful consideration as civil rights pressure grew. Connally still claimed that
"compromise" on any "anti-South" proposal would be an "opening wedge" for
further civil rights measures. Behind the scenes, however, southerners began
redefining their response to "anti-South" legislation. Although the antilynching
bill remained locked in committee during the Seventy-sixth Congress, southern senators knew they would face new threats. They did not have long to wait.[4]

In the 1940s, many activists sought to abolish the poll tax as a requirement for voting in federal elections. During World War II, statistics indicated
that an estimated ten million citizens did not vote because of the tax, and
white Americans comprised 60 percent of that total. Alabama, Georgia, Mississippi, South Carolina, Tennessee, Texas, and Virginia required payment of
a poll tax, which varied from one to two dollars, to vote in federal and local
elections. This seemingly small amount proved an unbearable burden for a
large percentage of blacks and poor whites who found themselves trapped
in sharecropping and crop-lien arrangements. For individuals locked in such
inequitable credit arrangements, cash remained a scarce commodity. Far better to use that money to purchase necessities than to pay a poll tax and go
once again to usurious furnishing merchants for basic foodstuffs and sup-
plies. What in effect existed in the South was a situation in which citizens in
poll-tax states needed to decide whether casting a vote was more important
than feeding their families. Many opted for the latter.[5]

Streamlining the voting process for U.S. servicemen attracted considerable attention in Washington and, in the process, provided a spur for the
anti-poll-tax push. During the summer of 1942, southern senators, after vo-

---

and ("We are doing . . ."). For a detailed analysis of how southern politicians injected race into
much of the legislation passed in the 1930s through 1950s, see Ira Katznelson, *When Affirmative
Action was White: An Untold History of Racial Inequality in Twentieth-Century America* (New York:
Norton, 2005).

4. TC to Charles C. Huff, 30 January 1940, Box 127, "Civil Rights Anti-lynching Bill" Folder,
Connally MSS ("compromise") and ("opening wedge").

5. Statistics from *Newsweek*, 30 November 1942, 37.

ciferous protest, permitted the Soldiers Vote Act to pass without a filibuster, although the legislation eliminated payment of the poll tax for military personnel. On this occasion, southerners responded by taking a holistic view of the legislative situation. A filibuster against a bill providing absentee ballots to servicemen would appear unpatriotic and could alienate northern colleagues, coming as it would against legislation clearly tied to the war effort. Also important, the bill would not become law until after the southern states held their congressional primaries that year. Not for another two years, therefore, would the legislation take effect and by that point many thought the war might be over. Despite all of their bluster about drawing a line in the sand, the southern delegation for the first time broke with the concept of defeating all civil rights bills. Although they remained steadfast in the belief that one civil rights bill would beget another, the political situation demanded a new approach. They had successfully stymied the antilynching campaign in 1938 and yet failed to arrest the attack on Jim Crow. Southern senators opted for a new strategy, a strategy of delay they would maintain until the last stages of the civil rights fight. Capturing the essence of strategic delay, one southern senator noted regarding the Soldiers Vote Act, "A filibuster could not have succeeded at this time and an attempt to filibuster under the circumstances, would likely have alienated senators whom we are hopeful of having on our side" when measures for the abolition of all poll taxes, not just those for servicemen, reached the chamber. Southerners now recognized that caution sometimes proved the better part of valor when dealing with civil rights. Within the context of strategic delay, they often adopted a conciliatory approach in which they gave ground on some occasions to create goodwill that might prove helpful when they faced more sweeping legislation. Having garnered considerable approval for their restraint during debates concerning the Soldiers Vote Act, they responded to the broader assault against the poll tax with their customary fervor.[6]

On 13 October 1942, the House of Representatives passed by a 254 to 84 margin California Democrat Lee E. Geyer's bill that banned the poll tax

6. Lawson, *Black Ballots*, 66. The Soldiers Vote Act passed, forty-seven to five. *CR*, 77th Cong., 2nd sess., 25 August 1942, 6972. Lister Hill (hereafter cited as LH) to Horace C. Wilkinson, 11 September 1942, Box 376, Folder 1, Lister Hill Collection, W. S. Hoole Special Collections Library, University of Alabama, Tuscaloosa (hereafter cited as Hill MSS) ("a filibuster could . . .").

in federal elections. Several days later, the Senate Judiciary Committee favorably reported its own anti-poll-tax bill that replaced the language of the Geyer bill with that proposed by Florida's Claude Pepper. After release of the committee report, southern senators from states that employed the tax undertook a series of parliamentary maneuvers designed to kill the bill. With the Seventy-seventh Congress in its waning stages and with adjournment slated for 31 December 1942, they realized that they needed to postpone Senate action on the bill until the termination of the session when the legislative life of the anti-poll-tax bill would end. Once a session of Congress adjourned, all unaddressed bills had to be reintroduced at the start of the next session. Before engaging in parliamentary maneuvers clearly designed to waste time, several southerners addressed the inadequacies of the proposal.[7]

Striking the first blow against the legislation, Tom Connally, who now served as chairman of the Foreign Relations Committee, contended that only nine of the Judiciary Committee's eighteen members voted for the measure in person; the rest did so by proxy. According to the Texan, a constitutional majority of ten, or one more than half of the whole committee, was not present and thus a quorum had not existed, making the committee's actions unlawful. He based his arguments on Senate Rule 25, which permitted each committee to determine the minimum number of senators in attendance necessary to transact its business. Since the committee did not specify what it defined as a working quorum, Connally claimed that a constitutional majority served as the standard in the absence of a guideline, an argument that committee chairman Frederick Van Nuys overruled. Unbowed by the ruling, Connally revealed that he had more than procedural qualms with the legislation.[8]

After losing his point of order, the Texan resorted to the familiar tactic of placing the civil rights fight in constitutional rather than moral terms. Connally's opening maneuvers revealed a central aspect of the southern opposition; southern senators, as in 1938, would fight the battle largely on constitutional grounds, not on the basis of race. "The question is not whether we favor a poll tax," he noted, "the question is simply whether or not each state,

7. For the House vote, see *CR*, 77th Cong., 2nd sess. (all subsequent *CR* citations refer to the 77th Cong., 2nd sess. until otherwise noted), 13 October 1942, 8174; *Newsweek*, 26 October 1942, 36–37; *New York Times*, 27 October 1942, 21.

8. For Connally's account of Judiciary Committee actions and for his maneuvers, see *CR*, 26 October 1942, 8659–8660.

within its own sovereign rights, shall determine the question whether there should be a poll tax." Article I, Section 2 of the Constitution that stipulated that members of the House of Representatives "shall have the qualifications requisite for electors of the most numerous branch of the state legislature" served as the foundation of his claim. Connally argued that the article granted individual states the right to determine voter qualifications in both federal and local elections. Federal incursion into the electoral process, as exemplified by the effort to repeal the poll tax, contravened the intent of the framers, who wrote their desire for state control over suffrage requirements into the Constitution. Following his Senate colloquy, the southern leader issued a press release condemning the proposal in which he claimed "however, obnoxious may be poll tax requirements, they are not as bad as federal bayonets at the voting booths." Confident in the legal merits of their arguments, southerners doubted that the lame-duck Congress would act on such a volatile issue, but senators from Dixie would leave nothing to chance.[9]

On 13 November 1942, Senate Majority Leader Alben Barkley motioned for the consideration of House Resolution 1024, the anti-poll-tax measure. Again, Connally voiced his objections to the Judiciary's handling of the legislation. Speaking of the efforts of civil rights advocates, the Texan stated, "I plea with senators in their mad rush to cram this bill down the throats of unwilling but innocent victims, they at least observe the form of the constitution." Following Connally, Theodore Bilbo took the floor. As a champion of white supremacy, Bilbo thought the central reason for the bill, increasing the number of black voters, a case of misplaced activism. Poor whites had the most to gain from the elimination of the poll tax, and for Bilbo it remained this group that deserved the most attention in the debate. Nonetheless, he announced that he could not support the poll tax repeal on constitutional grounds. Despite his opposition to the tax, which cut directly into his core constituency, he felt it remained the states' responsibility to end it. And he assured his few listeners, one day all states would. Should poll-tax opponents push the issue, the Mississippian warned he would force the chamber to vote on an amendment calling for the reduction of the voting age from twenty-one to eighteen. According to his logic, if eighteen to twenty year olds could fight

9. *CR*, 26 October 1942, 8659–8660 ("The question is . . ."); *New York Times*, 27 October 1942, 21; press release, 26 October 1942, Box 559, "Statement on Poll Tax" Folder, Connally MSS ("however, obnoxious . . .").

in the war, then surely they should obtain the right of suffrage. At the time, the idea of such a reduction was preposterous, which of course was exactly what Bilbo intended. In his eyes, it was no more outlandish than a federally mandated abolition of the poll tax since the passage of either bill would represent a violation of the Constitution. The chamber recessed after the first portion of Bilbo's address with the Mississippian still holding the floor.[10]

The next day Bilbo was ready for another extended discourse, but many senators did not prove similarly prepared to listen. Only twenty-six members answered the initial roll call to establish a quorum. Another effort to reach a quorum likewise fell short. Majority Leader Barkley then ordered the sergeant at arms to search for stragglers in the Senate cloakrooms and offices. Even after this effort, the chamber still fell five short of a working majority. Angered by the situation and especially by the convenient absence of many southerners, Barkley requested that the vice president issue arrest warrants for eight senators known to be in Washington. Several more members soon arrived, reducing the number needed to establish a quorum. Only Tennessean Kenneth McKellar was officially "arrested" at his hotel room and escorted to the chamber. With a quorum finally established by McKellar's presence, Theodore Bilbo continued his oration with the better part of the legislative day at an end.[11]

Bilbo spoke for two hours on 14 November, explaining why he thought the poll tax fight represented nothing more than a ruse to curry favor with black voters. According to Bilbo, both blacks and whites paid a poll tax in Mississippi and "if that were the only thing that stood in the way of Negroes voting in my state they would be voting as freely and as frequently as do members of the white race." Here Bilbo stressed that passage of an anti-poll-tax bill would do nothing to expand the black electorate. Indeed, in Mississippi and in many other states, literacy qualifications most often thwarted black registration. In addition, he believed the measure would undermine domestic harmony by provoking a white backlash against what he labeled the "Hitler domination" of the region. Even worse, according to Bilbo, it would lead to further civil rights activism. Should Congress pass the bill, he

10. Move to consider: *CR*, 13 November 1942, 8814–8815; *CR*, Connally, 13 November 1942, 8822 ("I plead with . . ."); *CR*, Bilbo, 13 November 1942, 8833 (poor whites), 8835 (state repeal), 8830 (eighteen to vote).

11. *New York Times*, 15 November 1942, 1, 48; *Newsweek*, 23 November 1942, 35.

observed, "the first step to a centralized government and the wiping out of state lines would occur." At six o'clock that evening, the Senate adjourned, a maneuver that removed Bilbo and Barkley's motion to consider the poll tax bill from the floor. Bilbo believed that the future would permit him further opportunities to pontificate. Later that day he informed a Washington Post reporter that he needed at least thirty days to adequately address himself to the bill. Testifying to his physical competence for such an ordeal, he noted that his physician informed him that "I had absolutely no defects, except one—my mind. I told him that I didn't need my mind very much in the Senate, so that was all right." Circumstances in the days that followed proved that the Mississippian would not need his voice either. With the end of the session approaching, southerners wanted to buy time. Unlike the 1938 anti-lynching bill, which at least initially had considerable support, many senators in 1942 did not back the poll tax repeal since they viewed the legislation of dubious constitutionality. On this occasion, southerners recognized they had greater leeway in how they conducted their opposition. They responded with a wordless filibuster in which they slowed the legislative process by employing arcane parliamentary rules.[12]

Following a Sunday recess, Barkley again attempted to bring up the poll-tax legislation. Southern senators responded by invoking a rarely used chamber rule that required at a member's request on any Monday a vote on all bills previously reported. Such a motion held priority over all other motions, in this case Barkley's poll-tax motion, and could only take place during morning hours—the period between twelve and two o'clock at the start of a legislative day in which senators introduced bills, presented petitions and memorials, and during which no debate occurred. When southerners advanced their motion on Monday, 16 November, sixty-seven bills antedated the poll-tax measure on the Senate calendar. Under chamber rules, the Senate could not return to the poll-tax question until it passed judgment on these measures. By this point in the Seventy-seventh Congress, only minor legislation remained on the calender; however, dispensing these items required time, something the southerners hoped to buy. With the difficulty experienced on previous occasions gathering a quorum, a vote on all sixty-seven bills could take several days. In an effort to bypass this problem, Barkley adjourned the Senate,

12. *CR*, 14 November 1942, 8839 ("if that were . . ."), 8840 ("Hitler domination"); *Washington Post*, 14 November 1942, 1, 4 ("I had absolutely . . .").

a move that superceded the southern motion and that killed his own effort to consider the poll-tax bill. Another day had passed with little accomplished.[13]

The next day southerners employed another delaying tactic. As they had in 1922, they demanded the reading and correcting of the previous day's *Senate Journal*, focusing particular attention on minute concerns such as the proper placement of punctuation marks. For five hours on 17 November, the Senate remained in session and again accomplished nothing. At that point, sources indicated that Barkley recognized that the poll-tax bill held little chance for success, but he planned on continuing the fight, hoping that the Senate debate would rally national support for a future repeal effort. Although the wordless filibuster precluded widespread discussion, several southerners offered brief comments regarding the proposal that demonstrated the central reasons for their opposition. One of the South's rising stars, Richard B. Russell, availed himself of the opportunity to defend his state's use of the poll tax.[14]

Russell began his address with a touch of irony. In Georgia, he observed, Reconstruction leaders headed by "Negroes, carpetbaggers, and scalawags" framed the 1868 constitution that included the state's first poll tax. Russell, of course, always condemned the excesses of Reconstruction, but in this instance, he used the period to demonstrate that more than racism dictated his opposition to the poll tax. Its continued use in the twentieth century served the same purpose as it had during Reconstruction—underwriting social services. Subsidizing the Georgia educational system, not disfranchisement, represented the only purpose of the poll tax. The Georgian also denounced the vanguard nature of the attempt to outlaw the small suffrage fee. Poll-tax advocates "propose to follow it by other legislation which would wipe out all our registration and qualification laws" and allow "the federal government to take charge of all of our election machinery." Conspiratorial visions of a ravenous federal government continually usurping state prerogatives continued as a central feature of the southern opposition. What Russell and others could not understand was how those beyond the Mason-Dixon line could overlook the great strides made by the region in establishing amicable race relations. According to Russell, "any fair-minded man who will study

13. For the delaying tactics, see *CR*, 16 November 1942, 8861–8864.

14. For southern tactics, see *CR*, 17 November 1942, 8899–8922; *New York Times*, 17 November 1942, 21; *New York Times*, 18 November 1942, 18; *Newsweek*, 30 November 1942.

the history of the last 75 years would commend the South on the great work we have done." His comment on the glories of the South begged a rejoinder from civil rights advocates that highlighted the region's ongoing racial violence, mass disfranchisement, and stunted economy. No critique of Russell's dubious contentions emerged, however. With the session winding down, senators focused their attention elsewhere. Unlike most senators who lacked the desire for a protracted fight, southerners from poll-tax states saw their actions as part of a campaign to safeguard the region's sacred institutions as well as the sanctity of the Constitution.[15]

The next day, Mississippi's lame duck senator, Wall Doxey, who had assisted Connally in the argument over Rule 25, expanded the purview of his fight. Appointed to fill the unexpired term opened by the death of Pat Harrison in 1941, Doxey lost his reelection bid to James Eastland. Despite his defeat, the Mississippian remained committed to the southern cause, delivering a five-hour oration in which he raised several points of order that challenged the circumstances surrounding the bill's appearance before the chamber. Congress, he claimed, had no right to even consider the legislation since voting qualifications remained the exclusive domain of individual states. Only a constitutional amendment banning the poll tax, he argued, would legitimize efforts to remove the tax. Next he turned to an old charge in the southern arsenal—the question of political expediency. The clear unconstitutionality of the measure demonstrated, according to Doxey, that advocates of the legislation had no other purpose behind their actions than procuring political advantage. Supporters of the bill, the Mississippian noted, acted out of ignorance of the southern racial order. White supremacy represented a central feature of the southern worldview, a concept inextricably connected to the region's social system. "We intend to keep control of our state and see that it always remains under the domination of Anglo-Saxon supremacy," Doxey commented, adding that "we of the South know that our civilization and way of life are actually at stake." Doxey's address indicated that many southerners not only believed in Jim Crow but also viewed its perpetuation essential for the region's future. Advocates for the bill failed to match the intensity of the southern senators in defense of the principles that led them into the fight. Instead of challenging the southern position, most northerners proved tepid

15. *CR,* 17 November 1942, 8902 ("Negroes, carpetbaggers . . ."), 8903 ("propose to follow . . ."), 8904 ("any fair-minded . . .").

in their support for civil rights and put up a limited offensive. Widespread enthusiasm in the Senate for the proposal simply did not exist and it showed. Without a committed opponent, southern confidence soared.[16]

So optimistic did southerners become that they planned to drop their opposition to Barkley's motion, allowing the poll-tax bill to become the Senate's pending business. This represented a major concession that underscored southern confidence. Based on the Rules of the Senate, a cloture petition applied only to measures, not to motions. As a result, southerners could "debate" a motion to consider a bill without fear of cloture. In 1942, Connally and his colleagues recognized that the votes simply did not exist for cloture, so they planned on removing their opposition to making the bill the Senate's pending business and thus also making it subject to Rule 22. Supporters of the legislation would then push a cloture petition that would surely fail, but, at the same time, they would bolster their credentials as civil rights advocates. By defeating the petition, southerners would kill the bill for that session, buying themselves breathing room and the admiration of their constituents. All participants in the struggle would gain from this arrangement, except the group with the most at stake—black Americans.[17]

On Friday, 20 November 1942, Tom Connally convinced Majority Leader Barkley to enter an agreement that committed the southerners to withdraw their opposition to taking up the bill, if proponents of the measure agreed to a prompt cloture vote at 1:00 p.m., Monday, 22 November. A corollary to the agreement stipulated, albeit tacitly, that a failed cloture bid would end for that session further discussion of the anti-poll-tax bill. Flush with victory, the southern forces received added assistance from Wyoming Democrat, Joseph O'Mahoney. To the Senate, O'Mahoney delivered a speech raising arguments that reflected those made by southerners in which he emphasized the unconstitutionality of the proposal. Following the Democrat's address, Connally sent a note to the press gallery requesting that the major news outlets give adequate coverage to the Wyoming senator's speech. He noted that O'Mahoney's critique of the measure "prove[s] we have real grounds for opposing this bill and we are not a mere bunch of legislative ragamuffins." Further adding to

16. *CR*, 18 November 1942, 8933 (beyond congressional jurisdiction), 8945 ("We intend to . . .") and ("we of the . . .").

17. Since its adoption in 1917, Rule 22 was generally understood to apply only to pending measures, not procedural motions. Riddick, *Senate Procedure*, 303.

the dismay of anti-poll-tax advocates, President Franklin D. Roosevelt distanced himself from the civil rights debate. When asked about the Senate proceedings, the president refused to comment on the filibuster and claimed ignorance of both the southern effort and the legislative item itself. Roosevelt kept his distance from a bill certain to arouse enmity at a time when national unity proved vital. Against this backdrop, southern senators had every reason to feel "cocksure" that cloture would fail.[18]

With the date for the cloture vote established, senators used the intervening period to discuss the bill. The possible long range implications of the proposal figured prominently in these orations. Theodore Bilbo noted that he personally loathed the poll tax, but he opposed federal legislation to repeal it more because if it succeeded "it will be possible to pass a bill to remove some other qualifications we have in Mississippi." South Carolina's ailing "Cotton Ed" Smith also warned of the vanguard quality of the bill, observing that the movement to repeal the poll tax proved symptomatic of a "gradual but very persistent encroachment upon our dual form of government." He further warned, "We will wake up some morning and find that the power of the states has gone, and that their affairs are being conducted by bureaucrats in Washington." Alabama's Lister Hill addressed similar concerns.[19]

Born in 1894, Hill entered the Senate in 1937 and quickly won the favor of chamber liberals for his ardent support of the New Deal. Serving as Democratic party whip during World War II, the Alabama patrician proved unfailingly courteous and good humored in his dealings with his colleagues. Despite his liberal credentials and warm personality, Hill towed the southern line when civil rights became an issue. In most instances, he relegated his civil rights orations to the legalistic shortfalls of the legislation at hand. Since he often proved less vocal than some of his more outspoken regional colleagues, he received correspondence throughout his career that questioned his loyalty to Jim Crow. One civil rights advocate went so far as to claim that Hill "had not the slightest touch of racial prejudice in his heart." The point

18. For the agreement, see *CR*, 19 November 1942, 8962–63; *CR*, 20 November 1942, 9023; *Time*, 30 November 1942, 22; *Newsweek*, 30 November 1942, 37 ("prove we have . . ."); *New York Times*, 21 November 1942, 11; TB to George Washington Williams, 20 November 1942, Box 1077, Folder 6, Bilbo MSS ("cocksure").

19. *CR*, Bilbo, 19 November 1942, 8957–58 ("it will be . . ."); *CR*, Smith, 21 November 1942, 9043 ("gradual but very . . .") and ("we will wake . . .").

remained, however, that he participated whenever called upon to defend southern racial norms. He simply chose to convey his points in muted tones that deemphasized race. Hill, like the others, viewed the poll-tax fight as part of a long-term process. Regarding the issue, he observed that "the moment it is admitted that Congress" can prescribe voter qualifications, "the Federal Government becomes sovereign in that field, and can exercise any power and do anything it wished to do." As their speeches indicated, precedent altering legislation most concerned southerners, who themselves relied on tradition not only to safeguard their parliamentary advantage in the Senate but also to uphold segregation. Indeed, the *Plessy v. Ferguson* decision that formed the foundation of the entire Jim Crow edifice remained the South's preeminent defense of its racial order. Any allowance of a precedent that questioned, even if only tangentially, the legitimacy of that order weakened the sanctity of *Plessy*. The anti-poll-tax fight represented such a challenge.[20]

One southerner saw no reason to fear the abolition of the poll tax by federal decree. For Florida's Claude Pepper, the man who had sacrificed his convictions to procure electoral success in 1938, the time to defend principle had arrived. Pepper's advocacy of repeal, particularly as one of the bill's main sponsors, alienated him from his southern colleagues and raised speculations that his actions jeopardized his political future. In private the Floridian labeled southern tactics against the bill "vicious and determined." The filibuster prompted him to realize "the vital need for a change in the Rules of the Senate to prevent such abuses of power by a minority." Rule 22, which safeguarded the filibuster, represented an essential protection for southern senators. Securing it demanded constant vigilance lest its weakening precipitate action on legislation aimed at Jim Crow. That Pepper championed the anti-poll-tax bill proved bad. That he also supported a change in Rule 22 demonstrated rank apostasy. Pepper's native Florida had already expunged the poll tax from its constitution, thus making his stand consistent with the policies of his home state. To his southern colleagues the issue was not whether individual sovereign states could prescribe their own requirements for voting; few of them would argue that basic point, although many of them indicated their desire to see the requirement abolished provided it was done constitutionally by state authorities. What made Pepper's position so contentious was

20. Van der Veer Hamilton, *Lister Hill*, 1–111; Douglas, *In the Fullness of Time*, 228 ("had not the . . ."); *CR*, 21 November 1942, 9044 ("the moment it . . .").

his desire to permit the federal government to interfere with a state's constitutional right to set its own standards for suffrage. Once the federal government gained a foothold in the field of voter requirements, even in the case of the widely unpopular poll tax, according to many southern senators, it would establish a precedent for further interference in the process until the states lost control over the whole system. Making matters worse, Pepper wanted to achieve this unconstitutional goal by destroying the Senate Rules, rules that protected southern interests not just in this case but also in all matters regarding race. Reflecting a growing sentiment in the southern ranks, Theodore Bilbo observed, "I am so thoroughly disgusted with Claude Pepper . . . until I think we ought to ostracize him politically." Washington journalist William White wrote that the increased antipathy toward the Floridian stemmed from a "belief . . . that Pepper was fundamentally un-Southern."[21]

On 21 November, Pepper publically addressed himself to the legislation that bore his imprimatur. Speaking before the Senate, he emphasized the mild nature of the bill, arguing in its defense that "no sovereignty can be great enough to impose conditions which are a burden upon the enjoyment of those constitutionally accorded privileges to the citizen." As for the actions of his southern colleagues, he remarked that "today we have seen a destruction and frustration of democracy in what has been called in a better day the greatest deliberative body in the world." Pepper made good on his private critique of Rule 22 by vowing to introduce legislation to change the existing cloture rule that would reduce the requisite for curtailing debate from two-thirds of those present and voting to a simple majority. Explaining his activism, he commented, "It is because I love my South that I believe this issue worth fighting for," noting also that "the liberal tradition was born in the South. . . . I prefer to believe that it is again the mission of the South." With these words' Pepper vied for control of the South's historical memory, as well as its immediate future, with the region's conservative leaders such as Tom Connally and Richard Russell. If anything, however, southern politics after the late 1930s drifted from the liberalism espoused by Pepper. The Floridian moved away from the white South's unequivocal defense of Jim Crow segregation and its satellite institutions at great risk to his political future.

21. CP Diary, 16 November 1942, Series 439, Box 1, Folder 6, Pepper MSS ("vicious and determined") and ("the vital need . . ."); TB to J. C. Hamilton, 19 October 1942, Box 1077, Folder 10, Bilbo MSS ("I am so . . ."); White, *Citadel*, 79 ("belief that Pepper . . .").

Although in step with the march of history, he was slowly moving out of step with the sentiments of his constituents. As he undoubtedly expected, his impassioned pleas proved futile in changing the region's commitment to the status quo or in altering the tactics of Dixie's Senate delegation. His was a quixotic battle, a campaign against "southern reactionaries" who represented the "South's worst enemies." He would wage his fight without regard for the consequences or the prospects for victory. Writing about the pending cloture vote, he recorded in his diary, "it will admittedly lose but we have advanced the cause." His forecast proved accurate.[22]

On Monday, 23 November 1942, the Senate voted, thirty-seven to forty-one, against cloture. Again, not even a majority, let alone two-thirds, of those present saw the need to terminate debate on a civil rights bill. Political partisans often relish chiding their opponents on how they fail to live up to their respective rhetoric. Republicans believed that Democratic sectionalism delayed advances. Liberal Democrats, on the other hand, pointed to the conservative coalition of Republicans and southern Democrats as the basis of civil rights failures. An analysis of the 1942 cloture vote reveals that a bipartisan consensus sided with the southerners. Although a majority from both parties favored cloture, a sizable percentage, ten of twenty-four Republicans and thirteen of thirty-four nonsouthern Democrats, assisted the segregationists. Here was a voting pattern that defied generalization. New Englanders, midwesterners, southwesterners, and mountain state senators, regardless of party, allowed the filibuster to continue. Claude Pepper labeled the decision "a Phyrric victory for my southern friends," a comment rooted in his knowledge that supporters of the legislation would renew their efforts. Not necessary, Tom Connally countered, for "it would be a waste of time to bring it up again in the next Congress or any other time." Despite the Texan's comments, federal intervention in the voting process remained a contentious question in the next congressional session.[23]

As in 1942, Congress tackled legislation in 1943 designed to streamline

22. *CR*, 21 November 1942, 9046 ("no sovereignty can . . ."), 9047 ("today we have . . ."); Pepper Article, *Washington Post*, 22 November 1942, 35 ("it is because . . ."); *CR*, 21 November 1942, 9049 ("the liberal tradition . . ."); CP Diary, 20 November 1942, Series 439, Box 1, Folder 6, Pepper MSS ("it will admittedly . . .").

23. *CR*, 23 November 1942, 9065 (cloture vote); CP Diary, 23 November 1942, Series 439, Box 1, Folder 6, Pepper MSS ("a Phyrric victory . . ."); *Newsweek* 30 November 1942, 38 ("it would be . . .").

the voting process for servicemen in time for the 1944 presidential election. When it did, southerners attempted to keep as much of the absentee ballot process in state hands as possible without filibustering the entire measure, since they recognized the necessity of maintaining the goodwill of their colleagues. The resounding victory in the 1942 poll-tax fight could easily evaporate if they pressed their luck on an issue closely linked with the war. Besides, they believed that the new Soldiers Vote Act provided a challenge to states' rights only so long as the country remained at war. Following an armistice, only a limited number of the millions of Americans under arms would continue in the service, rendering the issue moot. Long term southern predictions foresaw a renewed push for anti-poll-tax legislation, not to mention other measures that they found equally as contemptible. Preserving their political capital for the next sweeping legislative foray against segregation served as their only alternative. Employing the framework of strategic delay, they permitted further federal intrusion in the electoral process by allowing the new Soldiers Vote Act to pass in early 1944 without a filibuster. At the time, they had other issues to consider, issues over which they had no control.[24]

During World War II, southerners not only faced civil rights pressure in Congress but also, for the first time, experienced opposition from both the executive and the judicial branches. In order to forestall a massive black demonstration in the nation's capitol orchestrated by the March on Washington movement, Franklin Roosevelt in 1941 issued Executive Order 8102, which created a Fair Employment Practices Committee designed to eliminate discrimination in defense industries. The committee possessed investigatory powers to explore alleged episodes of discrimination in war industries, but it could only make recommendations, not compel compliance, with its findings. Later, in the 1944 case of *Smith v. Allwright,* the Supreme Court denied the constitutionality of the white primary. Prior to the decision, southern states defined the Democratic Party, or the only legitimate political organization in most of the region, as a private organization. As such, the party could make its own rules, including establishing who could or could not participate in its services. The Court ruled that political parties were public groups that relied on state funds and electoral machinery for their operation and thus could not discriminate on the basis of race without running afoul of the Fourteenth

24. Lawson, *Black Ballots,* 74. The Soldiers Vote Act of 1944 passed, 47 to 38. *CR,* 78th Cong., 2nd sess., 8 February 1944, 1406.

Amendment. *Smith v. Allwright* became the first of many higher court rulings that riled southerners, who increasingly viewed the federal bench as drifting from the bedrock principles of Anglo-Saxon jurisprudence. Both the creation of the FEPC and the *Smith v. Allwright* decision served as a warning to white southerners that the political climate continued to move against their interests. Even worse, they had no means of arresting these developments which took place outside of the legislative branch. When another civil rights bill appeared on Capitol Hill, they attempted to regain a level of control over the growing civil rights movement.[25]

After the Supreme Court decision, southerners faced another attempt to abolish the poll tax, this time in the form of House Resolution 7 drafted by New York representative Vito Marcantonio, which passed in the House, 265 to 110. Few observers considered Senate action on the bill anything but an election year ploy that would allow northern liberals to tout their civil rights credentials while also permitting southern Democrats to demonstrate their support for white supremacy. Despite the charade in 1944 of debating a bill with no chance of success, many southerners delivered speeches that illuminated their views regarding voting rights that they did not fully enunciate during the wordless filibuster of 1942. Ironically, southerners waxed long on how political opportunism served as the catalyst for their northern colleagues' drive to abolish the poll tax, at the very time they delivered speeches that served the primary purpose of grandstanding, of showing their constituents that they brooked no compromise on "constitutional" matters. Setting the tone for his colleagues, Tom Connally observed that southerners would resist the bill "bitterly" and would "win." Saber-rattling rhetoric aside, the poll-tax fight in 1944 required little in the way of an organized opposition. Widespread chamber apathy ensured its failure.[26]

On 9 May 1944, Democratic senator Patrick McCarran of Nevada mo-

25. Herbert Garfinkel, *When Negroes March: The March on Washington Movement in the Organizational Politics of the FEPC* (New York: Atheneum, 1969); Key, *Southern Politics,* 624; August Meier and John H. Bracey Jr., "The NAACP as a Reform Movement, 1909–1965: To Reach the Conscience of America," *Journal of Southern History* 59 (February 1993): 3–30; Reed, *Seedtime for the Modern Civil Rights Movement;* Neil A. Wynn, "The Impact of the Second World War on the American Negro," *Journal of Negro History* 6 (1971): 42–53.

26. For the House vote, see *CR,* 78th Cong., 1st sess., 25 May 1943, 4889; Newsweek, 22 May 44, 42; TC to W. C. Hartgrove, 28 April 1944, Box 126, "Negro: Supreme Court Decision" Folder, Connally MSS ("bitterly") and ("win").

tioned to consider House Resolution 7. After a preliminary canvass of the chamber revealed little support for the measure, southerners proved so confident that they could defeat a cloture bid and so sure that their Senate colleagues lacked the will for a fight that they did not resist the effort to take up the bill. Despite the absence of drama, Tom Connally played to his constituents. Again he noted the political expediency of his northern colleagues hunting for a campaign issue with the poll tax while the nation fought a "globe-shaking war." The Texan urged others to resist the snare of interest groups such as the NAACP that appeared bent on forcing legislators to surrender "their freedom as Senators." In his closing statement, Connally reached the crux of the matter in a way that highlighted the conspiratorial nature of the southern worldview. Every maneuver that places the right of defining "who may vote and who may not vote" in the hands of the central government, he argued, represented a step "toward the destruction of this Republic." The federal system created by the founders rested on a balance between state and federal legal jurisdictions, Connally contended. Upsetting that balance by funneling power into the central government, the Texan opined, would necessarily undermine the entire system. If the federal government could strip a state's right to set a poll tax, then it could infringe on other suffrage requirements and, by implication, interfere in matters beyond the voting booth. Southerners raised such concerns to alert their colleagues of the possible long range consequences of the legislation. During World War II, the South bore the brunt of federal initiatives, but at some future point, Connally threatened, the government might launch an assault on sacred institutions in other regions. All senators, according to the Texan, thus had a stake in checking the gradual accumulation of power by the central government. Connally provided the framework for the southern defense of the poll tax; his colleagues completed the picture.[27]

Most southern senators prefaced their remarks by claiming that they opposed the bill on constitutional, rather than racial, grounds. For example, Georgia's courtly senior senator, Walter George, observed that "there is no issue of race and no question of race, color, or creed involved in this discussion." The flamboyant Allen Ellender joined George in exclaiming, "I have

27. CR, 78th Cong., 2nd sess. (all subsequent CR citations from 78th Cong., 2nd sess. until otherwise noted), 9 May 1944, 4173 ("globe-shaking war"), 4177 ("their freedom as . . ."), 4183 ("toward the destruction . . .").

absolutely no bias one way or the other, but I am viewing it solely from a legal standpoint." Even South Carolina's usually rabid white supremacist Cotton Ed Smith softened his language. "So far as the race question is concerned," he said, "it is just a smoke screen; it has nothing to do with this horrible onslaught on the Constitution" brought on by the poll-tax fight. Anticipating that his colleagues would think the worst of him, Smith added, "I know that many . . . expected me to rant and rave about the Negro question," but instead he planned on sticking to the merits of the bill and fight against what he considered "an assault on the Constitution."[28]

More so than in 1942, the new battle over the poll tax demonstrated a different aspect of the long term concerns of southern senators. In this battle, they did not tout the benefits of segregation, since they asserted that race played no role in their fight. They would claim, as they would assert whenever voting rights issues came before the Senate, that Constitutional concerns and nothing else informed their opposition to federally mandated electoral reform. Simply put, southern senators argued that the Constitution invested state governments with the responsibility of establishing voter proscriptions. Any attempt to alter that arrangement short of an amendment was, according to the southern bloc, unconstitutional. Race was not relevant to the debate. Instead, they addressed the subject in sweeping terms, warning their colleagues that a federally mandated repeal of the poll tax threatened not just southern interests but also the very foundation of the American political system. The members of the Seventy-eighth Congress had in their hands the power to safeguard the gift of the founders, while a failure to act could lead to terrible consequences. Walter George noted that passage of the bill would inevitably "hasten the day when the state and local communities will have lost all power and all control over their legislative bodies and over their own local affairs." Alabamian Lister Hill viewed the question in a similar vein, noting that state action or a constitutional amendment were the only means of repealing the troublesome poll tax that even most southerners denounced. To take any other action against the tax risked establishing a precedent in direct contradiction to the Constitution, and "to permit this camel to get his nose under the tent," Hill noted, "would be to start on a road which might lead inevitably and inexorably to the destruction of our great

28. *CR*, George, 10 May 1944, 4256 ("there is no . . ."); *CR*, Smith, 12 May 1944, 4387 ("I have absolutely . . ."); *CR*, Smith, 12 May 1944, 4402 ("so far as . . .") and ("I know that . . .").

Federal system." Louisiana's Allen Ellender, who in 1938 unabashedly championed white supremacy, also fought the battle along more edifying lines, depicting his opposition to the proposal in similar language to that of the more reserved patricians George and Hill. "If we should permit such an encroachment," Ellender observed, "it would be a direct curtailment of our dual system of government, and [I] predict that if we yield now this may be just the first of many similar attacks which may occur in future years." Despite the overall alteration in the thrust of southern arguments, some members of the caucus could not resist straying from legal critiques of the bill.[29]

Mississippi's junior senator, James Oliver Eastland, in many ways proved just the opposite of his state's flamboyant senior Senator Theodore Bilbo. The thirty-nine-year-old Eastland was by all accounts a "homebody" who preferred spending time with his wife and four children or in reading true life detective stories. To some observers, he seemed "taciturn and humorless," a man noted for his personal reserve along with an ever-present cigar. Eastland's restraint extended to his handling of his economic interests. Unlike Bilbo, no reckless financial endeavors threatened Eastland's fortune. He lorded over two sizable plantations in southern Mississippi valued at more than a million dollars. His five-thousand-acre plantation in the Mississippi Delta and his thirteen-hundred-acre cattle ranch near Vicksburg made him a man of considerable means. Financial security did not lead Eastland to adopt a paternalistic view of the black community. He never made an effort to hide his belief in white supremacy or in the innate depravity of the black race. Future president Lyndon Johnson observed of Eastland that he "could be standing right in the middle of the worst Mississippi flood ever known and he'd say the niggers caused it, helped out by some communists." Nonetheless, one northern statesman claimed that Eastland "was far more temperate in manner, if not in speech, and far more courteous in his personal relations" than the much maligned Bilbo.[30]

When confronted with the poll-tax issue, Eastland broached the unconstitutionality of the proposal, using the Nineteenth Amendment that granted

29. CR, George, 10 May 1944, 4256 ("hasten the day . . ."); CR, Hill, 11 May 1944, 4321 ("to permit this . . ."); CR, Ellender, 12 May 1944, 4387 ("If we should . . .").

30. Time, 26 March 1956, 26–29; Robert Sherrill, Gothic Politics in the Deep South: Stars of the New Confederacy (New York: Grossman, 1968), 174–210; Booth Mooney, LBJ: An Irreverent Chronicle (New York: Thomas Y. Cromwell, 1976), 49–50 ("could be standing . . ."); Douglas, In the Fullness of Time, 227 ("was far more . . .").

women's suffrage as an example of how the Seventy-eighth Congress should tackle the matter before it. According to the amendment, women could not be denied the right to vote so long as they met the requirements of the states in which they resided. The women's suffrage amendment, Eastland contended, therefore provided another precedent supporting the southern interpretation that Article I, Section 2 granted states the freedom to set voter qualifications. After dispensing with the illegality of the proposal, he turned to a subject in which he took particular interest—anticommunism. The "driving force behind this measure is the Communist Party, a group of aliens advocating an alien creed, who would attempt to destroy this country." He also read on the Senate floor a pamphlet published by the United Auto Workers, a branch of the Congress of Industrial Organizations (CIO). Eastland, of course, viewed the union as a Communist front, especially considering the organization's publication of a leaflet that called on Mississippians to remove him from office. He responded by noting, "I am proud that I am slated to be purged by the mongrel radical movement who today attempt to destroy the Constitution and the American way of life . . . the movement which advocates intermarriages and the amalgamation of the races and socialism in America." Others joined Eastland in labeling the Communist Party a catalyst behind the drive to abolish the poll tax. During the FEPC fight later in 1944, southerners would employ anticommunism with even greater fervor. Few matched the intensity or conviction of James Eastland regarding the alleged connection between communism and civil rights activism. Not even the intrigue imagined by Eastland, however, could save the anti-poll-tax bill.[31]

Majority Leader Barkley informed reporters on 9 May 1944 that he had a cloture petition ready for consideration. Two days later he forwarded the petition, where by the Senate Rules it had to remain on the legislative desk for at least two days before a vote. The showdown took place on Monday, 15 May, and provided no surprises. Only thirty-six senators voted in favor of cloture; forty-four voted against. Unlike the House, the Senate proved unprepared to tackle the question of civil rights. Eleven Republicans and fourteen nonsouthern Democrats voted with the segregationists. As in 1942, the votes

---

31. CR, 10 May 1944, 4258 (Nineteenth Amendment), 4264 ("the driving force . . ."); CR, 12 May 1944, 4403 ("I am proud . . ."). For other examples of anticommunism, see Richard Russell's comments in CR, 9 May 1944, 4178, and Kenneth McKellar's comments in CR, 11 May 1944, 4305–06.

against cloture lacked a readily discernible pattern. The caucus had support from all corners of the country. Few if any of the nonsoutherners who voted with the Dixie delegation would state that race served as the basis for their decision. Most Southerners did not even do that. Constitutional claims carried the day—as they had in 1938 and 1942. The southern defense of the poll tax proved logical, consistent, and ultimately convincing. It catered to the preexisting ideological predisposition of a broad consensus of senators and it came at a time when the nation, embroiled in a "globe-shaking" war—to borrow a phrase used by Tom Connally—sought unity instead of a divisive battle over civil rights. The voting rights of poor southerners both black and white simply remained too far off of the radar screen. Despite their victory in the sham poll-tax fight in 1944, southern senators knew that such efforts marked only the beginning of further legislative initiatives aimed at procuring black rights. Theodore Bilbo noted, "We have got the communistic anti-poll-tax crowd whipped for the present but we are not fooled—we know they will bob up again; if not this year, next year." Bilbo did not have long to wait. Concurrent with the poll-tax fight there developed an effort to cut appropriations for the FEPC, an action that, in effect, would nullify the executive order that created the agency. Although Tom Connally commanded the southern forces in the battle over the poll tax, Richard Russell's skillful handling of the FEPC question in 1944 hastened the Georgian's rise to power in the southern bloc.[32]

On 24 March 1944, Richard Russell orchestrated a parliamentary coup that placed the FEPC under the control of the legislative branch through an amendment to the Independent Offices Appropriations Act of 1915. In an Appropriations subcommittee, Russell received unanimous consent for a rider to the independent offices bill that prohibited the president from funding agencies that existed for more than a year without legislative approval. Prior to his action, Congress appropriated a sum of money to fund independent offices such as the FEPC and the executive branch then determined which agencies received funding from that pool of capital. Under Russell's proposal, Congress would hold the purse strings by determining the appropriations for most independent agencies. Many supported the amendment to check

32. *Washington Post,* 9 May 1944, 1; *Washington Post,* 14 May 1944, 1. For the cloture vote, see *CR,* 15 May 1944; TB to N. W. Rogers, 19 May 1944, Box 1076, Folder 6, Bilbo MSS ("we have got . . .").

Roosevelt's propensity for creating government agencies through executive decree. They viewed their vote as a means of reigning in presidential authority, an issue particularly relevant in light of Roosevelt's plan to run for a fourth term. For southerners, less lofty goals influenced their actions. They wanted to destroy the FEPC. After the approval of the Russell amendment, Congress controlled the fiscal solvency of the agency. It did not take long for Russell to move in for the kill.[33]

In June, the Georgian announced his opposition to the War Agencies Appropriations bill. In particular, he denounced its FEPC appropriation and introduced an amendment to cut its funding entirely. The relatively placid rhetoric of the earlier poll-tax fight gave way to a blunt discussion of southern racial views. Southerners did not filibuster this or other FEPC related appropriations during the war because funding for the commission came linked with funding for other wartime agencies. A filibuster against wartime legislation represented a sure way of appearing unpatriotic, while also increasing the likelihood of a successful cloture vote at a future point. Russell and other senators used the opportunity as a forum to air their grievances against the FEPC, but they stopped short of a filibuster. Here as in the poll-tax fight, strategic delay steered southerners away from their usual practices. They would save their filibuster weapon for fights against legislation designed to create a permanent FEPC. In his address that condemned the agency, Russell questioned the legality of the Executive Order that established the commission. According to the Georgian, the president of the United States could not arbitrarily create an agency designed to try American citizens without congressional approval. Even those senators who supported dismantling the Jim Crow system, he opined, had to recognize that "this end should be sought in a lawful way and not by an Executive order."[34]

After questioning presidential authority to create the commission, the Georgian turned to southern race relations and the threat the FEPC posed to it. The FEPC's activities, Russell charged, "have had the effect of alienating many of the best friends the Negro has ever had and have caused bad feelings between the races." Race relations even in the South had begun deteriorat-

33. William C. Berman, *The Politics of Civil Rights in the Truman Administration* (Columbus: Ohio State University Press, 1970), 24; *Newsweek*, 13 March 1944, 47–50.

34. *CR*, 78th Cong., 2nd sess. (all subsequent *CR* citations from 78th Cong., 2nd sess. until otherwise noted), 16 June 1944, 6032 (presidential authority exceeded), 6036 ("that this end . . .").

ing. Although Russell blamed the FEPC for the problem, the impact of the commission remained negligible. Something else was driving the discontent, something Russell did not publicly recognize, but hinted at in his address. The once largely northern civil rights struggle had migrated southward, upsetting the tranquility many southern senators once thought had existed in the region. By 1944, Russell fully grasped an important implication of the civil rights movement, something that Cotton Ed Smith had noted years before. "The white people have pride in their race, and they want the colored people to have pride in their race. We deal fairly with the colored people in our hiring practices," he claimed. In Russell's eyes, blacks needed racial pride for the Jim Crow system to work, but as his comments suggested, they as yet lacked this trait. White southerners thus had a vested interest in ensuring economic privileges for blacks so that the minority could build a sense of communal worth. Responsible white citizens in the South recognized this and sought to ensure that blacks in the region had job opportunities so that African Americans would have less reason to challenge the existing racial order. The FEPC, therefore, was not needed since the white South knew the importance of providing blacks gainful employment opportunities. If they failed in keeping blacks contented, they risked losing segregation. Like Russell, other southern senators conveniently blamed outsiders for the discord in the region.[35]

Mississippi's James Eastland denounced the FEPC, as he did the repeal of the poll tax, as a Communist conspiracy. "If given this appropriation," he stated, "these Communists . . . will use it . . . to displace management and control American industry." Georgia's Walter George also saw devious forces behind the FEPC. In George's eyes, the ultimate objective of the commission was "to strip owners of private rights in private property, and to convert the present economic system into a communistic or national socialistic system." As Eastland's and George's speeches revealed, strident anticommunism increasingly became an important political issue in Washington. Southerners did not differ from northerners in their assessment of the Communist threat. Because of the region's racial system, however, they also linked communism with, what they considered, the alien ideology espoused by civil rights advocates. Both communism and the civil rights movements, in white southern eyes, had as their final objective the dismantling of the nation's sacred governing principles. Many southerners viewed the Jim Crow system as one and

35. *CR*, 16 June 1944, 6034 ("its activities have . . .") and ("The white people . . .").

the same as free market capitalism or representative governing institutions. That southerners believed segregation an organic part of the nation's political heritage illustrates one reason why they so willingly employed the legacy of the founding generation to defend their own modern institutions in a manner that, to them, did not contradict that legacy. Some form of race-based social system had existed in the region since the colonial period. Twentieth-century southerners planned on maintaining their own unique system, as well as what they considered the real intent of the Constitution's framers, against all agents, Communist or otherwise. Unlike the poll-tax fight, which essentially followed constitutional lines, the FEPC question struck close to the Jim Crow citadel, too close from the southern perspective to granting the federal government a free hand in determining the appropriate nature of social relations. Its implicit challenge to Jim Crow made the committee a major threat.[36]

On 20 June 1944, the Senate voted, twenty-one to thirty-nine, against Russell's amendment to strip the FEPC of all funding. Russell did not expect his initiative to win. He nevertheless marked the occasion as an important step that officially recognized the legislative branch's control over the FEPC. Later, the Georgian advanced other amendments designed to limit its authority. He succeeded by a vote of twenty-seven to twenty-five in winning an amendment that protected Americans from losing their business for noncompliance with an FEPC ruling. By voice vote, the Senate also adopted an amendment that would withhold payment to any FEPC official who attempted to enforce commission rulings not in consonance with existing federal statutes. Although clearly unnecessary, the latter amendment symbolically demonstrated legislative hegemony over the agency. Power thus drained not only from the executive to the legislative branch on that day but also from the FEPC to the national legislature. Russell stripped the committee of its autonomy and reduced it to what amounted to a fiefdom of the legislative branch over which southern senators held the reigns of power.[37]

Southerners were still not happy. A year later they tried again to destroy the committee. Discord developed in their ranks over the scope of the effort to cripple the agency. For example, Kenneth McKellar of Tennessee, chairman

36. *CR*, Eastland, 19 June 1944, 6152 ("If given this . . ."); *CR*, George, 20 June 1944, 6256 ("to strip owners. . .").

37. For Action on the Russell amendments, see *CR*, 20 June 1944, 6264, 6268, 6269.

of the Senate Appropriations Committee, wanted quick action on the War Appropriations bill to keep the military funded in the latter stages of the war. In fact, most southerners recognized the wisdom of avoiding a protracted campaign to destroy the FEPC that would in turn prevent funding for more essential wartime agencies. Among members of this group, it proved axiomatic that with fiscal control of the committee in their hands, they could destroy it upon completion of the war. Far better to permit its existence for another year than risk angering their colleagues with a filibuster. Southern support for this conciliatory approach gained strength as several northern liberals increased their lobbying efforts for the creation of a permanent FEPC. The doctrine of strategic delay called for concessions on small issues, the appropriations measure, in order to procure the goodwill of the Senate for the larger issues, the anticipated fight against a permanent commission. Only Theodore Bilbo publicly threatened to reject a compromise. From the moment the Appropriations bill that covered the FEPC reached the chamber, he sought the destruction of the agency either by denying it all funding or by winning a guarantee that the appropriation for fiscal year 1946 would be its last. No matter the outcome, Bilbo hoped to push the committee into extinction. He never proved as reckless as he often feigned, however. Although troubled by the Mississippian's demagoguery, journalist Allen Drury wrote that Bilbo's "dangerousness is compounded by the fact that he is by no means unintelligent or stupid, but on the contrary shrewd and ruthless."[38]

Despite his stated intentions concerning the FEPC, Bilbo had ulterior motives that prevented him from undertaking a one man filibuster. At least on the surface, he stood alone, but he did so largely to prove to Mississippians his unequivocal opposition to any and all civil rights measures. With his reelection slated for 1946, a little grandstanding was in order. Despite all of his bluster about delivering a sixty-day speech against the appropriations bill, the Mississippian worked with the southern bloc. His correspondence reveals that he, too, accepted the strategic vision of his colleagues. Although southern senators would protest funding for the temporary FEPC, they would not filibuster. "Our strategy is to make the best fight we can under the circum-

38. *Washington Post*, 29 June 1945; *New York Times*, 1 July 1945, 16. Senate debate begins on H.R. 3368—the War Appropriation Bill, *CR*, 79th Cong., 1st sess. (subsequent *CR* citations refer to the 79th Cong., 1st sess., until otherwise noted), 26 June 1945, 6724; Drury, *Senate Journal*, 187 ("dangerousness is compounded . . .").

THE ORIGINS OF STRATEGIC DELAY 83

stances . . . for the effect it will have on the big fight to create the permanent FEPC." Strategic delay propelled the southern group toward a compromise orchestrated by Majority Leader Barkley that halved the initial $500,000 appropriation. Provided with an excuse not to filibuster, Bilbo conceded to the new figure since the FEPC "won't be able to function much" with such a small budget. Again southerners granted a concession in exchange for assistance against a larger question. By this time, action on a permanent FEPC bill loomed, but as southerners prepared for another civil rights battle, the nation readied itself for peace.[39]

The end of World War II in August 1945 changed political discourse in America. Where once national legislators focused on winning the war, they now faced the task of guiding the transition to peace. Soldiers returning to the United States took advantage of the Servicemen's Readjustment Act, or the GI Bill of Rights, which afforded them unprecedented opportunities to receive college degrees, low interest rate mortgages, and other services designed to smooth their transition to the civilian world. Involvement in overseas combat awakened many blacks to European cultures more tolerant, at least by American standards, of racial differences. For the first time, they experienced life outside of the socially enforced code of racial etiquette that demanded their subservience. Of all the members of the southern bloc, few were as blunt in offering his assessment of the implications of African American participation in the war effort as Bilbo. Even before hostilities ceased, the Mississippian sensed what the future held. On one occasion he noted, "we are headed for all sorts of race trouble especially when the war is over and these negro soldiers get back home" because they have "been cajoled and coddled and their minds poisoned with all sorts of talk dished out by their negro intelligentsia and the Jews and Quisling whites." Black servicemen, he claimed, "are going to be sore and resentful when their dreams don't come true that hell is going to break loose from Maine to San Francisco." If the war raised the expectations of African Americans that greater social equality would soon follow, then the conflict also steeled the resolve of southern legislators bent on maintaining the status quo. A major confronta-

39. TB to C. Norwood Hastie, 7 July 1945, Box 1024, Folder 1, Bilbo MSS ("our strategy is . . ."). Barkley compromise: CR, 28 June 1945, 6922–23. Vote on Barkley amendment (forty-two to twenty-six): CR, 30 June 1945, 7065–66. TB to C. Norwood Hastie, 15 July 1945, Box 1024, Folder 14, Bilbo MSS ("won't be able . . .").

tion seemed inevitable. In 1946, southern senators again faced a civil rights showdown.[40]

Senate activity on 17 January 1946 began with little fanfare as the chamber leisurely proceeded through the morning hour. Few expected anything out of the ordinary since Majority Leader Barkley promised that no controversial measures would be taken up until after President Harry S. Truman delivered his State of the Union message. Not everyone agreed with Barkley's plan, though. New Mexico Democrat Dennis Chavez rose, received recognition, and motioned for the consideration of Senate Bill 101—a bill to create a permanent FEPC. During the morning hour, the Senate Rules forbade debate, making Chavez's motion subject to an immediate vote. Caught unprepared, southern senators looked on in dismay as the Senate voted, forty-nine to seventeen, in favor of the motion. The South had lost an important tactical advantage. Based on Senate Rule 22, cloture did not apply to parliamentary motions to consider legislative items. Only a measure officially before the chamber fell under its auspices. Southerners had hoped to kill a permanent FEPC by filibustering the motion to consider it, knowing that their colleagues could not stop them. In an astute parliamentary maneuver, Chavez beat the southerners at their own game. Now the southern bloc faced a battle on the measure itself, a battle whose outcome remained unclear with the added threat of an all-or-nothing cloture vote that would create a federal commission to ban job discrimination based on race or creed. A direct assault against Jim Crow, they speculated, would surely follow passage of the legislation. Not since 1938 had, they faced a similar challenge. When they recovered from the shock of Chavez's maneuver, southern senators prepared their defensive with an eye on regaining their parliamentary footing.[41]

For several days, southerners resorted to the same wordless filibuster techniques that typified the 1942 poll-tax fight. Immediately following Chavez's initial motion, southerners sought to perfect the *Journal,* ensuring that the morning prayer, punctuation marks, and other inane matters contained in the minutes were flawless for "the benefit of posterity." Senator John Overton

40. For background, see chap. 2, note 1; TB to B. E. Reid, 21 June 1944, Box 1022, Folder 8, Bilbo MSS ("we are headed . . ."); TB to C. Norwood Hastie, 7 July 1945, Box 1024, Folder 3, Bilbo MSS ("been cajoled and . . .").

41. *CR,* 79th Cong., 2nd sess. (all subsequent *CR* citations refer to the same session and Congress until otherwise noted), 17 January 1946, 81 (Chavez's motion); *Newsweek,* 28 January 1946, 23; *New York Times,* 18 January 1946, 1, 4; *Time,* 28 January 1946, 22.

of Louisiana, who spearheaded this phase of the southern resistance, wryly told reporters, "We are going to make that Journal a perfect work of art." By 21 January, southern senators were ready to face the FEPC bill, although they theoretically addressed the legislation as part of the debate to amend the 17 January *Journal* since action on the minutes fell beyond Senate Rule 22. Not willing to concede their regained parliamentary strength, they would not permit approval of the *Journal* until they felt confident that an FEPC cloture vote would fail. Richard Russell, not Tom Connally, unleashed the opening broadside against the measure. For the first time in almost a decade, someone other than the cantankerous Texan, who was then in San Francisco assisting in the organization of the United Nations, led the southern forces in a major civil rights fight. A new era had begun. Russell's command of the southern opposition in 1946 heralded the end of Tom Connally's control of Dixie's Senate delegation. The Texan's absence from the chamber during the debate only solidified the Georgian's hold on the group. And when Russell took control, he had no intentions of relinquishing it. Although Connally had begun the process of shifting southern rhetoric away from overt racism, it was Russell who would complete the transition. Russell's innovative handling of the FEPC appropriations fight in 1944 illustrated to the majority of the southern bloc that he possessed the necessary foresight to lead the delegation in the uncertain times that lay ahead. Even more important, the southern caucus itself was changing. By 1946, many of Connally's staunchest advocates had either died or retired. A new generation of southerners born and raised under the Jim Crow system entered the Senate and they naturally gravitated toward the leadership of the aristocratic Georgian, who was more their contemporary than the septuagenarian Tom Connally. When Connally tried to reassert himself two years later, it was already too late. The southern caucus had abandoned him.[42]

Now in command, Russell set the tone for southern senators following Chavez's surprise motion. He conceded to the chamber that the maneuver "caught us flat-footed." Despite the setback, defiance marked Russell's statement. In response to threats by civil rights advocates that they would force round-the-clock sessions to break a filibuster, he sneered, "[We] are not in the least impressed or intimidated. We will be here." The following day the Georgian announced the beginning of an "educational campaign" that would bring the bill's "iniquities out into the full light of day." He also made clear

42. Twelve new faces had joined the caucus during the period 1938 to 1948.

that southern speeches would generally take the high ground by pointing out the bill's faults in an effort to win their case on its merits. Senators should consider, Russell observed, that if the American people voted on the bill in a popular referendum, it would convincingly fail. Americans, he believed, would certainly reject a bill that removed their right to hire who they wanted and that stripped them of their freedom to use their property, in this case their business, as they saw fit. Under Richard Russell's leadership, it became clear that swaying opinion, which the Georgian generally felt sided with the South on racial matters, took a high priority. If they could win the sympathy of their colleagues and the public, they felt they could defeat the FEPC.[43]

Like Tom Connally in 1938, Russell organized the southern bloc so that the group's "moderate" contingent spoke early in the "educational debate." Keeping Theodore Bilbo muzzled posed a particular dilemma for Russell, as it had for Connally before him. Animosity in the Senate against Bilbo had grown in the 1940s as his speeches became more lengthy and more reactionary. Russell needed to control him and, for the most part, he kept The Man in check. As for the other southerners, they worked together in the FEPC fight. For many of them, the onslaught against Jim Crow had already begun. The antilynching and poll-tax fights, although important, had taken place on the periphery of the Jim Crow edifice. The FEPC appeared to them as a precursor to segregation's destruction. Russell believed in the gravity of the threat, considering the FEPC a harbinger of doom. Responding to those who thought the South should accept the inevitability of "amalgamation," he said "we will starve to death before we will strike down the bars and let white and blacks go to school together." With the FEPC bill pending, southern senators prepared their defense with a conviction that they were entering the final battles in defense of the white South.[44]

Lister Hill of Alabama opposed the FEPC from its inception, working with Russell as Democratic party whip to rally votes for the Russell amendment, which placed the temporary FEPC under congressional supervision. According to Hill, the committee "has aggravated situations and irritated people" and "should be abolished." When he addressed the chamber on 28

43. *New York Times*, 19 January 1946, 3 ("we are going . . ."); *CR*, 21 January 1946, 160 ("caught us . . ."), 161 ("are not in . . ."); *CR*, 22 January 1946, 183 ("iniquities out into . . .").

44. For the effort to muzzle Bilbo, see *Washington Post*, 30 January 1946, 1; *CR*, 29 January 1946, 507 (popular referendum); *CR*, 25 January 1946, 380 ("we will starve . . .").

January, he placed the FEPC fight in the context of the Cold War, but un-like the chamber's more notorious Red-baiters, he chose not to categorically denounce communism or its followers. FEPC advocates, Hill contended, created domestic turmoil by enraging the South, something he felt "hin-ders our capacity to play our part in giving the leadership to the world in the manner of building the peace." As for the legislation itself, he labeled it another "force act" aimed at "bludgeoning" the South into submission. "Pa-tience" and "good-will," he claimed, represented the only way of addressing the racial issue. Federal compulsion only bred violence. Far from solving the question of discrimination, a permanent FEPC would only exacerbate soci-etal tensions, leading to an erosion in peaceful southern race relations. The potential disruption in the southern social order that the FEPC threatened was not the only argument raised by Dixie's senators.[45]

Senator Olin Johnston of South Carolina was a newcomer to the southern group. Nicknamed "Olin the Solon" more for the sobriquet's alliterative ap-peal than for any particular astuteness on the part of the South Carolinian, Johnston, then forty-five years old, spoke in a slow, deliberate southern drawl with little inflection. A former mill worker, Johnston endured a hardscrabble youth that made him particularly attentive to the plight of the poor. Ris-ing above the conditions of his birth, the South Carolinian ascended to the governor's chair before moving on to the U.S. Senate in 1944. Regarding the FEPC, he wrote in 1945, "I am convinced that it will cause strife, trouble, and probably a revolution in South Carolina." But left on its own, he believed, the South could handle its alleged racial problems as "we have always been able to take care of them." His speech against the permanent FEPC in 1946 represented his freshman effort in a filibuster.[46]

When he took the floor on 25 January 1946, Johnston pointed to the vio-lence of Reconstruction as a warning for twentieth-century politicians con-cerning the risk associated with pushing legislation so clearly at odds with the mores of a particular region. Five days later, he continued in the same vein, at one point even pondering whether the South would have been better

45. LH to M. W. Smith Jr., 1 April 1944, Box 376, Folder 2, Hill MSS ("has aggravated . . ."); CR, 28 January 1946, 455 ("hinders our capacity . . .") and ("force act . . .") and ("Patience . . .").
46. Olin Johnston (hereafter cited as OJ) to C. Norris Hastie, 18 April 1945, Box 3, "Legisla-tion—1945—Labor—FEPC" Folder, Modern Political Papers, South Caroliniana Library, Uni-versity of South Carolina, Columbia (hereafter cited as Johnston MSS) ("we have always . . .");

off "if the Confederacy had won the Civil War." A permanent FEPC, he concluded, "is but the culmination of a series of discriminatory acts against the
South which extended as far back as the Reconstruction days." By way of further explanation, the senator contended that since Appomattox, northerners had systematically punished the South. Sectional prejudice, he argued,
represented a central feature of northern economic policy, a fact reflected in
discriminatory freight rates and the deliberate effort to keep industry out of
the South. Westerners had better prepare themselves, Johnston warned, lest
they too fall prey to the depredations of northern financiers. The time for the
West to align itself with the South had arrived. Johnston's speech fit clearly
in the context of strategic delay. By appealing to senators from outside the
region on the common ground of economic discrimination, he hoped to win
converts to the southern fight and, in the process, prevent serious inroads
against Jim Crow. After his second address, he felt the tide turning in the
South's favor. "I honestly feel that our small band of ardent Southern Senators is winning favor every day," he wrote a constituent, adding that "many of
the supporters of the bill appear to be weakening." Time would tell whether
the South Carolinian accurately captured the mood of the Senate. Until then
Johnston did not stand alone in condemning the long string of discriminatory political and economic practices against the South.[47]

Like Johnston, Lister Hill bemoaned economic discrimination against the
South that effectively blocked the region from gaining access to the lucrative
consumer markets of the northeast. Implicit in both Hill's and Johnston's
denunciations of such policies was a belief that the South could solve its
own problems. Indeed, from their perspective only the impediments placed
before the region by outsiders accounted for the troubles below the Mason-
Dixon line. Grant the region an unfettered opportunity at internal improvement and the region would advance the status of both its black and white citizens, albeit in a segregated fashion. A change emerged in southern rhetoric
that signified the realization of the staggering odds arrayed against them. By
this time, southerners slowly began erecting a wall. Whereas in 1938 Dixie

---

OJ to Frank Dana, 6 April 1945, Box 3, "Legislation—1945—Labor—FEPC, #1 of 4" Folder,
Johnston MSS ("I am convinced . . .").

47. *CR*, 25 January 1946, 401 (Reconstruction); *CR*, 30 January 1946, 564 ("if the Confederacy . . ."); OJ to Robert J. Gantt, 31 January 1946, Box 7, "Legislation 1946—Labor—FEPC, #2
of 2" Folder, Johnston MSS ("I honestly feel . . .").

senators had denounced northern politicians from urban centers for pushing civil rights, in 1946 they criticized the entire region. They now faced what they considered a battle to the death against an aggressive northern society bent on keeping the South reduced to colonial status. Northern champions of civil rights soon learned just how far the white South would go in defense of the region's interests.[48]

Born in 1887, Virginian Harry F. Byrd was one of the chamber's wealthiest members. A high school dropout, Byrd rose to the Virginia governorship, all the while accumulating wealth from the apple orchards he inherited from his father. In 1933 he entered the U.S. Senate, where he gained a reputation for supporting balanced budgets and spending cuts, as well as a peculiar physical trait—rosy cheeks that matched the hue of his famous apples. Often brusque when pressed, his colleagues nonetheless appreciated the Virginian's "rugged personal honesty" and "general air of courtesy." Although a member of the Senate for over a decade, he rarely participated in southern filibusters. When he did speak against "anti-South" legislation, he delivered short addresses, often less than thirty minutes in length, denouncing the measure before resuming his silence. With national pressure for civil rights now rising, the Virginian, from this point forward, had to play a more active role in the southern fight.[49]

On 1 February 1946, Byrd took the floor announcing that Dixie's senators "stand together on the [FEPC] question as firmly as on any issue affecting our southern people which has ever been raised." Here Byrd placed the region's opposition clearly in the context of the South's martial heritage, comparing the steely resolve of southern senators with the courage of Confederate general Thomas J. "Stonewall" Jackson at Manassas. Byrd and other southerners grew up in a region that glorified the memory of what they all called the War Between the States. Twentieth-century southerners considered their struggle against civil rights legislation as a continuation of the same patriotic fight.

48. *CR*, 28 January 1946, 456 (Hill and economic discrimination).

49. Heinemann, *Harry Byrd of Virginia*, 5–108. Douglas, *In the Fullness of Time*, 228 ("rugged") and ("genial"). As governor, Byrd championed a state antilynching law; see speech, Harry Byrd to Virginia General Assembly, 26 January 1928, Additional Papers, Box 4, "Lynching" Folder, Special Collections Department, Alderman Library, University of Virginia, Charlottesville (hereafter cited as Byrd MSS). Byrd considered returning the nation to a more conservative fiscal approach his "main fight" in Washington. See HB to W. C. Caudill, 29 March 1938, Box 157, "Caudill, Dr. W." Folder, Byrd MSS.

They too fought with determination and with a conviction in the righteous-ness of their cause. Like others, Byrd emphasized the tremendous advances made by the region after the Civil War. As for the pending FEPC bill, he noted, "We want Negroes to work. My principal difficulty is to get them to work. That is the only real trouble we are having."[50]

After castigating the shiftlessness of the black race, the Virginian added a warning to fellow Democrats representing states beyond the Mason-Dixon line. Byrd claimed that "the South is the backbone of the Democratic Party." Without its support the organization would collapse. Why then, he won-dered, would northern Democrats continue pushing civil rights legislation knowing that they risked alienating the party's most loyal constituency? Byrd never explicitly threatened a southern bolt from the party, but his speech proved fraught with implications. He spoke directly to that segment of the southern population disenchanted with the direction of the party that once had served its interests so well. In part, this animosity stemmed from long simmering concerns over the sweeping power granted the government dur-ing the New Deal that stripped autonomy from state and local institutions. Civil rights only exacerbated tensions as the northern and western wings of the party began adopting the cause of black equality as their own. An im-plicit threat lay not so hidden in his warning. Continue neglecting southern interests and representatives from the region would bolt the party. Southern senators offered multiple reasons for their colleagues to vote against cloture that ranged from Hill's and Johnston's cries of economic discrimination to Byrd's threats of political retribution. Although infrequently discussed, the question of race also remained an integral, if veiled, aspect of the fight.[51]

Louisiana's Allen Ellender rarely minced words. Both in public and in private, his blunt approach to racial issues enabled him to say confidently, "I have always voted for white supremacy." According to Ellender, race rela-tions in the South generally remained peaceful. That situation began chang-ing, however, as northerners moved South, acting as "a disturbing element." Were it not for such individuals, the Louisianan contended, any existing ra-

50. CR, 1 February 1946, 719 ("Stonewall" Jackson) and ("we want Negroes . . .").

51. Ibid. ("the South is . . ."). Southern threats of defection from the party were, of course, not new. During the 1938 filibuster, for example, Josiah Bailey warned the Democratic Party about alienating the South, a threat that he and others would restate during subsequent civil rights fights.

cial problems would rectify themselves. The Great Migration to the North also threatened the South's contented black populace. Although the pace of black flight increased after World War II, a considerable number of the migrants returned South either to encourage their families to pursue a similar relocation or, in some instances, to remain after finding the North less hospitable than promised. Whatever the reason for their return to Dixie, African Americans accustomed to the absence of a strict racial etiquette in the North often experienced difficulty readjusting to the Jim Crow system. "A southern negro is polite by instinct," Ellender observed, "but when he comes up north he gets as sassy as a flea, and with that condition trouble follows." Regardless of such private sentiments, Ellender and other southerners made every effort to demonstrate their personal regard for African Americans when talking on the Senate floor. Dropping the overt racism he employed with constituents, Ellender observed to his colleagues, "We of the South have treated colored people well; we love them; but we do not associate with them on the same social basis." Despite the alleged good treatment, Ellender argued that southern blacks would inevitably want more protections should the FEPC pass. When off of the Senate floor, the Louisianan returned to more graphic racial rhetoric. As for why he condemned the measure, he outlined a long term process in which each small step toward black equality would lead to something worse. Summarizing the contours of the suspected attack on segregation, he wrote, "It is my view that political equality would lead to social equality and social equality to a degradation of our race."[52]

Some questioned whether expositions on the glories of Jim Crow proved germane to discussions concerning a commission designed to end discriminatory hiring practices. For most southern senators, the answer proved an unequivocal yes. Strategic delay necessitated viewing the civil rights movement in a holistic manner in which all legislative items posed a potential threat to the volatile racial system that they defended. No facet of the Jim Crow

52. Allen J. Ellender (hereafter cited as AE) to W. F. Motley, 16 March 46, Box 1280, "Education and Labor #2, FEPC" Folder, Allen J. Ellender Archives, Allen J. Ellender Memorial Library, Nicholls State University, Thibodaux, Louisiana (hereafter cited as Ellender MSS) ("I have always . . ."); CR, 6 February 1946, 963 ("disturbing element"); AE to H. A. Ghislain, 2 February 1946, Box 1280, "Education and Labor #2 FEPC" Folder, Ellender MSS ("a southern negro . . ."); CR, 7 February 1946, 1050 ("we of the South . . ."); AE to Margaret A. Haines, 29 January 1946, Box 1280, "Education and Labor #2 FEPC" Folder, Ellender MSS ("it is my . . .").

system—from voting regulations to antimiscegenation laws—existed independent of its relationship to the whole. Southern senators, with the exception of Bilbo and at times Eastland, announced their admiration for African Americans, but they increasingly noted how developments outside the South and agitators who infiltrated the region awakened southern blacks from the contentedness they once knew under segregation. In 1937, Cotton Ed stood alone in his concern over black loyalty to the social order predicated on white supremacy. A decade later, many southerners saw evidence of grass-roots unrest. They still could not accept that this agitation came from the iniquities of the system. It had to come from without. Regional insulation marked Ellender's racial views, just as it marked that of many of his colleagues. Like Hill, Johnston, and others who blamed sectional economic discrimination for the region's problems, senators like Ellender accused those beyond the Mason-Dixon line of deliberately fomenting unrest where peace once prevailed. In neither instance did they consider an alternative explanation for the souring of southern race relations and, until the end, they never would. Their system had worked for years and they saw no reason to change it now. After weeks of debate, southern senators began feeling confident that if they had not swayed their colleagues with their arguments, they had at least convinced them that the proposal required greater deliberation off of the Senate floor. In the meantime, they believed the chamber should move to other business, leaving the fate of the FEPC bill for another Congress to decide.

After conferring with Majority Leader Barkley and Republican Steering Committee chair Robert A. Taft on 7 February 1946, Richard Russell decided that the moment to accept the *Journal* for 17 January had arrived. The consultation with the two party leaders revealed to the Georgian that the votes for cloture did not exist. Another southern filibuster appeared on the verge of success. A cloture petition originally put forth on 4 February but ruled out of order because of the pending *Journal* revisions, now rested before the chamber. With southern victory assured, the cloture vote on 9 February proved anticlimactic. The forty-eight to thirty-six vote failure to limit debate, however, was a substantive change in the Senate's voting behavior. For the first time on a civil rights cloture vote, advocates of racial equality mustered more than a majority. The perquisite two-thirds necessary to invoke cloture remained a good deal off, but the tide was certainly changing. From this point forward, it became a death race for the southern forces with the crossover point, at which the majority of the Senate would favor cloture, now reached. Twenty-six Republicans and twenty-two nonsouthern Democrats, along with one in-dependent supported the petition. Only eight Republicans and nine northern Democrats sided with southern senators. In just two years, a profound voting realignment had taken place with the margin of southern victory rapidly shrinking. Many factors accounted for this change. Pure partisanship ranks high on the list. The Republican Party, experiencing a renaissance following World War II, felt confident it could become the majority party by exploiting the sectional schism in the Democratic ranks. Also, the temporary FEPC cre-ated during the war proved far less odious than southerners depicted it. Few feared its implication in spite of alarmist southern rhetoric. Most important was the issue itself. Southern claims concerning antilynching and anti-poll-tax bills were pointed, coherent, and focused on a conservative rendering of the Constitution. Race was effectively removed from the equation formulated by segregationists on those issues. When it came to matters touching more directly on segregation, southerners could not avoid at least some discussion of race, a development that invariably hurt their efforts. To be sure, they tried to stick to legal concerns, but any analysis of southern business and industry demanded an exposition on Jim Crow. There was no getting around it. As a result, discussion necessarily drifted from legal matters to racial matters. By its very nature such debate minimized support for the segregationist forces. Only those senators who unequivocally championed unlimited debate, such as those from the desert southwest, had serious reservations about voting for cloture on the FEPC. Aside from highlighting the even more difficult road ahead in southern minds, the vote also revealed just how detrimental discus-sions of race really were to the southern position. When race found expres-sion on the Senate floor, southerners lost support. It was that simple. At the same time, they could not altogether avoid it owing to the nature of a bill and because of pressure from home. Constituents expected it thus regional racial beliefs had to be voiced. But it hurt every time. Making matters worse, a southern senator supported curtailing the debate.[53]

53. *Washington Post*, 21 January 1946, 3; *Washington Post*, 24 January 1946, 15; 7 February 1946, 1; 8 February 1946, 1; *New York Times*, 19 January 1946, 3; 5 February 1946, 14; 7 February 1946, 4; *Time*, 28 January 1946, 22; CR, 4 February 1946, 802 (initial cloture appearance); CR, 6 February 1946, 951 (chair ruling on petition); CR, 7 February 46, 1063 (*Journal* approved); CR, 9 February 1946, 1219 (cloture vote).

Claude Pepper represented the South's lone renegade in the FEPC fight. Although he disapproved of the commission, the Floridian supported the failed cloture petition but did not vote because he was paired with the absent Tom Connally. Had the Floridian participated, he would have voted yea. Connally, of course, would have voted nay. Pepper attempted to defend his stand. Voting in favor of appropriations for the temporary committee as a wartime necessity, he harbored reservations concerning a permanent FEPC since he believed in the legality of segregation and feared that the commission would threaten the southern racial system. Nonetheless, he argued that the filibuster undermined the political process, stalling action on matters supported by a large majority of the chamber. He did not believe that a handful of obstructionists should prevent the chamber from passing judgment on the FEPC even though he personally opposed it. During the debate, he noted concerning the filibuster that it was a "doggoned shame—offense against parliamentary government and democracy." A degree of hypocrisy surrounded Pepper's position since a successful cloture bid would have led to the FEPC's prompt passage. Pepper's conviction regarding the Senate's cloture rule remained strong. This belief led to his later participation in a drive to change the chamber's rules, a step that so completely alienated him from mainstream white southern opinion as to cost him his Senate seat. But that remained in the future. In the immediate aftermath of the cloture vote, one of the South's preeminent champions of white supremacy experienced difficulties of his own that transcended ideology.[54]

With the FEPC destroyed, Theodore Bilbo prepared for his reelection bid that culminated in his success amidst widespread accusations that he had illegally solicited campaign funds from government contractors. Resolution of the dispute in the form of a Senate debate over the seating of The Man failed to occur. Unbeknownst to his colleagues, 1946 marked Bilbo's last filibuster. During that year, the Mississippian had taken several leaves from the Senate for what he euphemistically called "a new set of teeth." In actuality, the senator left to receive treatment for mouth cancer. Rather than conduct hearings on the Mississippi election, Senate leaders opted to wait until Bilbo's health improved. It did not, and on 21 August 1947, Bilbo died of the illness, an

54. *CR*, 25 January 1946, 410 (explains position); CP Diary, 21 January 1946, Series 439, Box 2, Folder 2, Pepper MSS ("doggoned shame . . .").

ironic culmination to the life of a man who spewed venomous racial invective. His passing marked the end of an era in the Senate. As the last of the loose cannons in the southern bloc, he had increasingly found himself out of step with the rigid order Russell began imposing on the caucus. After Bilbo died, no one remained to challenge Russell's authority. The troops now under Russell's command followed his dictates almost without question. The fate of the South's racial system rested with the aristocratic Georgian.[55]

Before his death, Bilbo left what amounted to a final testament to what he and his southern colleagues wished to accomplish. Although they differed in personal style, the overwhelming majority of southern senators in the 1940s agreed with Bilbo's assessment that "we are not going to stand for the abolition of segregation in the South and we are not going to permit social equality, and intermarriage to be forced upon us by the Congress or any of our Northern friends." Despite their aspirations, doubt crept into the southern ranks. Allen Ellender, for one, observed in 1947 that "we have been battling the negro question for quite some time. I am sorry to say, however, that our ranks are diminishing. With the Republicans in power it may be an uphill fight." The new leader of the southern group, Richard Russell, also expressed concerns for the future. Just prior to the cloture vote on the FEPC in 1946, the Georgian commented on the growing strength of pressure groups and especially of black voting blocs: "We have seen the beginning . . . of delegations coming to Congress to sandbag senators and intimidate them into voting against their better judgement." But pressure groups in Washington were not all that he feared. He worried too about the impact of "professional South haters throughout the nation" in influencing public opinion. Pressure from all quarters seemed aimed at the South. As commander of an army that viewed Washington politics in conspiratorial terms and that followed a tactical approach in which the worst case scenario was always presupposed, it is not surprising how the man who proved so instrumental in formulating the southern strategy considered the political landscape. Later events demonstrated that he had good reason for concern.[56]

55. Drury, *Senate Journal*, 81 ("a new set . . ."); Green, *Man*, 109–111.

56. TB to Eunice Morrow, 14 February 1946, Box 1022, Folder 14, Bilbo MSS ("we are not . . ."); AE to Mordaunt Thompson, 8 May 1947, Box 1028, "FEPC 1947" Folder, Ellender MSS ("we have been . . ."); CR, 9 February 1946, 1218 ("We have seen . . ."); RR to C. W. Sherlock, 26 December 1947, Box 1, Folder 4, Russell MSS ("professional South haters").

During World War II, southern senators linked their fears of the 1930s with the new political realities of the 1940s. They still believed that one civil rights bill would lead to another, but they added corollaries to that belief reflected in the concept of strategic delay. Where once they sought to defeat all proposals with civil rights implications, they now permitted action on minor bills in an effort to accrue Senate support for later battles against more sweeping measures. Even if they defeated one bill, they now recognized, new initiatives would follow—until Jim Crow fell. Southerners hoped to contain that trend by granting limited concessions to delay, at least temporarily, the inexorable push against segregation. Astute political observers, southern senators nonetheless realized that civil rights activism would begin again in spite of their efforts. They would, of course, continue to defeat the large proposals and thereby delay the push against Jim Crow, but they no longer believed that they could completely thwart the assault. Banking on the goodwill of their colleagues and the apathy of the American public, they considered all legislation with even a remote connection to civil rights in relation to their long-term goal of preserving the status quo for as long as possible. Southerners knew they could not stop senators from states such as New York and Illinois from voting for civil rights, but they did hope to convince representatives from less industrialized locales that battles for the antilynching and poll-tax-bills were chimeras for the larger goal of social equality. Southern senators sought assistance where they could find it. Excluding statesmen with large black constituencies, they believed that the rest of their colleagues, as well as the majority of the American people, felt as they did. All the while, they knew that ceaseless agitation against the region would continue until they failed. Defeat served as the only possible outcome. In the meantime, they planned on preserving for as long as possible the racial order they were charged with defending.

3. The Battle Broadens

AT THE END OF 1946, President Harry S. Truman established a civil rights commission in an effort to renew the then expired FEPC and, as he explained, "to get the facts and to publicize as widely as possible the need for legislation" aimed at ameliorating the plight of black Americans. After investigating the problem, the commission released its findings under the title *To Secure These Rights*. The document analyzed all facets of America's racial situation, just as it made specific suggestions on how to better race relations. Legislative initiatives, including a permanent commission on civil rights, an antilynching law, the repeal of the poll tax, and a renewed FEPC, figured prominently in the report. Requesting action in 1948, Truman sent a civil rights message to Congress that read, in part, "We shall not . . . finally achieve the ideals for which this nation was founded so long as any American suffers discrimination." For white southerners, the president's proposals underscored the central premise of strategic delay—that civil rights pressure would not cease until the Jim Crow system fell. During the previous decade, southern senators had defeated antilynching, anti-poll-tax, and FEPC bills, yet advocates of the legislation had not given up hope that these measures would one day pass. Now the president of the United States placed the full weight of the executive branch behind the civil rights cause, increasing the likelihood that Congress would enact at least some of the desired bills. More than a little political opportunism guided Truman's actions. With an election looming and public support for his administration waning, Truman needed to solidify the New Deal coalition forged by Franklin Roosevelt that included organized labor, farm workers, and especially African Americans if he hoped to win. By pushing civil rights in 1948 he was following the blueprint of a plan aimed at procuring victory. In November 1947, presidential counsel Clark Clifford drew up a forty-three-page memorandum in which he urged the president to make "new and real efforts" to appeal to northern blacks lest they "go Republican." Truman followed the advice to the letter, a fact that ensured that civil rights opponents would face their most difficult challenge yet.[1]

Southern senators responded to the threat on 6 March 1948 by holding a meeting in the office of Harry Byrd attended by all senators from the eleven states of the former Confederacy except Claude Pepper. During the caucus, they organized to fight the proposals and selected Richard Russell to oversee their strategy, making official the leadership role that he had held for several years. When confronted with Truman's civil rights package, the southern leader noted that many of the proposals had appeared before, only this time the political landscape had changed. The pressure for civil rights, he claimed, had "become more acute with the infiltration of a dangerous radical element into the Democratic Party which is willing to sacrifice the integrity of our institutions for supposed political advantage." Russell, along with other southerners, recognized a liberal shift in the ideological orientation of the national party. More than any other issue, civil rights created a schism in the party's ranks that would culminate in a political realignment decades later. Based on the prevailing southern assumption that the American people remained fundamentally misinformed about the nature of the civil rights crusade, the caucus planned to make frequent appearances on nationwide radio broadcasts to alert those beyond the Mason-Dixon line of the threat posed by the Truman program. Russell proved pivotal in the decision to mount a counteroffensive over the air waves as he had long claimed that the national media grossly distorted white treatment of southern blacks. The public relations offensive served as an adjunct to the legislative wing of the southern fight.[2]

1. Donald R. McCoy and Richard T. Ruetten, *Quest and Response: Minority Rights and the Truman Administration* (Lawrence: University Press of Kansas, 1973), 103; David McCollough, *Truman* (New York: Simon and Schuster, 1992), 586–589; Harry S. Truman, *Memoirs of Harry S. Truman: Years of Trial and Hope* (New York: Doubleday, 1956), 180 ("was set up . . ."); *New York Times*, 23 February 1948, 22 ("we shall not . . ."); all Clark Clifford quotations from Clark Clifford, *Counsel to the President: A Memoir* (New York: Random House, 1991), 191–192.

2. For background on the caucus, see Fite, *Richard B. Russell, Jr.,* 232; Mann, *Walls of Jericho,* 42; RR to F. M. Dancy, 3 September 1948, Box 26, Folder 12, Russell MSS ("become more acute . . ."). For another example of Russell noting political expediency, see RR to Roy F. Morgan, 14 February 1948, Box 1, Folder 4, Russell MSS.

Although proponents of the civil rights measures claimed that the legislation only sought to make minor improvements in the lives of African Americans, caucus members believed that they confronted proposals aimed at achieving full legal and political equality for southern blacks. The arguments Russell and other southern senators would employ against the Truman bills represented the distillation of southern thinking forged in the previous ten years of combating civil rights, arguments that would remain essentially the same through the 1960s. Of the nineteen southerners who participated in the filibuster against the Civil Rights Act of 1964, twelve of them attended the 1948 meeting. Continuity not only marked the southern ranks but also the nature of the bills they would encounter after World War II. Expanding suffrage and dismantling segregation slowly emerged as the twin objectives of civil rights advocates. Southerners, in turn, met these later proposals by drawing on the same constellation of ideas that informed their arguments during the Truman years. Immutable principles, they believed, guided their opposition, making their recurring rhetoric all the more noble, in their minds, since it proved consistent with the intentions of the founding fathers. Unlike civil rights advocates, they believed they did not need to change their core values to satisfy minority voting blocs. It did not take long before they had to put their ideals to the test in the crucible of debate, the U.S. Senate.[3]

A bill to repeal the poll tax became the first of the Truman-backed proposals to reach the Senate. Approved by the House 290 to 112, it stood little chance of passing the upper chamber during the special session called by President Truman before the national nominating conventions. The southern response to the poll-tax bill that reached the Senate in late July 1948 served as the prototype for their fight against later suffrage legislation. Since voting rights did not directly involve the region's system of segregation, southern senators deemphasized the question of race as they had when faced with similar legislation to repeal the poll tax in 1942 and in 1944. Convinced that the majority of white northerners would repudiate the legislation if they became aware of the bill's ramifications, the caucus attempted to reveal the

3. The southern senators present at the 1948 meeting who would participate in the 1964 filibuster were John Sparkman and Lister Hill of Alabama, John McClellan and J. William Fulbright of Arkansas, Spessard Holland of Florida, Richard Russell of Georgia, Allen Ellender of Louisiana, John Stennis and James Eastland of Mississippi, Olin Johnston of South Carolina, and Harry Byrd and A. Willis Robertson of Virginia.

forces that agitated for the repeal of the poll tax through what they again labeled an "educational campaign." Southern senators alleged that northern politicians proved willing to flout constitutional strictures in order to win the favor of black voting blocs. Even worse, southerners claimed that these very same lawmakers knew even before the bill reached the Senate that it would never pass, a fact that further illustrated that political expediency underlay the civil rights crusade. Although not addressing the issue themselves, they accused northerners of playing the race card not necessarily because they wanted more blacks to vote, but because they wanted African Americans to vote for them. Two distinct but interrelated themes thus emerged in southern arguments. First, they claimed that Truman and Senate civil rights advocates pushed the legislation in 1948 only because they wanted black support in the forthcoming elections. Second, they argued that northern politicians, in their blind rush to procure temporary political advantage, never considered the long-term consequences of tinkering with the electoral process that they believed the Constitution clearly left in the hands of state governments. Diligent southern senators claimed a host of threats to the American political system posed by a federally mandated voting rights law.[4]

As in the 1942 and 1944 battles over the poll tax, southerners hinged their case on Article I, Section 2 of the Constitution, which granted individual states the right to prescribe voter qualifications. They argued that a congressional repeal of the impost would not only impact the states that still retained the fee but also, in effect, repeal an entire section of the Constitution, not to mention those segments of state constitutions that mandated the tax. Such a course of action would, southerners warned, set a precedent for future Congresses to arbitrarily remove portions of the Constitution at their discretion, just as it would one day enable "unfettered, unbound, unregulated, and unrestricted" federal access to the voting statutes of the sovereign states. They said the bill's passage would undermine the entire concept of federalism that undergirded the American political system since the nation's found-

4. For House vote on H.R. 29, see *CR*, 80th Cong., 1st sess., 21 July 1947, 9551. For the motion to consider the bill in the Senate, see *CR*, 80th Cong., 2nd Session (all subsequent *CR* citations refer to the 80th Cong., 2nd sess. until otherwise noted), 29 July 1948, 9480. For examples of southerners claiming northern political expediency, see *CR*, 2 August 1948, 9605 (Robertson); *CR*, 3 August 1948, 9668–9669 (Hill); RR to Roy F. Morgan, 14 February 1948, Box 1, Folder 4, Russell MSS.

ing by further centralizing power in Washington, a trend that southerners had challenged since the late New Deal. Taking the argument to its logical extreme, southerners contended that by the simple act of repealing the poll tax, Congress would open "the gates for an unlimited invasion of the powers which the Constitution carefully reserves to the States." Based on southern contentions, the bill no longer represented a measure to grant poor southern blacks the right to vote, it became a proposal "striking at the very base of the temple of American rights and American freedoms." Southerners, therefore, claimed that their fight in 1948 expanded well beyond narrow sectional concerns, it encompassed the preservation of state and individual rights from an ever expanding federal government. Protecting the American political system served as the publically stated rationale for opposing the bill, but regional concerns remained an integral, if veiled, facet of their arguments.[5]

The Jim Crow system rested on the Supreme Court's ruling in the 1896 *Plessy v. Ferguson* decision. Following that decree, segregation laws proliferated in the South based on the premise now codified by the judicial branch that "separate but equal" facilities did not violate the equal protection clause of the Fourteenth Amendment. Concurrent with the proliferation of segregation statutes emerged laws that removed African Americans from the voting rolls in a manner that did not violate the Fifteenth Amendment, thus ensuring that the region's black population would lose its political voice and thereby its ability to alter the emerging Jim Crow system. Southerners interpreted the Fifteenth Amendment, as the Supreme Court did the Fourteenth Amendment, in narrow terms, considering it a negative mandate. The Fifteenth Amendment, according to southerners, did not say that all blacks possessed the right to vote, it merely stated that race could not be a factor in the voter qualification process. Literacy tests, understanding clauses, and poll taxes were, at least in theory, hurdles that all potential voters, regardless of race, had to face and therefore not in violation of the Constitution. If Congress could repeal the poll tax, southern senators recognized, it could revoke other suffrage laws, and if it could do that, it could also take action against segregation. The southern racial order existed primarily because of the judicial

5. For examples of arguments stressing the bill's broad implications, see *CR*, 28 July 1948, 9463–9464 (Russell); *CR*, Stennis, 29 July 1948, 9496 ("unfettered, . . ."); *CR*, 29 July 1948, 9499 (Stewart); *CR*, 30 July 1948, 9578 (Maybank); *CR*, Robertson, 2 August 1948, 9621 ("the gates for . . ."); *CR*, Hill, 3 August 1948, 9668–9669 ("striking at the . . .").

branch's narrow construct of the law, as well as the Tenth Amendment, which afforded the states sovereignty over matters not specifically granted the central government by the Constitution. Federal incursion into state jurisdiction on the poll-tax question threatened the foundation on which white southerners had constructed their racial system following Reconstruction. Should they relent now, they risked losing everything. The caucus had its own plan to abolish the poll tax, an imposition even most southerners considered unnecessary, which reflected their states' rights interpretation of the Constitution.[6]

Repealing the poll tax through constitutional amendment became the method preferred by southerners for lifting the impost. For them, an amendment would prevent the establishment of a precedent that permitted unrestricted federal access in the electoral process by leaving it up to the individual states to repeal the tax. By abolishing the impost through an amendment, the Constitution would remain unsullied and the southern racial order unchallenged. As for their long-term goals, the drive for an amendment served as another tactic in the southern strategy of delay. At the start of the next session, southerners introduced Senate Joint Resolution 34, which called for a constitutional amendment to abolish the poll tax in federal elections. Caucus members headed by Spessard Holland of Florida agitated for a repeal of the tax in federal elections until they finally succeeded in winning its ratification as the Twenty-fourth Amendment in 1964. Hoping to demonstrate that they adhered to the constitutional principles they often touted, southerners viewed their repeal initiative as serving the larger purpose of stemming the tide threatening segregation. By demonstrating that they could accept at least some changes in their political system, they sought to slow the push for civil rights. In the short term, the drive for a constitutional amendment garnered the support of many moderates, such as Claude Pepper, who were previously inclined to a legislative measure repealing the tax. With even former advocates of a legislative repeal breaking ranks, positive action on civil rights in the special session looked bleak.[7]

6. Edward L. Ayers, *The Promise of the New South: Life After Reconstruction* (New York: Oxford University Press, 1992); C. Vann Woodward, *Origins of the New South, 1877–1913* (Baton Rouge: Louisiana University Press, 1971); C. Vann Woodward, *The Strange Career of Jim Crow,* 3rd ed. (New York: Oxford University Press, 1974); OJ to R. Carl Griffith, 16 February 1948, Box 13, "Legislation, 1948, Civil Rights, General" Folder, Johnston MSS.

7. *CR*, 28 July 1948, 9464 (Pepper advocates a constitutional amendment); *CR*, 29 July 1948, 9496–9497 (Stennis advocates amendment). The poll-tax amendment was sponsored by Hol-

Many journalists at the time labeled the southern "educational campaign" a "leisurely" filibuster. One reason for the "leisurely" debate remained the precedent that the Senate's cloture rule only applied to measures. For years, southerners had relied on a strict interpretation of Rule 22 that excluded procedural motions from cloture, a loophole that enabled them to filibuster efforts to consider civil rights legislation without fear of reprisal. This narrow construct had its opponents. Some argued that based on the southern interpretation, Rule 22 proved useless since no measure could fall under the cloture guidelines without a motion first placing it there and southerners could indefinitely filibuster all motions to consider civil rights legislation. On 2 August, supporters of the poll-tax bill advanced a cloture petition during the southern filibuster against the motion to consider the legislation in an effort to receive a favorable ruling that would reverse the precedent that excluded motions from Rule 22. Not surprisingly, Richard Russell challenged the petition. Michigan Republican Arthur Vandenberg, president pro tempore of the Senate, upheld Russell's interpretation of the rule, recognizing that debate over parliamentary motions fell beyond the cloture guidelines. Vandenberg's ruling signaled the end of the battle. If civil rights advocates had no chance of forcing a cloture vote, they could not pass repeal of the poll tax unless southerners capitulated and gave up their filibuster. Two days later, supporters of the bill withdrew the measure from consideration. Southern forces again won a civil rights fight, but they quickly faced the consequences of their triumph.[8]

Following Vandenberg's decision, serious discussion concerning a change in Rule 22, which had so long blocked civil rights advances, filled the chamber. Even Arthur Vandenberg, who had upheld the southern interpretation, noted that the rule required improvement to close the existing loophole. From the southern perspective, any change would weaken their ability to thwart civil rights legislation. By refusing to concede any ground, southerners risked losing everything especially considering that some liberal sena-

---

land (Fla.), George (Ga.); Connally (Tex.), Ellender and Long (La.), Hoey (N.C.), Broughton (N.C.), and Robertson (Va.). *CR*, 81st Cong., 1st sess., 13 January 1949, 176.

8. *Newsweek*, 9 August 1948, 18; *Memphis Commercial Appeal*, 30 July 1948, 1; Riddick, *Senate Procedure*, 303. For the cloture petition, see *CR*, 2 August 1948, 9598. For Russell's challenge, see *CR*, 2 August 1948, 9600–9601; *CR*, 2 August 1948, 9602–9604 (Vandenberg); *CR*, 4 August 1948, 9736–9738 (H.R. 29 withdrawn).

tors favored cloture by a simple majority for both motions and measures. Although not likely to succeed, pleas for a drastic change emerged from a climate of opinion that favored some alteration in the existing rule. Richard Russell's forces confronted an important decision directly related to their ability to defend "the southern way of life." A wrong move might hasten the demise of all they had fought to protect. As on previous occasions, they faced the dilemma of appearing too intransigent if they fought such a minor alteration of the rule. Should they prove too stubborn, southerners feared that the chamber might punish them by adopting majority cloture. With a fight over Rule22 likely at the start of the next Congress, southerners had all the more reason to view the November 1948 elections as an integral component of their resistance efforts. Where many statesmen on the local level demanded a southern break from the Democratic Party, most of Dixie's national legislators proved more cautious. Expanding the concept of strategic delay outside of the legislative arena, southern senators approached the 1948 election with an eye on how their actions would influence their continued ability to halt civil rights advances in Washington.

Bold as President Truman's civil rights advocacy was in early 1948, he nonetheless needed to win an election later that year. Truman staffers contemplated the question of how best to handle civil rights at the party's nominating convention in Philadelphia, Pennsylvania. Southern Democrats had obviously let their displeasure be widely known in both large and small ways. For the biggest event on the Democratic Party's social calendar, the annual Jefferson-Jackson Day dinner, South Carolina senator Olin Johnston purchased tickets for an entire table in front of the speaker's dais. Neither Johnston nor any of his "guests" attended the banquet, leaving instead a silent protest in the form of an empty table. Johnston's message offered the president and rank-and-file Democrats a powerful visual reminder of just how passionate racial matters remained in the South. Even more, the gesture portended potential difficulty at the Democratic nominating convention.[9]

At the convention, the Truman camp, recognizing trouble ahead, opted to support a rather vague civil rights plank for the party's platform. Truman, of course, insisted he remained committed to equality and to the sweeping array of civil rights proposals advocated by the Civil Rights Commission he had created. At the same time, southern bluster on civil rights found its opposite

9. Clifford, *Counsel to the President,* 207–208.

in growing liberal protestations that the Democratic Party finally take a principled stand for equality. Leading the charge was Minneapolis, Minnesota
mayor and Senate hopeful Hubert H. Humphrey. Most observers considered
the driven Minnesotan a rising star in the Democratic ranks. As such, he
was cautioned not to be too vocal in his civil rights protests so as not to raise
the ire of the southern delegation. In caucus, convention liberals heatedly
debated how to approach civil rights. Rather than postpone their push to redirect the Democratic Party away from its states' rights southern wing, they
wanted action and would send Humphrey, who was already scheduled to
speak, before the delegates to demand it. A more provocative course of action
could not have been envisioned. Unlike the administration that attempted
to placate the southern arm of the party, its liberal wing led by Humphrey
decided the time for delay in actualizing the goal of "human rights" and
abandoning "states' rights" had arrived. The eloquent Humphrey stirred the
party faithful from their staid convention. So much for suggestions that he
soft-pedal the civil rights question. In response to his fiery speech, the Democratic convention adopted the far more activist Humphrey-inspired civil
rights plank and abandoned Truman's mild proposal. Every word of the plank
stung southern delegates. The Democratic Party, once labeled the "White-
man's Party," had just committed itself to the belief that "racial and religious
minorities must have the right to live, the right to work, the right to vote, the
full and equal protection of the laws." Portions of the Alabama and the entire
Mississippi delegation left the convention hall in protest, as their regional
cohorts sat aghast. Any hopes that Truman harbored of reconciliation with
the southern wing were now gone.[10]

Despite the convention chaos and the partial southern bolt, Harry Truman received the Democratic nomination with little fanfare. Remaining
southern delegates nominated their own rising star, Richard Russell of Georgia, a man who had long proven his credentials as a defender of the "southern
way of life." Clearly Russell would not win, but the 263 votes he garnered—
votes that were never altered to make Truman's nomination unanimous as
per custom—reflected the depths of southern animosity. This would be no
ordinary election.[11]

10. Ibid., 217–220; Mann, *Walls of Jericho*, 17–21; Merle Miller, *Plain Speaking: An Oral
Biography of Harry S. Truman* (New York: Putnam, 1974), 252.
11. Key, *Southern Politics*, 335.

The 1948 presidential election pitting Truman against the Republican challenger Thomas Dewey has received considerable scrutiny from both historians and political scientists. Another aspect of the campaign, the Dixiecrat revolt, has also become the subject of scholarly discussion. Research on the Dixiecrat movement often fails to address the large number of southern leaders who remained in the Democratic fold. Despite the much studied fragmentation of the Democratic Party in 1948, J. Strom Thurmond of South Carolina, who served as the States' Rights Candidate, only won four southern states. One reason for Thurmond's limited success was the decision of many of the region's U.S. senators to remain out of the contest. Most southern senators condemned the president's civil rights activism but stopped short of abandoning the Democratic cause since they viewed the seniority privileges granted them by their party affiliation a paramount concern in the wake of increased civil rights pressure. Many southern senators refused to campaign for Truman as they had in the past for other Democratic candidates, but many of them also did not offer their assistance to the Dixiecrat ticket. Senators recognized that the preservation of segregation required that they maintain their party loyalty to safeguard their power base in the U.S. Senate. Although a break from the party might play well with constituents in the short term, it would weaken the southern fight in the long term. Protecting segregation demanded a strong southern presence in the Democratic Party regardless of the national organ's civil rights position. When these Washington lawmen withheld their support from the Thurmond ticket, the States' Rights Party lost the backing of the region's most esteemed and, in many cases, most influential statesmen.[12]

12. Emile B. Ader, *The Dixiecrat Movement: Its Role in Third Party Politics* (Washington, D.C.: Public Affairs Press 1955); William D. Barnard, *Dixiecrats and Democrats: Alabama Politics, 1942–1950* (University: University of Alabama Press, 1974); Robert A. Divine, "The Cold War and the Election of 1948," *Journal of American History* 59 (June 1972): 90–110; Gary A. Donaldson, *Truman Defeats Dewey* (Lexington: University Press of Kentucky, 1999); Kari A. Frederickson, *The Dixiecrat Revolt and the End of the Solid South, 1932–1968* (Chapel Hill: University of North Carolina Press, 2001); Robert A. Garson, *The Democratic Party and the Politics of Sectionalism, 1941–1948* (Baton Rouge: Louisiana State University Press, 1974); Zachary Karabell, *The Last Campaign: How Truman Won the 1948 Election* (New York: Knopf, 2000); Irwin Ross, *The Loneliest Campaign: The Truman Victory of 1948* (New York: New American Library, 1968); Harvard Sitkoff, "Harry Truman and the Election of 1948: The Coming of Age of Civil Rights in American Politics," *Journal of Southern History* 37 (November 1971): 597–616; Allen Yarnell,

Although Alabama gave its electoral support to the Dixiecrats, Lister Hill questioned the efficacy of this decision. "I do not believe that it is to the interest of Alabama and the South for us to split up among ourselves." Like Hill, Virginia senator Harry Byrd vehemently opposed Truman's civil rights proposals and for a time thought that "powerful influences" in the Democratic Party would prevent the incumbent from winning the presidential nomination in 1948. When that failed to occur, Byrd stayed out of the campaign, choosing neither to endorse Truman nor to publicly support Thurmond. Unlike Hill's Alabama, Byrd's Virginia pledged its support for the incumbent Truman. Arkansas' James William Fulbright, who remained a favorite of the northern intelligentsia for his internationalist foreign policy preferences, also urged caution in the face of southern extremism. "I doubt," he said of the Dixiecrat revolt, "that withdrawing from the party or any other such move will achieve any beneficial results." In addition, Fulbright felt the movement would dissipate as the election approached and that "very few, if any, responsible people are going to walk out." For the Arkansan, moderation represented the best approach to southern racial difficulties. Despite deteriorating race relations, even the region's most liberal senators did not dare denounce segregation during the campaign except in the most tangential of ways.[13]

The 1948 election placed Florida's Claude Pepper in a difficult situation. Many southern citizens, and indeed many of the region's statesmen, viewed Truman's legislative initiatives as a possible catalyst for segregation's demise. Attempting to curtail suspicions that he did not wholeheartedly endorse Jim Crow, Pepper noted that "the idea that the president has ever recommended or Congress could make compulsory the abolition of segregation . . . is utterly preposterous." In Florida, nevertheless, Pepper fell victim to a smear campaign that conflated his former support for abolition of the poll

---

Democrats and Progressives: The 1948 Presidential Election as a Test of Postwar Liberalism (Berkeley and Los Angeles: University of California Press, 1974).

13. LH to J. H. Alexander, 11 February 1948, Box 492, Folder 4, Hill MSS ("belong to the . . ."); LH to S. U. Vines, 3 March 1948, Box 492, Folder 5, Hill MSS ("I do not . . ."); HB to Preston Collins, 22 March 1948, Additional Papers, Box 4, "Presidential Election 1948" Folder, Byrd MSS ("powerful influences"); J. William Fulbright (hereafter cited as JF) to Suzanne Lighton, 28 February 1948, BCN 38, Folder 1, J. William Fulbright Collection, Special Collections, Mullins Library, University of Arkansas, Fayetteville (hereafter cited as Fulbright MSS) ("I doubt that . . .").

tax through legislative decree with support for the entirety of the Truman initiatives, including social equality. To this charge, Pepper stated, "Don't believe that! That is not true!" Should the government attempt such an imposition on the South, he reassured constituents, "I would be the first to oppose it as a basic usurpation of power." As for the Truman candidacy, Pepper opposed his nomination at the Democratic convention, but following the sitting president's selection, he rallied behind the Missourian. His acceptance of Truman as the party's standard-bearer carried with it a heavy political price tag. Pepper considered himself a transitional figure at a time in southern history when "the progressive and the reactionary forces" battled "to determine which shall be dominant." He knew that southern liberals such as himself had little chance after the "explosive race issue" became a central feature of southern elections. Ten years earlier, in 1938, Pepper had allowed his upcoming reelection bid to influence his decision to close ranks with his regional colleagues against the Wagner–Van Nuys antilynching bill. By 1948, he proved more willing to stand by his convictions. His southern colleagues also prepared to uphold what they considered the core principles of the region, making Pepper's position the subject of intense scrutiny for its departure from the rhetoric utilized by other Dixie statesmen.[14]

Although tepidly supporting the Dixiecrat revolt, South Carolina's Olin Johnston viewed the effort as a temporary protest, not a permanent solution. Johnston informed one South Carolinian that "we have enough southerners in the Senate—good southerners—to vote down or talk down any attempt at passage of the antilynch, anti–Jim Crow, or other anti-southern legislation." Aside from pointing to the obvious importance of the Senate in the civil rights fight, his comments highlighted a new trend in southern thinking. By observing the presence of "good southerners," he deliberately cast politics in the region as a sharp dichotomy between right and wrong. Although he did not mention him directly, Johnston left little doubt that he considered

14. CP to James A. Davis, 16 December 1948, Box 57, Folder 12, Pepper MSS ("the idea that . . ."); transcript, undelivered radio address, 26 July 1948, Series 431A, Box 6, Folder 2, Pepper MSS ("don't believe that . . .") and ("I would be . . ."); CP to Richard O. Coffeen, 2 September 1948, Series 201, Box 25A, Folder 3, Pepper MSS (Truman support); CP to D. Lee Jones, 3 August 1948; Series 201, Box 26, Folder 3, Pepper MSS (Truman support); CP to Samuel S. Talbert, 16 August 1948, Series 431A, Box 6, Folder 3, Pepper MSS ("the progressive and . . .") and ("explosive race issue").

Claude Pepper a "bad southerner" for his heretical beliefs. Indeed, under the definition of "southern" offered by Johnston, only staunch supporters of segregation and all of its satellite systems represented the best interests of the region. His reflections embodied the political parlance of the era by castigating even mild defectors from regional norms in stark terms as traitors to the South. Unless one spoke long and loud about the glories of Jim Crow, he or she lost his or her bona fides as a "good southerner." Beyond the peculiar logic that informed the emerging definition of what "southern" meant, most senators from the region remained loyal to the party, adopting a wait and see approach to the election. Despite concerns over the future of the Democratic Party, southern senators in 1948 still viewed the legislative wing of their fight against civil rights as their primary line of defense.[15]

In the wake of Truman's stunning victory over Dewey in the 1948 presidential contest, some speculated that the election served as a mandate for the president's programs. At the time, few knew exactly how the triumph would translate into legislative action. J. William Fulbright sensed where the potential for trouble lay. "The difficulty is going to be with people like [Hubert] Humphrey [Democrat from Minnesota], [Paul] Douglas [Democrat from Illinois], et cetera, and the Administration. We ought to know in a few days what the intention of the President is," he wrote. With the election over, southerners recognized that the black vote proved pivotal in Truman's election. Based on this development, they feared that the number of senators firmly committed to civil rights would increase as both parties vied for the support of black voting blocs in future electoral contests. The 1948 election that placed Truman in power also added two new faces to the southern ranks, both of whom figured prominently in subsequent civil rights fights.[16]

Born in 1918, Russell Billieu Long of Louisiana bore a close physical resemblance to his famous father Huey P. Long, who had once served in the U.S. Senate. Holder of a law degree from Louisiana State University, Russell Long served in the U.S. Navy during World War II. As commander of a small landing craft, he saw action throughout the European theater, receiving four battle stars for bravery during the 1944 invasion of France. After the war, he

15. OJ to A. G. Kennedy, 5 February 1948, Box 13, "Legislation 1948 Civil Rights, General" Folder, Johnston MSS ("we have enough . . .").

16. JF to Harry S. Ashmore, 3 January 1949, BCN 48, Folder 2, Fulbright MSS ("The difficulty is . . .").

opened a small law firm before becoming engaged in his uncle Earl Long's successful 1948 bid for the Louisiana governorship. A few months later he entered a special election to fill the remaining two years of the Senate term opened by the death of John Overton. Although the question of Truman's civil rights proposals concerned Louisianans, Long steered his campaign toward substantive social issues that reflected the influence of his father's Share Our Wealth program. Far more reserved than his father, Long did not seek a complete overhaul of the economic system, but he did promise voters he would "work for greater federal aid to education, for social security and old age benefits and for our school lunch program."[17]

Another southerner with similar liberal tendencies joined the thirty-year-old Long in starting his Senate career at the beginning of the Eighty-first Congress. Lyndon Baines Johnson of Texas, who had spent the previous decade in the House of Representatives, entered the Senate under a cloud of suspicion. Victory in his 1948 Senate race came by a mere eighty-seven votes, raising charges of rampant electoral fraud. Overlooking significant evidence that Johnson's voters included the dead and noncitizens, the Texas Democratic Executive Committee permitted the result to stand. Using his Texas heritage and conservative civil rights record from his House service, Johnson actively courted the Senate's southern patriarchs. After taking the oath of office, he received a letter from Mississippi senator John Stennis, a member of the Committee on Rules and Regulations, which adjudicated contested elections, that read, "Of course I am not judging the case until the facts are in but as far as our personal relationships are concerned, I just have a feeling that we have a lot in common." This regional kinship with seniority rich southerners smoothed Johnson's transition to the Senate. Some of Johnson's liberal admirers from his youthful incarnation as an ardent New Dealer questioned his open alliance with the Senate's reactionary element and his plans to assist them in the anticipated fight over Rule 22. The junior senator from Texas responded to such criticism simply: "It is indeed a heavy price for me to pay, but the price of our freedom is worth it." The man who

17. Keith M. Finley, "Balancing Liberal and Conservative Policy Preferences: Russell B. Long's Early U.S. Senate Career, 1948–1957," *LA History* (Winter 2003): 11; press release, Russell B. Long (hereafter cited as RL), 2 July 1948, Box 591, Folder 2, Russell Long Collection, Special Collections and Archives, Hill Memorial Library, Louisiana State University, Baton Rouge (hereafter cited as Long MSS) ("work for greater . . .").

became an outspoken civil rights supporter as president began his Senate career espousing a diametrically opposed position. Whatever combination of ambition and idealism dictated his later actions, Lyndon Johnson, upon arriving in the Senate, fell directly in the mainstream of southern thought on the racial issue by unequivocally supporting Jim Crow, along with all of the mechanisms that guaranteed its continuation. As his House voting record testified, Johnson qualified, in the words of South Carolina's Olin Johnston, as a "good southerner." Southern leaders, however, did not dispense favors without expectations of future compensation. Johnson did not have to wait long to uphold his end of the bargain by participating in the next southern defense of regional interests that seemed less certain of victory than in previous years. The outcome of the fight hinged on the always suspect resolve of self-proclaimed civil rights advocates.[18]

J. William Fulbright claimed that northern Democrats and "some" Republicans "gave lip-service" to civil rights but never made serious efforts to pass such legislation. Even with the protection afforded the South by the Senate's cloture rule, Fulbright believed that "if the Republicans and northern Democrats were really determined to pass these laws they can do so and they could have done so in the past" through the use of round-the-clock sessions to

18. Robert A. Caro, *Years of Lyndon Johnson: The Path to Power* (New York: Knopf, 1982); Robert A. Caro, *The Years of Lyndon Johnson: Means of Ascent* (New York: Knopf, 1990); Paul K. Conkin, *Big Daddy from the Pedernales: Lyndon Baines Johnson* (Boston: Twayne, 1968); Robert Dallek, *Lone Star Rising: Lyndon Johnson and His Times, 1908–1960* (New York: Oxford University Press, 1991); Ronnie Dugger, *The Politician: The Drive for Power from the Frontier to Master of the Senate* (New York: Norton, 1982); Roland Evans and Robert Novak, *Lyndon Johnson: The Exercise of Power* (New York: New American Library, 1966); Doris Kearns, *Lyndon Johnson and the American Dream* (New York: Harper and Row, 1968); Merle Miller, *Lyndon: An Oral Biography* (New York: Putnam, 1980); Alfred Steinberg, *Sam Johnson's Boy: A Close-Up of the President from Texas* (New York: Macmillan, 1968); Irwin Unger and Debi Unger, *LBJ: A Life* (New York: Wiley, 1999); John Stennis to Lyndon Baines Johnson (hereafter cited as LBJ), 21 October 1948, Box 5, Congressional Files, Lyndon Baines Johnson Archives (hereafter cited as LBJA), Lyndon Baines Johnson Library, Austin, Texas (hereafter cited as LBJL) ("of course I . . ."); LBJ to Frank Baldwin, 10 March 1949, Box 214, "Speeches—Filibuster 1" Folder, Senate Papers, LBJL ("it is indeed . . ."). While a member of the House, Johnson voted against antilynching legislation during the 76th Congress and against anti-poll-tax bills from the 77th to the 79th Congresses. During the 80th Congress, he paired against a poll-tax bill. During his tenure in the House, Johnson did not face FEPC legislation. Memo, Walter Jenkins to LBJ, 28 February 1948, Box 165, "Civil Rights 1948" Folder, House of Representatives Papers, LBJL.

break southern filibusters. His observation carried grave implications. A central facet of strategic delay was the ability of southern senators to keep the majority of their colleagues from pushing civil rights measures by providing them with constitutional justifications for not supporting them. Fulbright recognized the efficacy of that approach but indicated that one day southern efforts would fall short. At the end of 1948, few knew whether those claiming to support civil rights had experienced a hardening in their convictions since the last battle. If they had, then Fulbright's concerns foreshadowed the possibility that some of Truman's initiatives had a legitimate chance. Either way, southern senators would not take any risks. Expecting debate on civil rights to begin at any time, Harry Byrd noted that "all of the Southerners have agreed not to leave Washington day or night . . . as we will have to make the fight of our lives." As they had expected, caucus members soon learned that a determined effort to amend the Rules of the Senate served as the administration's response to its election day triumph. Whether or not the announced supporters of civil rights were still only paying "lip-service" to expanding black rights remained unclear. Southerners would soon discover first hand if northern resolve had strengthened.[19]

Georgian Richard Russell had always asserted that the rules represented "the last weapon against the tyranny and statism and the mood of the mob." During the Truman years, those very rules came under assault. To a constituent he remarked, "We are in a desperate situation here, and are casting about for any means which will enable us to protect ourselves from an overwhelming majority of the Congress who are either misguided or seeking political support." Most northern Democrats and Republicans, he speculated, desired a change in Rule 22, and if "they succeed by force of numbers in doing this, it will be very simple for them to pass so-called civil rights measures." At one point, the Georgian indicated that he had grave doubts that his troops could prevail. "We must bravely face discouragement and probable defeat in our fight to stave off this vicious legislation." This remarkable concession by the southern leader underscored the importance with which the region's senators viewed the pending fight. Not since 1938 had they faced such pressure and,

19. All Fulbright citations from JF to Clarence Byrns, 18 May 1948, BCN 48, Folder 2, Fulbright MSS; HB to James Robertson, 26 April 1948, Box 190, "Robertson, James" Folder, Byrd MSS ("all of the . . .").

unlike in the past, the opposition did not seem willing to relent. The level of commitment for the rule change appeared strong, crossing partisan lines— the very same lines that southerners traversed when they successfully undermined previous cloture efforts. The South could no longer count on sizable Republican assistance as that party had begun contesting the Democrats' hold on black voters and forcing the spotlight on that party's regional schism ever since Truman succeeded Roosevelt. For southerners, protecting their besieged citadel seemed all the more difficult in an atmosphere charged with activism.[20]

To a man, the southern caucus agreed with Russell that the defense of segregation hinged on the rules governing the Senate. Olin Johnston, for example, observed that "our protection still lies in the ability of southern senators to hold the line in the U.S. Senate." As "long as we have [the] filibuster available as an effective weapon of defense and there are enough of us within the ranks," the president's civil rights package would fail. Lister Hill also saw the fight over Senate rules as an essential component of the southern opposition. Should things go wrong, Hill claimed, "the chances for passage of the so-called civil rights bills is greatly enhanced." Everything hinged on the outcome of the battle. Alabama's junior senator, John Sparkman, shared many of the same liberal tendencies as his colleague Hill and like Hill he knew the attendant risks associated with the cloture fight. Surveying the past decade of civil rights activism in Washington, Sparkman noted that despite considerable support for such legislation in both parties, a sizable number in the chamber had remained "sympathetic" to the South. In 1949, he found less reason for optimism. To a constituent, the senator wrote, "Frankly, I am very much afraid that the situation now is different and that we have very little sympathy to expect from either the Republicans or the Democrats." Somewhere southerners had to find a solution that would maintain the status quo in the Senate so that they could safeguard their social system at home.[21]

20. RR to B. W. Duncan, 5 March 1949, Box 25, Folder 6, Russell MSS ("the last weapon . . ."); RR to H. C. Bartlett, 26 February 1949, Box 25, Folder 9, Russell MSS ("we are in . . ."); RR to R. M. Harper, 14 February 1949, Box 26, Folder 3, Russell MSS ("they succeed by . . ."); RR to C. E. Baker, 6 January 1949, Box 26, Folder 5, Russell MSS ("We must bravely . . ."). For another example of his pessimism, see RR to C. D. Foster, 28 January 1949, Box 26, Folder 4, Russell MSS.

21. OJ to C. R. Dent, 29 January 1949, Box 13, "Legislation 1948, Civil Rights, General" Folder, Johnston MSS ("our protection still . . ."); OJ to Joseph W. Brooks, 8 March 1949, Box 17, "Legislation, 1949, Civil Rights" Folder, Johnston MSS ("as long as . . ."); LH to Geoffrey Birt, 26

On 17 February 1949, the Senate Committee on Rules and Administration chaired by Democrat Carl Hayden of Arizona favorably reported Senate Resolution 15, a bipartisan resolution designed to close the loophole in Rule 22 that exempted procedural motions from cloture. Debate on the measure did not begin until the last day of February. Like the question of voting rights, efforts to alter Senate Rule 22 became a recurring challenge faced by the southern caucus for the remainder of the legislative struggle over civil rights. As with suffrage bills, southern senators relied on a corpus of arguments, stressing historical precedent and potential long-term consequences of a rule change, that they trotted out whenever the Senate's cloture guidelines became the subject of debate. The founding fathers, southerners argued, designed the Senate as a refuge for minority interests, an institution meant to check the temporary passions of the mob. Although the founders fashioned the Senate as a bulwark of a particular form of minority interest—the landed gentry, twentieth-century southerners expanded this definition to include religious, racial, and, most important, sectional minorities. In so doing, they depicted themselves as the guarantors of liberty for all Americans by transmogrifying their opposition from a narrow sectional defense of segregation to a more broadly national fight that appealed directly to the legacy of the Revolutionary generation. If they acquiesced to a rule change, they would not only be perverting the intent of the framers, they would be turning their backs on all present and future interest groups that did not support the opinion of the majority then prevailing. In 1949, southern senators warned that civil rights advocates wanted to change the very nature of the chamber as conceived in 1787 for the dubious objective of passing the Truman proposals.[22]

February 1949, Box 492, Folder 7, Hill MSS ("the chances for . . ."); John Sparkman (hereafter cited as JS) to W. R. Withers, 22 January 1949, Box 113, 16-C-8, "Civil Rights—Jan.–Feb. 1949–8 Feb. 1949" Folder, John Sparkman Collection, W. S. Hoole Special Collections Library, University of Alabama, Tuscaloosa (hereafter cited as Sparkman MSS) ("sympathetic") and ("frankly I am . . ."). Although open to the public, the Sparkman papers are not catalogued. Citations from the collection are based on the system employed by the senator's staff at the time of his retirement. To best find the material, accession numbers along with box and folder numbers are included since the box numbers are not sequential and often overlap across accession blocks.

22. Bill reported: *CR*, 81st Cong. 1st sess. (all subsequent *CR* citations from 81st Cong., 1st sess. until otherwise noted), 17 February 1949, 1327. For examples of arguments regarding the intent of the founders and the protection of minorities, see *CR*, 2 March 1949, 1717 (Long), 1725 (Hoey); *CR*, 4 March 1949, 1872 (Fulbright); *CR*, 9 March 1949, 2043–2045 (Johnson); *CR*,

Although southerners generally cast their arguments in national terms, sectional interests also figured prominently in their defense of Rule 22. According to southern senators, civil rights advocates not only sought to undermine the institutional structure of the Senate, they also aimed to destroy the South's racial order. Southerners, of course, could not leave uncontested northern claims that racial injustices in the South necessitated a rule change so that the Senate could act on legislation to ameliorate the plight of the region's black populace. Discrimination in Dixie, southerners argued, proved a chimera constructed by civil rights advocates that bore little resemblance to the state of race relations as it existed on the ground. As North Carolinian Clyde Hoey observed, "Some persons seem to entertain the idea that we in the South get up early in the morning to see how we may oppress the Negroes on that day, and study how many things we can do to discriminate against them." Segregation's defenders maintained the myth that the region's black and white populations lived together in perfect harmony, each accepting its societal role with little complaint. Northern statesmen, they claimed, sought to upset southern racial tranquility by pushing a rule change that would inevitably lead to the passage of civil rights legislation. Caucus members had long held that social equality represented the end goal of civil rights advocates no matter what those activists publically stated. One way to expedite the process of ending segregation would be to change Senate Rule 22, which served as the South's most important weapon in thwarting civil rights advances. Dixie's Senate delegation made little effort to conceal its speculations regarding their opponents's intentions. What its members attempted instead was to tie their sectional interests to the concerns of the national body politic.[23]

Southern senators knew that the chamber's more liberal members such as Hubert Humphrey aimed not just to open motions to a cloture vote but also

14 March 1949, 2362 (Ellender); see also TC to Roy Terrell, 5 March 1949, Box 230, "General Legislation—Filibuster, Cloture" Folder, Connally MSS; TC to Wilbert Davis, 10 March 1949, Box 230, "General Legislation—Filibuster, Cloture" Folder, Connally MSS; JS to Henry D. Davidson, 8 February 1949, ACC 16-c-8, Box 113, "Civil Rights—January–February 1949" Folder, Sparkman MSS. For claims that civil rights was at the heart of the rule change initiative, see CR, 1 March 1949, 1632 (Connally); CR, 2 March 1949, 1721 (Long).

23. For examples of the southern use of race, see CR, 5 March 1949, 1911 (Fulbright); CR, 9 March 1949, 2047 (Johnson), 2067 & 2086 (McClellan); CR, 12 March 1949, 2335 (Eastland); CR, Hoey, 2 March 1949, 1730 ("some persons seem . . .").

to permit cloture by a simple majority in which one more than half of those senators present and voting could limit debate compared to the two-thirds margin then in place. Although little evidence exists that such sentiment proved widespread, southerners hoped that by emphasizing that their opponents sought a more fundamental change they would frighten enough moderate and conservative senators into opposing even a slight alteration. Of the major ideas stressed by the southern caucus, none received as great attention as the question of majority cloture. Such a dramatic rule change, according to southerners, would impact all Americans. Of course, an alteration would impact the South by making the passage of civil rights legislation almost certain, but it also had national ramifications because it threatened the constitutionally mandated purpose of the Senate. Precedent remained a vital concern for southerners, who viewed any break from established norms a potential catalyst for sweeping changes in America's political system. During the Truman years, the South fell under attack. Southern senators sought to convince western senators and conservative Republicans that one day they too might fall victim to the fleeting desires of a "transient majority." Their arguments proved particularly convincing to Senate Republicans, who only a few short years before had been a decided minority during the New Deal. Had southern senators abandoned what they considered their role as defenders of the Constitution then, who could tell what mischief the Democratic majority might have accomplished. Southerners now asked their colleagues, who had not yet become beholden to black voting blocs, to consider the long-term implications of a rule change. By permitting a narrow alteration in 1949, the Senate would establish a precedent that would inevitably result in majority cloture. In the process, the very balance of government power would shift and the legislative branch would become a mere subsidiary of the executive once the Senate lost its mandate as a preserver of minority rights. Richard Russell and his forces urged the Senate to step back from the propaganda of civil rights advocates and consider just how far-reaching Senate Resolution 15 really was. If all of their arguments failed, the caucus had one final reason the southern racial order, and therefore the Senate Rules, needed no changing.[24]

24. For examples of threats of majority cloture, see *CR*, 28 February 1949, 1608 (George); *CR*, 1 March 1949, 1649 (Russell); *CR*, 2 March 1949, 1717 (Long); *CR*, 3 March 1949, 1796 (Holland); *CR*, 5 March 1949, 1913 (Fulbright); *CR*, 14 March 1949, 2362 (Ellender); *CR*, 15 March 1949, 2464 (Robertson); *CR*, Fulbright, 5 March 1949, 1911 ("transient majority").

During the debate, devout Baptist A. Willis Robertson of Virginia added a religious component to what had previously been a secular defense of Jim Crow conducted by southern senators. According to Robertson, God deliberately made the races different because he did not wish to "mongrelize" them. Efforts by civil rights advocates, who pushed social equality, transgressed God's intentions by trying to "effect a purpose which He himself did not adopt." Moreover, the Virginian continued, the Bible provided "no evidence that it would be pleasing to him" if the South accepted blacks as equals. Southern religious denominations had a long and strained relationship with the region's racial systems. As Anne C. Loveland noted in *Southern Evangelicals*, nineteenth-century clergymen buttressed the slave system by providing biblical sanction to the status quo. During the antebellum period, the religious justification for slavery developed in conjunction with the emergence of the threat posed by the abolitionist crusade in the 1830s. Twentieth-century southerners were equally as pious as their forebears, making it not too surprising that they also turned to their faith when their racial system fell under attack. The defense of Jim Crow remained largely a secular concern until southerners again perceived a significant challenge to their way of life in the form of the Truman proposals. At that point, the southern populace turned to their faith at the very same time that growing numbers beyond the Mason-Dixon line questioned the morality of the social system constructed by the region. For the southern Senate delegation in Washington as well as for white citizens throughout the South, being a "good southerner" meant not questioning the racial system and not looking so deeply as to expose its faults that lay just below the surface. Robertson proved no different, choosing to avoid assessing the status of race relations on the ground by finding support for Jim Crow's maintenance in the heavens. Religious justifications of segregation would grow increasingly important in the arguments of several southern senators as civil rights pressure expanded in subsequent decades. Since the legislative battle occurred in a secular milieu, however, southern senators remained attentive to the sentiments of their Senate colleagues.[25]

25. All Robertson citations from *CR*, 2 March 1949, 1727; Anne C. Loveland, *Southern Evangelicals and the Social Order, 1800–1860* (Baton Rouge: Louisiana State University Press, 1980); Donald G. Mathews, *Religion in the Old South* (Chicago: University of Chicago Press, 1977); I. A. Newby, *Jim Crow's Defense: Anti-Negro Thought in America, 1900–1930* (Baton Rouge: Louisiana State University Press, 1965); H. Shelton Smith, *In His Image but . . . Racism in Southern Religion, 1780–1910* (Durham, N.C.: Duke University Press, 1972).

For days, the southern bloc engaged in a filibuster against Senate Resolution 15 that proved remarkably germane compared to similar debates orchestrated by Tom Connally. Unlike the Texan, Richard Russell kept a watchful eye on speech length and the tenor of debate. No longer would individual southerners hold the floor for a series of consecutive days. During the first week, the southerners maintained an "insistent mumble" as they looked for an opportunity to shift Senate opinion in their favor. Several potential avenues existed for Russell and his forces to end the stalemate. The most likely scenario saw the mercurial Truman blundering and thereby providing the South a chance to capitalize on the president's indiscretions. Another, and less likely prospect, saw the administration growing weary of the filibuster and thus abandoning its endeavor. Then, on 3 March 1949, Truman made the mistake that Richard Russell expected from his former Senate colleague.[26]

At a press conference, the president, who had never revealed his personal desires concerning Rule 22, announced that he supported majority cloture. Quick to relay the news, Russell alerted the Senate chamber about Truman's comments. For almost a week, southerners had warned their colleagues that majority cloture, not the two-thirds stipulation of Senate Resolution 15, remained the true objective of civil rights advocates. In the absence of corroborating evidence, it became the word of southerners against that of those supporting the change called for in the resolution. The pugnacious president provided all the evidence Richard Russell needed. Through his poorly thought out comments, Truman had exploded the bipartisan coalition favoring a rule change. Most senators simply could not sanction a very public effort on the part of the executive to fundamentally alter the legislative branch. Truman's pronouncement struck many as differing in degree, not in kind, from Roosevelt's drive to alter the judiciary. Senators have a tendency to zealously safeguard their autonomy and prerogatives. Conservative Republicans drifted back to their customary arguments regarding the Rules of the Senate, which matched those raised by southern senators, save, of course, for the emphasis on race. As a former senator himself, Truman should have known better. Southern caucus members, who had once viewed the rules fight with trepidation, found renewed optimism. Again they appeared on the verge of victory.[27]

26. *Time,* 14 March 1949, 23 ("insistent mumble").
27. For Russell's comments, see *CR,* 3 March 1949, 1811.

On 9 March 1949, Democratic majority leader Scott Lucas of Illinois announced that he would circulate a cloture petition to break the southern filibuster. He hoped that, unlike what transpired in 1948, civil rights supporters would get a favorable ruling from the chair that procedural motions also fell under the existing cloture guidelines. Vice President Alben Barkely, who for several years led the Democratic majority, presided over the Senate throughout the rules fight. Now he held the key to undermining the loophole in the existing cloture rule. The following day, Lucas placed the petition before the chamber. Russell immediately raised a point of order, challenging the legitimacy of a cloture petition on the grounds that it violated Rule 22. Barkley, who did not relish his role, ruled in favor of accepting the petition. According to the vice president, southerners, as well as Arthur Vandenberg in 1948, misinterpreted the rule. Although the rule only addressed debate over measures, it did not specifically exclude cloture on motions. The absence of any direct mention of motions in Rule 22 led Barkley to believe that when the Senate adopted the guideline in 1917 it was understood that cloture applied to both motions and measures. If cloture could not apply to all facets of the legislative process, he stated, then the rule served no purpose. In the absence of an answer satisfactory to all disputants, a motion was made to put the question before the entire chamber. Barkley's ruling thus fell subject to Senate approval. In light of Truman's remarks, what should have become a resounding victory for civil rights advocates soon turned into an embarrassment.[28]

Two days later, the Senate overruled Barkley's position, forty-six to forty-one. Among those voting against the new interpretation was, of course, the entire southern delegation, minus Claude Pepper and Estes Kefauver of Tennessee. In addition, twenty-three Republicans joined forces with the southerners; only sixteen sided with the twenty-five Democrats in favor. The vote represented nothing less than a devastating blow to rule change advocates. Despite the decision, Majority Leader Lucas announced the Senate would continue debating the motion. Emboldened by their ever strengthening position, southern senators forged ahead with their filibuster. They held all the cards. Any change in chamber rules would first have to meet the approval of the southern bloc. Based on strategic delay, however, they knew that they would have to grant at least some minor concessions or risk appearing as

28. For the cloture motion and Russell's point of order, see CR, 10 March 1949, 2166. For the vice president's ruling, see CR, 10 March 1949, 2172–2175.

nothing but obstructionists. They had to accept a change if for no other reason then to convince their colleagues and the American people that the southern caucus consisted of reasonable men capable of temperate actions. A positive perception of them, southerners hoped, would prove beneficial in future civil rights battles. What they eventually offered as a compromise illustrated that they would not give without receiving much in return.[29]

At the close of discussion on 12 March 1949, Richard Russell announced his willingness to ponder "any reasonable compromise which will end this controversy and serve to protect the rights of Senators." Senate Leader Lucas and the majority of the bipartisan coalition that desired a rule change simply wanted cloture applicable to all phases of the legislative process. On the other hand, southerners would not agree to such a maneuver without some assurance that it would not lead to majority cloture. After a weekend of wrangling, the contours of a compromise emerged. At one point, Truman requested that the Senate withdraw Senate Resolution 15 so the chamber could begin action on other items on his legislative agenda such as rent control extensions. Rather than looking for an end to the fight, southerners would not allow the removal of the motion as they wanted to settle the rules issue for good with a lasting agreement. When a compromise finally emerged, the filibuster ended on 15 March and the Senate voted, seventy-eight to zero, to consider Senate Resolution 15.[30]

The so-called compromise proved heavily weighted in favor of the South. Russell's forces won their most important point—any subsequent discussion of Senate Rules would fall beyond the jurisdiction of cloture. In essence, Rule 22 would never again change so long as southerners maintained a filibuster against future alteration attempts. Although they relented in allowing cloture on motions as well as measures, they raised the standards regarding

29. *CR*, 11 March 1949, 2275 (vote); *Newsweek*, 21 March 1949, 22; *Atlanta Constitution*, 12 March 1949, 1. Republican Wayne Morse of Oregon later claimed that a deal between Russell and key Republican leaders led to the defeat of Barkley's ruling. According to Morse, Russell promised southern support to ensure the defeat of a federal power transmission line from Kerr Dam to Anaconda, Montana, so that the privately owned Montana Power and Light could handle the line. As a result, Morse alleges that nineteen Republicans joined with the South to defeat Barkley's ruling. *New Republic*, 12 May 1952.

30. *CR*, 12 March 1949, 2354 ("any reasonable compromise . . ."). For the vote to consider the resolution, see *CR*, 15 March 1949, 2509.

the maneuver, making two-thirds of the entire Senate membership, rather than two-thirds of those present and voting, the prerequisite to limit debate. With the new guidelines established, it now took sixty-four votes to invoke cloture. By a margin of sixty-three to twenty-three, the Senate voted on 17 March 1949 to accept the rule change. Few observers viewed the compromise as anything but a complete victory for the South. Georgia's Richard Russell stood triumphant. Expecting defeat, he had bided his time and made the most of every opening. Moments before the vote that ostensibly made a filibuster harder to break, Russell did not claim the total victory many civil rights advocates argued that he had won but chose instead to emphasize the sacrifices the southern group had to make. Strategic delay called for restraint, not gloating. "We have salvaged as much out of this situation as we possibly could, in view of the fact that there were only some 21 of us to oppose the entire membership of the Senate," observed the Georgian.[31]

Off of the floor, southern senators exulted in their latest triumph. Following the fight, plaudits poured into Richard Russell's office. Alabama's John Sparkman wrote the Georgian, "the whole southern group is deeply indebted to you and will always be. Your strategy, daring, tenacity and statesmanship could not have been surpassed." Virginian Harry Byrd proved even more effusive in his praise of both the southern triumph and Russell's leadership. Byrd called the cloture fight "one of the most notable victories in our history." Speaking of Richard Russell, he added that "he was superb in his tactics and just as effective in their execution, . . . I do not think that even Robert E. Lee had a more coordinated army or a more loyal following than Dick had." When southern senators described their fight in Washington, they increasingly did so in a manner reminiscent of historical accounts describing Robert E. Lee's Army of Northern Virginia. Like their Confederate forbears, caucus members fought against enormous odds and did so with aplomb, knowing that they operated under the skilled generalship of Richard Russell. The observations of Senator Allen Ellender of Louisiana capture how members of the southern caucus viewed their relationship with their commander. On 14 March 1949, Ellender delivered an oration against a change in rules lasting twelve hours and twenty-one minutes. The Louisianan still had eight hours remaining in his speech, but Russell intervened. "I received orders . . . that

31. For the vote, see *CR*, 17 March 1949, 2724, 2722 ("We have salvaged . . .").

should I continue it might endanger our cause," he commented, "so, like a good soldier, I reluctantly took my seat." During Connally's tenure as head of the caucus, similar descriptions of the Texan proved rare. Now, southern senators acceded to Russell's dictates, recognizing his parliamentary skills and accepting the discipline that he imposed.[32]

Caucus commander, Richard Russell did not allow victory to obscure the implications of strategic delay. Although he felt the 1949 fight left the South "in a position to carry on the battle," he more ominously added "this was only one battle in a war that will be waged increasingly against us." Thwarted for a moment, the civil rights crusade would restrengthen before too long. Hubert Humphrey, Paul Douglas, and other pro–civil rights senators vowed to renew their fight until they brought full legal and political equality to all Americans. They too would not sanction defeat, but at the time their prospects for victory appeared far more dim than that of the southern caucus. Despite southern contentions of being an embattled minority, the difficulty of the caucus' situation was not nearly as grave as that of their adversaries. To hear southerners speak, however, is to hear a much different depiction of the legislative situation. According to them, civil rights advocates proved more resourceful than ever in advancing their agenda. With most senators absent on the eve of the session's end, Indiana Republican Homer Capehart pressured Scott Lucas to address why the Senate had not acted on a list of legislative items, including several civil rights proposals. Had Lucas proved willing, the Senate could have easily passed an antilynching, anti-poll-tax, or FEPC bill that day by unanimous consent in the absence of southern resistance. Also in 1949, Republicans John Bricker of Ohio and Henry Cabot Lodge Jr. of Massachusetts attempted to exacerbate the sectional schism in the Democratic ranks by pushing antisegregation measures in federal housing and aid to education legislation. Although both efforts convincingly failed, southerners feared that liberal northern Democrats would attempt to reestablish their civil rights credentials called into question by their opposition to the Republican amendments by employing clandestine parliamentary tactics to pass "anti-South" legislation. Cognizant now that "eternal vigilance" represented the only way

32. JS to RR, 22 March 1949, 16-C-8, Box 113, "Civil Rights, March 1949" Folder, Sparkman MSS ("the whole southern . . ."); HB to JF, 16 March 1949, Series 71, Box 4, Folder 6, Fulbright MSS ("one of the most . . .") and ("he was superb . . ."); AE to J. E. Schoolfield, 19 March 1949, Box 603, "Civil Rights 1949" Folder, Ellender MSS ("I received orders . . .").

of defending "the southern way of life," Russell reinstituted the use of "floor guards" so that whenever the Senate convened a representative from Dixie remained in the chamber to prevent any further "legislative trickery." The implementation of guard duty occurred frequently in future years, taking place whenever Russell deemed the political climate grave enough to warrant close southern scrutiny of chamber activity. "Eternal vigilance" became the new reality for southerners as they faced mounting civil rights pressure.[33]

J. William Fulbright also sensed that the southern success in 1949 provided only a temporary respite. In particular, he feared that "as a result of the discussions in the Congress the desire to afford greater opportunities has been strengthened." Because of such fears, southern senators could not long enjoy their victory. They knew that antilynching and poll-tax bills represented gradual steps toward "the real offensive to abolish segregation" in the South. Although they did not advocate this yet, Russell Long noted that once the NAACP advanced beyond its current program, "the northern wing of our party cannot resist the pressure that will be brought for the total abolition of segregation." Speaking about more immediate concerns, Long observed, "I fear that we are going to lose a couple of rounds in the Civil Rights fight" before the end of the legislative session. Although all southerners agreed with Long regarding the long-term agenda of civil rights advocates, they did not necessarily accept his forecast of the region's short-term prospects.[34]

Based on the result of the rules fight, southerners experienced renewed optimism that they could defeat what everyone knew would come next, a bill to create a permanent FEPC. Spessard Holland, who unlike fellow Floridian Claude Pepper worked with the southern caucus, observed that the outcome of the rules fight provided the region better protection "against unwise legislation which would set back the solution of the civil rights problems, which is already moving ahead swiftly." At least in the short term, Holland believed the new rule provided the necessary protections for the region and he offered no indication that he anticipated southern defeat in the next civil

33. RR to John M. Holladay, 1 April 1949, Box 25, Folder 2, Russell MSS ("in a position . . ."); RR to W. B. Crawford, 30 March 1949, Box 25, Folder 2, Russell MSS ("this was only . . ."); CR, 24 August 1949, 12147–12149; RR to JF, 24 August 1949, BCN 48, Folder 2, Fulbright MSS ("eternal vigilance"); RR to HB, 7 June 1949, Box 30 Folder 9, Russell MSS ("legislative trickery").

34. JF to Lawrence A. Davis, 31 March 1949, BCN 48, Folder 2, Fulbright MSS ("as a result . . ."); RL to W. B. Webb, 30 March 1949, Box 11, Folder 38, Long MSS ("the northern wing . . ."); RL to Lawrence Eustis Jr., 25 March 1949, Box 10, Folder 32, Long MSS ("I fear that . . .").

rights fight. Joining Holland, Alabama's John Sparkman also felt certain that the FEPC "will not pass." Civil rights sentiment in the chamber was changing, but certainly not so fast as to reverse the outcome of the 1946 FEPC cloture fight, a fact that led Olin Johnston to announce, "I predict that victory will again be ours." Nonetheless, all southerners knew that every success came at a considerable cost. Each victory the southern group wrested from civil rights supporters further dramatized the racial problems of the South. Americans beyond the Mason-Dixon line witnessed southern obstructionism in every legislative battle, just as they received a barrage of propaganda from those advocating civil rights that illustrated discrimination in Dixie. A major concern of southerners thus became how long the nation would stand apathetic in the face of their intransigence. Developments in the 1950s proved Americans could wait a very long time. The battle over the FEPC in 1950 foreshadowed the apathy that would mark the legislative struggle over civil rights for the remainder of the decade.[35]

Prior to the start of the second session of the Eighty-first Congress in 1950, southerners privately grappled with their fears that federally mandated social equality would inevitably result if the FEPC legislation succeeded. In a region where race shaped identity, the FEPC represented an affront to southern interests far in excess of what the bill's provisions actually sought to accomplish. For all the lofty rhetoric regarding the Constitution and the sanctity of the Senate that took place in 1949, the majority of the southern caucus conceptualized the FEPC in racial terms. Richard Russell argued he would do all that he could to improve the economic status of blacks, however, he added, "I could never bring myself to accept the idea that these United States would be a better country if populated by a mongrel race." As for an end to segregation, which southerners believed the bill threatened, Louisiana's Allen Ellender enunciated a typical refrain: "To be frank . . . my brand of democracy does not encompass social equality among the negroes and whites." True enough southerners loved the Constitution, but they also

35. Spessard Lindsey Holland (hereafter cited as SH) to George E. Goldthwaite, 29 March 1949, Box 818, Folder 53, Spessard Holland Collection, Claude Pepper Library, Florida State University, Tallahassee (hereafter cited Holland MSS) ("against unwise legislation . . ."); telegram, JS to Geoffrey Birt, 24 February 1949, ACC. 16-C-8, Box 113, "Civil Rights—Jan.–Feb. 1949–8 Feb. 1949" Folder, Sparkman MSS ("will not pass"); OJ to C. G. Dowling, 11 May 1950, Box 22, "Legislation—1950—FEPC" Folder, Johnston MSS ("I predict that . . .").

viewed the maintenance of segregation as an essential mission of the South that complied fully with the nation's founding principles. Many southerners considered themselves "Jeffersonian Democrats" and as such favored a strict construction of the Constitution. To them fell the task of maintaining the balance of power among local, state, and national institutions as the founders intended. Since the New Deal political power had shifted to the federal level, a development they clearly viewed as a transgression of the intent of the framers. The assault against Jim Crow represented one facet of an even larger drive to strip states, and eventually individuals, of their freedom. Southerners believed that their ideals represented American ideals and that their defense of segregation was not just a battle for an antiquated regional custom but a fight to preserve the sanctity of the American political system. If segregation fell, the forces that favored centralization would continue chipping away at local, state, and individual autonomy. The equal parts racism, constitutionalism, and patriotism southerners expressed in private would become the cornerstone of their arguments in opposition to the FEPC when that legislation reached the Senate. Although faced with a bill unlikely to pass, veteran filibusterers knew that they could take nothing for granted in their fight to preserve southern and, therefore, what they considered American ideals.[36]

During the 1949 Christmas season, A. Willis Robertson dropped a line to his Virginia Senate colleague Harry Byrd. Robertson indicated that he had concluded work on a 180-page speech on the FEPC bill. He added, "I hope to have the leg power as well as the lung power to deliver it before the roll is called on a bill that is unconstitutional, socially and economically unsound and smells to high heaven of political demagoguery." The tandem from Virginia, along with the rest of the southern caucus, prepared for yet another civil rights battle at the start of the second session of the Eighty-first Congress in January. Although the outcome of the rules fight buoyed their resolve, they knew this would not spell the end of civil rights advocacy. Pressure would continue to mount as it had done since the New Deal. If uncertain about the future, they were prepared for the present.[37]

36. RR to William Dickey, 17 February 1950, Box 23, Folder 11, Russell MSS ("I could never . . ."); AE to M. Columba, 16 March 1949, Box 603, "Civil Rights 1949" Folder, Ellender MSS ("To be frank . . .").

37. A. Willis Robertson to HB, 19 Dec. 1949, Box 204, "Robertson, A. Willis" Folder, Byrd MSS ("I hope to . . .").

On 5 May 1950, the Committee on Labor and Public Welfare reported out Senate Bill 1728, the FEPC bill. The measure would make the nation's employers liable to fines and imprisonment if they discriminated on the basis of race or religion. Majority Leader Lucas immediately motioned to consider the bill. The official commencement of the southern filibuster was on 8 May 1950. As for the stated purpose of the bill, creating job opportunities for African Americans, caucus members maintained that no employment discrimination existed in the South, a fact that made the measure superfluous. The precedent the FEPC threatened to create became the subject of much southern exposition. If the government could tell people who they could or could not hire, then, southerners said, it could also force them to associate with individuals against their will. Jim Crow could not long survive once the government had a right to limit one's freedom of association. In short, the bill, according to southerners, represented the long feared thrust against the southern racial order.[38]

Federally mandated social equality served as the preeminent concern of the southern caucus and indeed of the white South in general after World War II. Uniform southern apprehensions regarding a post–Jim Crow South, however, never led to the formulation of a singular argument that encapsulated the diversity of explanations found in the region for the existence of segregation. Throughout their careers, individual caucus members fluctuated in their arguments defending segregation, fluctuations that reflected the difficulty of championing to the nation a race-based social system unknown outside the region. Caucus members could always defend Jim Crow and its satellite institutions by employing their own narrow interpretation of the Constitution as well as that held by the pre–Earl Warren Supreme Court, but when it came to dealing with the moral aspect of segregation they often found it difficult to craft a cohesive argument that reassured outsiders of the righteousness of the southern cause. Products of their time and place, southern senators exhibited many of the characteristics that most twenty-first-century Americans consider racist. They believed that blacks differed from whites in manifold ways and that these distinctions made segregation essential. Many caucus participants had long attempted to deemphasize the notion that white racism necessitated Jim Crow by arguing that southern

---

38. *CR*, 81st Cong., 2nd sess. (all subsequent *CR* citations from 1950 refer to the same Congress and Session), 5 May 1950, 6491 (reported out), 6497 (Lucas motion).

blacks had no objections to the prevailing racial system. Under this construction, white southerners absolved themselves of any guilt they might
feel concerning their subjugation of African Americans. Arguments that
heralded black support for Jim Crow proved difficult to document and the
least likely to sway national opinion because of the existence of what caucus
members called a "hate the South" campaign orchestrated by the northern
media and other "self-righteous reformers." Liberal news outlets beyond the
Mason-Dixon line, southerners contended, deliberately sensationalized isolated episodes of racial violence in the South, creating a perception among
northerners that such occurrences represented the norm rather than the
exception in the region. They had to find a different argument if they hoped
to convince northerners that tranquility, not oppression, marked race relations in the region.[39]

Paralleling the mythological portrait of black and white contentedness
under Jim Crow, stood the more ambiguous argument that cultural norms
and precedents made separation of the races a part of the southern social fab-
ric and thereby something that could not and should not be abolished overnight. Customs that limited social intercourse between the races, according
to southerners, did not in any way undermine opportunities for the region's
large black minority. In the 1940s, southern blacks had greater economic
and educational opportunities than they had ever experienced in the South.
Things were changing in the region, southern senators claimed, and they
would continue to do so for the betterment of African Americans without
outside pressure. Southerners asked northerners to assist them in ensuring
that blacks held a similar standard of living as whites, albeit in the context
of a segregated society. Alabama's Lister Hill summarized this perception,
remarking "it is not token legislation that will improve the lot of the Negro
and other minority groups. It is constructive, affirmative programs—education, hospitals and health centers, public health and prevention of disease—
decent homes and housing on the farm and in the city, adequate wages and
economic security under our American free-enterprise system. These are

39. For southern emphasis on tranquil race relations, see relevant passages from the discussion of the 1949 rule change fight. For examples stressing the existence of an anti-South
propaganda campaign, see *CR*, 8 May 1950, 6623 (Russell); *CR*, 12 May 1950, 6995 (Johnston);
and RR to Roy F. Morgan, 14 February 1948, Box 1, Folder 4, Russell MSS ("self righteous . . .").
See also RR to C. W. Sherlock, 26 December 1947, Box 1, Folder 4, Russell MSS.

the substance. Senate bill 1728 is the shadow." Caucus members in this mold such as Hill, J. William Fulbright, and Russell Long believed that instead of pushing civil rights bills, northerners should stress education and infrastructure improvements in the South so that the region's black population could further lift itself out of the poverty that followed emancipation. However, these same solons warned that trying to push social equality on the region would provoke great unrest since it would threaten the long-entrenched regional custom of a race-centered social system. Segregation permeated all phases of southern life from education, restaurants, conveyances, to many other public accommodations. An effort to change that custom through legislation such as the FEPC bill would at best produce chaos, at worst an apocalyptic race war. Far better, this more moderate branch of the opposition argued, to allow long-term shifts in southern sentiment to dictate the pace of change in the region than to compel integration through legislative fiat.[40]

When mythological and cultural arguments failed, some southerners sought to capitalize on the thinly veiled northern racism that all caucus members believed existed. Although the civil rights crusade in the late 1940s had its origins in the North, southern senators could not help but believe that most whites outside of Dixie harbored the same prejudices found below the Mason-Dixon line, especially concerning the sexual taboo of interracial coupling. Amalgamation became the issue that southerners such as Richard Russell and Spessard Holland often emphasized during the FEPC debates. They warned that the bill would lead to social equality and inevitably spawn amalgamation of the races. Reaching back to the era of Theodore Bilbo, these southerners resorted to turn-of-the-century racist scholarship that linked the offspring of interracial unions with what they called "mongrelization" and the eventual degradation of history's great empires. Unlike Bilbo, these southerners did not offer a detailed analysis of the subject, they simply outlined the formula that amalgamation precipitated mongrelization and social decline. The fact that they never felt the need to elaborate this theme illustrates that in part they did not have to, that this allegedly south-

40. For examples of the cultural approach, see JF to Lewis M. Layer, 28 May 1948, Series 63.1, Box 1, Folder 2, Fulbright MSS; JF to Ward McCabe, 18 March 1948, BCN 48, Folder 1, Fulbright MSS; JF to John Welton, 9 August 1948, BCN 48, Folder 2, Fulbright MSS; CR, Hill, 9 May 1950, 6719 ("it is not . . ."); RL to J. C. Durrett, 5 July 1949, Box 10, Folder 27, Long MSS; CR, 17 May 1950, 7183 (Long).

ern view of race was not a regional peculiarity at all but a national belief shared throughout the country regardless of locale. It was the question of mongrelization that senators such as Russell wanted northerners to consider, not the "shadow" issues fashioned by northern liberals and media outlets. The phrase "civil rights" itself proved misleading, according to southerners, for on the surface it entailed only the idea that blacks should not face violent oppression and that they should posses the same opportunities as whites. But that was only part of the objective of those advocating civil rights. Liberal activists ultimately wished to erase all racial distinctions. Social equality thus became a euphemism for "social admixture" in southern arguments. Spessard Holland, for one, noted that "the people of the South know that the preservation of racial purity on both sides, the white on the one and the colored stock on the other, is fully involved in this argument." Although rarely explicitly stated, southerners believed that black Americans who clamored for legal and political equality also desired equality in the bedroom. Russell and like-minded southerners wanted northerners to realize that the pressure for civil rights would not abate until amalgamation became an accepted practice. The taboo concerning interracial unions represented one of many concerns for southern whites who found themselves engulfed in what they considered a sea of black faces. In comparison, northern blacks were concentrated in large urban centers far removed from the white world that encircled them. This residential separation made social intercourse between the races minimal above the Mason-Dixon line. The racial divide in the North proved problematic for the defenders of segregation. Although sharing the interracial sexual taboo with the South, most northerners tended to find the excesses committed in the name of white supremacy in Dixie disturbing, a fact that encouraged many Yankees to support legislation aimed at rectifying the most glaring injustices perpetrated against black Americans. Southerners needed to find a way to convince northerners that their racial system proved the best, and indeed the only option when dealing with a large black population. Richard Russell had devised a plan to lay on the North's doorstep the problem that inspired Jim Crow in the first place.[41]

41. For arguments stressing amalgamation, see RR to Martha Steele, 5 April 1950, Box 23, Folder 1, Russell MSS; RR to William Dickey, 17 February 1950, Box 23, Folder 1, Russell MSS; CR, 8 May 1950, 6626 (Russell); CR, Holland, 16 May 1950, 7099 ("social admixture") and ("the people of . . ."). Lister Hill referred to the FEPC as a "shadow" issue; see CR, 9 May 1949, 6719.

Both privately and publically, Russell exclaimed that the South would not accept "miscegenation and amalgamation of the Negro race with the white" as a solution to the nation's race problems. His reasoning for southern opposition to the FEPC embodied the principles of strategic delay as well as the long-term trends it anticipated and sought to arrest. We "shall oppose it unalterably and to the end," he declared, "because it will have, and has, as its primary purpose, the breaking down of separation of races which we regard as necessary to our progress and peace in the South." Russell expressed the fears of many southerners in noting the inherent connection between segregation and social stability. Northerners, who did not live around large numbers of blacks, could not understand the potential for racial violence in the South. To rectify the trouble, Russell, in 1949, had introduced legislation similar to Theodore Bilbo's repatriation scheme. Instead of returning the black population to Africa, Russell unveiled a program to evenly distribute the nation's black population, then so heavily concentrated in the South, throughout the country. His plan aimed to create parity across America in which each state had an identical percentage of its population comprised of African Americans. In what was certainly not his finest hour as a statesman, Richard Russell produced large charts and maps as exhibits while explaining his plan. Although he made only passing reference to the scheme during the FEPC filibuster, the premise remained the same. Northerners should pass judgement on the South only after they had experienced the difficulties of living with a sizable black population. Southerners such as Russell contended that the northern populace would adopt the same tactics employed in the South if they too lived among a numerically large black citizenry. Already holding a disdain for interracial unions, northerners were far closer to the racial sensitivities expressed in the South than many above the Mason-Dixon line proved willing to admit. Although Russell's plan never came to a vote, he hoped to illustrate that hypocrisy informed the northern position on civil rights by emphasizing that northern statesmen could easily champion black equality because they had few minorities in their baliwicks. If the proportion of blacks increased in the North to levels approaching those found in Dixie, then the civil rights crusade would cease as northerners began recognizing the enormous shortfalls of African Americans that southerners believed made their racial order so essential. Russell thus sought to make his belief in the existence of universal American racism a central feature of the FEPC debate, but he and his southern cohorts were not without other arguments rooted in post–World War II necessities.[42]

During the debate, many southerners argued that a commission on employment practices would hamper the country's conduct of the Cold War since America's economic and industrial prowess served as the most effective deterrent to Soviet aggression. An FEPC bill, they claimed, would strip private enterprise of its autonomy and presumably of its ability to expand or improve its operations. Communists desired such oppressive bureaucratic regulation since it would reduce the effectiveness of American industry. Again, southern forces depicted the civil rights movement as an "un-American" threat to fundamental national principles such as free market capitalism. Exemplifying southern use of the Red peril, Spessard Holland noted that "there is no doubt in the world that this proposal . . . comes from communist inspiration." Communist forces, according to southerners prone to Cold War moralizing, had a larger plan, a plan highlighted in 1938 by Richard Russell, who argued that the ultimate destruction of Jim Crow served as the end goal of not only all civil rights activists but also all Communists. Belief in the existence of a clandestine civil rights agenda never died and, indeed, remained an integral aspect of southern opposition, codified in the very tactical model that informed their legislative activities—strategic delay. It seemed only rational, according to some, to assume that Communist insurgents fomenting unrest could be the only reason why southern blacks demonstrated resentment against what white southerners considered the benevolent Jim Crow system. Later, when evidence of black resistance occurred with greater frequency across the region, white southerners, still unwilling to accept the fundamental inequality of segregation, blamed agitators bent on sparking a race war. The myth of amiable southern race relations under Jim Crow proved too strong and too integral to regional identity to permit a detached analysis of its shortfalls. To do so would place social stability in the balance. With the majority of the white population at least suspicious, if not convinced, of the innate depravity of the black man, tinkering with segregation risked precipitating a destructive wave of violence. No one wanted

42. CR, 8 May 1950, 6626 ("miscegenation and amalgamation . . .") and ("shall oppose it . . ."). For Russell's relocation plan, see CR, 27 January 1949, 570–572. For Russell's private views on his relocation plan, see RR to W. B. Strickland, 26 February 1949, Box 25, Folder 9, Russell MSS.

to take that risk. The southern fear of change carried over to their party allegiance.[43]

From the beginning of the FEPC filibuster, it became apparent that the Democratic Party suffered from a serious sectional schism precipitated by civil rights. Reaching noticeable levels in 1948, the party's fragmentation continued even after the Dixiecrat revolt netted no appreciable gains for the South. Arkansan J. William Fulbright blamed Truman for the deterioration in interregional accord, claiming that the "President rather enjoys the division that has arisen and he makes little effort to cure it." At the time Fulbright speculated that Truman hoped to again use the civil rights question as a campaign issue should he decide to run for reelection. Despite their continued problems with the Democratic Party, many southern senators harbored no further designs of bolting. Olin Johnston, for one, reaffirmed his conviction that the fate of southern interests remained tied to the U.S. Senate. Putting it bluntly to a constituent who questioned the wisdom of Johnston's Democratic loyalty, the South Carolinian wrote, "I believe that, if we pull away from the Party and thereby lose all the strategic positions which our southern senators now hold, this legislation [civil rights] would pass very soon thereafter." While southerners struggled with the growing tension in the Democratic Party, Senate Republicans sought to aggravate the ideological schism in their opponents' organization.[44]

Republican statesmen made cloture the issue on which they hoped to assist their own electoral fortunes. Learning a valuable lesson from their defeat in the 1948 presidential election, they would not again grant their Democratic rivals a free hand in courting black voters. On 17 May 1950, Democratic Leader Scott Lucas placed a cloture petition before the chamber in order to break the filibuster against the motion to consider the FEPC legislation. Republican Leaders Robert Taft of Ohio and Kenneth Wherry of Nebraska, seeking to make political hay, pleaded with their cohorts to vote favorably on the petition regardless of their personal beliefs for the good of the party. When the chamber voted on 19 May 1950, the cloture petition fell

43. *CR*, 8 May 1950, 6619–6620 (Russell and Communists); *CR*, 12 May 1950, 7009 ("hate mongers") and ("vicious fascistic . . ."); all Holland citations from *CR*, 16 May 1950, 7097.

44. JF to Walter Lippmann, 27 March 1950, Series 61:2, Box 2, Folder 2, Fulbright MSS ("President rather enjoys . . ."); OJ to C. G. Dowling, 11 May 1950, Box 22, "Legislation 1950, FEPC" Folder, Johnston MSS ("I believe that . . .").

to a fifty-two to thirty-two defeat, twelve votes short of the newly established perquisite of sixty-four. The vote revealed the divisions in the Democratic ranks as twenty-six members of the party cast votes against cloture with only nineteen in favor. On the other hand, the Republican Party proved more consistent with thirty-three of its Senate delegation voting cloture compared to only six who joined the southerners. The Party of Lincoln demonstrated that it had yet to fully concede the black vote to the Democrats. Indeed, their stance in 1950, albeit predicated more on political expediency than actual conviction, points to the desire of the party's leadership to court black voters. At the same time, it revealed that many Democrats lacked a firm commitment to the president's civil rights agenda. Presiding over a party with irreconcilable sectional differences, Majority Leader Lucas found himself in an impossible situation. After the vote, he announced his intention of removing the FEPC bill from consideration, but he vowed he would force another fight on the issue later in the session.[45]

Caught between a polarized party in the Senate and a stubborn chief executive, the hapless Scott Lucas made good on his promise, motioning in July for the chamber to reconsider the FEPC bill. Concurrent with his motion, Lucas filed a cloture petition since debate on the issue had already taken place and thus, he argued, the Senate required no further discussion on the subject. Not surprisingly, the chamber voted fifty-five to thirty-three against cloture, again falling short of the necessary two-thirds. If the 1946 FEPC cloture vote boded ill for the future, the 1950 votes on the same question even more dramatically highlighted the plummeting fortunes of the white South. By 1950, few could claim that a definable conservative coalition was in operation on civil rights. The vast majority of Republicans and nonsouthern Democrats favored cloture. Speculation popular among chamber liberals held that if a vote looked uncertain, southern politicians need only request it and support would allegedly materialize for them—such was the alleged reach of their power. Those making these claims never offered anything but anecdotal evidence. Southern senators themselves mentioned nothing either in public or in private that remotely intimated that they held such power. Short-term success remained theirs, but that victory came leavened with heightened knowledge that the bell tolled for them. At the very mo-

45. Cloture petition: *CR*, 17 May 1950, 7183; *Newsweek*, 29 May 1950, 14; *Time*, 29 May 1950, 16; first cloture vote: *CR*, 19 May 1950, 7299–7300.

ment southern senators foresaw inevitable defeat, Washington civil rights advocates, after years of struggle, lost their direction. Resurgent southern senators under the principle of strategic delay had beaten back all threats to segregation. They were rewarded with the one commodity they desired most—time.[46]

Despite the FEPC victory, Richard Russell still exhibited a pessimism that illustrated his realization of things to come. Although pleased with the outcome, he recognized the inexorable nature of the civil rights movement. "We have held the bridge up until now," he said, but "it is disheartening to see how the advocates of this monstrosity [FEPC] increase in strength each year." Being an astute observer of the political scene, Russell undoubtedly recognized that not all of the Republican votes favoring cloture in 1950 represented legitimate support for the legislation, a fact that underscored southern contentions that political expediency, not principle, dictated civil rights activism. Nonetheless, he still contended "the odds against us are very heavy," in part, because now, unlike on previous occasions, the South's defensive perimeter rested on the doorstep of its Senate citadel. As northern opinion gradually drifted toward support for civil rights, only southern senators and their filibuster weapon stood in the way of social equality. Because of the significance placed in strategic delay by Russell and his cohorts, the southern legislative caucus remained vigilant for opportunities that might help it prolong the life of Jim Crow. Throughout the South, white citizens did the same and began crystallizing their ideological defense of segregation to meet the threat posed by civil rights. The editorial board of the *Atlanta Constitution* saw this as a positive step, believing that the South had legitimate arguments for its racial system that the nation should hear. As the region began to define its interests exclusively in terms of defending Jim Crow, internal dissenters against the status quo appeared all the more heretical.[47]

During the FEPC filibuster, liberal southerners Frank Graham of North Carolina and Claude Pepper of Florida both suffered reelection defeats. Southerners could accept liberalism regarding some social issues as seen by

46. Second cloture petition advanced: *CR*, 10 July 1950, 9753. *CR*, 12 July 1950, 9982 (cloture vote).

47. RR to Frank M. Scarlett, 24 July 1950, Box 23, Folder 9, Russell MSS ("We have held . . ."); RR to Bessie M. Carrutte, 21 April 1950, Box 23, Folder 11, Russell MSS ("the odds against . . ."); *Atlanta Constitution*, 4 March 1949, 12.

the electoral success of Lister Hill and Russell Long, but they would not succor similar views regarding race. Pepper's Senate campaign proved particularly ferocious in which his opponents slandered the incumbent as a Communist and a champion of integration. Pepper strived to counter this propaganda, proclaiming often on the stump "I don't believe in abolishing segregation," adding, "I will fight anyone who tries to change this." Despite his best efforts, Pepper could not break the negative image of him created by the campaign of his main opponent George Smathers. His belated effort to portray himself as a "good southerner" proved too little too late. Following his defeat, Pepper surveyed the political landscape. "I am troubled," he wrote a friend, "by the southern attitude of intolerance which seems to be so manifest today. I just can't bring myself to be a bigot on the racial question, and it looks like the South demands that today of its public men." On another occasion he observed the existence of a "trend against the liberal point of view in the South," a development he found discouraging but not so much as to lose his faith in the region. The Floridian stated that change had occurred in the South, but "the rate of change is rather slow and we oughtn't to slip back part of the way." Pepper anticipated that the South would modify its racial views much faster than it did, nonetheless, the region never fully slipped back as Pepper feared. It still elected a progressive coalition of legislators, including John Sparkman, Lister Hill, Olin Johnston, Russell Long, Lyndon Johnson, and J. William Fulbright. These senators remained staunch defenders of white supremacy at the same time in which they championed many liberal social programs. Pepper refused to balance such conflicting ideological viewpoints, a decision that ended his Senate career. In 1944, Pepper narrowly won reelection despite advocating a repeal of the poll tax. Six years later his luck ran out. A scion of the South had lost his Senate seat by questioning the fundamental principles of the region's social system at a time when race took on preeminent importance. By the 1950s, Dixie no longer sanctioned traitors.[48]

48. For examples of the positions that led to Pepper's political troubles in Florida, see CP to W. G. Carleton, 12 August 1948, Box 57, Folder 15, Pepper MSS; transcript, CP speech, Montgomery, Alabama, 7 October 1948, Series 401B, Box 3, Folder 1, Pepper MSS; White, *Citadel*, 79; *CR*, 10 March 1949, 2133–2134; CP to T. W. Beasley, 12 May 1950, Series 201, Box 60, Folder 3, Pepper MSS; CP, campaign speech, n.d., Series 401 B, Box 3, Folder 1, Pepper MSS ("I don't believe . . ."); CP to John Duss, 17 July 1950, Series 439, Box 21, Folder 12, Pepper MSS ("I am

Pressure to defend Jim Crow without reservation might also have prompted individual caucus participants to repress any personal reservations they had concerning Richard Russell's view of how to best defend segregation. Did Russell's unquestionably good track record at a time when Jim Crow seemed under sustained attack blind his colleagues to an alternative way of conceptualizing the civil rights struggle that went beyond strategic delay? In 1949, Arkansas Representative Brooks Hays advanced a compromise approach to civil rights that Richard Russell found intriguing. Hays's proposal, which became known as the Arkansas Plan, had as its primary objective ending civil rights pressure on the South. The main features of the proposal included a repeal of the poll tax through constitutional amendment, an antilynching law with less federal intervention, a voluntary, noncoercive FEPC, and an emphasis on allowing individual communities to decide what, if any changes, should occur in local racial etiquette. At its heart, Hays's plan left the task of tackling Jim Crow to churches and civic organizations. Sweeping federal legislation, he argued, would only incite violence. Nonetheless, under the plan, the South would permit minimal changes to the status quo by accepting items such as an antilynching bill as a sign of their good faith in improving the condition of the region's black population. In exchange for this legislation, northerners would leave the South alone. For a period, Russell hoped that Truman would go along with such a program, thus allowing the South considerable autonomy to work out its own destiny. When Russell and Truman deadlocked over the FEPC, the southern leader abandoned any pretext of following the conciliatory Arkansas Plan. The Georgian's belief that he could only slow, not stop, the drive against Jim Crow grew stronger, making the premises that undergirded strategic delay all the more salient.[49]

Truman's civil rights initiatives provided the South with its greatest threat since Reconstruction. Although none of the bills became law, the margin of southern victory in the Senate steadily deteriorated. Spared for the moment, southern senators became increasingly aware of their vulnerability. They still believed that the majority of the American population agreed with them, but owing to their conspiratorial view of politics, they were convinced that

troubled . . ."); CP to Howard Hughes, 19 July 1950, Series 439, Box 21, Folder 12, Pepper MSS ("trend against the . . .").

49. Brooks Hays, *A Southern Moderate Speaks* (Chapel Hill: University of North Carolina Press, 1959), 44–49; Berman, *Politics of Civil Rights*, 160–161.

the media and black interest groups were deliberately keeping the southern message concealed from the nation. To foster favorable sentiment, southerners in Washington and Dixie began consolidating their corpus of beliefs regarding segregation and making frequent appearances on nationwide radio broadcasts to better convince outsiders that righteousness rested with the South. As they viewed it, only southerners prevented an assault against every American's right to associate with whom they wanted and to use their property as they saw fit. More than "the southern way of life" was thus at stake in the civil rights fight, the entire American political system faced a serious threat from a "dangerous radical element." They hoped that the 1952 election of the war hero turned president, Dwight D. Eisenhower, would finally halt the excesses wrought in the name of civil rights and return the nation to the bedrock principles of the founders, principles that southerners attempted to convey in their defense of Jim Crow. For the region, the initial euphoria that accompanied the new administration's ambivalent approach to civil rights soon turned to paranoia following a single Supreme Court ruling. The long-prophesied assault against segregation was about to begin.

4. Division in the Ranks

THE SUPREME COURT DECISION in the 1954 *Brown v. Board of Education of Topeka, Kansas et al.* case offered a powerful judicial challenge to the segregation statutes sanctioned by the 1896 *Plessy v. Ferguson* ruling. "Separate but equal" schools as existed under the Jim Crow system, the court held, were "inherently unequal" and in violation of the Fourteenth Amendment, which afforded all Americans equal protection under the law. At the time of the verdict, the court announced that it would provide a temporal framework for desegregation at a later date. The next year the court issued an ambiguous edict that called for "all deliberate speed" in the integration of public schools. The absence of a clear timetable in the implementation edict only invited defiance. And there would be plenty of it. Some wondered how President Dwight D. Eisenhower, a Republican who enunciated a strong states' rights position during his 1952 presidential campaign, would respond. *Brown* forced Eisenhower to address the social issue he had, up to that point, avoided. In a case of circumstances making the man, Eisenhower set the tone for desegregation in the 1950s, a tone that for several years lacked much if any "deliberateness." But an effort, albeit haltingly, was underway. Finding an appropriate response to the judicial branch's decree became the immediate problem facing southern statesmen. Dixie's Senate delegation proved no different.[1]

1. Richard Kluger, *Simple Justice: The History of Brown v. Board of Education and Black America's Struggle for Equality* (New York: Knopf, 1976); Salmond, *"My Mind Set on Freedom"*; J. Harvie Wilkinson III, *From Brown to Bakke: The Supreme Court and School Integration, 1954–1978* (New York: Oxford University Press, 1979); Williams, *Eyes on the Prize*; Wolters, *Burden of Brown*. All citations from the verdict taken from the text provided in *New York Times*, 18 May 1954, 15.

After the first *Brown* decision, many caucus members searched for some action—any action—they could take that would demonstrate their opposition to the ruling. Olin Johnston of South Carolina, for example, wrote a constituent, noting that "we Southern Senators have been working together trying to draw up a plan whereby something could be done to help the Southern people" in the school desegregation fight. Although several caucus members took independent action following the first ruling by questioning the verdict on the Senate floor, the caucus as a collective entity remained silent until the announcement of the implementation phase of the decision. Once that edict arrived, they began considering a possible rejoinder. Confronted with the greatest challenge to Jim Crow they had faced thus far, southern senators had difficulty reaching a consensus on a plan of attack. Some in the group pushed for a collective statement condemning the verdict, while a smaller minority advocated no response. Members of both factions, however, recognized that their constituents demanded at least some action by their national legislators as many southern leaders on the state level had already promised.[2]

Cataloguing caucus members following the *Brown* verdict by their racial views and their level of support for massive resistance proves difficult since their positions often fluctuated over time. Excluding the question of civil rights, southern senators differed greatly in their ideological orientation, ranging from liberal to conservative and all points in between. The diversity found in southern voting behavior regarding most issues did not manifest itself as fully when they confronted challenges to regional racial norms. A senator's overall ideological predisposition, however, often impacted the intensity of his support for Jim Crow. The caucus' political conservatives tended to focus on the "many, many differences" between the white and black races that they believed made Jim Crow essential, just as they tended to support the campaign of massive resistance in the South. On the other hand, the South's ideological liberals centered their arguments on the cultural significance of Jim Crow, without dwelling on alleged racial distinctions. At the same time, they voiced private disapproval of lawlessness designed to thwart integration efforts. The caucus' ideological moderates held racial

2. OJ to G. P. Hill, 9 July 1954, Box 40, "Legislation—1954—Civil Rights—School Segregation" Folder, Johnston MSS ("we Southern Senators . . ."). The day after the verdict, Senators Price Daniel of Texas, Richard Russell, and John Stennis delivered speeches that denounced the decision. *CR*, 83rd Cong., 2nd sess., 18 May 1954, 6742–6750.

views that fluctuated between the southern bloc's polar wings. In the main, their rhetoric most often differed in degree, not in kind, from that employed by their more conservative colleagues and at times the rhetoric of the two groups proved indistinguishable. In the 1930s and 1940s, the question of social equality remained a feared but intangible concern. The Supreme Court's edict transformed the threat against Jim Crow into a very real problem that heightened all of the passions associated with race in the South. After the verdict, southern senators deliberately contrived public displays of unanimity that concealed fundamental differences in how individual caucus members privately viewed the emerging campaign of massive resistance. In essence, therefore, only two clearly definable divisions in the southern ranks existed when the caucus confronted challenges to the region's racial order in the post-*Brown* era: a conservative one that supported a strong response to the Supreme Court decision and a moderate one that, at least in private, opposed a hardline stand against integration. When it came to formulating the caucus' response to *Brown*, the group's ideological moderates most often sided with its conservative wing, leaving only the small number of racial moderates as a counterweight to extremism. The concerns of racial moderates, however, rarely found full expression outside of their musings to their close associates. How Dixie's senators would ultimately respond to the *Brown* decision resulted, in large part, from the influence of two new conservative additions to the southern opposition.

Born in 1896 in the mountains of western North Carolina, Sam Ervin immediately became an influential member of the southern caucus following his 1954 appointment to the Senate after the death of Clyde Hoey. First a lawyer, then a justice on the North Carolina Supreme Court, Ervin's legal knowledge made him an indispensable asset to Richard Russell in the southern fight against civil rights. Always bookish, the jowly North Carolinian lived a frugal life and loved to spin yarns drawn from biblical stories and from his experiences in the courtroom. His practical yet folksy wisdom would later make him a national celebrity when he oversaw the Senate Select Committee's investigation of President Richard M. Nixon. But when he first arrived in Washington, he already often affected the poor country boy persona popularized in the Watergate hearings. Ervin had a quick wit that through the course of a meandering story he employed with biting efficiency on his opponents, who often underestimated the North Carolinian's intellect. Not everyone found his personal characteristics endearing. Lyndon Johnson, for one, described Ervin as "a lightweight" and "a windbag." Regardless of how others perceived him, Ervin concerned himself with one thing—fighting the Supreme Court's decision. By 1955 he had joined the ranks of those who contended that "the South ought not to take things lying down." Ervin had company in desiring a strong response to *Brown*.[3]

Born in December 1902 in Edgefield County, South Carolina, James Strom Thurmond learned the art of politics at an early age from his father, who served as a state legislator, and from "Pitchfork" Ben Tillman, who lived near the Thurmond home. Following a term as South Carolina's governor and an abortive presidential bid heading the States' Rights ticket in 1948, Thurmond won election in 1954 to the U.S. Senate as a write-in candidate to fill the vacancy opened by the death of Burnet Maybank. He resigned in April 1956 after completing the remaining year of Maybank's term only to be reelected later that November. With a six-year term ahead of him, the South Carolinian focused on civil rights, observing that "our struggle will be long and unending, but the ends and purposes it seeks to achieve and preserve are well worth the struggle. We must never cease to fight." The reaction of Ervin and Thurmond to the *Brown* decision did not reflect the sentiments of all southern senators.[4]

In response to a constituent query regarding his relative quiet on the desegregation question, Allen Ellender, whose past rhetoric on racial matters proved anything but reserved, urged caution. "I frankly can see no good results," he wrote, from adopting a hardline approach. "All that can happen

3. Paul R. Claney, *Just a Country Lawyer: A Biography of Senator Sam Ervin* (Bloomington: Indiana University Press, 1974), 25–153; Dick Dabney, *A Good Man: The Life of Senator Sam J. Ervin* (Boston: Houghton Mifflin, 1976); Sam J. Ervin, *Preserving the Constitution: The Autobiography of Senator Sam J. Ervin, Jr.* (Charlottesville, Va.: Michie, 1984); Mooney, *LBJ*, 49 ("lightweight") and ("windbag"); Sam J. Ervin (hereafter cited as SE) to J. Bruce Eugene, 25 July 1955, Box 9, Folder 166, Sam J. Ervin Papers, Southern Historical Collection, University of North Carolina, Chapel Hill (hereafter cited as Ervin MSS) ("that the South . . ").

4. Cohodas, *Strom Thurmond*, 26–205; Sherrill, *Gothic Politics in the Deep South*, 239–252; J. Strom Thurmond (hereafter cited as ST) to James R. O'Daniel, 20 January 1955, Box 33, "Segregation and States' Rights, Folder I," Strom Thurmond Collection, Special Collections, Clemson University, Clemson, South Carolina (hereafter cited as Thurmond MSS) ("our struggle will . . "). The Thurmond collection is chronologically arranged, and the boxes are renumbered each year. Every year thus contains a Box 1, 2, 3, and so on. Box numbers in the citations refer only to the year in which the cited letter was written.

is that many southerners will become aroused and excited and we will have violence. . . . It would worsen rather than improve our position." J. William Fulbright also preached restraint, only in constructing his argument he employed the memory of the Civil War that usually served as a spur to southern resistance. "Once before," the Arkansan noted, "when the South disagreed with the policies of the Federal Government, we took matters into our own hands but did not succeed very well. I believe we will have to find some better way to meet this difficulty." For all the talk of maintaining white supremacy uttered by some, the statements of Ellender and Fulbright reveal something less than a monolithic opinion among the region's senators. Many southerners recognized that the *Brown* decision would precipitate some change and that the region risked imperiling its future through a campaign of massive resistance. Ellender, for one, believed that not only did an overwhelming majority of the white population oppose integration, so too did "99.9%" of the black population. Therefore he thought some form of accommodation advisable, perhaps through local option, allowing individual communities to settle their disputes in a manner that reflected the interests of all involved. Reactionary elements both in Washington and at home, however, pushed more moderate statesmen into condemning the Supreme Court. For cross-pressured senators who struggled between the sway of the demagogue and their own reservations regarding extremism, the task became mitigating the caucus's response by reigning in as much as possible those advocating massive resistance. Despite the best efforts of caucus moderates, the creation of the Southern Manifesto illustrated that a tempered approach to *Brown* was, in the eyes of many, not an option.[5]

Questions persist regarding the creation of the Declaration of Constitutional Principles, better known as the Southern Manifesto, that served as the southern rejoinder to *Brown*. Some argue that the impetus behind the document was a desire to reelect Walter George of Georgia, whose alleged racial liberalism placed his 1956 campaign in jeopardy. To strengthen his reputation as a champion of segregation, some caucus members pushed for a denunciation of *Brown* in which he would play a major role. More important,

5. AE to Reuben T. Douglas, 3 June 1954, Box 668, "Legislation—Civil Rights–1954" Folder, Ellender MSS ("I frankly can . . .") and ("All that can . . ."); JF to George Yarbrough, 28 June 1955, BCN 19, Folder 14A, Fulbright MSS ("Once before when . . ."); AE to Reuben T. Douglas, 3 June 1953, Box 668, "Legislation—Civil Rights–1954" Folder, Ellender MSS ("99.9%").

George allegedly had the support of the southern leader Richard Russell, who clearly disagreed with *Brown* and who had a personal stake in George's reelection. Aside from his respect for the modest George, Russell disapproved of George's opponent, Georgia Governor Herman Talmadge. Herman Talmadge's father Eugene, as Georgia's governor, had opposed Russell's reelection in 1936 in a fierce campaign that featured considerable mudslinging. Most galling to Russell were accusations that he was "soft" on the race question. Adopting his father's strategy, Herman cast similar aspersions on the genial George. Seeking to settle an old score, Russell, although initially unenthusiastic about the idea, allegedly consented to a written declaration to assist his beleaguered colleague. The prominent role later given George in crafting the declaration indicates that key members of the southern caucus wanted him to get credit for orchestrating the manifesto. Not all sources place George at the center of the southern effort, however.[6]

Many claim that Strom Thurmond served as the primary catalyst behind the Southern Manifesto. Throughout his career, Thurmond advocated a uniform southern response to all challenges against segregation. In keeping with this desire, he wrote in early 1956 of his plans to forge the southern caucus into a solid phalanx against desegregation. The South Carolinian anticipated that the meeting might lead to a statement by the group that included interposition, but, at the time, he planned on withholding his personal preferences until he had an opportunity to gauge the inclinations of his southern colleagues. Before the caucus gathered, Thurmond drafted the prototype of what became the declaration; it proved so incendiary that his compatriots sought to temper the document, which resurrected John C. Calhoun's doctrine of nullification. At that meeting, he recruited the assistance of caucus veterans to pressure the remainder of the group into support for a strong statement decrying the Supreme Court verdict. One of the veteran caucus crusaders who sided with Thurmond has also received attention as one of the primary forces behind the manifesto.[7]

6. For an account that emphasizes saving George, see Randall Bennett Woods, *Fulbright: A Biography* (New York: Cambridge University Press, 1995), 207–209. In his memoirs, Albert Gore Sr. noted Richard Russell's initial lack of enthusiasm for a manifesto. Albert Gore, *Let the Glory Out: My South and Its Politics* (New York: Viking Press, 1972), 103; Key, *Southern Politics*, 108.

7. For accounts emphasizing Thurmond's role, see *Time*, 26 March 1956, 25; Fite, *Richard B. Russell, Jr.*, 333; Gore, *Let the Glory Out*, 103; Mann, *Walls of Jericho*, 161–162; ST to Felix Morley, 3 February 1956, Box 12, "Segregation, Folder I" Thurmond MSS.

J. William Fulbright, who unlike George and Thurmond did not seek to gain political favor from the manifesto, credited the document primarily to the machinations of Harry Byrd of Virginia. Although others drafted the document, no one, according to Fulbright, played a bigger role in the manifesto's formative stage than the Virginian. Opposed to the document's release, Fulbright contended that "under the leadership of Senator Byrd, some 12 or 15 of the Senators were determined to make a statement, so the best we could do was try to keep it within reasonable bounds." Further questioning the actions of the Virginian, who by this time had already gained credit for coining the phrase "massive resistance" to the Supreme Court's ruling, the Arkansan observed, "Senator Byrd, I believe, is inspiring an extreme position which may well result in great harm to the South and the nation." Little evidence, however, exists to validate Fulbright's claim. Byrd did not assist in drafting the actual statement, and none of the members who wrote it mention him in describing the birth of the manifesto. If anything Byrd agitated for a statement at Thurmond's suggestion, but like his efforts in southern filibusters, he left it up to his colleagues to perform the lion's share of the work that, as it turned out, proved considerable.[8]

What transpired at the official caucus meeting to address the *Brown* decision in the first week of February provides some support for both the accounts that credit George and the ones that credit Thurmond. From the outset, disagreement in the caucus on the appropriate tenor of the statement was evident with a reactionary element on one side and a more moderate wing on the other. The hardliners, headed by Thurmond, stressed resistance at all costs, even if it meant nullification or dismantling the public school system. Southern moderates believed that further agitation in the form of a manifesto would exacerbate existing tensions in the region, resulting in violence and, even worse, federal intervention. To end the impasse, the caucus gave Walter George the responsibility of appointing a committee to draft a statement that became the manifesto in order to prevent Thurmond from forging ahead with a document that advocated lawlessness. The very fact that the caucus chose George, who played only a limited role in previous

8. Most historians and journalists who argue that Byrd played a pivotal role link his involvement with that of Thurmond, see Fite, *Richard B. Russell, Jr.,* 333; Heinemann, *Harry Byrd of Virginia,* 335–336; all Fulbright quotations from JF to Joe Barrett, 10 March 1956, Series 61:2, Box 2, Folder 6, Fulbright MSS.

civil rights fights, points, at least in part, to the existence of a campaign ploy to reelect the affable Georgian. George, in turn, selected for inclusion on the drafting committee caucus members who specialized in constitutional, not racial, defenses of segregation. He chose Sam Ervin, along with Richard Russell and Mississippi's John Stennis as part of a "committee to represent the southeastern senators to consider all the various problems regarding the segregation decision of the Supreme Court." George's part in organizing the committee does not, however, negate Thurmond's role in pushing the caucus into a more extreme position. Those advocating an activist approach placed disproportionate pressure on the drafting committee, a fact that troubled caucus moderates. By the time moderates voiced their discontent, it was already too late.[9]

Typical of caucus procedure, each member received a specific assignment whenever the group acted. To Strom Thurmond fell the chore of collecting signatures on the statement drafted by the committee. In a confidential letter dated 2 March 1956 and delivered to all the southern senators, the South Carolinian implored his colleagues to affix their names to the document, just as he pledged them to secrecy until George released the statement. At the time the letter was sent, George, Russell, Stennis, Ervin, and Thurmond had already signed aboard. Some southerners remained hesitant about joining the others. Despite the presence of "some objectionable spots," reluctant caucus members Price Daniel of Texas, George Smathers, John Sparkman, Spessard Holland, and J. William Fulbright, who all initially advocated no response to the *Brown* verdict, eventually signed it. Bowing to political pressure, southern moderates, ignored their reservations and followed their more reactionary colleagues, a decision that further diminished the already dwindling possibility of a peaceful integration process. As crafted, the manifesto was intended exclusively as a Senate document and the drafting committee received no assistance beyond that offered by caucus participants. Later, southern House members, hearing rumors of the manifesto, requested their inclusion in the statement and were allowed to sign. With the almost unanimous approval of the region's House and Senate delegations, Dixie's national legislators hoped the document would demonstrate southern resolve in the face of the *Brown* ruling. Wedded now to a staunch opposition, southerners

9. Walter George to SE, 9 February 1956, Box 15, Folder 1119, Ervin MSS ("committee to represent . . ."); SE to N. N. Perkins, 10 February 1956, Box 15, Folder 1119, Ervin MSS.

confronted the latest challenge to segregation with what, at least on the surface, appeared a considerable degree of solidarity.[10]

On 12 March 1956, Walter George presented the Declaration of Constitutional Principles signed by nineteen senators and seventy-seven representatives. In it, southerners condemned the Supreme Court's ruling as "a clear abuse of Judicial power," since nowhere in either the Constitution or the debates surrounding the Fourteenth Amendment was the subject of education broached. Anglo-Saxon jurisprudence, they contended, involved interpreting legal statutes by analyzing the "intent" of the original lawmakers. Segregation statutes hinged on the Fourteenth Amendment and, as such, had their origins in the Reconstruction era. The very Congress that created the amendment, they argued, provided for the establishment of a segregated school system in the District of Columbia. According to southerners, this illustrated that the Reconstruction Congress viewed segregation in consonance with the philosophical conception of equality before the law. Furthermore, the manifesto claimed that the Supreme Court justices "substituted their personal political and social ideas for the established law of the land." Departing from the Anglo-Saxon common law tradition, the justices abandoned judicial precedent in exchange for sociological and psychological treatises such as Gunnar Myrdal's *American Dilemma*. Aside from condemning the legal arguments that resulted in the verdict, the document also stated that the decision led to a deterioration in the formerly amicable state of southern race relations and precipitated an influx of "agitators" into the region bent on instituting "immediate and revolutionary changes in our public-school system." Near the conclusion of the statement stood the pivotal passage that indicated the influence of more moderate southern senators: "We pledge ourselves to use all lawful means to bring about a reversal of this decision which is contrary to the Constitution and to prevent the use of force in its implementation." One drafter of the declaration, Sam Ervin, noted that the phrase "all lawful means" emerged from the difficulty encountered in fashioning a statement that "would satisfy in full measure the views of a score or more persons." This phrase revealed that the region's national legislators

10. ST to JF, 2 March 1956, Series 61:2, Box 2, Folder 6, Fulbright MSS (manifesto signature letter); JF to Joe Barrett, 10 March 1956, Series 61:2, Box 2, Folder 6, Fulbright MSS ("some objectionable spots"). Sam Ervin noted that the Manifesto was originally intended as a Senate document. SE to W. E. Debram, 15 May 1956, Box 15, Folder 1126, Ervin MSS.

planned on stopping just short of openly flouting the court's decision. Its inclusion proved pivotal—an olive branch meant to illustrate that the region would resist the implementation of *Brown* only through legal channels. As further evidence of their good faith in seeking a peaceful resolution to the integration problem, Dixie's national legislators concluded the statement by urging their constituents to "refrain from disorder and lawless acts."[11]

Louisiana's Russell Long was one senator who urged caution. His comments following the announcement of the Southern Manifesto emphasized the importance of undermining the decision through legal means. In a press release concerning the *Brown* ruling, he said, "Although I completely disagree with the decision, my oath of office requires me to accept it as law." Parallels with another era in southern history proved unavoidable. Just as the brave Confederate forces valiantly fought against a numerically superior force, so too would the South's new soldiers—only this time without resorting to secession. Lest one miss the historical similarity, Long declared, "General Robert E. Lee accepted the verdict of a decision made in blood and pleaded with all of his beloved comrades to accept once and for all the authority of the Union. Anyone who would make us pay the price of learning that hard lesson again will have to do it against my advice." Long's fellow Louisianan, Allen Ellender, also deplored the ruling but believed that "nothing short of a constitutional amendment" could overturn the Court. Adopting a pessimistic tone, Ellender wrote, "I have never believed that I should mislead the people whom I represent by creating and fostering hope of Congressional relief when I know deep down in my heart that there is no hope of obtaining such relief." At least in private he hoped that moderate white southern leaders would steer the region toward a nonviolent solution that would enable segregation to survive within the context of the *Brown* ruling. Like Ellender and Long, J. William Fulbright worried that the manifesto would provide a stimulus "for everybody to continue to make speeches about it and dare the other side to do its worst." As Fulbright feared, the desired moderating impact of the phrase "all lawful means" was lost on many northern senators

11. All manifesto citations from *CR*, 84th Cong., 2nd sess., 12 March 1956, 4160. The text of the manifesto bore the imprint of Richard Russell. Indeed, most of its major points were a distillation of Russell's remarks following the first *Brown* decision. For the text of that address, see *CR*, 83rd Cong., 2nd sess., 18 May 1954, 6748, 6750; SE to Fred B. Helms, 13 March 1956, Box 15, Folder 1120, Ervin MSS ("that would satisfy . . .").

hearing the Southern Manifesto for the first time. Independent Wayne Morse of Oregon, who was a staunch supporter of civil rights, observed regarding the statement, "You would think today Calhoun was walking and speaking on the floor of the Senate." According to Morse, the manifesto represented the repackaging of an old idea—nullification. If the caucus's moderate membership sought to avoid fanning the flames of racial tension, the manifesto that they reluctantly supported produced just the opposite result. Tensions rose, while the prospect for a solution outside of total southern capitulation diminished. Anticipating the racial violence that resulted, some southerners avoided any involvement with the manifesto.[12]

The decision of three southern senators not to sign the document became an important side story to the manifesto's release. Tennessee's senior Senator Estes Kefauver, long known as a maverick, simply stated he disagreed with the premise of the declaration. Of course, his desire to win the Democratic nomination later in 1956 might have also influenced his decision. Furthermore, Kefauver never represented a solid vote for Richard Russell. As a representative and as a senator, the Tennessean supported legislation to abolish the poll tax, at the same time in which he followed more traditional southern behavior in opposing the FEPC and a federal antilynching law. Kefauver, who also eschewed the filibuster, proved unpredictable and few southerners expected his support.[13]

Fellow Tennessean Albert Gore Sr. also left his name off of the document. Gore too had established himself as somewhat of a maverick upon his arrival in the Senate after defeating the longtime incumbent Kenneth McKellar in 1952. Gore portrayed himself as a moderate on the segregation question, claiming, "I am not numbered among the extremists who refuse to recognize that discrimination and injustice to the negro race do exist. Neither am I numbered among the extremists in the other direction." As for why he

12. Press release, "Supreme Court Decision," n.d., Box 556, Folder 55, Long MSS ("although I completely . . ."); speech, 1956, Box 556, Folder 50, Long MSS ("General Robert . . ."); Finley, "Balancing Liberal and Conservative Policy Preferences," 26; AE to Frank Voelker, 28 February 1956, Box 668, "Legislation—Civil Rights–1956" Folder, Ellender MSS ("I have never . . ."); JF to Theo Epperson, 11 February 1956, BCN 19, Folder 45, Fulbright MSS ("for everybody to . . ."); CR, 12 March 1956, 4462 ("you would think . . .").

13. Joseph B. Gorman, *Kefauver: A Political Biography* (New York: Oxford University Press, 1971), 236; see also Dallek, *Lone Star Rising*, 496; Caro, *Master of the Senate*, 786.

did not sign the declaration, Gore offered several explanations. In one he claimed that when he received Thurmond's letter asking him to support the manifesto "not one single Tennessean had communicated to me his or her sentiment with respect thereto." Weighing the apparent lack of concern on the part of his constituency with the manifesto's implicit challenge to the rule of law, the Tennessean withheld his support. He of course recognized that his action "negated or counterbalanced" in the minds of some constituents many of his accomplishments on behalf of the state. "The affixing of my signature quickly and as publicly as possible would have been the easy and, at least for the moment, the politically appealing course of action," Gore said, but he had reservations. He felt the manifesto would provoke unrest, and although he had not yet declared an interest in the presidency, he was not without aspirations. To liberal constituents he proved more critical, describing the term "manifesto" a "misnomer"; it should have been "stump speech," he said, considering the electoral advantage some of the declaration's signers hoped to gain by its release.[14]

Regardless of which side of the fence he engaged at any given point, Gore's statements regarding race in Tennessee proved consistent with the political situation on the ground. In short, although important, race simply did not consume Volunteer State politics as it did deep South ones. More important, mountain regions throughout eastern Tennessee routinely turned out Republican majorities, a remnant of that region's disdain for slavery and prounion sympathies from the antebellum era. Tennessee blacks did vote with fewer impediments, especially in more populated communities. Both Gore and Kefauver's civil rights positions thus fell within the confines of the permissible in their home states.[15]

14. Kyle Longley, *Senator Albert Gore, Sr.: Tennessee Maverick* (Baton Rouge: Louisiana State University Press, 2004); Albert Gore Sr. (hereafter cited as AG) to Lilla M. Galvan, 2 December 1953, B 46, "Legislation 1954—Judiciary—Civil Rights, 1 of 1" Folder, Albert Gore Collection, Albert Gore Center, Middle Tennessee Sate University, Murfeesboro (hereafter cited as Gore MSS) ("I am not . . ."). The Gore collection is not contained in boxes but in a series of drawers. AG to Russell M.D. Bruce, 29 March 1956, Special Series 20, D 32, "Segregation" Folder, Gore MSS ("not one single . . ."); AG to Hewitt P. Tomlin Jr., 28 March 1956, Special Series D 31, "Segregation" Folder, Gore MSS ("negated or . . .") and ("The affixing of . . ."); AG to Jennings Perry, 17 March 1956, Special Series D 31, "Segregation" Folder, Gore MSS ("misnomer") and ("stump speech").

15. Key, *Southern Politics*, 58–81.

A final southern senator with presidential ambitions, Lyndon Johnson, did not sign the document. Johnson's actions remain the subject of much debate. Many view his decision not to participate as a calculated ploy to attain distance from his regional colleagues and a first sign that he supported civil rights. Others contend that Richard Russell allowed the omission to protect Johnson's national role as majority leader. Numerous journalists erroneously placed great emphasis on the initial portion of Johnson's official press statement in which he claimed, "I have neither seen this document, nor have I been asked to sign it." Yet they overlook the remainder of the release that clearly showed he in no way altered the states' rights stance that typified his previous civil rights position. In the latter part of his public statement, he declared that "in my opinion, the solution of the problem [segregation] cannot be found on the federal level, for it involves basic values reflected in the sovereignty of our states." Responding to a constituent inquiry, the Texan wrote that the Supreme Court's ruling left him "shocked and dismayed" and that he regretted "institutions which have worked well for so many years be disrupted by an arbitrary decision." Far from striking out on a course of greater civil rights activism, Johnson conveniently found a position that did not undermine his standing as the Senate's Democratic leader or unduly enrage his constituents. To those Texans still doubtful about his fidelity to regional norms, he reassured them—"My record on all the controversial issues is entirely clear"—then added the names of segregationist senators who planned to support him for the presidency. In the end, Johnson succeeded in avoiding the adoption of a controversial position regarding the *Brown* verdict. Indeed, while serving as the majority leader of the U.S. Senate, Johnson faced the civil rights controversy not from an ideological perspective, but from the vantage point of the pressing demands such legislation placed on his leadership position within the Democratic Party and from the need to placate his more conservative Texas constituency.[16]

16. For an example of Johnson distancing himself from his southern colleagues, see Monroe Billington, "Lyndon B. Johnson and Blacks: The Early Years," *Journal of Negro History* 62 (January 1977): 26–42. For an example of Russell granting Johnson permission, see Dallek, *Lone Star Rising*, 509. For an example of abbreviated usage of Johnson's press statement, see *Baton Rouge Advocate*, 12 March 1956, 4A; press statement, LBJ, 10 March 1956, Box 423, "Reedy: Southern Manifesto" Folder, Senate Papers, LBJL ("I have neither . . .") and ("in my opinion . . ."); LBJ to Judge H. R. Wilson, 28 May 1954, Box 252, "Legislation—[Social Welfare]—Segregation" Folder, Senate Papers, LBJL ("shocked . . .") and ("institutions which have . . ."). Johnson boasted the

Johnson, Gore, and Kefauver all took a calculated risk in not signing the Southern Manifesto. Although departing from regional orthodoxy with their decision, they, nonetheless, avoided playing a substantive role in the integration crisis, a course of action that, for the most part, had few deleterious consequences on the ground in their respective states. But in the deep South, the absence of a moderating voice often proved disastrous. Fearing to appear too moderate on racial matters, senators such as J. William Fulbright, George Smathers, and John Sparkman abandoned their initial reservations regarding the manifesto and joined with those who favored defiance. Caucus members across the ideological spectrum believed that the majority of their constituents demanded a battle to the end in defense of "the southern way of life" and they proved more than willing to give the electorate just such a spirited opposition. From that point forward, racial moderates in the caucus chose silence over even a limited critique of southern intransigence. By adopting a hands-off approach to the political situation in Dixie, southern senators, who opposed massive resistance, permitted state-level officials to shape the region's response to *Brown,* and many of these officials, who operated in isolation hearing neither northern nor southern voices of criticism, chose defiance. The contempt for federal authority that undergirded the campaign of massive resistance finally forced the nation's chief executive into reluctant action.

President Dwight Eisenhower received widespread criticism for his administration's slow response in implementing the *Brown* decision. Although raised in Abilene, Kansas, he spent most of his professional life on military bases in the South and served in a segregated army throughout his career. Many of his friends came from the South and he, due to his background, harbored some of the same racial sensitivities. Historian Stephen Ambrose claimed Eisenhower "was trapped by his own prejudices, a prisoner of his own limited view." Although calling for the desegregation of schools within the District of Columbia, he never openly supported the *Brown* ruling because he believed the process of school integration required considerable deliberation. Adding to the clamor for executive action in the field of civil rights was the acquittal by an all white jury of the individuals accused of lynching the black youth Emmett Till in Mississippi. What made the incident

support of Harry Byrd (Va.), Richard Russell (Ga.), Strom Thurmond (S.C.), George Smathers (Fla.), Willis Robertson (Va.), and John McClellan (Ark.). LBJ to Caroline Hazel, 15 May 1956, Box 567, "1956 General Files: Civil Rights" Folder, Senate Papers, LBJL ("my record on . . .").

most shocking was that one of the defendants later admitted his guilt and even bragged about his involvement in *Look* magazine. White southerners took advantage of presidential inertia and the court's vague implementation ruling by challenging the rule of law. *Brown* would have created social unrest in the South regardless of federal activism, but the absence of a powerful federal response to white resistance when it initially emerged compounded the problem. For the remainder of the 1950s, many white southerners harbored the misbegotten notion that through legal and extralegal forms of resistance, they could block integration. The slow response from Washington only fueled this dangerous perception. To some, the Till case represented a sign of things to come if the national government did not take a strong stance against southern resistance. Public outrage over the miscarriage of justice in Mississippi, therefore, led to an outcry for federal intervention to address racial unrest in the South. The growing pressure finally forced the president's hand, but it was a hand forced reluctantly and only after considerable prodding.[17]

Eisenhower called upon his Attorney General Herbert Brownell, who had encouraged the president to act sooner in advocating racial change, to draft civil rights legislation that, after several heated cabinet meetings, emerged as a voting rights measure. Brownell had sought a more sweeping proposal, while others sought to rein in the attorney general, believing that any administration bill would face difficulty in a Democrat-controlled Congress. In the end, caution proved the better part of valor on civil rights. Suffrage, Eisenhower wrote in his autobiography, "was the overriding provision of the bill . . . with his right to vote assured, the American Negro could use it to safeguard his other rights." The administration touted the bill as extremely "mild," but according to the president, "at the time, these proposals were little less than revolutionary." Public announcement of the bill came at a 9 April 1956 press conference in which Herbert Brownell outlined the measure and emphasized "the right to vote is one of our most precious rights. It is the cornerstone of our form of government." The legislation consisted of four sections: the establishment of a nonpartisan civil rights commission, a provision for an assistant attorney general to head a new civil rights division

17. Stephen Ambrose, *Eisenhower: Soldier and President* (New York: Touchstone Books, 1990), 410; Sherman Adams, *Firsthand Report: The Story of the Eisenhower Administration* (New York: Greenwood, 1961), 331–334; Stephen J. Whitfield, *A Death in the Delta: The Story of Emmett Till* (New York: Free Press, 1961); *Look*, 24 January 1956, 44–50.

in the Justice Department, a statute to expand the right of the attorney general to expedite cases involving alleged civil rights violations, and a means to secure and protect the right to vote. With the administration's plans now public, the question of the legislation's prospect in Congress became the primary concern. The institutional structure of the House that favored the more populous North guaranteed the bill would make it through that body, regardless of southern opposition, by the end of the session. Even if it did, the feasibility of Senate action on the eve of the 1956 presidential nominating conventions struck most observers as an overly optimistic goal. Further heightening doubt regarding the bill's future, southern senators wasted little time voicing their disapproval of the proposal.[18]

Virginian Harry Byrd called the civil rights bill the most "vicious legislation" he had seen in his political career; it sought to "humiliate and destroy the South" for the sake of "collecting Negro votes." Louisianan Allen Ellender contended that Americans should not permit the expansion of the federal government through civil rights legislation based on "highly publicized but rare and isolated incidents like the Till case." Adding to the chorus of complaints, Georgia's Herman Talmadge, who forced George to withdraw from the 1956 election despite Russell's assistance, claimed that the bill illustrated "our system of government as wrought by the founders is under sustained attack." The southern bloc's most respected member among Senate liberals, Alabama's Lister Hill, also viewed the political situation as becoming increasingly unfavorable to the region. As in no other period in recent southern history, the rapid succession of events such as the *Brown* case, the Southern Manifesto, and the Till lynching had brought the region's race relations to a boiling point. Now more than ever, the Alabamian sensed the importance of controlling caucus rhetoric. "Our whole southern group," Hill wrote, "have to shape our words and actions in light of the situation facing us." On previous occasions, they had "held the line against" civil rights; however, "we must recognize that we have been effective with some of our Senate colleagues from out of the South

18. Adams, *Firsthand Report*, 335–336; Ambrose, *Eisenhower*, 408; Neil R. McMillen, *The Citizens' Councils: Organized Resistance to the Second Reconstruction, 1954–1964* (Chicago: University of Illinois Press, 1974); Adams, *Firsthand Report*, 337; Dwight D. Eisenhower, *The White House Years: Waging Peace, 1956–1961* (Garden City, N.Y.: Doubleday, 1965), 156 ("was the overriding . . ."), 153 ("at the time . . ."); press release, Herbert Brownell, 9 April 1956, Box 567, "1956 General Files: Civil Rights" Folder, Senate Papers, LBJL ("the right to . . ."). The civil rights commission was to consist of six members with no more than three from the same political party.

and have gotten their help." Strategic delay figured prominently in Hill's personal outlook on the civil rights fight. In order to sway Senate votes, the southern caucus needed to raise the plane of their rhetoric to a more lofty level by deemphasizing even further the question of race that, nonetheless, remained an integral component of their opposition. Only by doing this could the South expect to avert the implementation of legislation detrimental to the region.[19]

Following the Southern Manifesto's release, southerners found themselves in a conundrum. They faced the challenge of balancing their rhetoric as never before between placating their constituents, now hypersensitive to threats to segregation, and convincing their Senate colleagues, who slowly started getting pro–civil rights pressure from their respective electorates, that the foundation of southern opposition rested on sound constitutional grounds. Striking a balance proved just as difficult as it did for the manifesto drafting committee that sought to reconcile the political demands of the eighteen unique personalities that comprised the caucus, but they met the challenge with their customary thoroughness. "We are in close contact and consultation," Lister Hill said in relation to the southern caucus, "and we are striving to wage the most effective battle possible for the preservation of our southern customs, traditions and way of life." With a presidential election scheduled later in 1956, the question of civil rights and especially of the Eisenhower proposal that neared passage in the House, became a chief concern in Washington. Although the bill received much attention, its issuance late in the second session of the Eighty-fourth Congress foreordained its defeat, at least for the year.[20]

Senate debate on the civil rights bill failed to occur in 1956 because of a desire to preserve Democratic unity on the eve of the party's August convention in Chicago. With passage of the Eisenhower proposal in the House a

19. Speech, 25 July 1956, Box 410, "Statement—July 25, 1956—on the so-called civil rights legislation" Folder, Byrd MSS ("vicious legislation") and ("humiliate and destroy . . ."); AE to Anderson Washington, 8 March 1956, Box 688, "Legislation—Civil Rights—956" Folder, Ellender MSS ("highly publicized but . . ."); speech, Herman Talmadge (hereafter cited as HT), to Richmond Kiwanis Club, 29 April 1957, Box 303, Folder 3, Herman Talmadge Collection, Richard Russell Library, University of Georgia, Athens (hereafter cited as Talmadge MSS) ("our system of . . ."). The majority of the boxes that contained information from Talmadge's early Senate career, including the years covered in this study, were lost in transit from Washington to Athens. LH to Jesse W. Mabry, 2 July 1956, Box 493, Folder 34, Hill MSS ("our whole southern . . .") ("held the line . . ."), and ("we must recognize . . .").

20. LH to Jesse W. Mabry, 2 July 1956, Box 493, Folder 34, Hill MSS ("We are in . . .").

foregone conclusion, the Senate Democratic Policy Committee convened to discuss a course of action once the bill reached the upper chamber. Minutes of the 27 June meeting clearly indicate the threat that the measure posed to party cohesion. A civil rights debate would lay bare before the nation the ideological divide that polarized the northern and southern wings of the party. Democratic leaders decided it was far better to postpone the issue until after the election than to risk sabotaging the party's prospects in 1956 with an intramural schism over civil rights. After weighing the available options, Carl Hayden of Arizona succinctly stated, "My judgement is to get the money bills passed and to get out of here." Richard Russell echoed Hayden's sentiments, adding that "if we get into civil rights, we will have trouble even recessing over the Convention." A handful of civil rights activists planned on delaying the adjournment date planned by the Policy Committee.[21]

On 23 July 1956, House Resolution 627, the Eisenhower civil rights proposal, passed in the House of Representatives. By tradition the Speaker of the House appoints an employee of that body to walk a newly passed bill over to the Senate where it is then referred to committee. Senate liberals planned to use this tradition to keep the bill from its expected destination, the Judiciary Committee chaired by staunch segregationist James Eastland of Mississippi. Prior to becoming chairman, Eastland headed the Judiciary's Subcommittee on Civil Rights and refused to convene the group for three years. He even bragged to Mississippians that he had extra pockets sewed into his trousers so as to better hide civil rights bills. Regardless of the truth surrounding Eastland's pants, so long as he oversaw the Judiciary no civil rights measure would likely emerge from it. Senate liberals hoped to keep House Resolution 627 out of Eastland's civil rights "graveyard," but they did not realize that the southern caucus was already one step ahead of them.[22]

On the morning of the House vote, Eastland convened the Judiciary, which included the planned floor leader for Resolution 627 in the Senate, Tom Hennings of Missouri. Realizing this conference conflicted with the pending civil rights vote in the House, Hennings dispatched Paul Douglas of Illinois to accompany the bill to the chamber. If Douglas accomplished his mission, the

21. All quotations from Committee Minutes, 27 June 1956, Box 364, "Senate Democratic Policy Committee Minutes of March 8, 1955–June 24, 1960" Folder, Senate Papers, LBJL.

22. For the House vote, see CR, 23 July 1956, 13937; Sherrill, *Gothic Politics in the Deep South*, 210 (Eastland's trousers).

liberals intended to precipitate discussion on the measure by voicing opposition to the customary unanimous consent request to send all newly passed House bills to the committee with jurisdiction over it. Majority Leader Johnson used his close personal friendship with Speaker Sam Rayburn of Texas to stymie the civil rights advocates. As Douglas casually walked to the House, Rayburn oversaw an unusually rapid vote on the bill. After its passage, Rayburn handed the bill to a waiting Johnson aide who hurried the document out a side door, passing Douglas along the way. Minutes later, Douglas entered the House chamber and, after realizing what had transpired, rushed back to the Senate. In the absence of opposition to Johnson's unanimous consent request, the bill was read twice in the upper house and placed in the Judiciary Committee. During the remainder of the session, a handful of civil rights advocates attempted to wrest the bill from the committee, but they lacked sufficient support for their maneuver. The Eighty-fourth Congress expired on 27 July without Senate action on the Eisenhower civil rights bill. Southern senators had won a temporary respite, but their leader recognized that the group would undoubtedly face yet another civil rights battle at the start of the next Congress.[23]

By the late 1950s, Richard Russell had adopted a lifestyle that reflected his status as a confirmed bachelor. Spartan by nature, the Georgian resided in a small hotel room in which he spent most of his time perusing works of history, especially Civil War monographs. Often he completed his ten hour days on Capitol Hill with several glasses of Jack Daniels whisky before grabbing a quick meal at a nearby restaurant on his route home. A lifelong smoker, his habit had escalated to two packs of cigarettes a day. His long since thinning hair was now almost completely absent on top, which only added to the angularity of his prominent nose and the size of his protruding ears. Despite the enormous political prestige he enjoyed in the U.S. Senate, he remained a lonely man when the chamber adjourned. He loved the Senate, considering it his life and work. Inside that chamber, Russell possessed the wherewithal to continue defending his beloved South.[24]

23. Evans and Novak, *Exercise of Power*, 123; *New York Times*, 24 July 1956, 12. For Douglas's version of events, see *CR*, 85th Cong., 1st sess., 17 June 1957, 9348. Hennings, Douglas, and Herbert Lehman of New York led the effort to extricate the bill from committee.

24. Fite, *Richard B. Russell, Jr.*, 199–207; Douglas Kiker, "The Old Guard at Its Shrewdest," *Harper's Magazine*, September 1966, 101–106.

Russell knew the importance of segregation to the white South and recognized that its defense fell to him. A series of Gallup polls conducted in 1957 revealed that 70 percent of southerners disapproved of the *Brown* verdict. More ominous, 51 percent of southerners believed race relations would further deteriorate in the coming year. In the face of intense regional concern regarding the issue, Russell had grave doubts about his ability to successfully engage the enemy considering the climate of opinion following *Brown* outside of the South where only 20 percent of nonsoutherners disapproved of the court decision. Though happy with the shelving of the civil rights bill in 1956, he noted, "I am sorely concerned about the sword hanging over the heads of the white people of the South for if this bill ever comes to a vote in the Senate under the present conditions, political expediency and the whip of Party leadership will drive a majority of the Senate to support it." More than ever, Russell sensed that trouble lay ahead. On another occasion he lamented the unprecedented pressure for enactment of a civil rights bill, not to mention the "lost support of even some Southern Senators. The situation is becoming increasingly ominous." Before 1957 he had thwarted civil rights advances through the use of all of the parliamentary tricks he had learned early in his Senate career. Now at the pinnacle of his power, he found his leverage on the one issue he held most dear—segregation— waning. At the same time, he hoped that he would lead the South fully back into the body politic by erasing the stigma attached to the region following the Civil War. In all previous civil rights battles, Richard Russell had conceptualized the southern opposition as a national, rather than a sectional, fight, making his drive to put a representative from the region in the White House a logical manifestation of how he viewed the battle for Jim Crow. Someone needed to return the country to its core principles and who better than an individual from a region devoted to the Constitution as wrought by the founders, Russell pondered? He wanted a southerner elected president of the United States, and not one like Woodrow Wilson, who although born in Virginia spent most of his life in the company of northeastern intellectuals. No, Russell sought to place a real southerner in the post, one who had grown up in the region, understood its culture, and respected its history. In 1952, he had hoped that he would be that candidate, but popular support for his presidential bid never ignited above the Mason-Dixon line. Orchestrating the southern defense of segregation in the Senate made him too southern for acceptance by the rest of the country. Russell did not lose sight of his goal and found Texan Lyndon Johnson perfectly suited to fill the role.[25]

Many have chronicled the close relationship between Johnson and Russell. The friendship between them proved complex but, in the end, a two-way street. As many have stated, Johnson's precipitous rise to power could not have occurred without the intervention of the Senate's most powerful man. Indeed, Johnson's position as Senate majority leader resulted largely because of Russell's efforts, as well as the Georgian's own disinclination for the post. By the same token, Russell fulfilled his own interests by delaying the final assault against segregation and raising a southerner to the White House by using Lyndon Johnson. In the long-term, Russell got much more than he bargained for from Johnson after the Texan became president. During the latter half of the 1950s, he got exactly what he wanted—time. Russell needed to slow the civil rights pressure that threatened the South. Faced with the Eisenhower proposal, the Georgian began to believe that some form of a civil rights compromise in 1957 would grant the region breathing room, but he could not accomplish this goal alone. Lyndon Johnson provided the answer, in part, because the Texan also needed civil rights legislation to pass in order to solidify his position as the Democratic leader in the Senate and to further his presidential ambitions. As 1956 drew to a close, Russell's pupil proved reticent regarding his civil rights intentions. When asked by a reporter whether he planned to push the Eisenhower bill during the next session, Johnson wrote, "I know of no such plan, favor no such plan, am participating in no such plan." Civil rights advocates would soon force Johnson into a different position.[26]

In 1949, an overwhelming majority of the upper house had voted in favor of amending Rule 22. Despite the alteration, Senate liberals lamented the inherent difficulty of procuring the necessary sixty-four votes to stifle debate and loathed the exemption of rule changes from cloture petitions. At the start

25. When asked whether they approved or disapproved of the *Brown* verdict, 67 percent marked their disapproval in April, and 72 percent did in September 1957. George H. Gallup, *The Gallup Poll: Public Opinion, 1935–1971*, vol. 2, *1949–1958* (New York: Random House, 1972), 1507, 1518; RR to Lila Benton, 31 July 1956, Box 21, Folder 2, Russell MSS ("I am sorely . . ."); RR to Ruby Dobyns, 24 July 1956, Box 21, Folder 2, Russell MSS ("lost support of . . .").

26. For a sample of the many works that emphasize Johnson's relationship with Russell, see note 14, chapter 3, as well as Goldsmith, *Colleagues;* LBJ to Robert Allen, 26 December 1956, Box 567, "1956 General File" Folder, LBJL ("I know of . . .").

of the Eighty-fifth Congress in 1957, New Mexico Democrat Clinton Anderson introduced a resolution that would require the Senate to adopt new rules at the beginning of each Congress subject only to majority approval. Advocates of the change centered their arguments on the question of whether or not the Senate was a continuing body. Unlike the House of Representatives, where all members sought reelection every two years, the Senate maintained a staggered system where only one-third of the chamber campaigned in the biennial congressional referendum. At the commencement of each new Congress, the House adopted new rules to reflect the changed nature of that body, whereas the Senate maintained its existing protocols since two-thirds if its members carried over from one election to the next. Liberals claimed that the Senate, despite its staggered election cycle, became a new body at the start of each Congress, thus making its rules subject to change by majority vote. Few senators accepted this argument. With only limited support for such a change, Lyndon Johnson easily gained permission from the Senate hierarchy for a unanimous consent agreement for six hours of debate on 4 January regarding the Anderson proposal, followed in turn by a vote to table the motion for further deliberation in the Rules Committee. A successful fifty-five to thirty-eight vote led to the tabling of the Anderson measure. For southerners, the maneuver safeguarded their filibuster weapon, which they fully expected to use when the Eisenhower civil rights bill once again arrived in the chamber. Before that time, they explained to constituents the reasoning behind their tactics and the possibility of a civil rights defeat later that year.[27]

Some southerners found it difficult to comprehend the apparent lack of combativeness on the part of their Senate delegation. Many of them wrote their senators demanding to know why they took no legislative action to protect regional interests. This belief stemmed in large part from differences between state and national politics. On the state level, local officials operated with others of like mind on racial matters, a fact that allowed them to take a hardline stand on the question of integration with little political risk because the overwhelming majority of the region's black population lacked access to the ballot box. National statesmen operated in a milieu that contained a wide

27. For the Anderson proposal, see *CR*, 85th Cong., 1st sess. (all subsequent *CR* citations refer to the same Congress and session until otherwise noted), 4 January 1957, 153; Howard E. Shuman, "Senate Rules and the Civil Rights Bill: A Case Study," *American Political Science Review* 51 (1957): 955–975. For the vote to table, see *CR*, 4 January 1957, 214.

variety of conflicting interests. Being a decided minority, southern senators could not produce the changes necessary for the preservation of white supremacy through legislative initiative. They could only fight a rearguard battle, but that fight proved equally as important for the maintenance of segregation as anything accomplished on the state level. Failure by Dixie's national legislators would mean the end of Jim Crow. No similar threat informed state-level decision making. Remarking on the obvious reason for a policy centered on strategic delay, Lister Hill noted that "if we had a majority we could adopt a strategy and proceed in many ways now impossible for us." Because of the political situation in 1957, southern senators expected that "there will be further efforts during this session of Congress, both to kill the filibuster and to enact civil rights legislation." Summarizing caucus fears at the end of January, Allen Ellender pessimistically noted, "We have lost a few supporters in recent years and the outcome now is doubtful, to say the least." Things looked dim, leading some to consider a compromise on the Eisenhower proposal. Events on the ground further elucidated the need for restraint.[28]

For years, African Americans had vested their hope for greater opportunity in Washington politicians and in the legal system, but repeated disappointments soon steered them in a different direction. Even though the Supreme Court ruled school segregation unconstitutional, it quickly became evident that judicial verdicts alone would not change the "southern way of life." Something more, something larger that had the force of a moral imperative behind it was necessary to break through white southern obstructions. African American churches provided that catalyst. Evidence of a new consciousness in the black community began emerging as seen in the successful Montgomery Bus Boycott orchestrated by Martin Luther King Jr. In January 1957, the Southern Christian Leadership Conference (SCLC) formed to coordinate church action in the region in an effort to procure greater civil rights for black Americans and to capitalize on the momentum of the bus boycott. This group soon influenced other activist organizations, such as the Congress of Racial Equality (CORE) and the Student Non-Violent Coordinating Committee (SNCC), both of which would bring the policy of nonviolent resis-

28. LH to Arthur A. Adams Jr., 7 January 1957, Box 493, Folder 38, Hill MSS ("if we had . . ."); JS to John E. Walker, 12 January 1957, 16-A-9, Box 430, Folder 139, Sparkman MSS ("there will be . . ."); AE to W. R. Hynson, 31 January 1957, Box 705, "Legislation–Civil Rights, 1957" Folder, Ellender MSS ("we have lost . . .").

tance throughout the South. African American leaders now recognized that their success hinged on rallying popular opinion to their side. Without public pressure, Washington politicians seemed unwilling to break through southern obstructions.[29]

With the desegregation edict and fledgling black protest movement increasingly bringing national scrutiny on Jim Crow, southern senators knew the impact that regional intransigence was having. Southerners whipped into a frenzy by Citizens' Councils, formed to organize resistance to *Brown*, and opportunistic politicians, seeking to capitalize on white discontent, openly flouted federal authority, giving outsiders an impression that lawless reactionary forces reigned supreme. Dixie's U.S. senators knew from experience that too much massive resistance prompted charges of obstructionism, a development that could only hamper their battle in Washington. Fighting a battle based on moderation while representing a region degenerating into extremism posed a host of challenges for southern senators—and things kept getting worse.[30]

In early January 1957, Russell Long wrote former U.S. senator William Feazel of Louisiana, "this is the time for a tactical retreat. If Eisenhower's civil rights bill is anything like reasonable, I am going to advise our friends that I do not believe it wise for us to filibuster the bill. The point I have in mind is that we would do best to save our filibuster weapon against the day when it is desperately needed." Long, too, clearly recognized the impracticality of blocking all such measures because of the formation of a new civil rights coalition in the Senate that undermined southern strength. Some chroniclers of the 1957 civil rights fight point to Lyndon Johnson as the agent responsible for filling caucus members, especially the pivotal Richard Russell, with doomsday scenarios that precipitated their decision to compromise. What such an explanation overlooks is the trend in southern thinking since the 1940s that emphasized both the mounting pressure against them as well as the gradual loss of support from their traditional Senate allies. Long before

29. Clayborne Carson, *In Struggle: SNCC and the Black Awakening of the 1960s* (Cambridge: Harvard University Press); David J. Garrow, *Bearing the Cross: Martin Luther King, Jr., and the Southern Leadership Conference* (New York: Harper Perennial, 1999); Branch, *Parting the Waters*.

30. Numan V. Bartley, *The Rise of Massive Resistance: Race and Politics in the South during the 1950s* (Baton Rouge: Louisiana State University Press), 1999; Numan V. Bartley and Hugh D. Graham, *Southern Politics and the Second Reconstruction* (Baltimore: John Hopkins University Press, 1975); McMillen, *Citizens' Council*.

Johnson had designs on the White House and thus needed to establish his credentials as something other than a regional statesman by passing a civil rights bill, the caucus sought to slow civil rights activism through the use of strategic delay. Russell Long's insightful remarks underscored a central feature of that policy—the desire to extend the life of segregation by any means possible. Whether or not the legislative situation proved as grave as Long and others feared, the point remains moot since these grim forecasts clearly reflected the paranoid worldview that had long engulfed the southern caucus. Even if, as many argued, Johnson played a role in encouraging the group not to filibuster in 1957, his suggestions fell on fertile ground among a group prone to alarmism. Feeling their position threatened as never before in the wake of the *Brown* decision and the emergence of a strong bipartisan civil rights coalition, some southern senators considered a compromise the most effective way of prolonging the Jim Crow system. For the first time since the advent of the modern civil rights crusade, members of the southern caucus considered the possibility of allowing a substantive measure to come to a vote. In the eyes of some, desperate times demanded desperate actions. Not all caucus participants proved similarly inclined.[31]

Unlike fellow Louisianan Russell Long, Allen Ellender initially harbored no intention of compromising. Noting his advancing age, Ellender claimed, "I am still capable of talking for quite a long time, and I am prepared to fight this thing as long as I have breath in my body." Despite his bluster, he nonetheless recognized some of the factors that ultimately encouraged a compromise. "Our ranks of loyal southerners," he wrote a constituent, "are growing smaller and smaller with each session, making it increasingly difficult to fight these nefarious bills." Here Ellender specifically referenced the unreliability of the delegations from Texas, consisting of Majority Leader Johnson and the recently elected Ralph Yarborough, a confirmed liberal, and the duo from Tennessee, Albert Gore and Estes Kefauver. Now, four fewer senators would be on hand to sustain a filibuster. Despite the gloomy situation, South Carolina's Olin Johnston indicated his belief that the group could sustain a filibuster with a "lengthy educational program" and had a forty-hour speech prepared for just such an eventuality. Prior to the bill's arrival in the Senate, opinion in the caucus was divided regarding the appropriate course of action. John Sparkman best gauged the mood of the southern senators when

31. RL to William Feazel, 7 January 1957, Box 22, Folder 17, Long MSS ("this is the . . .").

he noted that "no one can tell what the outcome will be" in the anticipated civil rights battle.[32]

For Lyndon Johnson, 1957 brought him more than a doctrinaire internal conflict over personal ideology. To him, the sixty-four votes needed to invoke cloture against a southern filibuster seemed reasonably attainable. Further adding to the dilemma, proponents of the bill planned to avoid a repetition of the events that transpired at the end of the Eighty-fourth Congress when House Resolution 627 disappeared in the Judiciary Committee. Prospects appeared favorable for the passage of civil rights legislation during the Eighty-fifth Congress with or without his assistance. As party leader, Johnson encountered a challenge that not only tested his political acumen but also threatened to destroy his political career. Staunch support of the measure would win the plaudits of the liberal media and much of his party but hopelessly antagonize his constituents. If he remained faithful to the Senate's southern bloc and thwarted the legislation, a massive Democratic schism would emerge, leading to Johnson's ouster from power and the end of his presidential aspirations. The production of a weak civil rights measure, though still a risky undertaking, seemed infinitely more agreeable than the alternatives. Furthermore a carefully managed public relations campaign, coupled with the negligible impact of a watered-down bill, would erase any initial criticism by Johnson's constituents long before he faced reelection in 1960. With the fate of his political career hanging in the balance, Lyndon Johnson sought a compromise. Fortunately for him, much of the southern caucus sensed the need for negotiation.

Johnson settled on two crucial factors necessary to derive a compromise. First, he needed to convince those southern senators who did not yet sense the need to negotiate that an attempted filibuster would fail. Naturally, everyone expected southern senators to wax long against the measure for constituent consumption, but they could still make a strong record of opposition without resorting to blatant obstruction. In order to persuade the uncertain and to reinforce the conviction of the willing, Johnson, at the urging of his

32. AE to B. F. Walton, 28 June 1957, Box 705, "Legislation—Civil Rights—1957" Folder, Ellender MSS ("I am still . . ."); AE to D. L. Kerlin, 3 April 1957, Box 705, "Legislation—Civil Rights—1957" Folder, Ellender MSS ("Our ranks of . . ."); media script, 1957, Box 128, "Media Scripts 1957" Folder, Johnston MSS ("lengthy educational program"); JS to W. T. Rutland, 14 May 1957, 16-A-9, Box 430, Folder 115, Sparkman MSS ("no one can . . .").

trusted aide George Reedy, raised the possibility of harsh retribution if Senate moderates "are totally rebuffed." He strongly emphasized that the "[Joseph] O'Mahoneys, the [Clinton] Andersons, the [Mike] Mansfields . . . are willing to beat their brains out in the interests of prudent legislation," but if the South filibustered, "the moderates will then follow the extremists to the North because they have no place else to go." The second crucial factor shaping Johnson's maneuvers developed from intelligence reports indicating that most Republicans harbored serious reservations about the Eisenhower initiative. Numerous tips emanated from the opposition party that there existed "a complete lack of enthusiasm of Republicans for the bill." Although nominally paying lip service in supporting their party's highest official, many Republicans entertained significant doubts about the sizable expansion of federal authority mandated in the pending legislation. Armed with reluctant southern approval for a compromise and hedging Republican support for the measure, Johnson had the foundation from which he would forge the Civil Rights Act of 1957. Every step of the process surrounding the bill's passage stemmed from the majority leader's read of the political situation as well as on his ability to keep southerners and moderates appeased.[33]

In the meantime, at least one southern senator wanted to take immediate action. Following the cloture fight, southerners waited for the enemy to make a move. Growing tired of the inactivity, J. Strom Thurmond wrote Richard Russell that members of the southern bloc should "make a special trip to the White House to discuss with the president the grave implications" of the administration's civil rights bill. Believing that Attorney General Herbert Brownell had "brainwashed" the president, many southerners, including Thurmond, contended that if informed of the bill's provisions, Eisenhower would surely condemn it. Russell dismissed Thurmond's suggestion, claiming that "Brownell is the president's accepted oracle in this field and we know Brownell's views all too well." Later, when the bill came before the Senate, Russell did visit Eisenhower, but he did so alone. Thurmond, however, did not have long to wait before debate began on the president's proposal.[34]

On 18 June, the Eisenhower civil rights initiative, reintroduced as House

33. Memo, George Reedy to LBJ, n.d., "Siegel: Civil Rights," Box 404, Senate Papers, LBJL; George Reedy, *Lyndon B. Johnson: A Memoir* (New York: Andrews and McNeel, 1982), 95; memo, Willie Day Taylor to LBJ, n.d., "Siegel: Civil Rights," Box 404, Senate Papers, LBJL.

34. ST to RR, 6 April 1957, Box 13, "Legislation: Civil Rights, Folder II, 1957" Folder, Thurmond MSS ("make a special . . ."); RR to William T. Bodenhamer, 31 January 1957, Box 20,

Resolution 6127 at the opening of the Eighty-fifth Congress, passed in the House, 286 to 126. Northern Democrats and Republican leaders in the Senate attempted to keep the bill out of the Judiciary Committee by arguing that Rule 14 permitted the immediate placement of a bill on the calendar if a single member objected to a committee referral. Adhering to the remarks he made during the Eighty-fourth Congress, Lyndon Johnson denounced the liberal effort to force the bill on the calendar as an abrogation of orderly Senate procedure. To constituents, Johnson ridiculed the "ends justifies the means" doctrine employed by the "fervent advocates" of civil rights. Not surprising, Richard Russell joined Johnson in denouncing the liberal maneuver as threatening to establish "a precedent, in the Senate, which can only lead to chaos." Challenging the interpretation of Rule 14 advanced by civil rights advocates, the Georgian argued that Rule 25 produced as a result of the Legislative Reorganization Act of 1946, nullified the earlier code by specifically requiring the referral of all bills to the committee with jurisdiction over the matter. Unconvinced by Russell's logic, Senate civil rights advocates attempted to force the bill onto the calendar. The presiding officer of the Senate, Vice President Richard Nixon, ruled that since no clear precedent existed regarding Rule 14 the body needed to determine whether to place the bill in committee or directly on the calendar. Civil rights advocates won the day as the Senate voted to bypass the Judiciary, forty-five to thirty-nine. Twelve western senators sided with their southern colleagues to place the measure in committee. Under conventional circumstances such a vote would have provoked little controversy; however, the passage of the Hells Canyon hydroelectric dam bill the next day evoked widespread charges of vote trading.[35]

Legislation authorizing construction of the Hells Canyon dam along Idaho's Snake River failed in 1956 but passed on 21 June the following year, forty-five to thirty-eight. Five southerners who opposed the project during the Eighty-fourth Congress helped carry the measure in 1957 by suddenly reversing their votes. Many columnists viewed the dramatic shift in southern opinion as evidence of an unwritten gentleman's agreement whereby

Folder 7, Russell MSS ("brainwashed"); RR to ST 12 April 1957, Box 13, "Legislation: Civil Rights—Folder II, 1957" Folder, Thurmond MSS ("Brownell is the . . .").

35. For the House vote on HR 6127, see CR, 18 June 1957, 9518; LBJ to Henry Trantham, 13 June 1957, Box 289, "Judiciary—Civil Rights, #2 of 2" Folder, LBJL ("ends justifies . . .") and ("fervent advocates"); CR, 17 June 1957, 9260 ("a precedent, . . ."). For Russell's interpretation, see CR, 19 June 1957, 9627–9628; for the vote on committee referral, see CR, 20 June 1957, 9827.

southerners would help carry the dam and westerners would aid southern senators where practicable in the civil rights fight. Wayne Morse, one of the alleged conspirators, called the rumors "vicious" and "unwarranted," adding, "I have never traded a vote in the Senate." Idaho senator Frank Church, who won his election in 1956 on a promise that he would get the dam built, later related that "there was never any quid pro quo at all" attached to the passage of Hells Canyon. The correspondence of Russell Long, one of the alleged southern conspirators, provides a different interpretation.[36]

Long denounced Hells Canyon from the beginning, arguing that it represented a waste of taxpayers' money "in order to generate an extra tidbit of power." Even worse from his perspective was that a private power company had already promised to construct three smaller dams capable of generating an equivalent amount of power at less cost than the proposed federal project. As late as May 1957, Long remained adamant about the measure: "I think there is even less reason today . . . to vote for government construction of the project." One month later, he reversed himself and voted in favor of the bill. In response to a constituent letter concerning his change of heart, Long replied, "there are some occasions in the Senate where a great many things have to be taken into consideration on a particular vote and this particular vote was such an issue." Although purposely vague, Long's response suggested that he indeed viewed the vote on Hells Canyon as linked with the civil rights debate. This alleged agreement, of course, required no face-to-face meeting between southern and western senators. It was part of a tacit accord not verbalized but nonetheless binding. Enough southerners would alter their votes to carry Hells Canyon, an important water resource issue in western states, and westerners would assist the southern contingent on an issue that meant everything below the Mason-Dixon line—civil rights. The foundation for a civil rights compromise emerged from this alliance just in time for the start of Senate debate on House Resolution 6127.[37]

Richard Russell opened discussion on 2 July with his usual thorough cri-

36. For the 1956 Hells Canyon vote, see *CR*, 84th Cong., 2nd sess., 19 July 1956, 13498. In 1957, Eastland, Ervin, Long, and Smathers voted aye: *CR*, 85th Cong., 1st sess., 21 June 1957, 9977; Morse's comments appear in *CR*, 21 June 1957, 9987; transcript, Frank Church Oral History, 1 May 1969, by Paige Mulhollan, AC 78–37, 5–6, LBJL ("there was never . . .").

37. RL to L. G. Simms, 12 July 1955, Box 21, Folder 25, Long MSS ("in order to . . ."); RL Address to Mississippi Valley Flood Control Association, 13 January 1956, Box 593, Folder 96, Long MSS; RL to Farrar Armstrong, 24 May 1957, Box 91, Folder 7, Long MSS ("I think there . . .");

tique of civil rights legislation that touched upon many of the themes he emphasized throughout his career and outlined most of the central arguments that his colleagues would subsequently employ. Russell claimed that "the failure of the National Press, radio, and television to report the true facts" concerning the bill made it essential for him to deliver a "strongly worded speech" to "enlighten the people." He wasted little time placing the voting rights bill in a negative light, by arguing that it had far more insidious designs than safeguarding suffrage. Title III of the bill galled the Georgian most for it "was deliberately drawn to enable the use of the military forces to destroy the system of separation of the races in the southern states at the point of a bayonet, if it should be found necessary to take this step." The section to which he referred granted the attorney general power to use any means, even military force, to compel compliance with any civil rights order, not just those involving suffrage, as the administration had touted. Resurrecting the memory of Reconstruction, Russell said that "neither [Charles] Sumner nor [Thaddeus] Stevens . . . ever cooked up any such devil's broth as is proposed in this misnamed civil rights bill." The legislation, he argued, granted the attorney general "unprecedented power to bring to bear the whole might of the Federal Government . . . to force a commingling of white and Negro children" in public schools. Strategic delay figured prominently in his approach to the question since he saw the legislative item as another in a long line of attempts to undermine the Jim Crow system. Unlike other initiatives, Resolution 6127, as drafted, contained the apparatus necessary to "put black heels on white necks." Although the Eisenhower administration stressed the bill's suffrage protections, it became evident from Russell's speech that only Title IV of the bill, its final section, dealt exclusively with the franchise. Adding an air of gravity to his argument, the Georgian cautioned his audience to weigh heavily the points raised by his caucus in the coming weeks because the bill's passage would cause "unspeakable confusion, bitterness, and bloodshed . . . there will not be enough jails to hold the people of the South who will oppose the use of raw Federal power." Despite all of his bluster, the Georgian stopped short of calling for the outright defeat of the bill. He had other plans.[38]

RL to Q. T. Hardtner, 16 July 1957, Box 91 Folder 6, Long MSS ("there are some . . ."); Finley, "Balancing Liberal and Conservative," 32–34.

38. RR to Mark W. Fitzpatrick, 3 July 1957, Box 19, Folder 10, Russell MSS ("the failure of . . .") and ("strongly worded"); CR, 2 July 1957, 10771 ("Attorney General unprecedented . . .") and

The day after his speech, Russell gathered the caucus in his Senate office, room 205. Seated around a circular table, the group planned its opposition. As in all such meetings, only senators attended, no one took notes, and everyone received an assignment. This gathering, however, proved different from any previous one. Russell had convened the group not to orchestrate a filibuster, but to lobby for a compromise. He laid before them his reasons for such a course of action. Foremost in the Georgian's mind was the existence of strong Republican support for the measure. In years past, southerners had relied on GOP conservatives to vote against cloture. Now with a Republican administration pressing for party unity on the civil rights bill, Russell felt the risk of undertaking a filibuster too great. If the Senate invoked cloture, the chamber would pass the "sweeping" civil rights bill drafted by Brownell. The southern leader did not wish to take that chance. He suggested the caucus attempt to amend the bill in such a manner that what remained of it would produce little hardship in the South. Some in the group, including Strom Thurmond and Olin Johnston, questioned the Georgian, but Russell talked them out of their opposition, although he encouraged them to keep their filibuster material handy just in case. As the meeting drew to a close, Harry Byrd said, "Dick, it's up to you." With tacit accord to seek a compromise reached, the meeting adjourned. The rest of the Senate soon discovered that, at least for the moment, a filibuster would not take place.[39]

In a series of brief speeches, Richard Russell provided the Senate with a clear outline of the caucus' intentions. Southerners planned on making a distinct record of opposition, but their orations would approximate in length those given under ordinary circumstances. Furthermore, their addresses would be aimed at informing the Senate and the nation about the nuances of the bill. Ultimately, Russell hoped, "we may arrive at some meeting of the minds" on the most objectionable aspects of the bill. If that occurred, he revealed that the caucus would permit a vote on the measure. A filibuster would take place only if the Senate rejected southern demands. Throughout the debate, the caucus carefully divided its eighteen members based on their political temperament and on the ability of each individual. In order to sway

("black heels on . . ."), 10772 ("was deliberately drawn . . ."), 10774 ("neither Sumner . . .") and ("unspeakable confusion . . .").

39. *Time*, 12 August 1957, 11–16; Mann, *Walls of Jericho*, 195–196; Caro, *Master of the Senate*, 920–921.

their colleagues, they usually limited their speeches to one section of the proposed bill, rather than issue blanket denunciations of civil rights on principle. The Georgian's conciliatory attitude immediately began bearing fruit.[40]

Senate speeches rarely alter opinion, but Russell's 2 July analysis caused widespread introspection. The limited debate on House Resolution 6127 in the House left public perception intact that the bill aimed solely at the protection of voting rights. By highlighting the enormous power the bill would grant the attorney general, as well as by revealing the origins of that power—an 1866 Reconstruction statute—Russell's telling interpretation defied prevailing notions that the proposal focused exclusively on suffrage. At a press conference on 3 July 1957, a reporter asked Eisenhower if he believed the bill needed rewriting in light of the recent Senate discussion. A seemingly bewildered president responded, "Well, I would not want to answer this in detail, because I was reading part of the bill this morning and I—there were certain phrases I didn't completely understand." Eisenhower's garbled answer disheartened those expecting full executive support for the duration of the debate. Russell's arguments concerning Title III had struck a resonant chord. His southern colleagues further pressed the attack.[41]

The sweeping power Title III allegedly granted the attorney general to expedite civil rights cases became the subject of much southern attention. By focusing on it, southerners shifted the debate away from what would surely have been a less convincing defense of the region's voter registration process. The fact that thousands of black Americans residing in Dixie were deliberately denied the right to vote became a side issue as the Senate grappled with the legislation in a framework defined by southerners. To be sure, many caucus members broached the subject of minority suffrage, boldly claiming that blacks voted freely in the South and challenging the bill's supporters to provide more than anecdotal evidence that racial discrimination existed in the southern electoral process. In precincts where only a small percentage

40. For Russell's outline of the debate parameters, see *CR*, 3 July 1957, 10900–10901; *CR*, 8 July 1957, 10989–10990, 10991 ("we may arrive . . ."").

41. The rules limiting debate in the House prevented many southern congressmen from adequately addressing the faults of the bill, prompting them to send a lengthy critique of the legislation to Eisenhower. Southern congressmen to President Eisenhower, 12 July 1957, Box 58, "Judiciary Committee" Folder, James H. Morrison Collection, Center for Regional Studies and Archives, Sims Memorial Library, Southeastern Louisiana University, Hammond; *New York Times*, 4 July 1957, 13 ("well, I . . ."); *Time*, 14 July 1957, 17.

of African Americans cast ballots, southerners placed the blame not on local registrars but on the apathy of the black community. Only time would rectify this demographic imbalance in the region's voting rolls, they contended, as southern blacks gradually accepted the responsibilities of citizenship by participating in the electoral process. African Americans, southerners claimed, did not clamor for suffrage legislation because they already possessed the privilege of voting, although few of them saw fit to avail themselves of the opportunity. Fertile northern imaginations, they concluded, bore the primary responsibility for House Resolution 6127.[42]

During previous civil rights battles, southerners claimed that their northern counterparts deliberately used the question of race for their political advantage and returned to that argument in 1957. Throughout the debate, caucus members noted the presence of an "anti-South" propaganda campaign deliberately contrived to fool those beyond the Mason-Dixon line into believing that rampant discrimination existed in the South. For caucus members, this liberal duplicity had a deliberate purpose. Using Title III as a point of reference, they claimed that the oft-stated goal of protecting the right to vote stressed by advocates of the bill veiled the measure's true objective—destroying segregation. As drafted, caucus members claimed that the controversial section would permit the use of military force to compel compliance with all court orders, including those resulting from the *Brown* decision. Following this line of reasoning, southerners returned to their fear that "social admixture" served as the true purpose of civil rights activists. Title III provided all of the evidence the caucus needed. By stressing this point, southerners, albeit far less explicitly than during previous filibusters, again played to northern racism in the form of the interracial sexual taboo. Striving to maintain the perception that nothing but good intentions marked their own actions, caucus members observed that they had no qualms regarding black suffrage so long as the expansion of the franchise did not come at the expense of the region's racial order as House Resolution 6127 threatened. For northern moderates and conservatives, legislative action forcing integration remained an idea whose time had not yet come. Many members of both parties who initially supported a suffrage proposal found southern arguments

42. For examples of claims that southern blacks voted freely, see *CR*, 9 July 1957, 11086 (Fulbright); *CR*, 10 July 1957, 11195 (Sparkman); *CR*, 13 July 1957, 11600 (McClellan); *CR*, 15 July 1957, 11683 (Long); *CR*, 29 July 1957, 12919 (Talmadge); *CR*, 31 July 1957, 13152 (Thurmond).

concerning the section compelling and, like the president before them, began withdrawing their unequivocal support for the legislation. In the process, these northern politicians fell victim to the caucus's efforts to shift the debate away from the very obvious problem of black disfranchisement. At the time, southerners noted that their region bore the brunt of the *Brown* ruling, but should senators accede to the use of "storm troopers" to force compliance with the verdict in Dixie, they would set a precedent that would inevitably prompt similar action in the North, if not regarding civil rights, then certainly in relation to a cultural norm considered equally as important above the Mason-Dixon line as segregation proved below it. Few but the most liberal of senators in the 1950s could accept, upon further reflection, such a massive investment of power in the hands of a single, non-elected, official for a purpose that many northerners did not fully support.[43]

In order to illustrate their allegations concerning the bill's "true" designs, many southerners turned to the historical legacy of Reconstruction to highlight the deleterious consequences of allowing the political passions of an era to influence the legislative process. Although by the late 1950s Reconstruction historiography had progressed beyond the scholarship of William A. Dunning and his disciples, southern senators continued to employ the central interpretive themes of the Dunning school. According to Dunning acolytes, the Reconstruction era represented a dark chapter in the nation's history in which southerners, who had graciously accepted defeat after the Civil War, fell victim to corrupt carpetbaggers and scalawags under the direction of Radical Republicans. Rather than reconciling with their vanquished foes, Republican leaders imposed military rule on the South, reducing the region to a quasi-colonial status that stunted its development for decades. Furthermore, according to the Dunning interpretation, southern blacks, as yet unprepared for the responsibilities of citizenship, became nothing but

43. For examples of the emphasis on political expediency and an anti-South propaganda campaign, see *CR*, 17 June 1957, 9293 (Holland); *CR*, 19 June 1957, 9628 (Russell); *CR*, 2 July 1957, 10771 (Russell); *CR*, 8 July 1957, 10990 (Russell); *CR*, 10 July 1957, 11207 (Sparkman); *CR*, 11 July 1957, 11332 (Holland); *CR*, 13 July 1957, 11602 (McClellan); *CR*, 13 July 1957, 11612 (Scott); *CR*, 29 July 1957, 12880 (Eastland); *CR*, 29 July 1957, 12925 (Talmadge). For examples of southern explanation of the bill's "real" intent, see *CR*, 19 June 1957, 9627 (Russell); *CR*, 2 July 1957, 10771 (Russell); *CR*, 9 July 1957, 11085 (Eastland); *CR*, 11 July 1957, 11350 (Eastland), 11367 (Thurmond); *CR*, 12 July 1957, 11493 (Stennis); *CR*, 13 July 1957, 11607 (McClellan); *CR*, Talmadge, 12 July 1957, 11508 ("storm troopers").

pawns of the newly installed Republican governments throughout the region that lined their pockets with ill-gotten gains procured in the prostrate South. In the 1950s, southern senators employed the Dunning interpretation of Reconstruction to highlight what they considered a return to the policies and practices used against their region following the Civil War. Again it appeared that northerners were determined to return military rule to the South, as evidenced by Title III, or more specifically, to "place black heels on white necks," as Russell had earlier observed. Southerners believed that only they knew the best method of handling the region's black population, but as during Reconstruction, many northerners payed little heed to the inevitable consequences of forcing sweeping reforms on a region violently opposed to such an alteration. Frequent references to Reconstruction in southern speeches thus served as a warning to northerners. If civil rights activists succeeded in ramming through "force" bills aimed at punishing the South, then they risked inciting the sort of violence that precipitated the retreat from the first Reconstruction. As on previous occasions, caucus participants urged their colleagues to step back from the political passions of the moment and consider the consequences that southern senators proved all too happy to provide them. In an effort to further obscure the question of voting rights, southern senators also turned their sights on Title IV of the bill, the only section specifically related to suffrage, and transformed even discussion concerning that section into a debate on tangential issues that had little relevance to safeguarding the right to vote.[44]

North Carolinian Sam Ervin led the southern fight against Title IV by turning his years of experience as a constitutional lawyer on the question of jury trials in contempt proceedings. Ervin and his colleagues assured their listeners that the Constitution, not race, dictated their opposition to the pending measure. In particular, Title IV received exhaustive analysis because it granted the attorney general, in the name of the federal government, the right to institute a civil action or "other proper proceeding for preventive relief," including injunctions and restraining orders in cases involving the denial of suffrage. Opponents of the section argued that by tradition an aggrieved party must first exhaust all legal options on the state level before

44. For references to Reconstruction, see *CR*, 19 June 1957, 9627 (Ervin); *CR*, 2 July 1957, 10771 (Russell); *CR*, 13 July 1957, 11611 (Scott); *CR*, 15 July 1957, 11683 (Long); *CR*, 16 July 1957, 11817 (Byrd); *CR*, 18 July 1957, 12073–12074 (Russell); *CR*, 28 August 1957, 16216 (Talmadge).

resorting to the federal judicial system. Passage of House Resolution 6127 would short circuit this time honored precedent firmly established in American jurisprudence by usurping the authority of local legal systems. Also, by requiring that all such cases be brought in the name of the United States, not the injured party, the bill automatically deprived future defendants of the right to a jury trial in contempt proceedings resulting from the legislation.[45]

Southern senators, of course, objected to the premise that underlay the absence of a jury trial provision in Resolution 6127—that an all white southern jury would not convict one of its own in a civil rights case. They argued that the right to a trial by jury appeared in four places in the Constitution: Article III, Section 2, and the Fifth, Sixth, and Seventh Amendments; whereas the right to vote received no mention in the document. Even the Fifteenth and Nineteenth Amendments, they noted, as they had during the poll tax debates, did not guarantee anyone the right to vote. Instead, these amendments only stipulated that race and gender could not be a factor in whether or not one could vote. An individual, according to the southern interpretation, still had to meet all of the registration qualifications in the state in which he or she resided before obtaining the privilege of voting. Their arguments linked their fight with that of the founding fathers, who also considered the right to a jury trial essential for the preservation of liberty. Indeed, southerners noted that a central reason for the American colonists' break from Britain in the eighteenth century was the Crown's efforts to punish the provincials without jury trials. The Declaration of Independence itself illustrated this contention, making the claims of twentieth-century southerners all the more consistent with the ideological forces that led to the Revolution. As in previous years, caucus members made every effort to depict their fight as one that transcended narrow sectional prejudices by creating in the minds of Senate moderates a stark dichotomy in which southerners defended the most sacred of American principles, while their opponents sought unconstitutional means to bring about un-American ends. Civil rights advocates, caucus veterans claimed, proved willing to destroy the temple of democracy for the sole purpose of winning the favor of black voters. At least in 1957 many members of the Senate apparently accepted these southern claims, a fact that led Herman

45. For some of the less opaque legal critiques of Title IV, see CR, 8 July 1957, 10995–10996 (Ervin); CR, 9 July 1957, 11078–11081 (Fulbright); CR, 10 July 1957, 11195–11198 (Sparkman); CR, 10 July 1957, 11201 (Ervin).

Talmadge to opine that "it is not the people of the South who defy the Constitution, rather, it is we who uphold it."[46]

The extensive legal critique of the bill and its problematic Titles III and IV revealed that the southern bloc planned on resisting the bill largely on its shortfalls and that they believed, as Richard Russell observed in caucus, that they had a "good case on the merits." Caucus members demonstrated that they did not have to resurrect the race-centered arguments they had employed in the past. Nonetheless, they dissembled throughout the debate, deliberately avoiding a systematic analysis of what was clearly the discriminatory use of voter registration laws in the South. Although southern senators bear the primary responsibility for shifting the debate away from suffrage discrimination, it also remains true that only a small minority of northerners and westerners from either party made any effort to steer the debate back to the woefully low number of blacks registered in the region. By allowing the caucus to dictate the scope of the debate, senators from beyond the Mason-Dixon line permitted the moral imperative of ensuring equal access to the political process to slip from their grasp. Instead, chamber debate revolved around the question of jury trials in contempt cases and the manifold hidden threats that southerners claimed existed in Title III. With senators willing to debate the legislation within the southern framework, it became increasingly probable that the chamber would accept a compromise along the lines recommended by the caucus.[47]

On 16 July 1957, the Senate prepared to vote on two motions, one to make House Resolution 6127 the body's pending business and the other a proposal by Wayne Morse to send the bill to committee for further deliberation. Aware that the motion to take up the bill would succeed, Richard Russell pleaded with those outside of the South to deal with the proposal as if their state faced such "drastic" legislation. He did not expect to win the vote so

46. For references to the Revolutionary War generation, see CR, 8 July 1957, 10992 and 11003 (Ervin); CR, 9 July 1957, 11079–11080 and 11086 (Fulbright); CR, 10 July 1957, 11196 (Sparkman); CR, 13 July 1957 11590 (Ellender); CR, 16 July 1957, 11820 (Thurmond), 11822 (Byrd); CR, 25 July 1957, 12704 (Robertson); CR, 29 July 1957, 12881 (Eastland), 12896 (Long); speech, HT to American Legion Auxiliary, 1957, Box 303, Folder 5, Talmadge MSS ("it is not . . .").

47. Time, 12 August 1957, 16. Throughout the debate, Democrats Hubert Humphrey and Paul Douglas, along with Republican Jacob Javits of New York, were the most vocal of the senators who attempted to redirect Senate discussion to the question of black disfranchisement.

much as he sought to influence future action on the bill. To the surprise of no one, the first motion passed decisively, seventy-one to eighteen. Morse's motion to send the bill to committee, with an adjusted guideline to report its findings in seven days, failed, thirty-five to fifty-four. With the bill now opened to amendments, the Senate faced the challenge of deciding what kind of civil rights bill, if any, would pass. By not filibustering the motion to take up the bill, caucus members demonstrated their good faith that they sought a compromise. The task remained to find a consensus in the chamber for an alteration that at least proved palatable to the South.[48]

The process of amending Resolution 6127 had actually begun before the 16 July vote making the bill the Senate's unfinished business. Eisenhower's often disastrous press conferences during the early stages of the debate encouraged a major alteration in the bill's problematic Title III. When asked at a July news conference if he would implement the provisions contained in the section, the president replied, "I can't imagine any set of circumstances that would ever induce me to send federal troops . . . into any area. . . . I would never believe that it would be a wise thing to do." Indecisive administration leadership, in conjunction with Richard Russell's skilled orchestration of southern strategy, produced a noticeable diminution in support for the section. Damaged by the president's comments, the civil rights coalition faced further disruption with the introduction of amendments molded by Majority Leader Lyndon Johnson.[49]

When popular civil rights advocate Clinton Anderson approached Johnson with an amendment to strike the controversial Title III from the legislation, the majority leader seized the importance of finding a moderate Republican cosponsor to encourage a bipartisan consensus. Republican George Aiken of Vermont offered to assist with the amendment for the simple reason that it would limit House Resolution 6127 to the originally stated purpose of the bill, safeguarding suffrage rights. With support for the Anderson-Aiken amendment growing, Florida's Spessard Holland alerted the chamber that should the initiative fail a filibuster would commence post haste. Awakened to southern intentions, the chamber reached a critical juncture in the debate. Any-

48. *CR*, 16 July 1957, 11831 ("drastic"); for the vote on motion, see *CR*, 16 July 1957, 11832; for Morse vote, see *CR*, 16 July 1957, 11837.

49. *New York Times*, 18 July 1957, 12 ("I can't imagine . . .").

thing less than an outright concession to the South on the Anderson-Aiken amendment foreordained a filibuster that would threaten the entire bill.[50]

Refusing to relent without a fight, Republican leader William Knowland and civil rights activist Hubert Humphrey introduced an amendment calling for the repeal of the Reconstruction era statute tied to Title III in an effort to salvage what remained of the section. Richard Russell promptly dispelled any notion that the southern caucus would settle for such a compromise. Although he supported the Knowland-Humphrey amendment, Russell believed that even with the change, Title III still granted the attorney general inordinate power. On 22 July the Senate voted, ninety to zero, in favor of the Knowland-Humphrey amendment. The decisive vote to remove the Reconstruction statute, however, offered little insight concerning the Senate's overall attitude toward the Anderson-Aiken amendment. As the hour of decision approached on 24 July, Lyndon Johnson noted the significance of the pending vote, stating that it "may very well be the deciding factor on whether this Congress will pass any civil rights bill at all." The moderate appeals by Anderson-Aiken supporters proved successful as the Senate convincingly voted, fifty-two to thirty-eight, in favor of the amendment striking Title III. Minority Leader Knowland cringed as he witnessed seventeen Republicans vote in favor of removing the section. Debate concerning the amendment also proved noteworthy for the absence of significant southern speeches. Northerners and westerners from both parties supplied the majority of the arguments for the amendment, lending further support to southern contentions that the ramifications of the bill had national significance. By not participating in this facet of the debate, caucus members hoped to, and to a great extent succeeded in, removing sectionalism from the discussion. Much work remained before southerners would drop the ever present threat of a filibuster.[51]

As Spessard Holland warned, southerners would not permit a final vote on the bill if they did not receive concessions that many in the chamber considered exorbitant. As they approached the Anderson-Aiken vote and then

50. Johnson encouraged Anderson based on his opposition "to any legislation that would make it possible for the Army and Navy to be sent into the South." LBJ to Johnny Coomer, 10 July 1957, Box 289, "Judiciary—Civil Rights—1957" Folder, Senate Papers, LBJL; Evans and Novak, *Exercise of Power*, 131–132; *CR*, 16 July 1957, 11826–11827; Holland's warning: *CR*, 17 July 1957, 11982.

51. Johnson's warning and final votes appear in *CR*, 24 July 1957, 12564–12565.

confronted the more complex jury trial question, caucus members maintained the threat of a filibuster. Describing how the southern group perceived the legislative situation at that time, Olin Johnston observed, a "wrong move and we would get a bill that would probably reach farther than anyone can even see. . . . We have to shoot with care in this manner and I for one will not burn down the barn to destroy the rat." As for caucus decision making during the 1957 crisis, he noted, "What we do is being done by unanimous agreement and only after the most weighty consideration has been given." This accord in the caucus on strategic matters is not always evident in how individual southern senators addressed the question of a compromise. Despite the meeting in Russell's office, many continued taking a hardline stand when addressing constituents, claiming that they would never permit the passage of a civil rights bill, whereas others talked openly of a compromise.[52]

J. William Fulbright indicated throughout July 1957 that he remained "hopeful that our efforts in explaining the dangerous provisions of the bill will result in a compromise on its more obnoxious provisions." Fulbright's comments leave little doubt that for him a substantive compromise represented a victory in the civil rights fight. Success regarding Title III did not necessarily mean a similar result concerning Title IV, especially considering Knowland's efforts to keep Republicans from again straying from the administration bill as they had on the Anderson-Aiken vote. Failure in the jury trial fight would lead to a filibuster that many in the caucus still believed they could win. Louisiana's Allen Ellender observed, "It is my belief that they will again fail" in garnering the votes necessary for cloture. Strom Thurmond also found it expeditious to rattle his sabers. "I do not favor any compromise," he declared, adding that "although the Press has been carrying reports of compromise attempts none has been made to me." Despite his bluster, the South Carolinian did concede that "the fight will be harder this year than in the past," because many Republicans, who might have considered siding with southern Democrats, felt it their obligation to support the initiative since it emerged from their own party's administration. Several southerners thus balanced their approach, claiming a willingness to compromise when addressing their Senate colleagues, while, at the same time, reassuring constituents that they as yet had not given up hope of an outright victory. This bifurcated

52. OJ transcript—Radio and TV spot, n.d., Box 128, "Media Scripts—1957" Folder, Johnston MSS ("wrong move and . . .") and ("what we do . . .").

strategy would later require much explanation back in Dixie when a compromise bill eventually passed. In the meantime, it became evident that their restrained efforts at critiquing the legislation produced a positive response.[53]

Sam Ervin, for one, noted that "we have been able to bring some reason into the Senate by pointing out how this Civil Rights Bill would rob American citizens of their basic rights." With the contours of a compromise taking shape, the southern bloc still faced the difficult question of permitting the bill to pass and thereby setting a dangerous precedent. A considerable gamble marked the potential decision to abandon some of the precepts that encompassed strategic delay. Since the 1940s, they had blocked all major civil rights bills, while granting concessions on minor proposals that only tangentially impacted the southern racial order, based on the theory that allowing the passage of a substantive measure would encourage further activism. However, experience had taught them that defeating one bill did not abate the advancement of other measures. Indeed, over the years the flurry of legislation only increased in the face of southern victories. In 1957, southerners hoped that their willingness to permit the passage of an emasculated bill would blunt some of the impetus behind civil rights activism. A weak measure served the dual purpose of limiting the drive to amend Rule 22 by demonstrating that civil rights legislation could pass and by, at least in theory, encouraging northern liberals to grant the South a grace period before commencing their next attack. Summarizing the perils that still existed following the Anderson-Aiken vote, Harry Byrd wrote, "We must take nothing for granted." A jury trial amendment would go a long way toward relieving southern anxiety and thus increasing the likelihood of a compromise.[54]

Despite proudly announcing that the bill now simply represented a voting rights measure, Majority Leader Lyndon Johnson called for still further improvement. A jury trial amendment remained extremely important because with it, "it is doubtful that many people can legitimately oppose the . . .

53. JF to Frank Cantrell, 18 July 1957, BCN 126, Folder 18, Fulbright MSS ("hopeful that our . . ."); AE to Frank R. McLavy, Sr., 17 July 1957, Box 705, "Legislation—Civil Rights—1957" Folder, Ellender MSS ("it is my . . ."); ST to E. V. Conyers, 16 July 1957, Box 13, "Legislation—Civil Rights, #4" Folder, Thurmond MSS ("I do not . . ."); ST to F. E. Gibson, 1 July 1957, Box 13, "Legislation—Civil Rights—Folder 3, 1957," Thurmond MSS ("that the fight . . .").

54. SE to Frank Redmond, 22 July 1957, Box 22, Folder 1370, Ervin MSS ("we have been . . ."); HB to James Kilpatrick, 26 July 1957, Box 245, "Kilpatrick, James J." Folder, Byrd MSS ("we must take . . .").

measure." Fashioning a coalition for such an amendment proved far more thorny than for the Anderson-Aiken proposal because of the confusion surrounding jury trials in contempt cases. Attempting to unify his proposal with an earlier one introduced by Senator Joseph O'Mahoney of Wyoming, Tennessee's Estes Kefauver forwarded a jury trial amendment that covered all criminal contempt proceedings not just those involving suffrage. Kefauver concentrated on establishing a clear distinction between civil and criminal contempt cases, with the latter open to jury trials. As described by Kefauver, civil contempt proceedings aimed at assuring compliance with a court order. A judge, in such a case, may fine or imprison an accused individual, but once the defendant complied with the order he purged himself of contempt. As in civil actions, criminal contempt proceedings attempted to force an individual to obey a court order, yet differed by also punishing a person for past noncompliance. Majority Leader Johnson seized on Kefauver's distinction regarding the types of contempt proceedings, seeing the Tennessean's amendment as the possible foundation of a compromise. Intrigued by Kefauver's goal to expand the bill beyond civil rights, segments of organized labor also began expressing interest in rewriting the federal statutes on contempt proceedings.[55]

Labor interest in House Resolution 6127 stemmed from a long history of government intervention in union disputes. Prior to the 1914 Clayton Act, designed to abet workers prevented from unionizing by their employers, a clear distinction between criminal and civil contempt existed but the right to a trial by one's peers in such cases did not. The act established a new precedent by permitting jury trials in cases not maintained by the U.S. government. In order to further protect labor, the 1932 Norris-LaGuardia Act expanded the jury trial guarantee to include cases initiated by the federal government. The Taft-Hartley Act of 1947 revised the ruling of the Norris-LaGuardia Act, once again denying the right to a jury trial in cases initiated and maintained by the government. Jury trial supporters based their argument on the sole, overruled precedent established by Norris-LaGuardia. Their supposition proved tenuous because the 1932 legislation encompassed only those

55. For Kefauver's distinction, see *CR*, 17 July 1957, 11983; Walter Jenkins to Mrs. Eli Morgan, 1 August 1957, Box 289, "Judiciary—Civil Rights—1957" Folder, Senate Papers, LBJL ("it is doubtful . . ."). Johnson aide George Reedy claimed that his employer taught himself the distinction between criminal and civil contempt and could effectively argue the issue with the best of the Senate's lawyers. Reedy, *Lyndon B. Johnson*, 77.

contempt cases dealing specifically with labor injunctions. Although fashioning a legally weak argument in relation to House Resolution 6127, proponents of a jury trial amendment sought to coax the aggressive labor lobby into demanding an alteration of the legislation. Lyndon Johnson aided the cause by pressuring O'Mahoney and Kefauver to unify their proposals, while he personally sought to enlist maximum union involvement.[56]

The concerted effort to attract union interest in the amendment prompted condemnation from the NAACP, Walter Reuther of the United Auto Workers, Jim Carey of the International Union of Electrical Workers, and other leaders of the social reform movement in organized labor. Reuther and Carey, both vice presidents in the AFL-CIO hierarchy, issued a statement from the body's executive committee that the union "cannot and will not permit itself to judge the appropriateness of this proposed change . . . because of any possible advantage to organized labor." Disavowing the decree of the committee, John L. Lewis of the United Mine Workers (UMW), whose union suffered stiff penalties after flouting a restraining order during a 1946 strike, jumped at the opportunity to alter the injunction statutes. The railroad brotherhoods and the postal unions, both with special interest legislation pending in Congress, joined the UMW in announcing their support for the O'Mahoney-Kefauver amendment. Promoters of the initiative now depicted the issue as a battle pitting those in favor of jury trials against those in opposition, while purposely obscuring arguments pertaining to suffrage.[57]

Despite the effort to "fuzz up" the issue, considerable doubt remained in the chamber. Many felt the amendment as drafted too pro-southern; they wanted some assurance that suffrage cases would not be tried exclusively

56. For background, see Foster Rhea Dulles, *Labor in America: A History*, 3rd ed. (New York: Crowell, 1966). For a succinct overview of labor legislation, injunctions, and the question of jury trials, see *CR*, 25 July 1957, 12694–12695; see also memo, George Reedy to LBJ, August 1957, Box 420, "Reedy Memos—August 1957" Folder, Senate Papers, LBJL.

57. *CR*, 24 July 1957, 12570–12572; press release, AFL-CIO, 30 July 1957, Box 291, "Civil Rights—Public Reaction and Press" Folder, Senate Papers, LBJL; Evans and Novak, *Exercise of Power*, 137. Lobbyists from the railroad brotherhoods and the postal union descended on Washington to urge support for the amendment to curry favor with southerners who chaired committees overseeing the dispensation of legislation vital to them. For example, a 15 percent increase in retirement benefits for the railroad brothers sat in Lister Hill's Labor Committee and a bill raising the pay of postal workers remained in Olin Johnston's Post Office Committee. *Newsweek*, 12 August 1957, 26.

before all white juries. As Joseph O'Mahoney held the floor on the eve of the jury trial vote, Idaho's Frank Church, who benefitted from southern largesse in the Hells Canyon fight, introduced a proposal that would alter the federal code to prohibit states from prescribing the qualifications for federal jury duty. According to this scheme, all U.S. citizens over twenty-one immediately became eligible to serve on federal juries. By removing the possibility of a southern jury pool coming exclusively from the overwhelmingly white state voting rolls, the Church rider opened the way for Democratic liberals to support the measure without prompting southerners to abandon it. During the predawn hours of 2 August, the Senate passed the O'Mahoney-Kefauver-Church amendment, fifty-one to forty-two, a vote that featured the defection of twelve Republicans from Knowland's contingent. When President Eisenhower awoke on the morning of 2 August, he obtained the result of the jury trial vote, an outcome that he described as one of the worst defeats suffered during his presidency. He allegedly went on to state his utter disbelief that eighteen southerners could "bamboozle the entire Senate." In contrast to the mordant refrain emanating from the White House, an expansive Harry Byrd wrote Lyndon Johnson on the outcome of the vote, "No one living but yourself could have accomplished what was done last night. . . . I am glad to have had a small part in this great victory." After disposing minor amendments, the Senate, on 7 August, passed House Resolution 6127 seventy-two to eighteen, an event highlighted by the "yea" votes of five southerners: Senators Johnson and Yarborough of Texas, Gore and Kefauver of Tennessee, and George Smathers of Florida. Final enactment of the civil rights act remained unresolved pending the outcome of a joint House-Senate conference on the bill. While waiting for the report, caucus members assessed the 1957 civil rights fight.[58]

Richard Russell took pride in what the southern caucus had achieved. Following passage of the Senate version of the bill, he wrote that "it appears that we have almost accomplished the impossible" in emasculating the civil rights measure. As for the decision not to filibuster, the Georgian

58. CR, Hubert Humphrey, 26 July 1957, 12803 ("fuzz up"); CR, 31 July 1957, 13153–13154 (Church addition); for the result of the jury trial vote, see CR, 1 August 1957, 13296; Time, 12 August 1957, 12; CR, 1 August 1957, 13356; Evans and Novak, Exercise of Power, 128; Adams, Firsthand Report, 342–343 ("bamboozle the entire . . ."); Ambrose, Eisenhower, 444; HB to LBJ, 2 August 1957, Box 9, "Byrd, Harry, F." Folder, Congressional Files, LBJA, LBJL ("no one living . . ."); for final vote, see CR, 7 August 1957, 13900.

observed that many of those who assisted them in weakening the bill wanted something to pass. Rather than risk alienating these friends of the South, the caucus chose to permit a vote as "it was unanimously agreed that this was the wisest course." More than the influence of strategic delay informed this decision. "We never had the strength to kill a gag rule or cloture," served as Russell's assessment of the political situation that compelled the southern contingent to compromise. In early August, many caucus members echoed Russell's sentiments. J. William Fulbright viewed the accomplishments of the group with satisfaction, observing, "I feel that the southern senators have rendered a great service to the entire nation" by rectifying the grievous "defects in the original administration bill." John Sparkman also praised the revisions that emerged in spite of the president, who "put the full weight of his office behind the enactment" of the civil rights measure as originally drafted. Even Strom Thurmond joined his colleagues in celebrating their achievements, calling the jury trial amendment "a great victory for constitutional government." The South Carolinian tempered his praise. "I hope that we are ultimately successful in defeating the bill in its entirety," he stated. Thurmond still grasped at the prospect of victory, whereas the rest of his colleagues by that point had accepted a tactical draw. But Thurmond had great respect for Russell, who "did a magnificent job" in orchestrating the southern opposition, just as he did for Lyndon Johnson, who he deemed instrumental in the success of the jury trial amendment. Although he supported caucus actions thus far, Thurmond continued to question the benefits of a compromise in 1957. He would wait and see what resulted from the conference committee before making up his mind.[59]

After much wrangling, a bipartisan agreement emerged from the conference committee on 23 August. The conferees agreed to limit the jury trial right only to those criminal contempt cases that emerged directly from House

59. RR to David Tyner, 8 August 1957, Box 69, Folder 1, Russell MSS ("it appears that . . ."); RR to Roy V. Harris, 9 August 1957, Box 69, Folder 1, Russell MSS ("it was unanimously . . ."); RR to R. Pate Watson, 6 August 1957, Box 69, Folder 1, Russell MSS ("we never had . . ."); JF to William A. Duerson, 7 August 1957, BCN 126, Folder 9, Fulbright MSS ("I feel that . . ."); JS to Guy D. Roberts, 9 August 1957, 16-A-9, Box 43, Folder 112, Sparkman MSS ("put the full . . ."); ST to E. H. Bowers, 2 August 1957, Box 13, "Legislation—Civil Rights, #4" Folder, Thurmond MSS ("a great victory . . ."); ST to Walter J. Brown, 5 August 1957, Box 13, Folder 6, Thurmond MSS ("did a magnificent . . .").

Resolution 6127 in which the penalty would likely exceed three hundred dollars or forty-five days of imprisonment and to set the maximum possible reproof under the bill at one thousand dollars or six months' incarceration. On 27 August, the revised bill easily passed in the House. The Senate planned to debate the issue the following day. Southerners could still filibuster, an option made more likely by the changes made to the pivotal jury trial amendment. Caucus members found the alterations in the jury trial provision of Resolution 6127 disappointing. How could one put a price tag on the privilege of a jury trial, one of the most important rights afforded to all Americans, southerners wondered? But most in the caucus accepted the outcome, if for no other reason than Richard Russell thought it advisable. Upon receiving the conference report, the caucus met to discuss its response. At the time, the southern group decided not to conduct an organized filibuster, but agreed that each individual could voice his opposition to the bill as he saw fit. The meeting adjourned with that general agreement reached, as all caucus decisions, by unanimous consent. Several days later, Strom Thurmond began second guessing the group's decision. Concerned, he approached Russell and requested that the Georgian reconvene the group to consider a possible filibuster. Russell, however, had made up his mind and refused to hold another caucus meeting. Thurmond remained convinced that the South could defeat the bill, but for one impediment; Russell wanted to elect Lyndon Johnson president, and to do so he had to remove the sectional tint from his friend. Only one thing could help him accomplish that goal. Johnson had to be seen as a candidate who transcended his southern heritage by possessing a moderate civil rights record. A civil rights bill in 1957 that emerged as a result of the majority leader's actions would go a long way toward achieving that end. Unbowed, Thurmond decided he would observe the letter not necessarily the spirit of the caucus agreement.[60]

60. For background on the conference committee's actions, see *Time,* 12 August 1957, 11; *Newsweek,* 2 September 1957, 18–19; *Time,* 2 September 1957, 14; LBJ to Adlai Stevenson, 12 August 1957, Box 9, "Stevenson, Adlai [1952–1963]" Folder, Famous Names, LBJA, LBJL; statement, AFL-CIO, 13 August 1957, Box 289, "Judiciary—Civil Rights—1957" Folder, Senate Papers, LBJL. The House passed the amended bill, 279 to 97. *CR,* 27 August 1957, 16112–16113; for the actions of the southern caucus and Strom Thurmond, see Oral History, Strom Thurmond by Robert Mann, 10 August 1989, Robert Mann Collection, Oral History Collection, Hill Memorial Library, Louisiana State University, Baton Rouge. See also JS to the Editor, *Time,* 6 September 1957, Box 14, "Legislation: Civil Rights Filibuster, Folder 1" Folder, Thurmond MSS.

184 DELAYING THE DREAM

Early on 28 August 1957, Strom Thurmond headed to the Senate gymnasium for an extended bout in the steam room. Thurmond's office staffers knew his prolonged sauna visit could only mean one thing—he was readying himself for a filibuster. Throughout the legislative battle over civil rights, southerners adopted some unusual methods of ensuring that they could maintain extended speeches on the Senate floor. In perhaps an apocryphal story, Russell Long once recounted that his father Huey always wore dark suits on the days he planned on delivering lengthy speeches. Unbeknownst to his Senate colleagues, the dark clothing enabled Huey to urinate while standing at his desk without having to relinquish the floor. Others inserted catheters that connected to plastic bags taped to their legs. These senators could thus relieve themselves in a less unseemly manner than Russell Long's father. Either way, they achieved the desired result. Thurmond's choice of taking extensive steams went toward a similar end. The heavy perspiration produced in the sauna led to dehydration. By the time Thurmond ambled to the Senate with a handful of throat lozenges later that evening, he had experienced a considerable loss of water weight. When he began his speech at 8:54 p.m. on 28 August, Thurmond could occasionally sip water without fear of having to answer nature's call since his body absorbed the liquid like a sponge.[61]

Thurmond's method apparently worked, as he pilloried the civil rights bill in a record-setting twenty-four-hour, eighteen-minute speech that began with his reading all of the voting rights laws in the forty-eight state constitutions. With so many voting provisions on the books, he noted that a bill providing even further suffrage protections would achieve little. The uselessness of Resolution 6127 served as the meta-theme in his often rambling oration that denied the deliberate disfranchisement of southern blacks. Moments before he concluded, Thurmond noted to the chamber, "I expect to vote against the bill." Laughter followed the comment which seemed so self-evident at that point in the marathon oration. At the end of Thurmond's address, the Senate moved quickly to a vote on 6127 as amended by the conference committee. The bill passed by a margin of sixty to fifteen. George Smathers's decision to vote nay this time because of the change in the jury trial provision represented the only significant alteration in southern voting behavior.

61. For filibuster techniques, see Woods, *Fulbright*, 301, and especially the account of former Texas senator John Tower: John G. Tower, *Consequences: A Personal and Political Memoir* (Boston: Little, Brown, 1991), 167–168; for Thurmond's actions, see Cohodas, *Strom Thurmond*, 294–297.

Not surprising, Thurmond's actions produced some criticism against other southern senators from their constituents who questioned their decision not to join the South Carolinian.[62]

On 30 August 1957, Richard Russell leveled the final broadside against the civil rights measure, just as he addressed himself to the decision not to filibuster, now called into question by Thurmond's antics. The Georgian's critique of the bill rehashed the concepts he had earlier developed in that he denounced the legislation as a politically inspired effort to curry favor with bloc voters and as a ruse to place inordinate power in the hands of the attorney general to undermine the southern racial order. Although he never mentioned the South Carolinian by name, Russell reserved his harshest criticism for Thurmond. He contended that the caucus unanimously agreed to compromise, knowing that this decision would not play well in the South. They could not risk a filibuster that would so arouse Senate sentiment as to provoke a successful cloture bid and a move to return the teeth to the bill extracted during the debate. The caucus, according to Russell, lived "in mortal fear" during the previous few weeks of an attempt to return some portion of Title III that would approve "the race-mixing decision of the Supreme Court of May 1954." Political expediency dictated a filibuster, but Russell observed, had he bowed to such pressure, "I would have forever reproached myself for being guilty of a form of treason against the people of the South." This statement, by implication, accused Thurmond of undertaking just such a treasonable action, risking the goodwill of the Senate forged through compromise for temporary political advantage. Lest anyone doubt his fidelity to "the southern way of life," Russell concluded by explaining that he would part with his own life "if this would guarantee the preservation of a civilization of two races of unmixed blood in the land I love." His speech in many ways became a form of damage control, an effort to undermine the positive publicity Thurmond's actions received in the South. Other members of the southern caucus, recognizing the public relations nightmare unleashed by the South Carolinian, began formulating their own response to the controversy produced by the filibuster that never was, but, in the eyes of many, should have been. They prepared for a possible backlash that might lead to

62. Thurmond filibuster begins: CR, 28 August 1957, 16263. Thurmond filibuster ends: CR, 29 August 1957, 16456 ("I intend to . . ."). For the final vote, see CR, 29 August 1957, 16478.

their own electoral defeat with a propaganda campaign aimed at regaining any lost constituent support.[63]

In explaining their decision not to filibuster, participants in the southern caucus emphasized several themes First, they stressed that only through the goodwill of their colleagues were they able to remove Title III from the bill and to insert the jury trial amendment. They wished to maintain this goodwill for future legislative battles when they faced more insidious proposals. Second, they stressed the difficulty of maintaining a filibuster that theoretically would have had to last until 2 January 1959, the official end of the Eighty-fifth Congress. A cloture effort would likely have emerged to stop the filibuster before that point. Southerners feared that it might have succeeded and thereby created a precedent for such action in the future. If cloture failed, then undoubtedly there would emerge a new effort to drastically alter Rule 22 at the start of the next session. No matter which path they chose, many potential pitfalls existed. Following the dictates of strategic delay, the caucus opted for the one choice with the least potential for damaging their strength in future fights—compromise.

Noting the necessity of changing their tactics, Sam Ervin observed that "we no longer enjoy the benefit of conditions which used to exist . . . and that in consequence we will have to fight Civil Rights Bills in the future as we fought this particular bill, by appeals to the reason of our fellow senators." Circumstances had changed and, along with it, the southern caucus altered its tactics within the context of strategic delay. Their goal of preserving segregation remained the same, even though their means of achieving that end shifted from defeating all significant civil rights bills to emasculating substantive measures through compromises. Caucus veteran Allen Ellender depicted the southern strategy in 1957 as "a course of action designed to obtain the maximum results from the meager amount of bargaining power our small group possessed." Earlier in the year, Ellender believed a filibuster would succeed, only later did he change his course. Once he did, he attempted to convince himself and his electorate that a filibuster would prove disastrous. Also important, southern senators needed to reassure their constituents that they remained firmly committed to the preservation of regional racial norms. Another veteran caucus crusader Lister Hill, for example, calmed worried Alabamians

63. *CR*, 30 August 1957, 16660 ("in mortal fear . . .") and ("I would have . . ."), 16662 ("if this would . . .").

by employing the prevailing southern script. Stressing his undiminished fidelity to Jim Crow, Hill said, "I will continue to uphold and defend our southern customs, traditions and way of life, which are so dear to you, to me and our people of Alabama and the South." As for the man who spawned the filibuster furor, Thurmond refused then or ever after to question the justness of his position. "The South has already compromised too much," Thurmond stated, "and has received nothing in return therefor. I do not see how we can continue to compromise away our principles." Thurmond's analysis tends to obfuscate the realities of the situation. Once the caucus permitted votes on substantive amendments to the bill, they had then placed themselves in a position that they could not abandon. At the start of the debate, a majority of both parties supported the bill. By raising doubts about certain facets of the legislation, southerners succeeded in considerably weakening the proposal. Left with a mere stump of the original measure, they could not then decide, after pleading with their colleagues for assistance, to kill the entire bill. Such an action would certainly have elicited the dire consequences noted by Russell. In 1957, the southern caucus reached a grave decision and in the end adopted a course that very likely extended the legislative battle against civil rights for several years. They had fulfilled their objective of slowing the push against segregation within the framework of strategic delay by emasculating a bill that at the start of 1957 appeared destined for success.[64]

The southern caucus could not have achieved victory without the assistance of Lyndon Johnson who immediately became closely associated with the civil rights bill that derived in large part from his machinations. Accolades from Democratic congressmen and party officials poured into Johnson's office. Clinton Anderson called his handling of the bill "magnificent" and added, "I am sure you saved the Democratic Party from a serious split." Two-time Democratic presidential nominee Adlai Stevenson wrote Johnson that "the civil rights debate certainly has been another major test of your extraordinary management of our Democratic majority." Former secretary of state

64. SE to Robert D. Keziah, 16 September 1957, Box 22, Folder 1378, Ervin MSS ("we no longer . . ."); AE to J. P. Sanders, 1 September 1957, Box 705, "Legislation—Civil Rights—1957" Folder, Ellender MSS ("a course of . . ."); LH to W. H. Bruce, 4 September 1957, Box 493, Folder 42, Hill MSS ("I will continue . . ."). For another example of the southern script, see JS to Loyd L. Riddle, 27 August 1957, ACC 16-A-9, Box 430, Folder 112, Sparkman MSS; ST to Thomas W. Waring, 4 September 1957, Box 14, "Legislation: Civil Rights Filibuster," Folder 1, Thurmond MSS ("The South has . . .").

Dean Acheson penned a hyperbolic tribute of his own, deeming the legislation as "among the greatest achievements since the war." In dealing with constituents, Johnson touted his role in removing the "notorious" Title III and in procuring a jury trial amendment. At the time, he did not intimate a shift toward support of civil rights, but offered instead the resigned comment: "I could not vote against a guarantee [the right to vote] which we deem essential for our Texas citizens." Johnson walked an ideological tightrope of satisfying the Democratic majority and placating his constituents in an effort to maintain his position in both spheres against the threat posed by civil rights.[65]

Despite his efforts to deflect southern criticism, Johnson could not avoid it since his role in the bill's passage had been the subject of national media attention. A comprehensive public relations campaign served as the only method of dispelling constituent doubts. He responded to the great number of accusatory letters from Texans by highlighting his role in improving a "vicious" piece of legislation against the combined weight of the "President, the Vice president and the Attorney General." Any question of his sponsorship of the bill elicited the comment: "After the House of Representatives had passed and sent to the Senate a bill I considered not a good bill, I worked hard to make improvements on it." In answering queries related to his reluctance to assist Strom Thurmond in filibustering, Johnson acceded to Richard Russell's authority, claiming that "he [Russell] demonstrates to my mind, conclusively that it was not possible to block this legislation" and "it would have been dangerous to allow the bill, restricted as it is, to die at this session of congress [sic]." As majority leader, Johnson certainly possessed the power to obstruct the legislation, but he demurred in order to avoid "a drastic bill which would have covered every phase of the segregation problem." An analysis of his correspondence reveals that Johnson routinely emphasized the bill's restricted nature, by frequently commenting, "this bill seeks merely to insure to all Americans what we in Texas already possess [the right to vote]." Continuing the stratagem of illusion, he once again obscured the bill's components by accentuating the baleful results his actions prevented. Like Tennesseans Gore

65. Clinton Anderson to LBJ, 12 August 1957, "Anderson, Clinton P.," Box 39, Congressional Files, LBJA, LBJL; Adlai Stevenson to LBJ, 19 August 1957, "Stevenson, Adlai [1952–1963]," Box 9, Famous Names, LBJA, LBJL; Dean Acheson to LBJ, 13 August 1957, "Civil Rights Correspondence," Box 408, Senate Papers, LBJL; LBJ to Wiley A. Dyer, 15 August 1957, "Judiciary—Civil Rights—1957," Box 289, Senate Papers, LBJL; LBJ to Sgt. Joseph R. Martin, 5 September 1957, LBJL.

and Kefauver, Johnson took tentative steps in the direction of civil rights, but he did not outpace the ideological tendencies of his fellow Texans. In 1957, Lyndon Johnson was a Texan first, a national politician second. As president in the 1960s, Lyndon Johnson reversed his outlook, being an American first and a Texan second. This shift in outlook would make all the difference in the world. Before the transformation, Johnson provided the southern caucus with crucial breathing room under the guise of compromise.[66]

Richard Russell received considerable praise for his actions as commander of the southern opposition. Lyndon Johnson, for one, wrote his mentor, "there is only one word to adequately describe Dick Russell—superb." Fellow Georgian Herman Talmadge also voiced his approval of the caucus leader, exclaiming "when the history of this century is written, it will have a prominent niche for the tremendous role which Dick Russell played in the preservation of constitutional government and the right of the people." Regarding the decision not to filibuster that ultimately rested with Russell, J. William Fulbright wrote the southern commander, "Your restraint and wisdom and good judgement have never been better, and I think we are in the best shape we have ever been in the country, thanks primarily to you." Fulbright perhaps overstated the outcome of the fight. Soon the impotence of the bill became readily apparent even before the commencement of litigation under the new measure.[67]

To most observers, House Resolution 6127 represented more symbol than substance. Once again the Senate had the opportunity to pass judgment on a significant civil rights bill passed by the House, and once again the chamber fell short of the mark. In 1957, the southern caucus wished to buy time in the legislative battle to preserve Jim Crow. For many years they succeeded in achieving this goal. Their actions in 1957 were designed to ensure the continuation of segregation by providing a sop to civil rights advocates that would

66. LBJ to John V. Levy, 17 September 1957, "Civil Rights Correspondence Related to LBJ's Senate Bill # 1 of 2," Box 290, Senate Papers, LBJL; LBJ to Paul E. Wise, 28 August 1957, "Judiciary—Civil Rights—1957," Box 289, Senate Papers, LBJL; LBJ to Joseph Dale, 17 September 1957, "Civil Rights Correspondence Related to LBJ's Senate Bill # 1 of 2," Box 290, Senate Papers, LBJL; LBJ to Luther B. Finley, 30 August 1957, "Judiciary—Civil Rights—1957," Box 289, Senate Papers, LBJL; LBJ to Margine S. Laidlaw, 29 August 1957, LBJL.

67. LBJ to RR, 8 August 1957, Box 3, Folder 5, Russell MSS ("there is only . . ."); HT to Harry O. Smith, 9 September 1957, Box 3, Folder 5, Russell MSS ("when the history . . ."); JF to RR, 30 August 1957, BCN 126, Folder 110, Fulbright MSS ("your restrain and . . .").

slow the existing activism. But Resolution 6127 barely increased the number of voters and in certain states such as Louisiana the number of registered blacks actually declined following the bill's passage. African Americans would have to procure justice on their own. A new and ultimately successful phase of the civil rights movement was about to begin, prompted in no small measure by southern successes in Washington. Civil rights crusaders now contested southerners for possession of time, only they sought to shrink the temporal distance required to achieve full equality, where Dixie legislators sought to expand it. The winner of the contest would decide the fate of Jim Crow.[68]

Caucus actions following the *Brown* verdict illustrate the powerful forces exerted on southern politicians in the era of civil rights. During the writing of the Southern Manifesto and the strategy meetings against the Eisenhower bill, southern senators battled, often heatedly, over adopting a hard line or a more conciliatory response. So long as Richard Russell headed the caucus, something like "moderation" usually won out. And for the most part, other southerners followed. Even the man credited with coining the phrase "massive resistance," Harry Byrd, fell in line with the rest. Temperate actions in Washington did not trickle down to the local level. As the grass-roots protest movement began revving up, employing the nonviolent strategy successfully demonstrated in Montgomery, Alabama, and Baton Rouge, Louisiana, many white southerners whipped to a frenzy by white activist groups, such as the Citizens' Councils, dug in, refusing to relent. Tensions steadily rose. Every moment the likelihood of violence increased.

68. In 1956, 155,460 black Americans were registered to vote in Louisiana. In 1959, that number decreased to 150,235. Pamphlet, Public Affairs Research Council of Louisiana, *Democratic Primary, 5 December 1959, PAR Analysis* (January 1960): 6–8, Box 556, Folder 26, Long MSS.

5. Victory through Compromise

ON 9 SEPTEMBER 1957, President Dwight Eisenhower signed House Resolution 6127 into law, an event marking the enactment of the first civil rights bill since Reconstruction. This noteworthy occurrence received limited media attention because, the previous week, Arkansas governor Orval Faubus had activated the National Guard, ostensibly to prevent violence following the federal court ordered desegregation of Little Rock Central High School. Although Faubus's actions prevented a violent clash at the commencement of fall classes, the Guardsmen's presence strained the administration's patience because they also hindered the enforcement of the court's order. After several failed attempts at reconciliation with the obdurate governor, Eisenhower sent in troops from the 101st Airborne and federalized the National Guard to force compliance with the desegregation order. The presence of federal troops in the South evoked parallels to Reconstruction and prompted widespread condemnation from segregationists. President Eisenhower's actions particularly surprised southern senators. During the civil rights debate earlier that year, the caucus succeeded in removing Title III from Resolution 6127 to prevent just such a use of force. At the time they did not fully recognize that the president already possessed the power to quiet domestic unrest through military action and that Eisenhower was prepared to use it.[1]

1. For a sampling of the literature dealing with Little Rock, see Adams, *Firsthand Report,* 351–359; Melba Beals, *White Is a State of Mind: A Memoir* (New York: G. P. Putnam's Sons, 1999); Branch, *Parting the Waters,* 222–224; Robert Burk, *The Eisenhower Administration and Black Civil Rights* (Knoxville: University of Tennessee Press, 1984); Ernest Q. Campbell, *Christians in Racial Crisis: A Study of the Little Rock Ministry* (Washington, D.C.: Public Affairs Press,

Following the Little Rock imbroglio, Richard Russell sent a blistering telegram to the president. In it, he condemned Eisenhower's "highanded and illegal methods" and speculated that the administration intended to "intimidate and overawe all the people of the country who are opposed to the mixing of races by force." When describing the incident to constituents, the Georgian labeled Eisenhower's tactics as "totalitarian" and "Hitler-like," stating that the president relied on "the American version of Storm Troopers" against "defenseless civilians." Far from achieving any positive end, Eisenhower's actions, according to Russell, not only set back southern race relations but also undermined national unity at the height of the Cold War.[2]

Harry Byrd, Virginia's champion of massive resistance, joined Russell in condemning the Little Rock episode. Rather than breaking the will of the South, Byrd speculated that Little Rock would "intensify existing bitterness, and will strengthen the resistance of the southern people to enforced integration." By the end of 1957 the Virginian's conviction had grown that the push for civil rights would "mellow" since he did not think "the President or anyone else realized the intense opposition on the part of the South until recent months." National outrage over the "invasion" of Little Rock, the unexpected strength of the southern fight against desegregation, and the Republican Party's failure to win over black voters despite its recent support for civil rights legislation would, Byrd believed, produce a slackening in the political pressure against the South. Massive resistance once more appeared to offer the promise of success. If the South continued demonstrating its fierce

1959); Tony Allen Freyer, *The Little Rock Crisis: A Constitutional Interpretation* (Westport, Conn.: Greenwood Press, 1984); John A. Kirk, *Redefining the Color Line: Black Activism in Little Rock Arkansas, 1940–1970* (Gainesville: University Press of Florida, 2002); Michael J. Klarman, "How Brown Changed Race Relations: The Backlash Thesis," *Journal of American History* 81 (June 1994): 81–118; George R. Metcalf, *From Little Rock to Boston: The History of School Desegregation* (Westport, Conn.: Greenwood Press, 1983); Reed, *Faubus;* Irving J. Spitzberg Jr., *Racial Politics in Little Rock, 1954–1964* (New York: Garland, 1987).

2. RR to Dwight Eisenhower, 26 September 1957, Box 133, Folder 6, Russell MSS ("highhanded") and ("intimidate . . ."); RR to Kenneth Westling, 26 September 1957, Box 133, Folder 6, Russell MSS ("totalitarian"); RR to Henry Kuizengg, 2 October 1957, Box 133, Folder 1, Russell MSS ("defenseless . . ."); RR to Zack D. Carvery, 4 October 1957, Box 133, Folder 1, Russell MSS ("the American version . . ."); RR to Zack D. Carvery, 4 October 1957, Box 133, Folder 1, Russell MSS; RR to Henry Kuizengg, 2 October 1957, Box 133, Folder 1, Russell MSS ("Hitler-like"); RR to Ken Westling, 26 September 1956, Box 133, Folder 6, Russell MSS (national unity).

opposition to integration, then it remained plausible that all but the most dedicated civil rights activists would relinquish their crusade. Southerners always devised their civil rights strategy with public opinion in mind. Some, such as Byrd, believed that most northerners did not support the objectives of the civil rights movement and would blanch in the face of stiff resistance, as had occurred during the first Reconstruction, rather than engage in a protracted war against the southern people.[3]

James Strom Thurmond could not have agreed more with Byrd regarding the efficacy of southern defiance. Unlike Byrd, however, Thurmond conflated the southern caucus's failure to conduct a campaign of massive resistance earlier in the year with the events in Arkansas. The South Carolinian claimed that the president's actions at Little Rock resulted, in part, from the "overwhelming" passage of the 1957 Civil Rights Act, a bill Thurmond believed the caucus could have defeated. Unchastened by caucus criticism of his renegade filibuster earlier that year, he publically stated that "the Congress . . . may have created a climate in which he [Eisenhower] and his advisors thought actions of this nature would meet approval." Despite Thurmond's speculation, his argument apparently did not strike a resonant chord with the majority of the southern electorate as most of Dixie's Senate delegation faced little criticism for their decision not to join the South Carolinian in his solo filibuster that year. Administrative assistants in the offices of Russell Long and John Stennis, for example, reported that they had "received almost nothing except commendation" from constituents regarding the southern compromise. Only Majority Leader Lyndon Johnson faced substantive constituent speculation that linked his role in passing House Resolution 6127 with Eisenhower's actions during the Little Rock crisis. Even this criticism, according to a Johnson staffer, proved far less than expected. While remaining taciturn to the national media, Johnson frequently explained to Texans that "all the actions now taking place have been performed under laws which have been on the books for many years." With the exception of Johnson, most caucus members simply dispelled any connection between their tacit acceptance of the Civil

3. Speech, 25 September 1957, Box 410, "Statement—25 September 1957 on sending Federal Troops into Arkansas to Enforce School Integration" Folder, Byrd MSS; HB to William M. Tuck, 10 December 1957, Box 262, "Tuck, William M., 1957–1960" Folder, Byrd MSS ("intensify existing bitterness . . ."); HB to James J. Kilpatrick, 8 November 1957, Box 245, "Kilpatrick, James J." Folder, Byrd MSS ("mellow") and ("the President or . . .").

Rights Act of 1957 and the events in Little Rock by promptly condemning the president's use of force. As some southerners denounced the federal "invasion" of Arkansas, others took a cautious approach, again illustrating that caucus opinion following *Brown* proved anything but monolithic.[4]

Arkansas Senator J. William Fulbright had a great deal of interest in the Little Rock confrontation. Only a few months before the event he had praised his constituents for meeting the *Brown* decision "with a minimum of rancor." By September 1957, the senator's assessment of race relations in Arkansas required some amending. Rather than denouncing the president like many of his colleagues, Fulbright focused his criticism on Governor Orval Faubus, whom he labeled "a small man from the hills." He observed, "The most dangerous thing is that I believe the Governor now senses he has a vehicle for publicity and notice, and that he will not permit it to be solved or even calmed down until after the next election." Although he lamented the media's portrayal of Arkansans as "narrow minded" and "bigoted people," Fulbright remained out of the controversy altogether, despite his strong belief that resistance to desegregation orders as attempted by Faubus inevitably produced violence.[5]

In subsequent years, other southern senators discovered that actions taken by racial demagogues in Dixie directly undermined their ability to convince their colleagues that the South could cure its own ills without outside intervention. Little Rock clearly revealed that, at least in certain southern locales, politicians and law enforcement officials lacked the resources, and very often the desire, to settle racial disputes in a calm manner. At the same time, southern moderates such as Fulbright bear at least some of the responsibility

4. *CR*, 85th Cong., 2nd sess., 18 August 1958, 18210 ("overwhelming") and ("the Congress . . ."); Joseph A. Todd to RL, 7 September 1957, Box 67, "Administrative Assistant Files" Folder, Long MSS ("received almost nothing . . ."); Mooney, *LBJ*, 99–100; LBJ to Young Democrats of San Angelo, Texas, 24 September 1957, Box 290, "Correspondence Related to LBJ's Senate Bill # 1 of 2" Folder, Senate Papers, LBJL ("all the actions . . ."); Robert G. Baker to LBJ, 20 September 1957, Box 1, "Baker, Robert G., 1953–1957" Folder, Pre-Presidential Confidential File, LBJL; LBJ to John Levy, 17 September 1957, Box 290, "Civil Rights Correspondence Related to LBJ's Senate Bill # 1 of 2" Folder, Senate Papers, LBJL.

5. *CR*, 23 July 1957, 12448 ("with a minimum . . ."); JF to H. Charles Johnston, 28 October 1957, Series 66:3, Box 8, Folder 3, Fulbright MSS ("narrow minded") and ("bigoted people"); JF to Fred M. Pickens Jr., 28 October 1957, Series 66:3, Box 8, Folder 3, Fulbright MSS ("a small man . . .").

for episodes of racial turmoil in the South. The Arkansan's actions following the federal intervention at Little Rock exemplified the failure of moderate leadership in the post-*Brown* South. As the situation in Arkansas deteriorated, Fulbright avoided taking a public stand, despite his private criticism of Governor Faubus. His silence spoke volumes, providing tacit support to the campaign of massive resistance orchestrated by the governor. The Arkansan feared making public his private sentiments because he believed his constituents would reward such honesty with an election day defeat. Racial moderation was a political death sentence for southern politicians because it often produced a reactionary counterpoise that appealed to the passions of the masses and thereby undermined the possibility of a rational analysis of the integration question. The defeat of racial progressives, Claude Pepper and Frank Graham, in conjunction with the post-*Brown* victories of Herman Talmadge, Strom Thurmond, and Sam Ervin, all of whom fiercely opposed integration, also reaffirmed the conception held by some moderates that southern opinion tended toward extremism on the race question. Rather than risk defeat, many moderates demonstrated their profound distrust of their electorates by allowing the demagogues to shape the region's response to integration. In a battle of ideas, moderates thought their constituents would chose extremism so these politicians frequently paid lip service to the reactionaries or remained silent.

After the tumultuous events of 1957, politicians who departed from the prevailing attitude of southern defiance sometimes faced difficulty. With his reelection pending in 1958, Albert Gore Sr. could not risk appearing too progressive on racial matters even in moderate Tennessee and especially not following Little Rock. Civil rights played a significant role in Tennessee's 1958 senatorial election as Gore's opponent in the Democratic primary, Prentice Cooper, made the incumbent's failure to sign the Southern Manifesto the central issue of his campaign. Sensing the strength of this argument, Gore deliberately distorted his role in emasculating the 1957 Civil Rights Act. "I worked vigorously to eliminate the extreme provisions" of the Eisenhower bill, he claimed, and "take pride in the fact that these efforts were successful." Gore did vote for the amendments that weakened the 1957 proposal, but he participated little in the debate and certainly far less than fellow Tennessean Estes Kefauver, whose jury trial amendment made the bill palatable to southerners. Like Claude Pepper in his ill-fated 1950 reelection bid, the incumbent downplayed the extent of his break from the southern caucus to salvage his political career. Unlike Pepper's efforts, however, Gore's attempt to whitewash his record proved successful. Despite his suspect civil rights stance in 1957, Tennesseans indicated that they accepted Gore's explanation by anointing him with another six-year term. His victory came by a narrower margin than he anticipated over a candidate who began the campaign with little name recognition. After six years of service, Gore only increased his share of the vote by 2.5 percent over his 1952 total, and in that election he faced longtime incumbent Kenneth McKellar. Nonetheless, his victory revealed that many Tennesseans did not cast their ballots based exclusively on a candidate's stand on racial matters. Had Gore hailed from the Deep South, he undoubtedly would have lost his seat. His triumph in the rim South highlighted a larger national political trend toward greater liberalism.[6]

Electoral returns in 1958 revealed a leftward turn in national public opinion, a shift that swelled the Senate's Democratic majority from two to thirty individuals. Lyndon Johnson, who had previously rallied party unity by stressing the slim Democratic hold on the chamber, soon found himself challenged by the influx of Senate liberals. Rumors circulated that the swollen liberal ranks would attempt to install one of their own in the majority leader post. But in 1959 Johnson had the backing of the Senate's most influential members who just happened to come from below the Mason-Dixon line and

6. For an example of Gore's explanation for his actions during the 1957 civil rights fight, see AG form letter, 26 July 1957, Issue Mail 1957, A22, Civil Rights, Gore MSS; for examples of Gore's emphasis on jury trial amendment and removal of Section III, see AG to B. F. Viar, 22 July 1958, Spec., D-31, "General—Civil Rights—1956" Folder, Gore MSS; AG to C. T. Osborn, 10 June 1958, Spec D-31, Folder: "General—Civil Rights—1956," Gore MSS; AG to James Stokely, 3 April 1957, B 53, "Legislation—Judiciary—Civil Rights—1957, 1 of 4" Folder, Gore MSS; AG to Claude B. Stevenson, 29 July 1957, B 53, "Legislation—Judiciary—Civil Rights—1957, 2 of 4" Folder, Gore MSS; AG to Lawrence D. Wilson, 22 July 1957, B 53, "Legislation—Judiciary—Civil Rights—1957–3 of 4" Folder, Gore MSS; AG to W. Houston Igou, 18 September 1957, B 53, "Legislation-Judiciary—Civil Rights—1957, 4 of 4" Folder, Gore MSS; AG to George Cloys, 2 August 1957," B 53, "Legislation—Judiciary—Civil Rights—1957, 4 of 4" Folder, Gore MSS; AG to C. T. Osborn, 10 June 1958, Special Series D-31, "General—Civil Rights—1958" Folder, Gore MSS ("I worked vigorously . . ."); see also AG to B. F. Viar, 22 July 1958, Special Series D-31, "General—Civil Rights—1958" Folder, Gore MSS. In 1952, Gore received 334,957 votes or 56.5 percent of the total. Six years later, his margin of victory expanded slightly to 375,439 votes or 59 percent of the total. Congressional Quarterly, *Guide to U.S. Elections* (Washington, D.C.: Congressional Quarterly, 1975), 916.

who found his moderate brand of leadership to their liking. Southerners still considered the Texan their best option for defeating substantive civil rights legislation. Considered by many the most powerful man in the chamber, Richard Russell believed Johnson, "who stands four-square against compulsory integration," the only Democrat suitable to hold the post of party leader. Keeping the Texan in the position thus became a priority for the Georgian, a goal he accomplished with minimal opposition at the Democratic caucus prior to both sessions of the Eighty-sixth Congress. The prospect of a southern victory in the ongoing struggle against civil rights seemed less certain.[7]

On the eve of the Eighty-sixth Congress in 1959, it became apparent that the southern compromise in 1957 did not arrest the forward momentum of the civil rights crusade. Advocates for black equality continued pushing their agenda, prompting North Carolinian Sam Ervin to note, "some members of both parties north of the Mason-Dixon line devote themselves principally to the task of reconstructing the South." Pressure to change the southern racial order had long troubled southern senators whose principle of strategic delay both recognized the inevitability of increased civil rights activism and aimed at mitigating its impact. Soon the caucus would face another effort to amend Rule 22, a parliamentary weapon they needed now more than ever because of the leftward shift in the Senate's ideological midpoint. To meet that challenge, southern senators would resort to many of the arguments they employed in the 1949 rules fight. How their line of reasoning would play before a Senate chamber considerably more liberal than its predecessors became the central question when Vice President Richard Nixon called the Senate to order at the start of the Eighty-sixth Congress on 7 January 1959.[8]

Southern leader Richard Russell claimed that those advocating a rule change "are dressing it up with camouflage and also with the racial question, and this of course weakens the influence of the southerners in the fight." Ac-

7. Mooney, LBJ, 108–109. Johnson would face liberal challenges to his leadership for the remainder of his Senate career. For some examples, see Dallek, Lone Star Rising, 539–540, 548–549, 561–562; Washington Post, 4 January 1960, A9; Washington Post, 8 January 1960, A1; see also William Proxmire of Wisconsin's scathing rebuke of Johnson's leadership: CR, 86th Cong., 1st sess., 23 February 1959, 2816; RR to J. A. Stubbs, 11 September 1958, Box 186, Folder 21, Russell MSS ("who stands . . .").

8. SE to K. B. Pace, 2 December 1958, Box 29, Folder 1648, Ervin MSS ("some members of . . .").

cording to southern senators, principle guided their opposition to an alteration of the Rules of the Senate, or at least that served as the public expression
of their beliefs. Unlike their northern counterparts, who cared only about
winning black votes, southern senators claimed they wanted to protect both
the sanctity of the Senate as crafted by the founding fathers as well as the interests of all minorities by preserving the strength of the filibuster. However
transparent their arguments proved to some, caucus members nonetheless
sought to provide their colleagues, especially the chamber's conservatives,
an edifying means of disagreeing with a rule change by appealing to their
shared ideological proclivities. At the same time, caucus rhetoric attempted
to deflect claims made by advocates of a rule change that the stringent guidelines governing cloture thwarted legislative action on measures designed to
cure racial injustice in the South. As in 1949, the caucus fought liberal appeals to morality by highlighting the long-term implications of even a minor
alteration in Rule 22. Once again they resurrected their habitual contention
that a limited change would set a precedent for majority cloture, an objective
some members of the Democratic left enthusiastically supported.[9]

Despite southern arguments, some change in the rule appeared likely
considering the circumstances surrounding Lyndon Johnson's 1957 motion to
table Clinton Anderson's resolution, which would have required the Senate
to adopt new rules by a majority vote at the start of each Congress. In 1957,
Johnson and Republican minority leader William Knowland of California
sponsored their own resolution, Senate Resolution 30 (reintroduced as Senate Resolution 5 in 1959), for consideration during the next Congress; when
compared to the alterations advocated by Senate liberals, it barely constituted a change at all. The resolution called for a reduction in the number
needed to invoke cloture from two-thirds of the entire Senate membership
to the same proportion of those present and voting, returning the standard
to its pre-1949 level. Advocates for a substantive change condemned this
provision, arguing that on a cloture vote concerning a major political issue,

9. RR to George L. Neale, 19 December 1958, Box 98, Folder 7, Russell MSS ("are dressing it . . ."); for another example that civil rights lay at the heart of the rule change effort, see CR, 86th Cong., 1st sess. (all subsequent CR citations from same Congress and session until otherwise noted), 12 January 1959, 477 (Ellender); for arguments stressing the sanctity of the Senate, see CR, 8 January 1959, 149–153 (Talmadge), 153–154 (Ervin); CR, 12 January 1959, 468 (Holland); for emphasis on majority cloture, see CR, 9 January 1959, 349 (Thurmond).

such as civil rights, all able-bodied senators would place themselves on record by answering the roll call to limit debate. A successful cloture petition, Senate liberals contended, would thus require an identical number of votes under the new standard as under the old. In addition, the Johnson-Knowland initiative would recognize the Senate as a continuing body, a condition that southerners considered essential. This portion of the resolution would lay to rest liberal efforts to force the chamber to adopt a new set of rules at the start of each Congress on the pretext that the Senate had become a new body. Recognizing that the resolution favored by the Senate leadership fulfilled the objectives of strategic delay, southerners hitched their fate to the ability of the master compromiser, Lyndon Johnson, to sell this mild cloture change to Senate liberals. Southerners, in turn, would not filibuster the proposed alteration in order to demonstrate that they were not obstructionists, all the while knowing that the rule change championed by Johnson did nothing to weaken their defense of segregation.[10]

On 12 January 1959, the Senate voted seventy-two to twenty-two in favor of the leadership-sponsored rule change. Along with the expected defection of the Tennessee and Texas delegations, the senators from North Carolina and Florida also voted yea. Of the twenty-two votes against the resolution, fourteen came from southern hands. These votes, however, proved largely symbolic. Most if not all southerners viewed Johnson's compromise as heavily weighted in their favor considering the ideological makeup of the chamber. They could expect little more. Caucus members who voted against Senate Resolution 5 merely wished to place on record that they considered even a minor alteration in the chamber's rules an assault against the sanctity of the Senate and a departure from the intent of the founders. Despite their public opposition, their private musings after the rules fight demonstrated that they viewed the outcome in sanguine terms. Although voting against the resolution, J. William Fulbright found the change "more acceptable to the South than any of us expected." The Arkansan added that Majority Leader Johnson "has convinced everyone that he is a political genius, not that this endears him to our friends." Louisiana's Russell Long lamented the further "chipping away" of unlimited debate but viewed Johnson's role as es-

10. Transcript, Hubert Humphrey Oral History, 17 August 1971, by Joe B. Frantz, LBJL; *Time*, 19 January 1959, 15. William Knowland did not run for reelection in 1958. The position of minority leader fell to Illinois Republican Everett Dirksen.

sential in preventing "something much worse" from being "forced upon us." Even Strom Thurmond thought the South "came out very well in the Rules change" fight, despite losing "some ground," as its "basic weapons" remained intact "to combat radical legislation."[11]

After the rules battle, the Senate experienced a short-lived lull in civil rights action. Despite the 1957 Civil Rights Act, rampant voter discrimination persisted in the South, as did manifold other forms of racial oppression. Recognizing the continued persecution of southern blacks, many liberal Democrats desired legislation that contained the controversial Title III, that permitted the use of force to compel compliance with judicial decrees, stricken from the 1957 bill. The NAACP also aggressively lobbied for the inclusion of this section in future civil rights proposals. In a press release, the organization claimed that the absence of the provision in subsequent bills would prompt "suspicion that it is a sugar-coated pacifier." Further civil rights legislation was clearly needed. In 1959, President Eisenhower, under pressure from civil rights advocates and cognizant that the 1957 legislation accomplished little, placed the weight of his administration behind several proposals relevant to the racial situation in the South. Taken together, these bills would make transporting explosives across state lines for the purpose of bombing schools or churches a federal offense, extend the life of the Civil Rights Commission created by the 1957 legislation through 1961, make interference with desegregation orders a federal crime, require local voting officials to keep their records for two years, offer financial support to communities undergoing school desegregation, provide federal assistance for the education of servicemen's children in jurisdictions where desegregation efforts disrupted schooling, and put Congress on record in support of the *Brown* decision. Most of the civil rights proposals backed by the administration, along with countless others offered by northern senators, languished for the rest of the year in James Eastland's Judiciary Committee. The Senate only acted favorably on the Civil Rights Commission, which received a

11. For the vote, see *CR*, 12 January 1959, 494; JF to Jack Pickens, 13 January 1959, BCN 99, Folder 4, Fulbright MSS ("more acceptable to . . .") and ("has convinced everyone . . ."); press release, 14 January 1959, Box 24, Folder 39, Long MSS ("chipping away . . ."); ST to Arthur D. Rich, 16 January 1959, Box 5, "Federal Government 2–1–1 (Rule 22—Filibuster) Jan.–Jan. 30, 1959" Folder, Thurmond MSS ("came out very . . ."); ST to Kenneth L. Ackerman, 13 January 1959, Box 5, "Federal Government 2–1–1 (Rule 22—Filibuster) Jan.–Jan. 30, 1959," Folder, Thurmond MSS ("some . . .") ("basic . . ."), and ("to combat . . .").

two-year lease on life. Despite the commission's release of a 668-page report describing the prevalence of discrimination in the South and recommending, among other things, a voter registrar plan, the caucus could not risk blocking its extension because the House prolonged the life of the agency by way of an amendment to the Mutual Security Appropriations bill. To kill the commission, therefore, the caucus would have had to block the entire appropriations measure, an approach that could only hurt their long-term goal of delaying the assault against segregation. As they believed in the past, southern senators hoped this small act would help them secure the goodwill of their colleagues when they faced more sweeping civil rights proposals. In the House, the Rules Committee chaired by archsegregationist Howard Smith of Virginia similarly dragged its feet on the Eisenhower supported initiatives. For progress on civil rights to take place, someone needed to take drastic action. The catalyst for such a push came from an unexpected source.[12]

On 14 September 1959, the last day of the legislative session, Lyndon Johnson, who planned on snaring the Democratic presidential nomination in 1960, announced that he would open discussion on civil rights in mid-February if no action occurred on the issue before that time. No matter what, the Senate would debate a civil rights bill in 1960, a fact that would lead to a new series of challenges as well as decisions for the southern caucus with direct bearing on its ability to maintain segregation. "Whatever legislation is offered," Russell Long noted, "will be met with very substantial opposition from Southern Senators." Caucus members "dodged the first bullet" of the Eighty-sixth Congress during the rules fight. They knew they would not dodge the second.[13]

In 1960, the Eisenhower administration unified its civil rights agenda into a single package and added a voter referee provision. The new addition to the administration's bill would allow federal referees to oversee the electoral ap-

12. Press release, NAACP, 22 January 1959, Box 408, "Civil Rights, Correspondence" Folder, Senate Papers, LBJL ("suspicion that it . . ."); Daniel M. Berman, *A Bill Becomes Law: Congress Enacts Civil Rights Legislation*, 2nd ed. (New York: Macmillan, 1966), 9. H.R. 8385, the Mutual Securities Appropriation bill that contained the amendment to extend the Civil Rights Commission passed in the House, 279 to 136: *CR*, 9 September 1959, 14627–14628. The commission's report became public on 9 September 1959 and H.R. 8385 passed 63 to 25 in the Senate on 14 September 1959. *CR*, 14 September 1959, 19569.

13. Press release, 21 August 1959, Box 595, Folder 42, Long MSS ("Whatever legislation is . . ."); JF to Jack Pickens, 13 January 1959, BCN 99, Folder 4, Fulbright MSS ("dodged the first . . .").

paratus in areas where a "pattern of discrimination" existed. Southern senators found the suffrage provision particularly galling since it resulted, in part, from the recommendation of the Civil Rights Commission—the very same commission the caucus enabled to survive by not filibustering its extension in 1959. Justice Department officials used the evidence of discrimination in the voter registration process uncovered by the commission as a pretext to add a suffrage provision to the president's civil rights package. Instead of the stronger registrar system advocated by the commission, the Eisenhower administration supported the use of court appointed referees, who would not be dispatched until after a lengthy legal process that included successful judicial action under the 1957 Civil Rights Act. Although milder than the registrar plan, the referee proposal alarmed the caucus.[14]

Southern senators responded in a variety of ways to the looming civil rights threat. Seeing no need to address the question of voting rights, which the administration now emphasized as the centerpiece of its civil rights initiative, John Sparkman of Alabama contended, "I believe that we will kill legislation proposed during this session that would mix the races." Despite a lack of germaneness, his comment revealed the true objective of the southern caucus and its strategy of delay. In 1960, maintaining segregation remained the foundation of southern efforts in Washington, just as it had twenty-two years before when the region faced antilynching legislation. So long as they protected Jim Crow, southern senators fulfilled their primary obligation to their white constituents. How long they could continue granting concessions on the periphery of the Jim Crow system as they had in 1957 emerged as an essential question with an uncertain answer. As Sparkman foresaw, southern senators would prevent legislation compelling integration in 1960, but the Alabamian offered his constituents no assurances regarding the immediate challenge of the Eisenhower bill. Unlike Sparkman, Russell Long dealt specifically with the issue at hand, claiming the new suffrage bill would "make it impossible to decline any moron, imbecile, or even convicted criminal the right to vote." Joining Long, Sam Ervin also confronted the question of voting rights. Sufficient legislation to protect an individuals' right to

14. Based on the recommendation of the House Judiciary Committee, the administration also dropped its request for sections that would provide financial support to areas in the process of integrating schools and that would put Congress on record in support of the *Brown* ruling. Berman, *Bill Becomes Law,* 44–45, 54.

vote already existed, the North Carolinian insisted, making further suffrage measures superfluous. His contention strained credulity in light of the low number of registered black voters in the South. Safe now in the Senate for another six years, Tennessee's Al Gore Sr. challenged the mythological portrayal of the region's racial order that Ervin employed by candidly addressing voting irregularities in the region. "Portions of the South . . . simply can not continue to get by with the denial of the right to qualify to vote," he declared. Gore thus openly professed that, except of course in his native Tennessee, discriminatory voting practices existed in Dixie, something his regional colleagues rarely admitted in public. "These are turbulent days for politicians," he lamented, "particularly those from border states who have a conscience." As mid-February approached with the administration backed civil rights bill still mired in the House Rules Committee, Lyndon Johnson took a step that added to the turbulence of the period.[15]

On 15 February 1960, Johnson opened House Resolution 8318, a bill to authorize the secretary of the army to lease a portion of the Fort Crowder military base to the Stella Reorganized School District in Missouri, to nongermane civil rights amendments. Richard Russell was stunned by Johnson's actions, believing his friend would commence the promised debate by preventing an independent civil rights bill, not a rider, from a committee referral as had occurred in 1957. Because of Johnson's maneuver, the southern caucus lost the opportunity to orchestrate a lengthy fight over procedural matters, such as the decision to bypass the Judiciary Committee and the motion to consider the bill. Even more galling to the Georgian, the Armed Services Committee he chaired reported the Stella proposal. Once he regained his composure, Russell denounced the maneuver, claiming that "southern Democrats" are "the only minority which is not supposed to have any rights whatsoever." For Johnson, the situation proved more ennobling than the blatant sectionalism perceived by his mentor, Russell. "The Congress took a long step in this direction [securing voting rights] in the 1957 act," Johnson noted, but "it is apparent that the step was not quite long enough. Further

15. JS to Paul Gunter, 11 January 1960, ACC 17-F-8, Box 349, "Civil Rights—2" Folder, Sparkman MSS ("I believe that . . ."); SE to Ida S. Franks, 1 February 1960, Box 46, Folder 2255, Ervin MSS (sufficient legislation exists); press release, 11 September 1959, Box 595, Folder 46, Long MSS ("make it impossible . . ."); AG to Creed C. Black, 18 January 1960, B 57, "Legislation—Judiciary—1960 (1 of 4)" Folder, Gore MSS ("Portions of the . . .") and ("These are . . .").

action is needed." The next day the Senate voted, twenty-eight to sixty-one, against Russell's motion to postpone consideration of the Stella school bill, a decision that, based on the recent change in Rule 22, indicated that a cloture petition in 1960 might indeed succeed. With that vote, civil rights became the central focus of the Senate. The strong vote against Russell's motion revealed that many in the chamber were, at least for the moment, ready to confront the question of civil rights. Caucus members kept the outcome of that vote close in mind as they mapped their strategy for the session.[16]

With the Fort Crowder bill opened to amendments, Senate civil rights advocates began attaching dozens of proposals to the measure that ran the gamut from new to long-stalled legislation to ameliorate the plight of black Americans. Opponents began referring to the Stella school bill not by name but by its weight, which they variously claimed at five to ten pounds. Olin Johnston noted that it seemed New York senators Jacob Javits and Irving Ives were in a race to see who could add more amendments. "The Senators from New York are the most prolific introducers of bills I have ever seen," he sarcastically observed. The omnibus bill grew cumbersome, making it difficult to discern which of the more than one hundred proposals attached to the Stella measure was actually under discussion at any given time. Faced with this sweeping array of legislation, members of the southern caucus responded with a monumental filibuster that more cynical observers considered their penance for the 1957 compromise. Southern senators could do little else. The ultimate objective of strategic delay remained slowing the legislative drive to abolish segregation by whatever means necessary. Sometimes circumstances demanded a filibuster. At other times a tactical retreat better served their interests. Caucus members recognized that as the omnibus Stella bill grew, it also became less acceptable to the chamber's moderate and conservative statesmen. Soon it appeared that only the most devoted civil rights advocates would support a cloture petition to quiet a filibuster against the ill-defined legislation. Southern senators thus had reasonable confidence they could block the measure

16. *CR*, 86th Cong., 2nd sess. (all subsequent *CR* citations from the same Session and Congress until otherwise noted), 15 February 1960, 2470 (Stella bill opened), 2470–2471 ("southern Democrats . . ."); *CR*, 16 February 1960, 2592 ("The Congress took . . ."); for the vote, see *CR*, 16 February 1960, 2620; *Time*, 29 February 1960, 20; Baton Rouge *States-Item*, 16 February 1960, 1A, 4A.

with an extensive "educational campaign." At the same time, they knew they would be unable to defeat outright a more reasonable proposal, such as the Eisenhower bill, should it reach the Senate. If confronted with the president's legislation, they would have to consider granting concessions because very few senators would look kindly on the obstruction of a mild measure. For the moment, however, no grounds for a compromise existed.[17]

Majority Leader Johnson soon placed a further challenge before the caucus. On Friday, 26 February, he finalized a joint decision with Minority Leader Everett Dirksen of Illinois to begin holding round-the-clock sessions at the start of the next week to break the southern filibuster then in its early stages. He alerted senators to be on call at a moment's notice to answer quorums at any hour of the night. The decision of the Senate leadership touched off considerable acrimony. In particular, several southerners emphasized the health risk posed to the chamber's older members by the pending twenty-four hour marathon sessions, a charge civil rights advocates promptly turned on southern senators, whose filibuster, they argued, precipitated the maneuver. The bill's supporters held that culpability for the deaths of elderly senators would reside with intransigent southerners who threatened to block action on legislation favored by a large majority of the chamber. Despite the risks, the Senate leadership forged ahead with the nonstop sessions, bringing in cots to accommodate civil rights advocates who searched for comfortable sleeping locations in hideaway offices and hallways. For a period, an air of excitement engulfed the chamber, drawing large numbers of visitors to the Senate gallery who desired to steal a glimpse of U.S. senators shuffling to answer quorum calls in pajamas and slippers.[18]

The round-the-clock sessions were far less taxing on the southerners than the maneuver's originators intended. To meet the leadership's challenge, Richard Russell divided his troops into three six-man platoons headed by Lister Hill of Alabama, Allen Ellender of Louisiana, and John Stennis of

17. CR, 4 March 1960, 4549 ("The Senators from . . ."). North Carolina's Sam Ervin estimated the number of bills attached to the Stella proposal at 175: SE to Louis R. Wilson, 3 March 1960, Box 46, Folder 2258, Ervin MSS; and the weight of the legislation at over five pounds: SE to C. H. Hamlin, 29 February 1960, Box 46, Folder 2257, Ervin MSS.

18. Johnson first announced his intentions for round the clock session: CR, 23 February 1960, 3320; debate over health risks: CR, 26 February 1960, 3576; Time, 14 March 1960, 19–20; Newsweek, 7 March 1960, 28–29.

Mississippi. Each team held the responsibility of covering the floor for a twenty-four-hour period, after which its members would disappear for the next two days, avoiding all quorum calls. A southern senator, therefore, would have to speak for no more than four hours every three days. Even this time was abbreviated with the assistance of teammates who spelled orators by asking long, intricate questions. With such organization, Russell's forces appeared unruffled by the extended sessions. But they ensured that their colleagues beyond the Mason-Dixon line received no respite. At irregular hours throughout the night, one caucus member relinquished the floor to another "southern patriot," who then suggested the absence of a quorum, forcing those senators sleeping throughout the building to answer the call. And they did not trifle with convenient times. On the evening of 7 March 1960, for example, the squad responsible for the night shift—John Stennis, Russell Long, and Herman Talmadge—requested quorum calls at 12:00 a.m., 2:30 a.m., and 4:00 a.m. Veteran filibusterers such as Allen Ellender also benefitted from the perks of seniority. The sixty-nine-year-old Louisianan with twenty-five years of Senate service lorded over a hideaway office that allowed him to duck quorum calls throughout the filibuster. In it, he had a couch, a fully stocked refrigerator, and a hot plate. Known for his culinary skills, Ellender often prepared Louisiana specialties for himself and for his southern cohorts during the debate. A new spirit of camaraderie thus took hold of the southern ranks as they rallied together in a fight deemed pivotal to Dixie's interests.[19]

In comparison to the military efficiency of Richard Russell's soldiers, the civil rights forces became frazzled as the filibuster dragged on. Caucus members had long contended that their opponents could break a filibuster if they showed the same level of determination displayed by southern senators. Circumstances in 1960 granted Senate civil rights supporters the opportunity to prove their mettle as the southern forces had done many times in the past. It quickly became apparent that yet again they could not match the well

19. In his memoirs, Herman Talmadge claimed that he suggested to Russell that the caucus divide its members into three teams to limit the strain on southern senators. Herman E. Talmadge, *Talmadge: A Political Legacy, a Politician's Life* (Atlanta: Peachtree, 1987), 185; memo, John Stennis to RL and HT, 7 March 1960, Box 557, Folder 6.1, Long MSS; Jacob K. Javits, *Javits: The Autobiography of a Public Man* (Boston: Houghton Mifflin, 1981), 339; Becnel, *Senator Allen Ellender*, 212; *Newsweek*, 14 March 1960, 24.

organized southern resistance. Faced with a chance to breach the southern citadel in the Senate, civil rights advocates instead grew haggard by sleep disturbing quorum calls. The sweeping scope of the legislation served as one of the primary reasons for their failure. As the Stella bill grew, the Senate's tepid supporters of civil rights lost the will to fight.

With the chamber plodding through marathon sessions, caucus members unleashed a fierce attack against the administration's bill, the civil rights movement in general, and the drive for social equality in particular. Ever since Richard Russell took command of the caucus, he encouraged his soldiers to couch their rhetoric against civil rights as much as possible in legal terms. During the twenty-four-hour-a-day filibuster in 1960, he relaxed some of that discipline, allowing his colleagues to wax long in their defense of Jim Crow. In large part, this departure from more edifying constitutional arguments reflected the nature of the legislative situation. Caucus members did not face a clear bill, but rather one hundred separate items, making a uniform legal critique impossible. More important, however, they recognized the limited prospect of a successful cloture vote. With little chance of the "gag rule" being imposed, they used the opportunity to reassure their constituents that they understood the importance of Jim Crow to the white South. By employing sectional rather than national arguments for significant portions of the Stella debate, southern senators accomplished two important objectives. First, they assuaged any lingering constituent doubts raised by the 1957 civil rights fight that the caucus had lost its resolve. By establishing their bona fides as staunch defenders of white southern interests early in 1960, they hoped their constituents would accept limited concessions later when they confronted the president's suffrage proposal. Second, they aimed to illustrate to outsiders why Jim Crow remained essential, and to do that they necessarily had to narrow the scope of their rhetoric. The emergence of the lunch-counter demonstrations conducted by African Americans against segregated dining establishments that commenced two weeks before Johnson opened the Stella bill to amendments dictated the hardening of southern rhetoric. Caucus members saw in the burgeoning grass-roots movement an enormous threat that called into question the idyllic portrayal of southern race relations that they had used to great effect in earlier civil rights battles. Their mythological depiction of black contentedness under Jim Crow had never faced such a public challenge. Before, protests remained limited to single communities. Now, demonstrations emerged across the South. More than ever, southern senators had to marginalize the protest movement, while attempting to reestablish the credibility of the central myths upon which they built their defense of Jim Crow. In 1960, the caucus came ready to fight.

As in 1957, southern senators drew parallels between the drive for civil rights in 1960 and the Reconstruction era. The Dunning school remained in session. Every challenge to the status quo began looking to white southerners as a potential catalyst for social upheaval. With the black population publically challenging white hegemony, the region's white citizens increasingly viewed legislative initiatives supported by the very outside agitators they believed responsible for the deterioration in southern race relations as designed specifically to punish the South. The term "Second Reconstruction" as employed by historians encompasses one perspective of the civil rights fight. For these scholars, the civil rights crusade in the 1950s and the 1960s succeeded in achieving full legal and political equality for African Americans where the first Reconstruction failed. Southerners also adopted the term "Second Reconstruction" to describe the same period, but they employed it to illustrate a very different point. The parallels they drew were unmistakable. Louisiana's Russell Long, for one, viewed the 1960 legislation as "a willful revival . . . of the philosophy and attitudes of the Reconstruction Era . . . and an attempt to capitalize on that discredited 'bloody shirt' type of political appeal." For the citizens of Dixie, the post-*Brown* era witnessed a precipitous increase in northern efforts to destroy the heritage of the region, just as the Radical Republicans attempted after the Civil War. In 1960, caucus members believed their opponents wished to remake the South in the image of the North. These fears grew more pronounced following the internal combustion of the southern racial order initiated by the proliferation of nonviolent student demonstrations against Jim Crow. Pressure from all angles threatened white southerners, but they had an example from their own region's history that ultimately pointed to the possibility for success. During the "darkest days" of Reconstruction, the white South maintained its struggle and, against what once appeared to them as insufferable odds, succeeded in restoring white rule to the region. Southern senators could not help but recognize the similarity between their fight and that of their ancestors, who returned white supremacy to the region through the Jim Crow system, which Dixie's politicians in the 1960s sought to protect. And what better way for caucus members to highlight their continuity with the principles of their forefathers than by beating back the second Reconstruction just as completely as their predecessors had defeated the first. Southern senators did not mince words when addressing what they considered the inevitable outcome of a federally mandated alteration in the region's racial order. If civil rights advocates continued pushing their proposals, they would not assist southern blacks, but only "roll back the years to 1870—and to engender the hate, the bitterness and the distrust that tore this nation asunder."[20]

Recognizing that voting rights would serve as the central issue in the 1960 battle, most southerners initially focused on the referee provision of the Eisenhower measure rather than the multitude of other proposals attached to the Stella bill. The broad scope of the president's legislation, southerners lamented, made the civil rights debate in 1960 a fight over "the most vicious, iniquitous, revolutionary series of measures" ever discussed in the chamber, including even those items debated during the Reconstruction era. In particular, they stressed that the president's bill struck them as perilously close to previous "force bills," especially the Lodge Fair Elections bill, both in its intent and in its origin. Considered by some the Republican Party's last initiative to preserve the rights it had secured for the freedmen during Reconstruction, the Lodge bill would have enabled circuit courts to appoint federal supervisors to investigate electoral fraud and claims of voter discrimination. In 1960, the administration's civil rights bill, according to caucus members, resurrected the central provisions of the bill that fell to defeat at the hands of a southern filibuster in the 1890s. From the southern perspective, the new referee provision further illustrated that some northerners intended to rally opinion behind a drive to punish the South. Making matters worse, the Lodge proposal applied only to federal elections, whereas the Eisenhower initiative covered the entire electoral process from national to municipal contests.[21]

20. For southern appeals to the historical legacy of Reconstruction, see CR, Long, 16 February 1960, 2613 ("a willful revival . . ."); CR, 17 February 1960, 2735 (Ellender); CR, 18 February 1960, 2866 (Talmadge); CR, 23 February 1960, 3186 (Eastland); CR, 26 February 1960, 3613 (Long); CR, 1 March 1960, 3946 (Hill), 3978 (Fulbright); CR, 8 March 1960, 4850 (Talmadge); CR, Ellender, 8 March 1960, 4950 (" roll back the . . .").

21. Michael Perman, *Struggle for Mastery: Disfranchisement in the South, 1888–1908* (Chapel Hill: University of North Carolina Press, 2001), 39–40. For some of the manifold uses the southern caucus made of the historical legacy of Reconstruction, see CR, 16 February 1960,

Antisouthern bias in line with that found during Reconstruction, caucus members theorized, served as the only explanation for the president's sweeping proposal. Drawing on the archetype of Radical Republican excesses as defined by the Dunning school, some caucus members made reference to Thaddeus Stevens, one of the most reviled men in the region's historical memory, in their orations. After all, it was Stevens who attempted to place "black heels on white necks" during Reconstruction—the very same result they believed their contemporary opponents hoped to accomplish. Stevens ironically faired better in the opinion of southern senators than among Dunning devotees, for even he, caucus members claimed, would never have dreamt of the schemes fashioned by twentieth-century civil rights advocates. In the 1960s, southern senators created their own Thaddeus Stevens by branding New York Republican Jacob Javits with all, and more, of the opprobrium they used to describe his ideological forebear from the Reconstruction period. Indeed, according to Sam Ervin, Javits's "monstrous" proposals "would make Thaddeus Stevens turn over in his grave for envy, out of not having thought of them himself." Through their analysis, caucus members attempted to make clear that civil rights supporters were nothing more than dangerous radicals who would rather divide the country along sectional lines for their own political advantage than seek any real improvement in Dixie. Instead of attempting to understand and assist the South, one caucus member speculated that "the North has arrogated unto itself the position of supervising human relations" in the region. "Sectional tyranny," southerners argued, served as the driving force behind the Eisenhower proposal spuriously labeled a voting rights measure.[22]

Although desirous of turning back the second Reconstruction, caucus members did not have a clear bill to oppose, making the rhetoric at this stage of the debate noteworthy for its absence of uniformity when compared to the 1957 fight. Despite the moniker "voting rights," which accompanied the administration's proposal, its "true object," as that of all civil rights proposals, re-

2613 (Long); *CR*, 17 February 1960, 2735 (Ellender); *CR*, 18 February 1960, 2866 (Talmadge); *CR*, 26 February 1960, 3613 (Long); *CR*, 1 March 1960, 3946 (Hill), 3978 (Fulbright); *CR*, 8 March 1960, 4850 (Talmadge), 4950 (Ellender); *CR*, Eastland, 23 February 1960, 3186 ("the most vicious . . .").

22. For references to Thaddeus Stevens, see *CR*, 18 February 1960, 2866 (Talmadge); *CR*, Ervin, 29 February 1960, 3760 ("monstrous") and ("would make Thaddeus . . ."); *CR*, Fulbright, 8 April 1960, 7732 ("the North has . . .") and ("sectional tyranny").

mained from the southern perspective "the mixing of the races in the schools of the South." Caucus members, of course, exaggerated the bill's contents, but as they conceptualized the civil rights fight, each "anti-South" proposal represented just one aspect of a larger process aimed at dismantling segregation. At the same time, southern senators believed they could not stop, only slow, the forces arrayed against them. These beliefs, codified in the southern doctrine of strategic delay, were the most important concepts in their resistance. They provided a framework from which caucus members since the 1930s had conceptualized their fight against civil rights. From the earliest stages of their struggle, Richard Russell and his colleagues had contended that civil rights advocates had the single objective of destroying segregation, no matter their stated intentions. Each broadening of the legislative battle heightened that perception, lending credence to the concepts that undergirded strategic delay. 1960 proved no different and southern senators viewed their fight that year as one that would have a serious impact on Jim Crow's future.[23]

During the round-the-clock sessions, southern senators focused considerable attention on the deterioration of racial accord in Dixie. Since the *Brown* decision, they argued that a fundamental distrust began permeating southern race relations. In 1937, South Carolina's Cotton Ed Smith was one of the first southern senators to recognize the rumblings of discontent in the black community. In 1960, those rumblings had become roars and few, if any, members of the caucus could then neglect it. At the same time, most southern senators still viewed the worsening relations as a byproduct of outside provocations. Despite evident signs of black unrest, all caucus members argued for the maintenance of segregation on the grounds that racial separation remained an integral component of southern life that, if removed, would result in a wave of violence both by whites angered by federal intervention and by blacks unaccustomed to living outside of the region's racial order. Individual senators, however, differed considerably in that portion of the segregationist ideology they emphasized on the Senate floor, reflecting some of the manifold permutations of the southern defense of Jim Crow.[24]

23. For examples of southerners claiming the "true" objective was integration, see *CR*, 27 February 1960, 3698 (Russell); *CR*, 1 March 1960, 3921 (Holland); *CR*, 8 April 1960, 7764 (Mc-Clellan); *CR*, Russell, 29 February 1960, 3761 ("the true object") and ("the mixing of . . .").

24. For examples of claims that race relations were deteriorating, see *CR*, 17 February 1960, 2734 (Ellender); *CR*, 26 February 1960, 3600 (McClellan); *CR*, 2 March 1960, 4105 (Johnston);

Richard Russell claimed that the push for civil rights in 1960 had a single objective—to "mislead the country into thinking that the South is perpetrating all kinds of horrendous offences against our colored citizens" when the record, he argued, indicated otherwise. The sit-in movement that emerged in conjunction with the filibuster particularly vexed the Georgian. African Americans who led the resistance effort, he noted, "were very anxious to start a race riot of terrible proportions." On many occasions during previous filibusters, he noted his "great affection for individual members of the Negro race." Taken collectively, however, he believed they fell far short of the ethical standards of other Americans. Crime statistics reported by Russell demonstrated to his satisfaction that blacks committed a disproportionate number of violent crimes. Therefore, despite individual cases of black exceptionalism, the bulk of the race, he theorized, conducted itself in a contemptible manner. It remained true for Russell that the mechanism of white dominance created by Jim Crow was essential for the maintenance of social stability. Getting to the heart of the matter, he argued that the "extreme high incidence of violence among members of the Negro race is one of the major reasons the great majority of the white people of the South are irrevocably opposed" to forced integration. Indeed, as Russell's comments illustrated, many white southerners in the 1960s still believed in the innate depravity of the black man, who, if left alone, would retrogress to his natural state of barbarism. Based on Russell's interpretation, Jim Crow, like the slave system before it, protected the white population from black depredations. What would happen in the South, Russell questioned, if the stability created by Jim Crow disappeared? In Russell's view, the prospect of a cataclysmic race war made segregation an absolute necessity.[25]

Whereas Richard Russell focused on black violence in his defense of segregation, Russell Long, at least in 1960, settled on a divine explanation for the Jim Crow system. On one occasion Long opined, "If the good Lord had intended us to be all alike he would have made us that way." Going further in this line of reasoning, he employed an ornithological framework, holding the

---

CR, 3 March 1960, 4380 (Talmadge); CR, 4 March 1960, 4455 (Smathers); CR, 5 March 1960, 4680 (Eastland), 4601 (Ellender).

25. CR, 26 February 1960, 3567 ("mislead the country . . ."); CR, 27 February 1960, 3699 ("were very anxious . . .") and ("great affection for . . ."); CR, 16 March 1960, 5721 ("extreme high incidence . . .").

fact that red birds and blue birds did not nest together as evidence that God did not desire the commingling of the white and the black races. "We believe," he observed, "without wanting to hurt anybody's feelings, that it is everyone's right to feel proud of his race and to preserve the purity of his race." According to Long, the only solution to the race problem, insomuch that he or any of his southern colleagues believed one existed, fell beyond the jurisdiction of the federal government. "Persuasion and education," not legislation, he noted, represented the most effective way that those above the Mason-Dixon Line could influence the racial situation below it. Only by appealing to white southerners' "sense of justice" might civil rights advocates convince anyone in the region to seriously consider changes to the racial order. And by this, Long did not mean social equality, only greater economic and educational opportunities for the region's black population. Anything beyond internal, gradual changes, he theorized, would necessarily produce violence.[26]

Unlike Long, who ultimately made God the architect of segregation, Spessard Holland of Florida more explicitly defined the Jim Crow system as a cultural construct, not a natural law, that if seriously challenged would collapse. Federal compulsion would not improve race relations in the South, he argued, because "these problems are in men's minds and hearts, in their emotions and traditions, in their customs and habits. They are deeply rooted. They are deep convictions." Holland's observation revealed that Jim Crow was an integral aspect of southern culture; it was at once a social system, a custom, and a way of life inculcated into white minds from cradle to grave. The effort to integrate public schools, from his perspective, directly challenged this most important regional custom. He speculated that many southerners might permit integration in eating facilities, but never in the educational system. He noted that school desegregation "is something that reaches into every home in the South; it affects the future of every child in the South; and it is contrary to the customs, beliefs, and convictions of most of our people, both white and colored." The unspoken rationale for that concern was that by attending integrated schools at an early age, white southern youths would lose the fear of the black man that marked the attitude of their parents. Should that happen through elementary school social engineering, then segregation as well as the taboo against interracial sexual unions would

26. CR, 2 March 1960, 4162 ("if the good . . .") and ("we believe . . ."); CR, 26 February 1960, 3613 ("persuasion and education") and ("sense of justice").

collapse, ending in amalgamation, mongrelization, and the eventual demise of American civilization. Jim Crow's maintenance, therefore, required that the youth of the region receive indoctrination into the racial order. Desegregating public schools would remove that stage in the formation of racial identity in which white youths received their first instruction in not only reading, writing, and arithmetic, but also in a fourth R—race. Without this initial training in racial etiquette, the Floridian recognized that Jim Crow would lose its next generation of adherents.[27]

Holland believed African Americans themselves made segregation essential. Although the Floridian found southern blacks "in the main to be a good people, happy people, people of deeper religious convictions than we have, people who are much more musical than we are . . . who have a much better sense of humor than most of us white people have," they nevertheless differed from whites "in many, many ways" that made equitable social relations impossible. Almost all caucus members prefaced their remarks on integration with assurances that they held blacks in the highest esteem. However, the "many, many" differences between the races, as Holland contended, necessitated Jim Crow in segregationist ideology. Caucus members proved less consistent in their explanation of those differences. Russell pointed to violence. Long cited natural law, which in his mind doubled as God's law. Holland never defined the nature of the differences but assured his audience that they did indeed exist. Although for different reasons, all three considered Jim Crow the best possible social system given the South's biracial demography and cultural inheritance.[28]

The paternalistic regard for African Americans claimed by Russell, Long, and Holland served as the public face of Jim Crow that southern senators presented to the nation. As the speeches of these three statesmen implicitly reveal the outward signs of conviviality between the races hid the terror upon which the system of segregation rested. White fears of black depravity often precipitated violence against "rebellious" blacks as a means of social control. In the process, the fears that marked the white relationship to Jim Crow became ingrained in the black community. Terror instilled among the region's black citizenry served as the linchpin of white dominance. White southerners went to great lengths to validate segregation in order to con-

27. CR, 1 March 1960, 3921 ("these problems are . . ."), 3927 ("this is something . . .").
28. CR, 3 March 1960, 4380 ("in the main . . .") and ("in many, . . .").

vince themselves and outsiders of the fundamental justness of an unjust system. Long's biblical references, Russell's emphasis on crime, and Holland's sociocultural exegesis all reflected subtle distinctions regarding the black image in the white southern mind. At the same time, their efforts at explaining the necessity of segregation sought to distort the true nature of the southern social system as it existed on the ground. In an unusual degree of candor, John McClellan of Arkansas most forcefully explained white racial views in a pseudo-biological manner without resorting to the rhetorical camouflages his caucus mates used to conceal their racism.

Born in poverty as the son of a sharecropper, McClellan, unlike some southern senators with an aristocratic upbringing, rarely hid his convictions behind a veneer of paternalism. Pursuing the issue to its very core, the Arkansan revealed the true foundation of the Jim Crow system stripped of all pleasantries. During the 1960 filibuster, he condemned civil rights advocates for their delusional belief that by passing legislation they could elevate blacks to a position "far in advance of what the process of evolution can do, are able to do, have done, or would be able to do for them." At the heart of segregationist doctrine, as McClellan's comment underscores, rested the quasi-biological theory that blacks were inferior and would always remain as such. Even if legislation afforded them an equivalent starting point with the white population, the Arkansan speculated, they would before too long fall behind. To drive home his point, he concluded, "You might as well pass a law directing the Potomac to reverse itself and empty into the Great Lakes. It would be just about as practical." Of course, the southern leader Richard Russell came close to making similar claims on many occasions, but the Georgian forwarded his arguments regarding what he perceived as the African American propensity for violence only after he had praised the black people he knew. McClellan bluntly stated his contempt for the black race and there remains little doubt that many of his caucus mates thought the same way even if they rarely said as much in public.[29]

Only a small percentage of southern senators consistently emphasized something other than the "many, many" differences between whites and blacks in their explanations for Jim Crow's existence. The racial moderates in the caucus, including J. William Fulbright of Arkansas, George Smathers of Florida, and Alabama's tandem of Lister Hill and John Sparkman, most

29. CR, 7 March 1960, 4695 ("far in advance . . .") and ("you might as . . .").

often defended segregation in a manner that did not make racial distinctions the centerpiece of their arguments. Instead, they focused on cultural claims, contending that segregation had existed for many decades and was preferred by all southerners regardless of race. Dismantling Jim Crow, the group speculated, would only hurt black southerners because of the fierce white backlash it would initiate. Although they spoke far less critically of African Americans than did Russell, Holland, and McClellan, they never called for an end to Jim Crow and never made any claims indicating that they held the black population in any higher regard than the South's more vocal race baiters. Even moderates could not break the chains of regional political constraints. Southern rhetoric in 1960, as on all previous occasions, revealed that Jim Crow demanded nothing less than a spirited defense on its behalf.[30]

When addressing their constituents in 1960, southern senators did not need to defend segregation since all parties in that political dialogue knew the reason for Jim Crow's existence. To their respective electorates, caucus members emphasized the glories of their own campaign of massive resistance played out on a national stage, even as they privately anticipated a future compromise on the administration bill. As the debate began, they warned their constituents of the enormous odds they faced. These initial apprehensions were well placed because a sizable majority of senators did indeed support at least a moderate civil rights proposal. Southern senators proved less than forthright in conveying to their constituents the possibility that the Stella bill might pass. Later in the filibuster, southern senators continued the deception by claiming their "educational campaign" had begun changing the minds of their colleagues. In the end they wanted their constituents to believe that only the caucus's herculean efforts, not the Stella bill's sweeping contents, had turned the tide. Early in the filibuster, Allen Ellender, for example, observed to a Louisianan that "it will be a long, hard battle for our little band of southerners, but we are determined not to compromise." Before the debate commenced, Olin Johnston claimed, "We are facing one of the worst times in legislative history." As the "educational campaign" wore on, the South Carolinian discovered a renewed spirit, noting, "this fight is so important until we Southern Senators forget how we feel because, when you are

---

30. For examples of moderate analysis that deemphasizes race, see *CR*, 26 February 1960, 3600 (Long); *CR*, 1 March 1960, 3978, 3993 (Fulbright); *CR*, 4 March 1960, 4436 (Hill); *CR*, 7 March 1960, 4717–4721 (Smathers); *CR*, 5 April 1960, 7332–7334 (Fulbright).

holding the battle line against an overpowering enemy in a righteous cause, strength seems to come from an unknown source." Since arriving in the Senate, Strom Thurmond frequently had lamented the apathy he perceived among his southern colleagues. During the 1957 debate, he struck out on his own, hoping to awaken his comrades to their responsibilities to the South. Three years later the caucus faced another push for civil rights, only this time it seemed imbued with a new sense of determination. The South Carolinian took the opportunity to make it appear that he helped rally southern resolve, even though the circumstances, not the man, dictated the defiant filibuster. Early in the 1960 debate, Thurmond observed that "if all of the southern senators will exert their utmost efforts and every means at our command it is not beyond the realm of possibility that we can win." Two weeks later, his modest optimism turned to euphoria. "The Southern Senators, due to their renewed unit[y] and determination, have the best chance in recent years of defeating all civil rights legislation," he touted, adding that "it is also my hope that this united effort will lead to a new realization of the power that lies in the Southern Senators through united effort." For Thurmond, those were glorious days; for some civil rights champions, the filibuster had pushed them to the limits of their patience. They wanted action.[31]

Despite the effort of Lyndon Johnson to stop him, Oregon's Wayne Morse gathered enough signatures to forward a cloture petition. Tired of the incessant filibuster as well as frustrated over the sluggish House response to the Eisenhower bill, Morse and company pressed the issue, a fact that compelled Johnson to cancel the round-the-clock sessions. On 8 March 1960, the cloture petition came before the chamber. Moments before the vote, the majority leader stated his opposition to the petition since it "will serve no useful purpose, so far as the Senate and the country are concerned." As expected, the cloture effort failed, forty-two to fifty-three. In a reversal of a recent trend that saw the numbers favoring cloture increase, civil rights advocates failed to even muster a simple majority to shut off debate, let alone procure the

31. AE to Guy Juenemann, 29 February 1960, Box 757, "Legislation—Civil Rights—1960, January–March" Folder, Ellender MSS ("it will be . . ."); transcript, radio broadcast, 18 February 1960, Box 128, "Media Scripts, 1960, Radio" Folder, Johnston MSS ("we are facing . . ."); transcript, radio broadcast, 3 March 1960, Box 128, "Media Scripts, 1960, Radio" Folder, Johnston MSS ("this fight is . . ."); ST to Kent Courtney, 27 February 1960, Box 3, "Civil Rights 1, Folder 1" Folder, Thurmond MSS ("if all of . . ."); ST to J. Clifford Miller, 12 March 1960, Box 3, "Civil Rights 1, Folder II" Folder, Thurmond MSS ("The Southern Senators . . .").

prerequisite support of two-thirds of those present and voting. Eleven northern Democrats and twenty Republicans sided with the once again solid bloc of twenty-two southerners against the petition. Victory in the cloture fight pleased the southern forces, but a long battle remained. Although Johnson ignited the civil rights debate, southerners knew that only through his actions on their behalf could they expect to weaken the forthcoming Eisenhower bill. Describing Johnson's crucial role in the southern fight, Alabama's John Sparkman observed, "I am now of the opinion" that Johnson and "the influence he has will probably be the difference between relatively mild legislation or the kind of legislation now being pushed by practically all of the Republicans with the help of some northern Democrats."[32]

After the Senate overwhelmingly defeated the cloture bid, Lyndon Johnson saw the compromise he desired in reach. Being an astute politician, he recognized that a majority of the chamber supported civil rights to varying degrees, but only a small percentage of that number could be qualified as true activists. Most senators held the customs and courtesies of the chamber in the highest regard. When Wayne Morse forwarded the cloture petition, senators responded to what they considered a premature effort to stifle the filibuster by voting against it. Also, the vote illustrated the disinclination of most senators to a sweeping civil rights proposal. Johnson, therefore, did not see the outcome of that vote as evidence that no bill would succeed; he viewed it merely as a warning that the majority of the chamber did not want the rights of their colleagues violated or too broad a measure passed. The majority leader would wait for his friend Speaker Sam Rayburn to direct the president's bill through the House of Representatives. After it passed in that chamber, the Senate could then drop its burdensome Stella school bill and begin debate on the Eisenhower initiative. A civil rights measure would likely pass as a result, making Johnson a strong candidate for the Democratic presidential nomination. At the same time, the Texan made it clear that neither he nor Dirksen had any plans of abandoning civil rights in the session. According to Johnson, the southern opposition would have to accept a bill since there existed no choice "between legislation or no legislation.

32. The round-the-clock sessions lasted a record setting 125 hours and 31 minutes without a recess. *CR*, 10 March 1960, 5116 ("will serve no . . ."); for the cloture vote, see *CR*, 10 March 1960, 5118; JS to Ralph B. Chandler, 2 March 1960, ACC 17-F-8, Box 349, "Federal Registrars—Civil Rights 4" Folder, Sparkman MSS ("I am now . . .").

The only real choice is between national legislation which reasonable men can support, or punitive legislation which will certainly ensue if any efforts are made to deprive Congress of the opportunity to consider the legitimate issue." A filibuster against the administration measure would surely fail and this warning came from one of the Senate's foremost nose counters. If Lyndon Johnson claimed he had the votes for cloture, then the prudent statesman would do best to accept the majority leader's claim. Southerners knew they would have to trust Johnson to orchestrate a compromise. Before long the caucus found evidence that it would again escape the enactment of what its members considered pernicious legislation.[33]

As the Senate waited for the House bill, it began work on a substitute for the administration's proposal offered by Everett Dirksen as an amendment to the Stella measure. By revising the Dirksen amendment that closely followed the president's proposal, Johnson hoped to expedite action on the administration's bill once it cleared the House. The caucus quickly learned that the majority of the chamber desired to strip the measure of its overtly sectional characteristics. In particular, the Senate voted to expand the section of the bill that made it a crime to transgress court orders involving desegregation cases to include all instances of willful violation of judicial decrees. Also, the chamber made all bombings, not just those involving schools or churches as originally constituted, subject to uniform punishment under the bill. This string of votes provided caucus members with an assurance that their colleagues recognized that a degree of antisouthern sectionalism existed in the proposal. By broadening the measure to apply nationally, the Senate also demonstrated it was in a hospitable mood. Once again it seemed that southern senators would wrest major concessions from their colleagues.[34]

In private, caucus members remained cautious. Richard Russell viewed the situation following the failed cloture vote with his customary reserve since he still believed "we are facing the greatest challenge of the era." Indicating that he, and therefore the rest of the caucus, would accept a compromise on the president's bill, he added, "I hope the victories we have won to date will not be later snatched from us." His observation that the caucus

---

33. *Shreveport Journal*, 7 March 1960, 4A ("between legislation on . . .").

34. By a vote of 65 to 19, the Senate agreed to make all violations of court orders a federal offense: *CR*, 11 March 1960, 5288; and to make all bombings involving interstate flight a federal crime, 85 to 1: *CR*, 14 March 1960, 5423–5424.

might lose ground revealed that he saw the possibility of more far reaching legislation forced upon the southerners if they proved unwilling to grant concessions. This fear resulted, in part, from uncertainty regarding the intentions of chamber Republicans. Southerners had often rallied members of the GOP to their side by making ideologically conservative arguments that depicted civil rights legislation as one manifestation of a larger drive to centralize power in Washington. With the civil rights bill in 1960 the product of a Republican administration, the caucus assumed that the proposal would receive more support from the president's party than usual. The risk of another protracted filibuster was too great. Compromise under the auspices of strategic delay again emerged as the best possible tactic. As in 1957, Russell staked the future of the southern defense of Jim Crow on providing a sop to the opposition in the form of a moderate voting rights proposal to slow the advance against segregation. Unlike in 1957, Richard Russell and his forces reached their decision without an intense intramural squabble.[35]

Like Russell, other southerners indicated that they believed caution proved the better part of valor in the crusade against the administration's proposal. Harry Byrd depicted the legislative battle in grave terms, noting that "the Southern Senators are fighting with our backs to the wall, but we are doing everything that can possibly be done to defeat this infamous proposal." Despite the legislative difficulties faced by the caucus, Byrd wrote following the outcome of the cloture vote and the modification of the Dirksen substitute, "We are making some headway in opposition to the iniquitous Civil Rights legislation." Similar to Byrd, Olin Johnston found the votes of the previous week encouraging, but not enough to erase his overall perception that "the outlook on civil rights does appear rather gloomy." Johnston also recognized that the caucus could not thwart enactment of the president's bill. One reason for the pessimism that led to another compromise in 1960, according to Sam Ervin, was the southern perception that "most of the Northern and Western members of Congress are supporting these bills," which by implication pointed to the possibility that civil rights legislation would pass regardless of caucus efforts. The more defiant wing of the southern resistance such as Byrd, Ervin, and Johnston clearly had difficulty digesting another compromise bill, but they recognized the risks associated with

35. RR to R. Aubrey Baker, 16 March 1960, Box 64, Folder 1, Russell MSS ("we are facing . . .") and ("I hope the . . .").

a renewed filibuster. Although ultimately accepting a compromise, they did so with some reluctance, especially considering the good press they received across the South for the Stella fight.[36]

More moderate southerners considered a compromise measure an unmitigated victory. Although he labeled the debate "burdensome," Florida's Spessard Holland felt the southern arguments bore "good fruit and may bear more before the battle ended." So long as the southerners pressed their case, Holland believed they would likely be left with a bill that would do little to impact the Jim Crow system. J. William Fulbright of Arkansas argued that the upturn in southern fortunes resulted from the earlier record setting filibuster. In a blunt appraisal of the situation, he noted that any bill would prove unacceptable, "but it at least will be better than what would have passed had there been no filibuster." Similar to Holland and Fulbright, Tennessee's Albert Gore also wished to settle on a moderate compromise such as occurred in 1957. Regarding the then-existing situation, he noted that "if the Congress has no alternative but to make a choice between the two extreme positions, I doubt that the majority . . . would favor the extreme position taken by some southerners." Although cognizant that many Tennesseans opposed civil rights, Gore knew that "passage of some legislation during this session is most likely, if not inevitable."[37]

Majority Leader Johnson figured prominently in all compromise discussions, but he could not unilaterally construct a legislative consensus on civil rights. To pass a modified version of the administration's bill, Johnson still needed at least tacit southern approval. But caucus consent, as always, came with a price. In the words of Allen Ellender, the Texan "missed the boat" in February by believing that the South would capitulate if confronted with a strong opposition. "He has been informed in no uncertain terms that we will not compromise on principle; that the fight will be continued as long as

36. HB to Gardiner Tyler, 1960, Box 262, "Miscellaneous Political Correspondence—J" Folder, Byrd MSS ("the Southern Senators . . .") and ("we are making . . ."); OJ to J. Robert Martin, 18 March 1960, Box 75, "Legislation, 1960, Civil Rights, 1 of 9" Folder, Johnston MSS ("the outlook on . . ."); SE to Billy T. Pope, 24 March 1960, Box 46, Folder 2261, Ervin MSS ("most of the . . .").

37. SH to George D. Auchter, 16 March 1960, Box 808, Folder 22, Holland MSS ("burdensome") and ("good fruit . . ."); JF to Harvey Adams, 21 March 1960, BCN 145, Folder 44, Fulbright MSS ("but it at . . ."); AG to Thomas M. Trabue, 14 March 1960, B 57, "March 1960" Folder, Gore MSS ("if the Congress . . .") and ("that the passage . . .").

necessary." Simply put, the Louisianan indicated that, as in 1957, no legislation containing sections objectionable to the South would make it through
the Senate without a filibuster. If Johnson wanted a compromise measure
to bolster his presidential ambitions, he would have to satisfy the caucus.
Should he fall short, the filibuster would resume. Cloture, as many fore-
casted, would likely shut off any renewal of the filibuster, but that would
only occur after weeks of rancorous debate, something neither the South nor
Lyndon Johnson wanted. After all, Johnson held the principal responsibility
for civil rights in the Senate in 1960 and, if the legislation foundered in the
face of a southern filibuster, he would reap much of the criticism, especially
since such a debate would divide the Democratic Party on the eve of its presidential nominating convention. Cognizant of the stakes involved, Johnson
employed his considerable influence in forging an agreement that at least
proved acceptable to all sides.[38]

On 24 March 1960, the House of Representatives voted in favor of House
Resolution 8601, the administration's civil rights bill, 311 to 109. Within ten
minutes, the measure reached Lyndon Johnson. The majority leader favored
a committee hearing on the proposal as he had its predecessor in 1957, but
aware that archsegregationist James Eastland's committee had jurisdiction
over the legislation, he called for a vote on a five day referral. By a margin
of eighty-six to five, Johnson's motion carried. Southerners would get their
committee hearing, but they could not drag their feet indefinitely in the face
of a five day mandate to report the bill. It became clear that most southerners, who had spent the previous two months conducting an "educational
campaign" against the referee provision along with a host of other items, felt
confident that the chamber had heard their arguments and they could wrest
from the body the necessary concessions. As a result, even the majority of
the caucus favored the motion for a five day referral. Making public their
private musings, southern senators revealed that, at least for the moment,
they would not filibuster.[39]

Following the brief Judiciary hearings, Johnson motioned for the Senate
to consider House Resolution 8601. Since no southerner protested, an action

38. AE to Bert Hood, 17 March 1960, Box 757, "Legislation—Civil Rights—1960, January–
March" Folder, Ellender MSS ("missed the boat") and ("He has been . . .").

39. For the House vote, see *CR,* 24 March 1960, 6512; for Johnson's motion, see *CR,* 24
March 1960, 6455; for the committee referral vote, see *CR,* 30 March 1960, 6455; *Time,* 4 April
1960, 12.

indicating the onset of a filibuster, the Senate voted overwhelmingly to consider the bill, seventy-one to seventeen. The chamber quickly reaffirmed its position taken on the Dirksen substitute by voting, sixty-eight to twenty, to amend the bill, making the violation of any court order a federal offense, instead of accepting the House version that limited the provision to school desegregation cases. For southerners, this vote proved pivotal. As originally constructed, the section could have been construed as a vote of confidence by the national legislature for the Supreme Court's *Brown v. Board* ruling. By expanding the scope of the section, senators obliquely indicated, at least according to the prevailing southern interpretation, that they did not wholeheartedly endorse the 1954 verdict. As for the other "sectional" provision that made the bombing of schools and churches a federal offense, the House had acted on its own, expanding the title to federalize all bombing episodes that involved interstate flight. Of all the difficulties surrounding the strange career of the administration bill, no one expected that an amendment added to House Resolution 8601 by the Judiciary Committee would have posed a problem, especially not one urged by Estes Kefauver, a man whom many considered friendly to civil rights.[40]

As his reelection approached in 1960, Kefauver studied the 1958 campaign of fellow Tennessean Albert Gore Sr. In light of that election, Kefauver, considered by many more of a maverick than Gore, shifted toward the southern mainstream on racial matters as his own campaign approached. He saw the Judiciary Committee's hearings on the administration's bill as a perfect venue to unveil his new found fidelity to southern racial norms. His amendment would open the hearings to the public and grant local registration officials the right to cross-examine plaintiffs in any proceedings conducted by federally appointed referees involving contested voter applications. Senate liberals immediately recognized the shortfall of such an amendment—it built white intimidation into the bill. What black citizen would pursue his or her case knowing that he or she would face a hostile inquisition at the hands of local white officials who would remain in the community long after the federal presence departed? Kefauver's amendment threatened to sabotage the entire referee provision of the House bill that permitted ex parte hearings. For Kefauver's reelection bid, the amendment demonstrated that he

40. *CR*, 30 March 1960, 6931 (motion to consider), 6957 (vote on court orders); Berman, *Bill Becomes Law*, 117–119.

had not completely abandoned the region. As for its prospects of remaining in the bill, most recognized that it would never last as initially drawn. Two days later, the chamber compromised on the amendment, voting, sixty-nine to twenty-two, to restore the ex parte nature of the hearings and to retain the public character of the legal proceedings that would result from the legislation. With that vote, the Senate reaffirmed its desire for a civil rights bill, while at the same time making clear that it remained unprepared to enact a measure capable of seriously threatening the southern racial order. As the upper house moved toward a workable compromise, southerners leveled their final barbs against the legislation. They would not filibuster, but they would not remain silent either.[41]

During the marathon debate earlier in the year, southern senators addressed themselves to all aspects of the civil rights question. With the House bill before the chamber and the prospect of a palatable compromise strong, southern forces reverted to their 1957 form, couching their arguments in constitutional terms to wrest maximum concessions from their Senate colleagues. Their rhetoric proved almost identical to that employed when they confronted the first civil rights bill offered by the Eisenhower administration. Again the caucus deflected attention away from the impediments placed before southern blacks who desired the right to vote. And again they blamed everyone and everything but white southerners for black discontent in the region. As in most previous civil rights discussions, southern senators linked their regional interests with those of the rest of the nation by claiming that the bill simultaneously threatened Jim Crow as well as the American political system as designed by the founders. Segregation also remained a primary concern, and they of course viewed House Resolution 8601 as another step toward the deliberate submersion of the southern racial order by "radical" and "un-American" civil rights crusaders. In essence, caucus members speculated that this one bill would set in motion a chain of events that would end in tyranny not just for the South but for the entire country. Through the referee provision, the bill would undermine the constitutionally stipulated right of individual states to oversee elections in their sovereign domains. This in turn would set a precedent for the federal government to establish its hegemony over other jurisdictions formerly relegated to the states. The

41. *Newsweek,* 11 April 1960, 38; Gorman, *Kefauver,* 326–331; for the vote on the compromise, see *CR,* 1 April 1960, 7153.

potential centralization of political power in Washington possible under the bill, therefore, threatened all Americans. With the state political machinery engulfed by a central bureaucracy, it went without saying that individual rights would soon fall victim to federal regimentation. All of these dire consequences, furthermore, would occur, caucus members warned, if northerners allowed the passions exacerbated by the sit-in movement to influence their voting behavior.[42]

Aside from constitutional claims, caucus members contended that adequate legislation to safeguard the right to vote already existed. In 1957, the Senate passed a suffrage measure, but before the first judicial decisions stemming from the legislation were given, civil rights advocates wanted further concessions, prompting southern speculation that activists believed "every member of the Caucasian race who happens to reside below the Mason-Dixon Line . . . a dishonorable character." Caucus members again raised charges that northern media outlets deliberately concealed southern arguments from their patrons. If northerners recognized the difficulties faced by white southerners because of the large black population in the South, they would demand the cessation of civil rights activism. To bring about this realization, caucus members had to pierce the wall around their arguments erected by civil rights advocates who "rivaled carnival sideshow hucksters" in their misrepresentation of the truth as understood by white southerners. Even if they ultimately failed in their defense of Jim Crow, southern senators believed that northern civil rights crusaders neglected a pivotal consideration that would make all of their proposals inoperable. Summarizing this theory, Louisiana's Russell Long observed that "the good will, sympathy, and cooperation of the white majority in the South is indispensable to the progress of the Negro citizen in that area." No amount of legislating could ensure the support of the white South; that required time and patience, something civil rights proponents lacked, according to southerners. If northerners pushed the South too far, they would meet fierce resistance that in the end would only hurt the black population the civil rights activists hoped to assist. The caucus therefore implied that its very own constituents would never accept the end of segregation without some form of retribution, whether social,

42. CR, 8 March 1960, 4845 (Hill); CR, 10 March 1960, 5088 (Talmadge), 5156 (Ervin); CR, 1 April 1960, 7130 (Stennis), 7148 (Thurmond); CR, 5 April 1960, 7345 (Ellender); CR, 7 April 1960, 7606 (Talmadge), 7617 (Stennis); CR, 8 April 1960, 7754 (McClellan).

political, economic, or even physical, against southern blacks. Although un-intentional, southern senators ironically argued what civil rights advocates had always claimed—that oppression undergirded the Jim Crow system.[43]

Despite southern warnings, civil rights activists pushed for stronger leg-islation. Following the compromise on the Kefauver addition, Lyndon John-son faced several amendments championed by staunch proponents of black equality. After having convinced caucus members that intransigence on their part would lead to a far worse bill, he had to warn Senate liberals that their own truculence might precipitate a filibuster and jeopardize even a mild voting rights proposal. Regarding an attempt by New York Republican Jacob Javits to inject an FEPC provision into the bill, Johnson commented, "I think we ought to proceed to vote upon the bill as it has been reported to us by the committee, without substantial changes, if we are to expect legislation this session." The majority of the Senate agreed with Johnson's call for modera-tion. In a series of votes, the Senate defeated Javits's FEPC proposal, Kenneth Keating's amendment that would place the chamber on record in support of the *Brown* decision, and another Javits measure to permit the attorney gen-eral to intervene in school desegregation cases as proposed in Title III of the Eisenhower administration's 1957 bill. Of the strengthening amendments, the most relevant to House Resolution 8601 came from Republican Thomas Hart of Connecticut. As the bill then stood, suits could not be initiated on behalf of the party discriminated against unless that individual requested federal assistance and, even then, only after the denied applicant made a sec-ond attempt to register. The Hart amendment would have permitted federal litigation against local officials whether or not a denied registrant filed suit. By a fifty-two to thirty-eight margin, the Senate tabled the Hart amendment. For southerners, the vote represented an important victory in that it pre-vented the government from using the legislation to arbitrarily punish the region as many caucus members believed it would if left unchecked. Unless a denied black applicant requested the federal government to assist him or her, nothing could be done. The climate of fear in the South made the likeli-

43. Adequate laws exist: *CR*, 4 March 1960, 4430 (Hill); *CR*, 7 April 1960, 7660 (Thur-mond); *CR*, Ervin, 31 March 1960, 7043 ("every member of . . ."); *CR*, Thurmond, 1 April 1960, 7148 ("rivaled carnival . . ."); *CR*, 8 April 1960, 7809 ("the good will . . ."). For an example of the southern belief in a media conspiracy, see HB, form letter, 3 March 1960, Box 412, "Release March 7, 1960" Folder, Byrd MSS.

hood of a black southerner availing himself or herself of federal assistance rather remote. Even if he or she did, the numbers making such claims would remain small, especially considering the public nature of the hearings, and the verdicts would take years to come down. Change under the bill would occur at a staggeringly slow pace.[44]

Southerners hoped to make this sluggish judicial process even less effective. Sam Ervin proposed to limit House Resolution 8601 only to national elections, but the chamber tabled the amendment, seventy-two to sixteen. Following Ervin's lead, Allen Ellender sought to exempt primaries and special elections from the bill, however, the Senate majority refused to budge, defeating this effort by a vote of sixty-eight to eighteen. Unbowed, Ellender forwarded another amendment that would have completely removed the voter referee section from the bill. Not surprisingly, it too fell to defeat, seventy-three to eighteen. By the end of the first week of April, Lyndon Johnson's brand of moderation dominated the chamber, as amendments on both extremes of the civil rights issue fell to easy defeat. Passage of a moderate bill was now beyond question. Only a final wave of southern speeches against the measure and a vote on the finished product remained. In an election year, the chamber appeared on the verge of successfully dispensing with the hot-button civil rights issue.[45]

On 8 April 1960, the Senate overwhelmingly supported the compromise civil rights proposal, seventy-four to eighteen. The finished product consisted of six sections few, if any, of which posed a challenge to the Jim Crow system. Titles I and II of the bill respectively made obstructing any court order and interstate flight in bombing cases federal crimes. Title III of the bill required local election officials to preserve for twenty-two months all voting records involving national elections for possible inspection by federal officials. The measure also increased the power of the Civil Rights Commission and provided funding for the continued education of servicemen's children in areas where integration efforts resulted in school closings. Title VI that pertained to the voting referees represented the most controversial section. Under its provisions, a complaint from a citizen denied the right to vote would set in

44. CR, 1 April 1960, 7153 ("I think we . . ."), 7166 (FEPC tabled: 48 to 38); CR, 4 April 1960, 7218 (Keating amendment: 61 to 30), 7225 (second Javits effort: 56 to 34), 7250 (Hart amendment).
45. CR, 6 April 1960, 7406 (Ervin), 7409 (Ellender); CR, 7 April 1960, 7500 (Ellender II).

motion a process whereby a federal court would attempt to discern if a "pattern of discrimination" existed in a given district. If so found, a judge would appoint referees to hear the complaints of other similarly aggrieved persons from the same locale as the original claimant. The referees could register qualified African Americans who proved their case under existing state laws. For civil rights advocates, the bill represented progress, albeit just barely. As NAACP head Roy Wilkins observed regarding the measure, "No bill which has even a grudging acquiescence of Russell, Eastland and company," as the 1960 legislation had, "can be acceptable to citizens for civil rights."[46]

For southerners, who heard nothing but pessimistic forecasts about their prospects before the 1960 debate began, the outcome proved better than they expected. Following the final vote, Harry Byrd inserted into the *Congressional Record* a tribute to the southern caucus that left little doubt that he considered the bill an unmitigated victory for Dixie that "demonstrated the effectiveness of courageous massive resistance." Facing the combined pressure of the federal government, many northern statesmen, and NAACP propaganda, southern senators stood together in removing "the more vicious proposals and the worst features" of the bill. Advocates for the legislation also recognized that the better end of the civil rights bargain in 1960 rested with the southerners. Pennsylvania Democrat Joseph Clark, one of the Senate's staunchest civil rights supporters, announced that he was surrendering his "sword" to Richard Russell for "surely the roles of Grant and Lee at Appomattox have been reversed." Despite what amounted to an overwhelming southern victory, some from the region, as in 1957, questioned why the caucus permitted the legislation to pass. Southern senators took an approach similar to the one they adopted three years before, with the exception that their descriptions of the legislative situation in 1960 proved even more grave than those they had employed in 1957.[47]

Southern leader Richard Russell observed, "We did do much better than

46. For the final vote, see *CR*, 8 April 1960, 7810–7811. The Wilkins quote is from a telegram sent by the NAACP head to civil rights advocates earlier in the debate that encouraged them not to compromise. Harry Byrd got his hands on a copy of it and promptly sent it to his southern colleagues. For a copy of the telegram and the Byrd attachments, see HB to RL, 4 March 1960, Box 556, Folder 36, Long MSS.

47. *CR*, 8 April 1960, 7814 ("demonstrated the . . .") and ("the more vicious . . ."); see also press release, 8 April 1960, Box 412, "Statement April 8, 1960" Folder, Byrd MSS; *CR*, 8 April 1960, 7768 ("the roles of . . .").

it seemed possible when we started out. After the majority found they could not crush us and wear us out, they did some listening." On another occasion, he depicted the 1960 battle in more dramatic terms, noting "our small band of eighteen southern Constitutionalists was able to strike down or substantially modify every major provision that was offered." As for what he considered the greatest accomplishment of the caucus, he claimed, "I hope at least that we have convinced the country that those of us who still believe in constitutional government are willing to defend the faith at any cost." Russell's soldiers mimicked the southern general's outlook. Unlike in 1957, Strom Thurmond accepted the decision of the caucus to compromise without a renegade filibuster. As related by Thurmond, southerners recognized that they had removed all they could from the administration bill and did not wish to alienate the majority and minority leaders, who proved essential in "fighting off bad provisions," with a filibuster. Thurmond added that Johnson and Dirksen had also served notice to the caucus that "they had the votes to apply cloture and asked that we not make them do so." Based on these threats by the Senate leadership, southern senators sought a quick vote on the bill to avoid any erosion in their legislative position. Russell Long also related southern fears that a cloture showdown on House Resolution 8601 ran the risk of failure, "thereby establishing perhaps a precedent that would do more harm to us in the future when there are other, more obnoxious bills before us." Long's fellow Louisianan Allen Ellender lamented that a bill passed, but "under the circumstances," he noted, "our little band of southerners gained a major victory." North Carolina's Sam Ervin echoed these sentiments, adding for the benefit of a constituent, "I doubt very seriously whether the provisions of this bill will ever be used in North Carolina." Ervin's comments illustrated what many civil rights advocates already knew—the bill would produce few changes in the South.[48]

Safeguarding segregation also figured prominently in many descriptions of the caucus's efforts in 1960. Several southern senators defined the legislative

48. RR to W. A. Bowen, 23 April 1960, Box 63, Folder 2, Russell MSS ("we did do . . ."); RR to Edgar W. Tison, 17 July 1960, Box 63, Folder 1, Russell MSS ("our small band . . ."); RR to W. C. Mundy, 11 April 1960, Box 63, Folder 3, Russell MSS ("I hope that . . ."); ST to Hugh Grant, 12 April 1960, Box 4, "Civil Rights Folder VI," Thurmond MSS ("fighting off . . .") and ("that they had . . ."); press release, 8 April 1960, Box 596, Folder 17, Long MSS ("thereby establishing perhaps . . ."); AE to James H. Ware Jr., 26 April 1960, Box 757, "Legislation—Civil Rights—1960, April through–" Folder, Ellender MSS ("under the circumstances . . ."); SE to John Q. LaGrand, 14 April 1960, Box 46, Folder 2263, Ervin MSS ("I doubt very . . .").

battle that year in a context that illustrated what they considered their primary achievement. Rather than stress the question of voting rights, they, as in 1959, noted their success in preventing any legislation designed to implement the *Brown* ruling. Such an emphasis comes as no surprise considering the importance of safeguarding Jim Crow embedded in the tactical approach of strategic delay. For years southern solons had blocked legislation they believed would force integration and 1960 proved no different. In that sense, total victory remained theirs in spite of the compromise suffrage measure. Sam Ervin, for one, noted, "I rejoice in the fact that both the House and the Senate have thus far excluded all reference to the school problem" from civil rights measures. Alabama's John Sparkman observed that "no integration forcing legislation has passed" because "we have conducted an effective fight to preserve our southern traditions." Even with the continuation of Jim Crow assured, at least for the immediate future, southern solons must have recognized that pressure against them would only mount as white resistance in Dixie steadily collapsed.[49]

By 1960, the campaign of "massive resistance" had lost considerable momentum. Virginia, which faced some of the earliest integration pressure, enacted legislation to withhold state funding to schools forced to desegregate. Virginians had drawn a line in the sand, vowing to abolish the public school system if forced to accept the *Brown* verdict. Other southern states adopted similar mechanisms designed to achieve the same end—the destruction of public education to forestall integration. In early 1959, both state and federal courts ruled Virginia's school funding legislation unconstitutional. Throughout the rim South, capitulation to integration thus began with tensions high in places but violence limited. Despite setbacks to their north, politicians from deep southern states vowed to carry on. Citizens' Council leaders lambasted those who had lost their resolve in the face of reversals, such as the political leaders in Virginia, while encouraging the faithful to maintain their fight. Ground was being lost and to any rational observer massive resistance had not and ultimately could not work. Nonetheless, once the path of resistance was undertaken, giving up represented an option fraught with potential political fallout, especially in states where race mattered most. The

49. SE to Arthur I. Boreman, 13 April 1960, Box 46, Folder 2256, Ervin MSS ("I rejoice in . . ."); JS to Sandra Carroll, 23 May 1960, ACC 17-F-8, Box 349, "Civil Rights II" Folder, Sparkman MSS ("that no integration . . .") and ("we have conducted . . .").

forces of massive resistance had sustained grievous setbacks. In the Deep South, however, their numbers remained substantive and their commitment unbroken. White supremacy would not die without a fight.[50]

During the Eisenhower years, caucus members granted civil rights concessions in the form of two suffrage bills; whereas, in the 1930s and the 1940s, their predecessors had given ground on minor measures only tangentially related to the southern racial order. When the political climate changed following the *Brown* decision, all-out resistance to substantive civil rights initiatives gave way to a series of deliberate compromises in an effort to slow the movement for black equality. The end goal of protecting segregation remained the same, but for a period, caucus members saw such compromises as their only alternative to integration. Capitulating on the periphery of the Jim Crow system failed to arrest black unrest and, in part, seemed only to increase it. Nonviolent sit-ins at segregated lunch counters across the South served notice to southern senators that their efforts to placate southern blacks with emasculated voting rights bills would not work. In an interview following the rash of racial disturbances in 1960, SCLC leader Martin Luther King Jr. observed that "this may be the beginning of a full-scale assault on segregation." For southern observers, King's comments appeared to condone the episodes of violence that they thought inevitably followed all allegedly "peaceful" black demonstrations. Social disruption increased and, in many southern minds, the self-professed nonviolent protest leaders were, despite their stated pacifism, primarily responsible for the lawlessness.[51]

During the 1960 civil rights debate, southern spokesman Richard Russell harshly condemned the emerging grass-roots protest effort. Black Americans, he argued, represented the only minority in the United States unwilling "to work and strive to earn recognition and acceptance." Instead, according to Russell, African Americans "have sought to strong-arm and use physical force to secure the right of association from the majority against the wishes of that majority." Russell saw in the burgeoning protest movement that disrupted southern life evidence of everything that the caucus had warned. In the late 1930s, southern senators argued that antilynching legislation represented the vanguard of a much larger effort to dismantle Jim Crow. Twenty-years later that forecast, in their minds, was proven all too true. Activist pressure

50. Bartley, *Rise of Massive Resistance,* 322–335; McMillen, *Citizens' Council,* 250, 310–312.
51. *Newsweek,* 29 February 1960, 25 ("this may be . . .").

continued unabated, until at the dawn of the 1960s, civil rights organizations made clear that they would not cease their crusade until African Americans achieved full legal and political equality. Despite all that he witnessed in 1960, Richard Russell still believed, as he would until the end of the civil rights fight, that the overwhelming majority of Americans, regardless of region, opposed forced integration. Because of this long-held sentiment, the Georgian saw a window of opportunity. Announcing his vision to a constituent, he wrote, "We have indeed come to sad days, but I am not completely without hope that there are enough thinking Americans left to correct the grievous wrongs being wrought in the name of 'Civil Rights.'" What Russell could not know then is that many of the "grievous wrongs" committed during the 1960s by white southerners would eventually rally many "thinking Americans" into at least some level of support for civil rights. For all the power the southern senators held in Washington, they could not control the situation on the ground in their home states. It was there that white southerners would lose the civil rights battle, not by capitulating but by disgusting the American public with their actions.[52]

52. CR, 16 March 1960, 5725 ("to work and . . .") and ("have sought to . . ."); RR to Neal P. Hodgson, 28 September 1960, Box 63, Folder 1, Russel MSS ("we have indeed . . .").

6. This Is Where the Battle Will Be Won or Lost

ON 4 MAY 1961, members of the Congress of Racial Equality headed south from Washington to test southern compliance with the Supreme Court's 1960 *Boynton v. Virginia* decision, which banned segregation on interstate bus lines and in interstate terminals. As the delegation moved through Virginia, the Carolinas, and Georgia, they encountered only limited opposition. When the Freedom Riders reached Alabama, the situation degenerated into a flurry of violence as white locals assaulted the activists. Only the deployment of federal marshals by a reluctant President John F. Kennedy restored order. Most northern media outlets depicted the racial violence in Alabama as a byproduct of white southern intolerance. On the other hand, many southern whites believed that they, not the black demonstrators, represented the true victims of the interracial strife. Furthermore, they argued that despite the alleged nonviolent philosophy of the protesters, the unrest had resulted from the provocations of outside "agitators," who deliberately fomented turmoil where tranquility once ruled. Although most considered the white response in Alabama excessive, the prevailing southern interpretation held that racial violence occurred only when intentionally provoked. Culpability for the assault on the Freedom Riders thus rested with the demonstrators.[1]

1. Inge Powell Bell, *CORE and the Strategy of Non-Violence* (New York: Random House, 1968), 10–11; Branch, *Parting the Waters,* 412–450; Carl M. Brauer, *John F. Kennedy and the Second Reconstruction* (New York: Columbia University Press, 1977); 98–112; Robert Cook, *Sweet Land of Liberty? The African-American Struggle for Civil Rights in the Twentieth Century* (New York: Longman, 1998), 123–125; Adam Fairclough, *Better Day Coming: Blacks and Equality, 1890–2000*

Not surprisingly, southern senators also blamed the Freedom Riders for the turmoil in Alabama. Allen Ellender, for one, bluntly proclaimed, "I have always said that if anyone goes looking for trouble, he is sure to find it. That is exactly what happened in Alabama." Lister Hill, who had a direct political stake in removing the federal presence in his bailiwick, pleaded with Attorney General Robert Kennedy to withdraw the U.S. marshals, just as he urged Kennedy to do "everything possible . . . to keep outside agitators out of Alabama." In keeping with his desire to quell the protests, Hill joined James Eastland, John McClellan, A. Willis Robertson, George Smathers, John Sparkman, John Stennis, and Strom Thurmond in cosponsoring an antidemonstration bill that would make it a criminal offense to travel across state lines "with the intent to make a riot." Like most white southerners, the drafters of the proposal recast the civil rights fight by labeling the demonstrators dangerous insurgents bent on flouting state law. Before the arrival of CORE activists, Hill asserted, peace had marked race relations in Alabama. The fact that social stability in the state deteriorated upon the arrival of the Freedom Riders proved evidence enough for Hill that external pressure played a central role in precipitating racial violence in the South. As the Alabaman's comments underscore, southern senators had yet to acknowledge that black resistance in the region resulted from its repressive racial order. They had very little choice. To admit that even a shred of injustice prompted the protest movement would be to undermine everything they had said and planned to say regarding civil rights. How could they argue that nothing was wrong and the South, if trouble emerged, could take care of its own problems "as it always has" if they were on record criticizing, even if only obliquely, the racial order they defended? Southern senators would remain, until the end of their struggle against civil rights, unwilling to deviate from their mantra that peaceful coexistence marked white and black social intercourse in the region. Disturbances, they would argue, stemmed from the agitation of outsiders. The mythological portrait of Jim Crow as a benevolent system that fostered idyllic race relations remained the foundation of southern arguments in defense of segregation.[2]

(New York: Viking, 2001), 253–256; August Meier and Elliott Rudwick, *CORE: A Study in the Civil Rights Movement, 1942–1968* (New York: Oxford University Press, 1973), 135–158; Stephen B. Oates, *Let the Trumpet Sound: A Life of Martin Luther King, Jr.* (New York: Harper Collins, 1994), 174–178.

2. Mississippi's John Stennis drafted the antidemonstration bill. For introduction of the proposal, see *CR*, 87th Cong., 1st sess., 24 May 1961, 8708; AE to D. T. McKearan Jr., 31 May

In private, some caucus members continued to question the standard southern denial of racial injustice in the region. J. William Fulbright, whose home state of Arkansas experienced a similar federal "invasion" during the 1957 Little Rock school integration episode, refrained from denouncing the Freedom Riders. When out of the public spotlight, the Arkansan viewed massive resistance as an impediment to his task of safeguarding segregation in Washington. "One of the greatest problems we southern members of Congress have is created by acts of violence. It is difficult to oppose legislation designed to punish the South in the face of such incidents as this one." His comment casts doubt on a central caucus argument—that the South could solve its racial problems without federal intervention. Lawlessness that was stilled only after the incursion of federal troops pointed to just the opposite contention—that at least regarding racial matters local officials lacked sufficient control over segments of the white population. As in 1957, Fulbright's private musings on the deleterious consequences of white violence remained conspicuously absent in his public expressions. He validated his silence on the grounds that emotions delimited the scope of racial dialogue in the South. As he saw it, a rational analysis of racial injustice in the region simply could not occur. Questioning any of the mechanisms designed to ensure white supremacy, even the assault on the Freedom Riders, the Arkansan feared, was to court certain electoral defeat. In the absence of a countervailing force provided by racial moderates, proponents of massive resistance inflamed segments of the white population, who responded to such passion plays with violence. Fulbright apparently did not see it as his responsibility to provide a counterweight to such extremism. And so it continued.[3]

Despite his lack of public fortitude, Fulbright privately sensed the development of an important shift in public opinion against the South resulting from episodes of racial violence, which he as a U.S. senator made no effort to quell. The national media, especially the ever-expanding television medium, provided significant coverage of civil rights demonstrations in the 1960s, bringing to the homes of many northerners powerful images of the excesses of Jim Crow. From Maine to California, Americans saw on the evening news

1961, Box 757, "Legislation—Civil Rights—1961" Folder, Ellender MSS ("I have always . . ."); LH to Forrest S. Fields, 26 May 1961, Box 376, Folder 10, Hill MSS ("everything possible . . ."); LH to James Ozier, 29 May 1961, Box 376, Folder 10, Hill MSS ("with the intent . . .").

3. JF to Bob E. Rice, 27 May 1961, Series 64:4, Box 9, Folder 14, Fulbright MSS ("One of the . . .").

and read in their local newspapers accounts of the brutality that had always marked southern race relations. As white southerners long feared, northern attitudes on the race question changed as a result of this exposure. Apathy above the Mason-Dixon line concerning the plight of southern blacks decreased in turn. Southerners had long banked on outside disinterest in racial equality. Every public airing of the region's dirty laundry, however, either in the form of Washington debate or increasingly in television footage, challenged the myths peddled by southern politicians. Astute civil rights activists pushed their crusade into ever more provocative locations, baiting southern racists to display their true colors. Racial tranquility became a difficult commodity to sell. Time was running out on Jim Crow.

In the fall of 1961, caucus leader Richard Russell remained steadfast in his crusade to "preserve the rights of the individual states, and to stem the tide toward an all-powerful centralized government here in Washington." Few doubted Russell's loyalty to the South's system of segregation, but the same could not be said for many of his soldiers in the southern caucus. Concerning his regional colleagues, Strom Thurmond observed that "too many are taking a defeatist attitude about the South's position at the present time," but "if our leaders and our people are alert and take a positive attitude, we may be successful." Thurmond's tempered optimism regarding the ultimate outcome of the integration fight apparently did not trickle down to his caucus mates. Addressing their apathy, he noted that "the southern will to resist in the Congress is not what it used to be and I am trying to refortify that." In particular, he thought southern legislators could better utilize their strength by acting in concert on all policy issues, not just when faced with an effort to change the Senate's rules or with a bill specifically labeled "civil rights." If any measure threatened to decrease the power of state government, Thurmond reasoned, the southern bloc should move en masse against it. As a result, the region's Washington delegation would hold the balance of power on a wide range of legislative issues, a fact that the South Carolinian believed would force northern politicians, as well as the executive branch, to grant concessions to the South regarding civil rights. The vote on the School Assistance Act of 1961, which provided $2.5 billion in grants for school construction and teacher salaries, demonstrated conclusively to Thurmond that "southern solidarity is not what some may think it to be." Four southerners voted in favor of the legislation that many others in the group opposed on the grounds that "the Federal Government ultimately controls any activity where it makes substantial federal contributions." With the purse strings of southern schools in its hands, the government could then expedite its drive to force integration in the region.[4]

Like Theodore Bilbo two decades earlier, Strom Thurmond wanted the southern caucus to take the offensive in its fight against civil rights. Bilbo failed in his endeavors; Thurmond faired little better. The South Carolinian's push to revive flagging southern morale fell short largely because many statesmen from the region had begun focusing greater attention on economic, not racial, concerns. Promises to expand social programs now served as a major feature of the campaign rhetoric employed by many southern politicians. Unlike Thurmond, southern liberals such as Lister Hill, John Sparkman, Russell Long, and George Smathers infrequently rolled out their states' rights arguments, except when confronting civil rights legislation. They would not risk jeopardizing the influx of federal money into the impoverished South based on the unproven assumption that a caucus counteroffensive as Thurmond proposed would prolong the existence of segregation. The southern caucus, in Thurmond's eyes, thus limped into the final stages of its fight with far less of the unity often ascribed to it by civil rights advocates. Subsequent events further tested the determination of the group in their battle to maintain "the southern way of life."

In 1962, the Kennedy administration timidly pushed a modest voting rights proposal that would have eliminated the use of literacy tests by adjudging anyone with a sixth grade education literate. Southern senators, with the assistance of most Republicans, easily defeated the legislation that had little backing even from the president who introduced it. As during the poll

4. RR to D. W. Warthen, 25 September 1961, Box 186, Folder 19, Russell MSS ("preserve the rights . . ."); ST to John B. Crouch, 30 March 1961, Box 3, "Civil Rights—January 14, 1961–[c. 1961]" Folder, Thurmond MSS ("too many are . . ."); ST to James F. Timmerman, 10 July 1961, Box 3, "Civil Rights 3 (Race Relations)" Folder, Thurmond MSS ("the southern will . . ."); ST to H. L Pratt, 2 June 1961, Box 3, "Civil Rights 4 (Freedom Riders)" Folder, Thurmond MSS ("southern solidarity is . . ."). For the vote on S. 1021, the school assistance bill, see CR, 87th Cong., 1st sess., 25 May 1961, 9054. Active caucus participants, Sam Ervin (N.C.), B. Everett Jordan (N.C.), Lister Hill (Aa.), and George Smathers (Fla.), voted for the proposal, as did rim South senators, Albert Gore Sr. (Tenn.), Estes Kefauver (Tenn.) and Ralph Yarborough (Tex.). HT to Fred Everett, 2 March 1961, III Civil Rights Series, Box 7, Folder 1, Talmadge MSS ("the Federal Government . . .").

tax fights in the 1940s, caucus members convincingly argued that Article I, Section 2 of the Constitution granted individual states the autonomy to set voter qualifications, a claim their Senate colleagues apparently accepted. 1962 also witnessed further civil rights demonstrations and, in September, another manifestation of massive resistance gone awry in a southern state that required a federal presence to end racial turmoil. Mississippi governor Ross Barnett's actions following the University of Mississippi's refusal to admit African American James Meredith touched off days of racial violence as members of a white mob, who arrived in the small college town of Oxford from throughout the South, indiscriminately assaulted blacks and U.S. marshals dispatched by the Kennedy administration. Only the presence of the National Guard and regular Army troops halted the mayhem. Again citizens outside of Dixie witnessed the spectacle of white southern lawlessness; in this instance, over the enrollment of a single black male at the state's flagship university. The contention that the white South could solve its own problems suffered yet another blow.[5]

Lister Hill, whose own state experienced a similar series of racial disturbances during the 1961 Freedom Rides, wired Governor Barnett, "Mississippi's fight is Alabama's fight. We support you in the principles that you are forcefully defending and we commend you for the courageous battle you are waging for constitutional government." Like other caucus members, Hill also reassured his constituents that he remained "unalterably opposed to the use of Federal troops against the sovereignty of Mississippi or any other state." Despite caucus denunciations of the federal intervention, Strom Thurmond again noted "a reluctance up here to really fight hard on this subject." At this time, the South Carolinian looked to the past, and to 1957 in particular,

5. The southern caucus handily defeated two efforts to invoke cloture by margins of forty-three to fifty-three and forty-two to fifty-two. On both occasions, they had the support of at least twenty-two of the Senate's thirty-six Republicans. For the first vote, see CR, 87th Cong., 2nd sess., 9 May 1962, 8058. For the second cloture vote, see CR, 14 May 1962, 8294. For some of the many works that address aspects of the Ole Miss controversy, see Henry S. Ashmore, *Hearts and Minds: The Anatomy of Racism from Roosevelt to Reagan* (New York: McGraw-Hill, 1982), 342–346; Mary Frances Berry, *Black Resistance/White Law: A History of Constitutional Racism in America* (New York: Appleton-Century-Crofts, 1971), 190–194; Branch, *Parting the Waters*, 647–672; Brauer, *John F. Kennedy*, 135–136, 181–204; Erle Johnston, *I Rolled with Ross: A Political Portrait* (Baton Rouge: Moran, 1980), 89–113; Fred Powledge, *Free at Last? The Civil Rights Movement and the People Who Made It* (Boston: Little, Brown, 1991), 430–437.

to highlight his point. From his perspective, the decision of his southern colleagues not to join him in his record-setting filibuster that year best illustrated his claim that a general malaise had settled over many in the group. Nonetheless, Thurmond still proved optimistic, noting, "I personally think that segregation is here to stay for many years yet, although in some areas various forms of segregation may be eliminated gradually." For all of his concerns over caucus indifference, he took heart in the fact that no antisegregation proposals appeared on the horizon. Like Thurmond, Louisiana's Russell Long observed, "we held our own this year as far as civil rights legislation is concerned" and should a threat emerge, "I will be ready to go all the way to defend the position of the South." Long could never have foreseen what would happen next. Episodes of violence in the early 1960s continued to alert the northern public regarding the pervasiveness of racial injustice below the Mason-Dixon line. Events in 1963 would heighten that awareness, pushing the timid New Frontiersman John F. Kennedy into action. The final struggle in defense of Jim Crow was approaching.[6]

Responding to the growing racial violence in the South, the president, on 28 February 1963, requested legislative action on a limited civil rights bill that would strengthen suffrage protections, extend the Civil Rights Commission, and provide assistance to communities that voluntarily integrated schools. In April and May, the nation stood transfixed as Birmingham's public safety commissioner, Eugene "Bull" Connor, unleashed all the weapons at his disposal, including billy clubs, fire hoses, and police dogs, to disperse the nonviolent protestors led by Martin Luther King Jr. On 11 June 1963, Kennedy responded to the outrage in Alabama by unveiling a new civil rights program that had as its cornerstone the end of segregation in public accommodations if a "substantial degree" of a business catered to interstate travelers or if a "substantial portion" of its goods and services had moved in interstate commerce. That same night in Mississippi, white perpetrators gunned down NAACP leader Medgar Evers outside of his home. The slaying

6. Telegram, LH to Ross Barnett, 26 September 1962, Box 376, Folder 14, Hill MSS ("Mississippi's fight is . . ."); LH to Ralston Long, 28 September 1962, Box 376, Folder 15, Hill MSS ("unalterably opposed to . . ."); ST to C. E. Tollison, 24 August 1962, Box 3, "Civil Rights 3; Folder I," Thurmond MSS ("a reluctance up . . ."); ST to Lyn Lawrence, 19 April 1961, Box 3, "Civil Rights 3 (Race Relations)" Folder, Thurmond MSS ("I personally think . . ."); RL to Lorena White, 19 September 1962, Box 713, Folder 42, Long MSS ("we held our . . .").

touched off a new flurry of demonstrations and a concomitant wave of white retaliations across the South. Two months later, civil rights activists followed the Birmingham protest with the 28 August 1963 March on Washington in which nearly 250,000 spectators gathered to hear Martin Luther King speak. After the event, the House Judiciary Committee broadened the president's bill by adding provisions that would create a permanent Equal Employment Opportunities Commission capable of issuing enforceable executive orders, make the Civil Rights Commission permanent, include the Title III provision stricken from the 1957 Civil Rights Act, and prohibit discrimination in any business operating with state authorization. Ironically, southern members of the House of Representatives assisted in broadening the bill's scope, believing that the sweeping additions would hamper legislative action on the proposal. Later that year, Governor George Wallace made good on his promise to "stand in the schoolhouse door" to thwart the integration of the University of Alabama. This time, the Kennedy administration responded swiftly by federalizing the Guard, a prompt reaction that prevented Wallace's theatrics from degenerating into mob violence as had occurred the previous year at Ole Miss. All of the unrest in 1963 provided a further spur to the drive for substantive civil rights legislation in Washington. In the final analysis, massive resistance had serious shortfalls as a strategy for maintaining white rule in the South. With a national audience looking on, it became increasingly difficult for white southerners to deny the brutality that undergirded the Jim Crow system. By challenging judicial authority and by blatantly denying African Americans basic constitutional rights, white southern extremists ensured the type of federal intervention that their campaign of massive resistance sought to prevent.[7]

7. For a sampling of works that address some aspect of the civil rights struggle in 1963, see Berry, *Black Resistance*, 196–198; Blumberg, *Civil Rights*, 117–121, 122–125; Branch, *Parting the Waters*, 673–887; Brauer, *John F. Kennedy*, 231–241, 252–259, 272–273, 290–293; Dan T. Carter, *The Politics of Rage: George Wallace, the Origins of the New Conservatism, and the Transformation of American Politics* (New York: Simon and Schuster, 1995), 110–155; Sean Dennis Cashman, *African-Americans and the Quest for Civil Rights, 1900–1990* (New York: New York University Press, 1991), 157–166; Cook, *Sweet Land of Liberty?* 130–138; Garrow, *Bearing the Cross*, 236–260, 265–288; Fairclough, *Better Day Coming*, 273–279; Inge, *CORE*, 11; Steven F. Lawson, *Running for Freedom: Civil Rights and Black Politics in America Since 1941*, 2nd ed. (New York: McGraw-Hill, 1997), 88–91; Loevy, *Civil Rights Act of 1964*, 150–158; Manning Marable, *Race, Reform, and Rebellion: The Second Reconstruction in Black America, 1945–1990*, 2nd ed. (Jackson: University Press of Mississippi, 1991), 77–81; Oates, *Let the Trumpet Sound*, 209–243, 255–264;

Defiance typified the responses of southern senators to Kennedy's civil rights proposal and to the other events of 1963. North Carolina's Sam Ervin found the legislation "incompatible with the federal system of government established by the Constitution" and condemned the "vast arbitrary and tyrannical powers" it vested in the hands of the president and the attorney general. The wave of demonstrations in the South, according to Ervin, would continue even if the Kennedy proposal passed and would not cease "until the white man had no other place to which he could flee." Following George Wallace's face-off with the Justice Department, Ervin found much to criticize in the governor's tactics, arguing that "such conduct seriously handicaps southern Senators in their fight against civil rights bills, and aids and abets those who advocate such bills." Northern and western senators, who on previous occasions had assisted the South, he speculated, would prove less likely to do so in the wake of the violent acts inspired by certain southern leaders. Nonetheless, Ervin, who had staked out a hardline position on integration early in his career, chose to keep these sentiments private. Like the more moderate J. William Fulbright before him, the North Carolinian would not risk castigating the white South out of fear of losing his Senate seat. Ervin did not publically condemn white lawlessness and through his silence helped to ensure that the violence he privately criticized would continue.[8]

Blind to the reasons behind the civil rights protest movement, Sam Ervin theorized that voluntary community initiatives to create an interracial dialogue offered the best means of diminishing racial tensions. Unlike the federal government, local administrators, the North Carolinian believed, knew their communities better than Washington bureaucrats, enabling them to best "shape their regulations to fit local needs and conditions." Ongoing racial violence revealed that the method of solving race problems preferred by many southern senators—local dialogue—often did not work. What the North Carolinian, along with the vast majority of his regional comrades,

---

W. J. Rorabaugh, *Kennedy and the Promise of the Sixties* (New York: Cambridge University Press, 2002), 67–125; Powledge, *Free at Last?* 481–513; Whalen and Whalen, *Longest Debate*, 29–70.

8. SE to P. W. Gaither, 16 July 1963, Box 85, Folder 3823, Ervin MSS ("incompatible with the . . ."); SE to Lewis Kaney, 7 August 1963, Box 85, Folder 3845, Ervin MSS ("vast arbitrary and . . ."); SE to Creighton Lacy, 17 June 1963, Box 85, Folder 3824, Ervin MSS ("until the white . . ."); SE to Mercer T. Blankenship, 23 September 1963, Box 86, Folder 3890, Ervin MSS ("such conduct seriously . . .").

never admitted was that southerners had been granted decades worth of opportunities to right the most pronounced racial injustices in the region and yet the very same local communities touted by Dixie legislators as the solution to the region's problems did little to improve the conditions that spawned the protests. Many state legislatures did indeed undertake significant efforts following *Brown* to rectify some of the grossest violations of the separate but equal doctrine by pouring money into long-neglected black schools. Initiatives to rectify the most obvious inadequacies of segregation proved too little too late, just as they failed to address the fundamental issues behind the black protest, such as the inherent inequality of a social order predicated on race. By touting the efficacy of handling racial tensions on the local level and then by failing to produce tangible results when permitted the autonomy to do so, southern leaders provided their opponents with all of the ammunition they needed.[9]

Proving equally as combative as Ervin, Russell Long issued a Louisiana-wide radio broadcast denouncing Kennedy's civil rights package in which he vowed he would "fight that proposition till hell freezes over and then I propose to start fighting on the ice." In more pensive moments, the Louisianan recognized the serious challenges confronting the South's system of racial segregation. The region usually relied on a mere eighteen senators, far too few to safeguard Jim Crow through legislative means. He grew doubtful whether southerners could sway their colleagues from voting against the Kennedy bill once civil rights emerged as a major issue in American politics. At best, Long remarked, "we might be able to convince enough Senators to join us to the extent of not voting for cloture." Economic considerations figured prominently in his conception of the pending civil rights fight. In particular, he felt that the public accommodations bill neglected the real issue that the "Negroes' problems lie primarily in the economic field." As he

9. SE to John C. Bernhardt Jr., 20 August 1963, Box 85, Folder 3856, Ervin MSS ("shape their regulations . . ."); see also SE to Elonzo McBroom, 6 September 1963, Box 86, Folder 3867, Ervin MSS. Tennessee's Al Gore proved much more forthcoming in addressing the situation in the South. Describing events on the ground , Gore remarked that "the white South felt put upon . . . instead of concentrating on correction, it entrenched and fought back." Gore, *Let the Glory Out,* 119. Moments before the Senate passed the 1964 Civil Rights Act, Gore echoed similar sentiments: "It is my belief that this sweeping civil rights bill is now nearing enactment largely because of massive resistance." *CR,* 88th Cong., 2nd sess. (all subsequent *CR* citations refer to the same Session and Congress until otherwise noted), 14439.

long asserted, increasing social programs remained a better way of assisting the region's black citizenry than the Kennedy proposal that diluted "our cherished rights of private property." Long vowed not to "fight the Negro" in the pending civil rights battle as "I have always been his friend and I will continue to be so." Issues he championed in Washington such as social security, the school lunch program, and affordable public housing, he frequently contended, helped the poorest of Americans, who he noted were frequently African Americans. In Long's mind, the assistance he gave the black community through his liberal social welfare agenda fulfilled his obligations to them. As 1963 drew to a close, Long stood solidly with his southern colleagues, observing, "I shall certainly do my bit to preserve the white race." His promise to fight a last-ditch battle expressed the sentiments of most of his caucus mates.[10]

Thirty-year Senate veteran Harry Byrd thought he had seen it all in his lengthy political career. The seventy-five-year-old Virginian, however, could not believe the content of the Kennedy administration's civil rights bill. "I am opposed to every line" of the legislation, he wrote, vowing that the southern caucus would "fight it to the bitter end." Furthermore, he remarked that he had "never seen such pressure exerted to pass legislation by any Executive" in his Washington experience. The extent of the political forces demanding a civil rights bill undoubtedly made some southerners apprehensive. Even the usually cocksure Olin Johnston offered a less-than-sanguine assessment of the situation. "I do not know what is going to happen in the future," he observed, before adding that the southern senators would attempt "everything we can to see that the way of life as we know it is preserved."[11]

Unlike many caucus members who condemned either the president or the protest movement for their plight, Alabama's tandem of Lister Hill and John

10. RL transcript, 11 July 1963, Box 598, Folder 38, Long MSS ("fight that proposition . . ."); RL to Gus Burandt, 24 July 1963, Box 558, Folder 6, Long MSS ("we might be . . ."); RL to Elmo G. Hollaman, 30 September 1963, Box 558, Folder 20, Long MSS ("Negroes' problems . . .") and ("our cherished rights . . ."); RL to A. L. Casselman, 20 August 1963, Box 558, Folder 26, Long MSS ("fight the Negro . . ."); RL to Robert S. Osborne, 13 September 1963, Box 558, Folder 22, Long MSS ("I shall certainly . . .").

11. HB to James A. Ferguson, 28 October 1963, Additional Papers, Box 1, "Civil Rights Correspondence" Folder, Byrd MSS ("I am opposed . . .") ("fight it to . . ."), and ("never seen such . . ."); OJ to J. A. Woods, 14 August 1963, Box, 88, "Legislation 1963, Civil Rights, 6 of 10" Folder, Johnston MSS ("I do not . . .").

Sparkman employed partisan arguments, blaming the Republican Party, not their own Democratic organization, for the tumultuous events of 1963. Lister Hill, for example, declared that "it was the action of a Republican President in Little Rock that set the precedent for the use of federal troops against our people. It has been Republican members of Congress, led by Senator Javits of New York, who have gone so far as to criticize the president [Kennedy] for not doing enough in the field of civil rights." Sparkman also noted that only one Republican, John Tower of Texas, planned on aiding the southern bloc in future civil rights battles. "Nearly all of the Republicans are against us as they historically have been," he less than truthfully added, apparently forgetting the pivotal role members of the GOP played in past southern triumphs. In the aftermath of the March on Washington, Alabama's Senate delegation remained steadfast. Echoing a common caucus sentiment, Hill defiantly observed, "No march, demonstration, mob or riot is going to persuade me or deter me in my fight" against civil rights. Far from capitulating in the face of growing turbulence, the Alabama senators, at least on the surface, appeared emboldened with a new spirit of resistance. Although on previous occasions, the two senators often proved mild in their anti–civil rights rhetoric, they adjusted with the times, increasing their level of defiance as the situation in the South deteriorated.[12]

Before the administration officially announced its legislation, Lister Hill had commented that "the Southern forces in the Senate are already preparing their combined opposition" to whatever measure they might face in order "to preserve the principles that mean so much to our people in Alabama." Echoing Hill's comments, John Sparkman stated, "We Southern Senators have been organized for a long time and are fully prepared for the fight that is coming." Tempered optimism marked Sparkman's response following the initial release of the president's proposals. Recalling the compromise bills during the Eisenhower years, he felt reasonably convinced that the southern forces would follow a similar course in the future and extract "the worst parts of the bill." Despite his convictions, he warned, "we are in the worst spot this year that we have ever been in" considering what initially appeared as sizable

12. LH to R.A. Boggs, 22 July 1963, Box 494, Folder 99, Hill MSS ("it was the . . ."); JS to Earl T. Rogers, 19 June 1963, ACC 66 A89 #3, 18-E-3, "States and Human Rights" Folder, Sparkman MSS ("Nearly all of . . ."); LH to G. Baxley, 3 September 1963, Box 494, Folder 100, Hill MSS ("no march, . . ."); see also LH to Garner Bigham, 30 August 1963, Box 494, Folder 99, Hill MSS.

Republican support for the proposal. Although recognizing the odds against them, both Hill and Sparkman believed that the pending fight would not prove wholly deleterious to the South. Veterans of many civil rights battles, the Alabamians held out hope that they would again triumph. On numerous occasions, the media as well as many of their Senate colleagues thought that the southern forces would fall short and yet each and every time they pulled out some semblance of a victory. Attorney General Robert Kennedy added to their confidence by meeting with the southern caucus on 10 June 1963 to assure them that the president only sought moderate legislation that would prevent further demonstrations. Southern senators, therefore, had reason to believe that the administration would permit the emasculation of the civil rights bill that emerged from the House Judiciary Committee. It was a slim hope, but it was all that they had left.[13]

Although most of his southern colleagues vowed a spirited fight against the administration's bill, Strom Thurmond continued to doubt their tenacity on the eve of their most important battle. According to the South Carolinian, the civil rights struggle represented "a political fight and we are losing it because we are not matching political power with political power." He leavened his correspondence during the period with the troublesome concern that had become his mantra since his arrival in Washington: "I don't think there is enough real strong determination up here" to combat the drive for black equality. Almost all of the civil rights battles Thurmond witnessed as a U.S. senator required, in his mind, lengthy filibusters since he failed to see the utility of strategic delay in postponing the assault on segregation. In 1964, he would get his wish for an all-out, last-ditch filibuster. The end result would not please him. Before then, however, he felt that if the southern senators employed all of the "weapons" at their disposal, the tide might yet turn in

13. LH to W.R. Swope, 11 June 1963, Box 376, Folder 3, Hill MSS ("the southern forces . . ."); LH to S. O. Bynum, 30 July 1963, Box 494, Folder 99, Hill MSS ("to preserve the . . ."); see also LH to S. J. Ingram, 8 July 1963, Box 213, Folder 19, Hill MSS; JS to Dalton Bedsole, 10 July 1963, ACC 66A 89 #3, 18-E-3, "States and Human Rights, June 27" Folder, Sparkman MSS ("we southern senators . . ."); JS to James L. Hardman, 28 June 1963, ACC 66A 89 #3, 18-E-3, "States and Human Rights June 27" Folder, Sparkman MSS ("the worst parts . . .") and ("we are in . . ."). The Kennedy administration also hoped that it could convince at least one southern moderate to support the civil rights bill. In particular, the president thought that Lister Hill of Alabama, J. William Fulbright of Arkansas, or George Smathers of Florida would defect from the caucus. None of these senators proved willing to take such a risk. Brauer, *John F. Kennedy*, 266–267.

their favor. Bearing in mind the attorney general's intimation that the administration only wanted a moderate bill, Thurmond hoped the caucus would rally together and "serve an ultimatum on the President that we will stymie the rest of his legislative program unless he withdraws his civil rights proposals." A united southern front, the South Carolinian speculated, would pressure the Kennedy administration to capitulate. Thurmond, and to a lesser extent many of his caucus mates, neglected the equally powerful pressure exerted on the president by grass-roots black activists and by changes in public opinion regarding civil rights. The bullying of peaceful demonstrators by white mobs could not continue without some federal response. Even if the president acquiesced to the strong-arm tactics proposed by Thurmond, the civil rights fight would go on and likely intensify. Wholesale northern neglect of the black community in the South was at an end. Many Dixie statesmen, particularly Thurmond, did not fully realize the growing northern disgust over southern violence. Now, he and his colleagues faced "the biggest fight on this subject that we have ever had" with a far less apathetic northern populace than they encountered on previous occasions. But for all of their concerns, a general faith still existed among caucus participants that they were not alone in opposing forced integration.[14]

Long before George Wallace attempted to capitalize on the prejudices of northerners in his presidential campaigns, southern senators had courted the same group of voters by appealing to the racial sensitivities they shared in common with southerners. More often than not, they employed code words, such as preserving constitutional government, states' rights, and fighting federal regimentation, rather than overt racial appeals, in crafting their arguments, but the message, however veiled, remained the same. Southern senators strongly believed that the overwhelming percentage of the white population in the United States harbored at least some degree of racism. Residential patterns in the North prevented the formation of as strong a sense of "race consciousness" as found in the South. Most white Americans

14. ST to Ben E. Thralkill Jr., 7 January 1963, Box 3, "Civil Rights, January 7–November 23, 1963" Folder, Thurmond MSS ("a political fight . . ."); ST to George Nichols, 14 June 1963, Box 3, "Civil Rights 1, Folder 1" Folder, Thurmond MSS ("I don't think . . ."); ST to Jerry F. Douglas, Box 3, "Civil Rights, Folder 1—June 1963" Folder, Thurmond MSS ("weapons . . .") and ("serve an ultimatum . . ."); ST to George Nichols, 14 June 1963, Box 3, "Civil Rights 1, Folder 1" Folder, Thurmond MSS ("the biggest fight . . .").

beyond the Mason-Dixon line had little interaction with blacks, but if they did, southerners theorized, they would adopt a system akin to Jim Crow. If alerted to the real objectives of the civil rights movement, if put on notice that even northern communities without a sizable black population were at risk, that busing and quotas would result from the Kennedy bill, then maybe those beyond Dixie's borders would halt the push for social equality. Bringing northern racism to the surface served as a central feature of southern opposition since the Truman administration. In light of the rash of sit-ins, protests, and other episodes of civil disobedience "perpetrated" in the name of civil rights, Allen Ellender, reflecting the thoughts of other caucus members, remained certain that national opinion would turn against the grass-roots movement. "I think the solid basis of truth for which white southerners have fought so long is going to be recognized more and more by the people of this country" as black protests shifted northward. Indeed, he believed the "pendulum would inevitably swing in the South's favor." The question was not if, but when. Southerners banked on a favorable surge in public sentiment in their direction in light of the events that year. Although northerners deplored white southern violence, citizens above the Mason-Dixon line had begun questioning whether or not African Americans were asking for too much, too soon and thereby creating a climate that ensured their own victimization. With a little pressure, caucus members hoped to bring this animosity to the surface, provoking a white backlash against the civil rights crusade. What they could not have known was that in a few short months the man who championed the desegregation bill, John F. Kennedy, would be gunned down in a Dallas street. His replacement, Lyndon B. Johnson, a man who offered the southern caucus considerable support when he served as Senate majority leader, would inherit Kennedy's legislative agenda, including the public accommodations bill. With Johnson, formerly considered a "good southerner," in the White House, southerners hoped that civil rights legislation would fall into disfavor. The incoming president quickly dispelled such notions.[15]

After Kennedy's assassination, Lyndon Johnson wrapped himself in the legacy of his fallen predecessor, vowing to keep the slain president's staff onboard and to fulfill his predecessor's political objectives. One item on that

15. AE to Ethel Perez, 7 August 1963, Box 821, "Legislation—1963—Civil Rights" Folder, Ellender MSS ("I think the . . .") and ("pendulum would inevitably . . ."); Mann, *Walls of Jericho*, 380–386.

agenda, civil rights, went to the top of the Texan's legislative wish list. Johnson vowed to pass the bill and, even worse for southern senators, he spurned the possibility of a compromise. At the prodding of one of the South's own, the final showdown over segregation had arrived. Disappointment permeated the southern ranks as they now realized that they would wrest no concessions from the new administration. Southerners once hoped they could pressure Kennedy into withdrawing his endorsement of the civil rights bill; they knew that Johnson would not acquiesce to such strong-arm tactics. Regardless of Johnson's hardline posturing, segregationists in Washington still needed favors for their home states and thus still sought executive aid. When architects of massive resistance, such as Harry Byrd and James Eastland, could casually converse on the telephone with a man vowing to end segregation and not even mention civil rights, the role of politician as rational actor becomes most salient. Criticize the president's stand in public—all caucus members did that—but at the same time these politicians knew how the political process worked and, most of all, they knew Lyndon Johnson was a man who could get things done for them in spite of his civil rights apostasy. In short, they needed him, and in turn Johnson needed them if he hoped to fulfill his legislative objectives. The president would not ask "a southerner to change his spots" and support civil rights, an action tantamount to political suicide.[16]

One caucus member, who figured prominently in Johnson's meteoric political ascent, in particular, found the new president's actions deplorable. When asked his views on the measure in light of the regime change, Richard Russell stated that "the civil rights bill was a monstrosity when it was introduced in the lifetime of President Kennedy and it is equally evil and bad under the administration of President Johnson." In spite of his friend's activism, the Georgian vowed that he would not deviate from his usual opposition, proclaiming, "I do not intend to waver in my effort to defeat it." He would fight the measure until the bitter end, recognizing that either an outright victory or a catastrophic defeat for the South would serve as the final outcome. While publically condemning his close personal friend, Russell went right on advis-

16. In the weeks leading up to debate on the civil rights bill, Johnson touched base with scores of politicians, many of them from the South, including Richard Russell, George Smathers, Harry Byrd, John McClellan, Russell Long, Spessard Holland, and J. W. Fulbright. Michael R. Beschloss, *Taking Charge: The Johnson White House Tapes, 1963–1964* (New York: Simon and Schuster, 1997), 148 ("a southerner to . . .").

ing Johnson on all other policy matters. As usual, the president sought the Georgian's advice often calling on him to perform duties that Russell would have preferred not to perform. But he did. And he would whenever his president asked. Russell hated Johnson for his position on civil rights, but loved him as a son. Even as president, Johnson played to Russell's paternal affections, observing, "You made me and I know it and I don't forget it." Civil rights strained their relationship but would not break it. Johnson did what he felt he had to do. Richard Russell did the same. These two men who lived for the ebb and flow of the political process understood that sometimes even friends stood on opposite sides of an issue. They would not get in each other's way. And when the dust settled, they would go right on with the business of running the country.[17]

Unlike in the past, strategic delay offered no immediate solution to the pending crisis. From its conception, the southern tactical approach aimed to arrest the drive to dismantle segregation through a series of minor concessions and deliberate compromises orchestrated by the caucus. Now with Jim Crow directly under assault, many southern senators believed that no option remained but to defeat the proposal outright. To many caucus participants, the fight that strategic delay was meant to postpone had arrived, rendering the organizing principle of southern tactics against civil rights obsolete. As for the bill's future in the Senate, Russell felt that there existed some Republican opposition to the public accommodations portion of the bill, and he hoped that that party's Senate leader, Everett Dirksen, might assist in striking the provision. "But, as things now stand, our prospects are not very good," he noted, considering the pressure for the bill's enactment from most national media outlets and from both political parties.[18]

17. Beschloss, *Taking Charge*, 69 ("you made me. . .").

18. For background on the transition from the Kennedy to the Johnson administrations, see Beschloss, *Taking Charge;* Taylor Branch, *Pillar of Fire: America in the King Years, 1963–1965* (New York: Simon and Schuster, 1998), 175–179; Robert Dallek, *Flawed Giant: Lyndon Johnson and His Time, 1961–1973* (New York: Oxford University Press, 1998), 46–71, 111–121; Eric F. Goldman: *The Tragedy of Lyndon Johnson* (New York: Knopf, 1969), 13–34; Lyndon B. Johnson, *The Vantage Point: Perspectives of the Presidency, 1963–1969* (New York: Holt, Rinehart and Winston, 1971), 29, 37–39, 157–169; Kearns, *Lyndon Johnson,* 190–192; Miller, *Lyndon,* 335–450; Tom Wicker, *JFK and LBJ: The Influence of Personality upon Politics* (Chicago: Ivan R. Dee, 1968), 154–182. RR to G. D. Locke, 14 February 1964, Box 49, Folder 3, Russell MSS ("the civil rights . . ."); RR to R. L. Hicks, 17 February 1964, Box 42, Folder 2, Russell MSS ("I do not . . ."); RR to E. D. Ricketson Jr., 14 February 1964, Box 49, Folder 3, Russell MSS ("But, as . . .").

Olin Johnston pointed out other reasons for concern—the near total loss of even limited support for caucus actions by Texas, Tennessee, and border state solons such as the once friendly Oklahoma and Kentucky delegations, in addition to his assessment that some "deep southern states have lost their ironclad opposition to some civil rights provisions." By 1964, even the combative Strom Thurmond began expressing some reservations regarding the final outcome of the battle. If all the southerners "give this fight everything, I think . . . there is some chance of success, although the odds are stacked terrifically against us." This shocking admission from one of the South's foremost spokesmen of resistance reveals that even he saw the writing on the wall. Segregation was entering its last days. Despite Thurmond's criticism of his colleagues, many caucus members, at least publically, beat a defiant drum, vowing a heroic resistance. Private doubts remained just that—private. When addressing the public, southern senators gave little indication that they expected to lose. Difficult times lay ahead and the legislative battle would prove bitter, caucus members alerted constituents. Nonetheless, they would fight with all the tools at their disposal. More important is what was not said. Amidst all the bluster, no one unequivocally promised victory. Russell Long reflected this hesitancy when he noted, "I predict that we'll make headway and I am hopeful that we'll defeat the whole bill . . . I think we have a chance to win." Southerners, as Long noted, did have a chance and as the legislative battle loomed most recognized it was only a slim one. For years, they succeeded in thwarting substantive civil rights advances. Now the region's entire white dominated social system rested on the backs of a handful of southerners facing a legislative situation that never looked so grim. All their years of battle came down to this final fight in which the fate of Jim Crow hung in the balance. North Carolina's Sam Ervin found the political battle too close to call: "Whether we are successful in this endeavor is something which time alone will tell." Dwindling confidence permeated the ranks of the vaunted southern caucus in the face of its most difficult challenge.[19]

Southern senators had good reasons for their concern. Never before had they confronted as sweeping a civil rights proposal as they now faced in the

19. Transcript, n.d., Box 128, "Media Script, 1964" Folder, Johnston MSS ("deep southern states . . ."); ST to Lowndes Daniel, 4 February 1964, Box 3, "Civil Rights 1, # II" Folder, Thurmond MSS ("give this fight . . ."); transcript, 16 February 1964, Box 598, Folder 65, Long MSS ("I predict that . . ."); SE to John A. Avery Jr., 13 February 1964, Box 98, Folder 4360, Ervin MSS ("Whether we are . . .").

administration sponsored ten section bill. Title I of the measure would require uniform implementation of a state's voter registration laws. Title II would prohibit discrimination in all public accommodations. Titles III and IV would respectively authorize the Justice Department to bring suit on behalf of individuals aggrieved under the public accommodations provision and enable the attorney general to intervene in desegregation litigation. The Civil Rights Commission would receive a four-year extension under Title V. Communities that discriminated on the basis of race in any program receiving federal funding would lose such assistance under Title VI until they complied with the law. Title VII would create a permanent Equal Employment Opportunities Commission to investigate discriminatory hiring practices. The Census Bureau would receive a mandate under Title VIII to compile voter registration and voter turnout statistics at the request of the Civil Rights Commission. Title IX would grant the attorney general the freedom to assist in private lawsuits involving alleged violations of the Fourteenth Amendment. Title X would create the Community Relations Service to assist locations undergoing disputes over discriminatory practices. Of the bill's provisions, only Title X found any support among caucus members, for it recognized the longstanding southern claim that local dialogue represented the best method of solving racial unrest. Aside from that section there existed nothing else in the measure even remotely acceptable to the caucus. While waiting for the debate to begin, southern senators prepared their speeches for what would surely prove a monumental battle, one without comparison in their long fight against civil rights.[20]

On 17 February 1964, Senate Majority Leader Mike Mansfield of Montana requested the first reading of House Resolution 7152. The bill was no ordinary legislative item, it was the public accommodations proposal recently passed by the House, 290 to 130. Mansfield refused the traditional second reading of the bill, an action that revealed the strategy devised by civil rights advocates. As in 1957, they would prevent the measure's referral to the Judiciary Committee chaired by archsegregationist James Eastland of Mississippi. Nine days later on 26 February, Mansfield asked for its second reading. By refusing the unanimous consent request for a second reading on 17 February, Mansfield argued that he could call for another reading of the bill at anytime, and since the Senate's rules proved silent on the proper procedure for

20. For the text of the bill, see *CR*, 29 July 1964, 17243–17244. Foster Rhea Dulles, *The Civil Rights Commission, 1957–1965* (East Lansing: Michigan State University Press, 1968).

a nonconsecutive reading of a proposal, he contended that he could then request the measure's immediate placement on the calendar, thus bypassing the customary committee referral. Richard Russell promptly objected, requesting adjudication by the chair, who ruled the Georgian's point out of order. Seeking to overrule the chair's findings, Russell pushed for a vote. By a vote of fifty-four to thirty-seven, the Senate upheld the ruling, thereby assuring that the bill would escape committee consignment. The first phase of the battle ended in victory for civil rights advocates.[21]

On 9 March 1964, Mike Mansfield planned to call up the civil rights bill during the morning hour as Senator Dennis Chavez of New Mexico had done with FEPC legislation nearly twenty years before. During the morning hour, a motion to introduce a bill was not debatable. Richard Russell had a plan of his own. When Mansfield asked for unanimous consent to dispense with the reading of the *Senate Journal* that morning, Russell objected. The crafty Georgian, a veteran of many civil rights struggles, was about to let his adversaries know that he too had a few tricks up his sleeve. The bill's supporters kept the proposal from the committee. Now it was time for the South to answer back. Winking at Hubert Humphrey of Minnesota, the bill's floor leader, the Georgian requested a slow reading of the minutes that consumed the better part of an hour. When the clerk finished, Russell proposed an amendment to the *Journal,* a maneuver that degenerated into a monologue in which the Georgian denounced the civil rights bill. By the time the southern leader completed his speech, the morning hour had ended. At that point, Mansfield motioned to consider House Resolution 7152 anyway, but coming as it did at the cessation of the Senate's morning hour, it now fell subject to debate and thus to a filibuster. Russell won some breathing room for his troops. As the situation stood, the southern forces could now conduct two filibusters, one versus the motion, and one against the measure itself. Russell knew, however, that if the caucus maintained a filibuster against the motion, cloture would result. He and his regional cohorts planned on debating the motion for a period before permitting it to carry. This would buy southern senators time without compelling their Senate colleagues to shut off debate in the face of southern intransigence. All caucus members believed that once

21. For the House vote, see *CR,* 10 February 1964, 2804–2805; *CR,* 17 February 1964, 2882 (first reading); *CR,* 26 February 1964, 3696 (second reading). For the vote on Russell's motion, see *CR,* 26 February 1964, 3719.

a cloture petition succeeded on a civil rights bill it would set a precedent for such action in the future. They could not lose this fight, for as they saw it, they would get only one chance. The battle that Russell long sought to avoid was finally joined. "The southern way of life," which permitted white hegemony over the social and political system, hung in the balance.[22]

All U.S. senators recognized that the 1964 filibuster would differ from those that preceded it, at least in terms of its length. To meet the new challenge, the southern caucus again divided its ranks into three, six man teams headed by Lister Hill, Allen Ellender, and John Stennis, with Richard Russell serving as a floater. As in the past, the quality of their speeches varied considerably, ranging from the serious to the more whimsical. But, this proved an unusual fight requiring a melding of all of the arguments they had used in the past with new claims regarding the bill's unconstitutionality and the ever broadening demonstration movement. Throughout the debate, an eclectic constellation of ideas filled southern speeches in the most desperate filibuster in the caucus's long fight against civil rights. For those inclined to listen, caucus members provided a detailed analysis of what they considered the principal stakes in the fight. From the beginning, southern senators attempted to obfuscate the question of racial injustice in the South by shifting attention to "vagueness" in the language of the bill that if applied as southern senators warned would produce unthinkable mischief. Caucus members wanted their colleagues to study the wording of the proposal very carefully for, as one southerner explained, the bill was "as full of legal tricks as a mangy hound dog is fleas." Unless they desired the country run by "tyrannical" federal bureaucrats, southerners noted, senators should carefully weigh the sweeping implications of the administration's bill before permitting the passion of the moment to propel them toward supporting a measure capable of destroying individual liberties.[23]

Something made the southern drive to define the parameters of the debate more difficult than ever before. For the first time, civil rights advocates organized a massive counteroffensive to steal the initiative from the caucus. Under the direction of Hubert Humphrey and Republican Thomas Kuchel of California, the civil rights forces divided their ranks to ensure that they

22. For Russell's actions, see *CR*, 9 March 1964, 4742–4754; *Time*, 20 March 1964, 25.

23. *CR*, Russell, 9 March 1964, 4745 ("vagueness"); *CR*, Ervin, 11 April 1964, 7699 ("as full of . . ."); *CR*, Eastland, 21 March 1964, 5865 ("tyrannical"); see also *CR*, 11 April 1964, 7697 (Ervin); *CR*, 15 April 1964, 8090 (Ervin).

would meet all quorum calls. More important, their troops defended the bill title by title and had a representative on the floor at all times to challenge both southern arguments regarding the bill's constitutionality as well as claims concerning the idyllic nature of the region's race relations. Southern senators, long accustomed to dictating the tenor of civil rights discussion in the chamber, now found themselves confronted with an aggressive opponent. And they were not only challenged on Capitol Hill. Humphrey and his forces also commenced a public relations blitz in an effort to receive the same favorable press coverage that they claimed, contrary to caucus arguments, generally fell to their opponents. At the same time they pressed the nation's religious denominations, which had remained largely quiet in past civil rights fights, into demanding the end of Jim Crow on moral grounds.

Despite their new fighting spirit, the bill's advocates remained aware of the lessons learned from previous battles. The 1960 civil rights debate, in particular, provided valuable clues on how to surmount southern obstructions. That year, a premature effort to shut off a southern filibuster led to the failure of a cloture bid and a subsequent compromise on President Eisenhower's proposal that proved quite favorable to the South. In 1964, proponents of racial equality would allow southerners to talk for an extended period until the caucus's "educational campaign" more clearly drifted into obstructionism. Once that occurred, they would consider forwarding a cloture petition, but only if they knew for sure that they possessed the necessary votes to carry the motion. Pivotal also in the decision to give southerners a long leash remained the importance of negating charges that the region's interests had not been given full expression, that the caucus was muzzled before its members could speak their minds. Everyone recognized the highly charged racial atmosphere found in the South. Any perceived "miscarriage of justice" in Washington in which southerners were "gagged" with undue haste could potentially touch off a wave of violence. Furthermore, civil rights advocates would not hold round-the-clock sessions as they did in 1960 because they recognized that such a maneuver tended to unduly tax those not engaged in the filibuster. During the debate, the caucus would thus be extended all of the senatorial courtesies so important to members of the chamber, but southern senators knew from the outset that their opponents were diligently working toward their defeat.[24]

24. Loevy, *Civil Rights Act of 1964*, 83–89, 176; Whalen and Whalen, *Longest Debate*, 121–148.

Most disturbing of all to the southern caucus proved the president's active assistance to the civil rights forces. Few, save perhaps Richard Russell, knew the intricacies of Senate rules better than Lyndon Johnson. Few too possessed Johnson's remarkable gift of counting noses, of knowing exactly who would vote for a bill, who would vote against it, and who could be swayed. As majority leader, Johnson helped the caucus get off easy in several legislative battles by putting his talents to use on their behalf. Civil rights bills passed in this period but not nearly as far-reaching ones as would have had he not assisted. Now as president, he refused to compromise. Johnson also ensured that civil rights advocates received the coaching necessary to succeed. Champions of equality such as Hubert Humphrey always had the passion for the issue but never an effective road map to realize their aspirations. It took time to break a filibuster. Johnson knew that; Senate liberals were learning that, but needed constant reminding that patience and hard work would ultimately reap advances. Lyndon Johnson steeled the resolve of the often-undisciplined civil rights forces.

The civil rights fight now became a chess match between Richard Russell and civil rights advocates as to who best could gauge the mood of the country and of their uncommitted colleagues. Just as civil rights advocates had a plan of attack, so too did the southern caucus. Russell felt confident that the civil rights coalition would fracture as Republicans and Democrats tried to outdo each other in demonstrating their support for black equality. Southerners also hoped the lobbying campaign by America's religious denominations would prove overzealous and thereby push those senators, who disdained strong-arm pressure tactics, against the legislation. Furthermore, caucus members knew that the bill's floor leaders in the House vowed not to accept significant alteration in the civil rights proposal that passed in that chamber. If the southern senators could amend the bill in any significant way, then it became possible that the resultant conference committee of House and Senate members would deadlock over which version of the measure to accept.

At the same time, Richard Russell had to contend with internal caucus pressure. He knew that it would be difficult to convince southern hardliners such as Strom Thurmond, James Eastland, and Sam Ervin that some concessions on the part of the southerners made good tactical sense. The region's most defiant statesmen proved unwilling to accept any option that required caucus concessions. Southern senators originally adopted strategic delay to postpone a direct assault against Jim Crow. With segregation now under attack, many caucus members believed that they could no longer sell their constituents another compromise, especially not one on a bill that struck at the heart of the region's racial order. This more reactionary wing handcuffed the Georgian, preventing him from conducting the flexible rearguard battle the situation demanded. The hardliners all but ensured that the caucus would undertake a lengthy filibuster. For them, compromise on any facet of segregation was unthinkable, akin in their mind to being half-pregnant. Some caucus participants, most notably Richard Russell, hoped to adapt the principle of strategic delay to meet the present circumstances by making limited concessions on segregation to extend the institution in some form. Russell could no longer convince many of his regional colleagues of the efficacy of compromise. Even if they had agreed, it is unlikely they would have reached a consensus regarding which portions of the bill they could accept. Many caucus participants further thought that their constituents would find a compromise, even one with the potential of hopelessly deadlocking a House-Senate conference committee, an unnecessary capitulation to black agitators. This, in their eyes, was not the time to appear "soft" on civil rights. Rather than self-destruct over strategy in the face of its greatest challenge, the caucus settled on an all-or-nothing filibuster, hinging Jim Crow's fate exclusively on the strength of southern arguments. Staunch civil rights supporters Hubert Humphrey and Jacob Javits both later considered southern tactics in 1964 the principal reason for the caucus's subsequent defeat. Had southerners permitted votes on at least some amendments during the debate, Humphrey and Javits believed the caucus could have fractured the fragile civil rights coalition. Instead, southern senators "just kept talking and talking" and thereby isolated colleagues who might have proven amenable to a compromise. In the end, time served as the main impediment in the caucus's undertaking. All caucus members recognized that civil rights advocates would not indefinitely postpone a cloture vote and the longer they obstructed the legislative process with a filibuster the more support they would lose. At some point, a cloture vote would come. Southern senators needed to rally their colleagues as well as national opinion to their side before that vote, or all was lost.[25]

25. Loevy, *Civil Rights Act of 1964*, 199, 300; Javits, *Javits*, 346; Humphrey, *Education of a Public Man*, 280 ("just kept talking . . .").

Recognizing the necessity of swaying their colleagues, southerners focused more attention on the bill's potential to upset the American political system than to any other concern, even the demise of segregation. The threat of miscegenation, long a mainstay in southern arguments, received little attention in the 1964 debate. Of course, southern senators evolved more subtle ways of exploiting American racism that they would soon unveil. This shift in rhetoric reflected the larger objectives of the group. Explaining to a constituent why caucus members did not devote themselves exclusively to defending Jim Crow in their "educational campaign," Strom Thurmond observed that "if we profess to be interested here solely in segregation, then we will get very few votes in our fight to prevent foreclosure of debate in the Senate." When faced with the gravest legislative threat against segregation, the southern caucus thus turned not to the memory of the Civil War or Reconstruction but to the American Revolution. In doing so, they attempted to transform the racism that created Jim Crow into a patriotic cause. Their self-professed fight against tyranny led them to draw frequent parallels between their struggle and the response of the American colonists to British oppression in the eighteenth century. All of the affronts against individual rights that southern senators claimed the civil rights bill contained undermined the republican ideology that proved so essential in the birth of the nation. Depicting themselves as the defenders of the American political system, caucus members staked a claim on the meaning of the Constitution that civil rights advocates felt southerners so flagrantly violated. Southern senators made every effort to link their cause with the cause of all Americans. They were not the ones trampling the Constitution; they were the ones defending it. Attaching their fortunes to the most cherished episode in the nation's historical memory, southern senators made a desperate effort to bridge the divide that separated the South from the rest of the country, to transcend the boundaries and prejudices of region that prevented them from finding the middle ground they all shared as white Americans.[26]

26. For some of the few direct references to miscegenation, see CR, 9 March 1964, 4751 (Russell); CR, 16 March 1964, 5408 (Holland); CR, 24 March 1964, 6073 (Long). ST to Hugh Grant, 10 March 1964, Box 3, "Civil Rights 1, Folder V" Folder, Thurmond MSS ("if we profess . . ."); For some examples of how southerners employed the heritage of the American Revolution, see CR, 9 March 1964, 4759 (Hill); CR, 14 April 1964, 7907 (Long); CR, 11 May 1964, 10524 (McClellan); CR, 20 May 1964, 11522 (Byrd).

Muting overt racial appeals, southern senators centered their arguments on the legal implications of the legislation. The entire bill, caucus members claimed, was "flagrantly and repetitiously in contravention of the Constitution." For southerners, the dramatic departure from what they considered the intent of the founding fathers contained in the legislation represented an unparalleled assault on the American political system. In their minds, southern society as constructed by the region's white citizenry remained fully in accordance with the Constitution; it both maintained and fulfilled the intent of the framers. As Harry Byrd succinctly remarked regarding the legal foundation of segregation, "Time and circumstances change, but principles do not." Southern senators thus challenged the assumption that civil rights advocates embodied the highest ideals of the nation. Instead, caucus members depicted themselves as the preservers of order, as the defenders of the Constitution, and as the embodiment of the Revolutionary credo. Something un-American, they held, lurked behind the intentions of the bill's supporters, something foreign to basic American values. In the late 1930s, southerners had recognized a break from what they considered the nation's founding principles as the federal government gradually, but continually, stripped power from local institutions. By the 1960s, the trend toward centralization increased to such a point where, under the rubric of civil rights, the Senate was prepared to destroy the entire political apparatus that had shaped the republic since its inception. Only southerners stood in the way of this trend, and they were not without hope that they could enlist others to their side by stressing the sweeping implications of the measure, at the same time that they downplayed the centrality of race in their opposition. When accused by civil rights advocates of wasting time, not defending principle, with their "educational campaign," southerners pressed the analogy of their ideological connection with the founders to extremes. Likening the southern filibuster to the defiance of the American colonists, John McClellan of Arkansas remarked that "it was called a Revolution when our forefathers went out, and fought, and died to establish liberty in this land." Claiming they were safeguarding the legacy of liberty inherited from the Revolutionary era, southern senators believed that they were undertaking a similar heroic battle.[27]

27. For context, see CR, 26 February 1964, 3714 (Ervin); CR, 17 March 1964, 5445 (Thurmond); CR, 24 March 1964, 6045 (Johnston); CR, 14 April 1964, 7909 (Thurmond); CR, 19 Mary 1964, 11296 (Talmadge); CR, Thurmond, 31 March 1964, 6641 ("flagrantly and repeti-

To illustrate their fidelity to the Constitution, all southerners focused particular attention on the perceived threat the bill posed to property rights. Once again, caucus members expanded the purview of the debate from a narrow sectional fight over Jim Crow into a conflict over the rights of every American. For southerners, preserving segregation remained their primary concern, but they knew that property rights and the free enterprise system remained sacred ideals to all senators, especially the chamber's conservative Republicans. Early in the debate, civil rights advocates also recognized that midwestern Republicans represented pivotal swing voters because the Senate's thirty-three GOP representatives held the balance of power on any cloture vote owing to the regional split in the Democratic ranks. If the proponents of social equality failed to convince this voting bloc that the bill would not destroy the cornerstones of capitalism and individual liberty, they would fail. At the same time, caucus members pressed their own attack to sway these pivotal Republicans through the use of arguments they had employed with great success in previous fights.[28]

Resurrecting old claims southerners appealed directly to chamber conservatives by arguing that Titles II and VII of the bill made federal authority supreme over an individual's private property. Time stood still when caucus members revisited such claims—claims that their predecessors had once used in defense of the South's other principal racial system—slavery. Indeed many of the caucus's arguments in the twentieth century could have just as likely been made in the nineteenth century. Immutable constitutional principles southerners would contest; intellectual stagnation their opponents

---

tiously . . ."); *CR*, Byrd, 20 May 1964, 11522 ("time and circumstances . . ."); *CR*, McClellan, 11 May 1964, 10524 ("it was called . . .").

28. *CR*, 9 March 1964, 4744 (Russell); *CR*, 13 March 1964, 5220 (Long); *CR*, 18 March 1964, 5606–5607, 5614 (Ervin); *CR*, 16 April 1964, 8169 (Tower); *CR*, 20 April 1964, 8444 (Hill). Southern leader Richard Russell encouraged some concerned constituents to contact Senate Democrats Quentin Burdick of North Dakota, J. Howard Edmonson of Oklahoma, and Gale McGee of Wyoming, along with Republicans Norris Cotton of New Hampshire, Carl Curtis of Nebraska, Barry Goldwater of Arizona, Roman Hruska of Nebraska, Edwin Mechem of New Mexico, Jack Miller of Iowa, Thurston Morton of Kentucky, James Pearson of Kansas, and John Williams of Delaware, and urge them to vote against the proposal. To these constituents, he made sure to add that "it would be disastrous if any of these people knew that I had given you this list, and it would be best not to mention my name in any of your correspondence." RR to Leonard Maxwell, 1 June 1964, Box 39, Folder 8, Russell MSS.

would counter. Nonetheless, the ghosts of the Old South still resonated in the new. Coerced desegregation of public accommodations, according to caucus members, resulted in business owners losing the right to decide who they wished to serve. Title VII, which greatly enhanced the powers of the EEOC in southern eyes, represented nothing but the repackaging of the old FEPC proposal and their arguments against it mirrored those employed in earlier fights. Again they claimed the EEOC, like its FEPC predecessor, threatened to destroy the right of private property by "taking the authority of management from the owner and placing it in a Federal commission." Never before, caucus members lamented, had the Senate faced legislation promising such an "out-and-out unconstitutional extension of Federal Government power over the private right of every single American citizen."[29]

By highlighting the threat to individual freedoms contained in the bill, caucus members laid the foundation for a broader exposition on the implications of the "notorious" legislation that they contended stemmed from the provocations of "un-American" civil rights activists. More fundamental changes in the nation's tripartite system of government, they speculated, loomed if the Senate enacted the proposal. Foremost, southerners claimed that the measure would erode the autonomy of the individual states by forcing their acquiescence to federal regimentation. Title VI of the measure, in particular, provided the central government a powerful stick to compel compliance with the legislation by granting it the right to withhold funding to communities that flouted desegregation efforts. Even worse, the bill divested the legislative branch of any role in overseeing the implementation of the measure. Instead, the executive branch, the EEOC, and the Civil Rights Commission would receive the power to initiate legal action under the legislation, a development that, caucus members contended, undermined the system of checks and balances ensconced in the Constitution. This abrogation of state, judicial, and legislative autonomy would ultimately lead to a single result from the southern perspective—"governmental tyranny." If senators did not pause, as southerners hoped that they would, and consider the implications of the measure, they would assist in destroying "the legal and political bedrocks upon which we base our American heritage of Freedom,

29. *CR*, 14 April 1964, 7875 (McClellan), 7909 (Thurmond); *CR*, 29 April 1964, 9590 (Fulbright); *CR*, Stennis, 20 March 1964, 5808 ("taking the authority . . ."); *CR*, Tower, 19 March 1964 ("out-and-out . . .").

progress, and opportunity: separation of powers, limited executive authority, no special privilege."[30]

When not addressing the constitutional implications of the bill, southerners attempted to depict themselves as even greater defenders of minority interests than their opponents. Throughout the debate, they found many groups worthy of inclusion in the legislation that the bill's drafters originally overlooked. Their arguments in these instances derived from their long-standing assumption that political expediency dictated the push for black equality. Unlike African Americans, other minority interests lacked a powerful lobbying campaign on their behalf, a fact that made them less important to northern politicians than well-organized black voting blocs. The nation's aged and Native American populations, for example, found southerners conveniently awakened to their plights during the 1964 debate. To further illustrate their point, southern senators made sure to add that even women were excluded from the original bill and would have remained as such were it not for Virginian Howard Smith's insistence that the House inject a provision into the proposal providing for gender equality. By championing the interests of various segments of the population, southerners hoped to make one point clear—that the pending legislation resulted because of intimidation, that the protest movement through its disruptive practices had cowed the U.S. Senate. Northern politicians, southerners speculated, were on the verge of passing unconstitutional legislation out of fear of reprisal by black voters. The fact that America's less organized special interests received no attention in the proposal only served to illustrate, from their perspective, what they had long contended—that political expediency dictated northern responsiveness to the demands of black pressure groups.[31]

If southerners heaped scorn on the bill's Senate advocates, they reserved

30. *CR*, 12 March 1964, 5091 (Robertson); *CR*, 24 March 1964, 6045 (Johnston); *CR*, 26 March 1964, 6456 (Long); *CR*, 31 March 1964, 6641 (Thurmond); *CR*, 8 April 1964, 7224 (Ervin); *CR*, 13 April 1964, 7776 (Tower), 7765 (Hill); *CR*, 14 April 1964, 7870 (McClellan); *CR*, 21 April 1964, 8623 (Sparkman); *CR*, 25 April 1964, 9083 (Gore); *CR*, 30 April 1964, 9681 (Long); *CR*, 19 May 1964, 11296 (Talmadge); *CR*, 20 May 1964, 11520 (Byrd); *CR*, 9 June 1964, 1964, 13133 (Byrd of W.Va.); *CR*, Hill, 23 March 1964, 5956 ("the legal and . . .").

31. *CR*, 31 March 1964, 6607 (Russell); *CR*, 10 April 1964, 7562 (Sparkman and Thurmond—Native Americans); *CR*, 21 April 1964, 8616 (Sparkman and Stennis—Age Discrimination); *CR*, 1 May 1964, 9824 (Byrd of WV); Bruce J. Dierenfield, *Keeper of the Rules: Congressman Howard W. Smith of Virginia* (Charlottesville: University Press of Virginia, 1987), 194–196.

even harsher invective for the protest movement that called into question their mythological depiction of the region's racial system. In particular, they noted that the civil rights organizations responsible for upsetting the region's racial order had already announced that House Resolution 7152 did not go far enough. No amount of appeasement, not the administration's bill or any other legislation, southerners warned, would satisfy their demands. This line of reasoning had a very specific purpose. President Kennedy offered his more stringent civil rights proposal in June 1963 in partial response to the violence surrounding Martin Luther King's Birmingham protest. The Kennedy administration, as well as all but the most hardcore champions of civil rights, southerners speculated, supported the bill under the false pretense that its passage would stop the protest efforts that so often provoked white violence. Southerners asserted that this mistaken assumption would only embolden the "militant Negro groups." The caucus proposed its own formula for ending the protests. If the Senate took a stand and demonstrated it would "not be intimidated into enacting unwise, socialistic, and unconstitutional legislation," the "agitators" would get the message in no uncertain terms that their tactics no longer worked. Indeed, from the southern perspective, the Senate had a constitutional mandate to resist the pressures of the mob by rising above the passions of the hour and by deliberating in a setting free from the demands of lobbyists. As in the past, Richard Russell's forces argued that the founders designed the Senate so that it would remain impervious to the whims of a "transient majority." Its staggered election cycle in which only one-third of its members campaigned in the biennial congressional referendum went toward ensuring government stability. In 1964, caucus members claimed that the chamber stood on the precipice of violating the very reason for its creation.[32]

Lest their colleagues still harbored doubts regarding the true intent of the nonviolent protest effort, southerners had a ready-made response that depicted the demonstrators as something less than idealistic crusaders. "We should stop kidding ourselves" that the ongoing civil rights protests "are in the finest tradition of American freedom," remarked Harry Byrd. From the southern perspective, the wave of demonstrations that continued unabated since the commencement of the lunch-counter sit-ins in February 1960 had

32. CR, 9 March 1964 (Hill); CR, 26 March 1964, 6455–6456 (Russell); CR, 14 April 1964, 7899 (Thurmond); CR, 17 June 1964, 14223 (Hill); CR, Russell, 9 March 1964, 4747 ("militant Negro groups"); CR, Eastland, 18 April 1964, 8356 ("not be intimidated . . .").

a single objective—obtaining radical social change through violence. Caucus members made plain their belief that the leaders of the allegedly nonviolent protest movement intended to spark a "race war" that threatened unprecedented "devastation." Even worse, the caucus argued that civil rights activists created a climate of extremism that diminished the tendency toward moderation that they held represented the natural inclination of both blacks and whites in the absence, of course, of outside provocation. Caucus members regularly claimed that the actions of extremists agitating for immediate change polarized the southern population along racial lines. White moderates, who might have assisted the African American community, southern senators argued, recoiled in the face of black radicalism and drifted toward the extremists from their own race. According to Florida's Spessard Holland, the protest movement "may put back for a hundred years the progress that has been made in racial relations and destroy the peace of our land." Far from advancing the cause of black equality, southern senators claimed that the spate of "insurrections" made white approval of black Americans increasingly remote. As with so much in the belief system that went into the construction of Jim Crow, white southerners often failed to consider that segregation itself constituted a form of discrimination. With no internal dialogue that addressed the grosser inadequacies of Jim Crow, many southern whites continued to believe that all was well with the racial order that they vigorously defended. Instead of looking inward at the shortfalls of segregation, caucus members had a suggestion for the black community, a recommendation that they offered, at least in theory, out of their paternalistic regard for African Americans. Rather than pressuring the nation to view them as equals, black Americans, southern senators asserted, should work toward achieving a general level of "acceptability" in the eyes of the white population.[33]

Although southern senators attempted to provide their colleagues sound arguments from which they might find grounds to vote against cloture and thereby keep their own prejudices hidden, race remained an unavoidable

33. CR, Byrd, 15 May 1964, 11004 ("We should stop . . ."); CR, Holland, 19 March 1964, 5711 ("devastation") and ("may put back . . ."); CR, 18 May 1964, 11234 (Long); CR, 9 March 1964, 4743 (Russell); CR, 7 April 1964, 7070 (Stennis); CR, 13 April 1964, 7755 (Holland); CR, 14 April 1964, 7903 (Thurmond); CR, 28 April 1964, 9306 (Stennis); CR, 7 May 1964, 10353 (Holland); CR, 19 March 1964, 5691 (Holland); CR, 23 March 1964, 5992 (Smathers); CR, 24 March 1964, 6073 (Long); CR, 13 April 1964, 7791 (Smathers); CR, 17 April 1964, 8294 (Stennis).

component of the debate. In the end, the Johnson civil rights bill aimed directly at segregation so the defenders of that order simply could not debate the legislation without also putting themselves on record regarding Jim Crow. According to most caucus members, this represented a battle between conflicting cultures and many white southerners had little doubt that their's best suited the biracial demography of the region. Unlike northerners, who sought to impose their value system on the South, southern senators had no desire to export Jim Crow. Southerners, as Olin Johnston noted, "seek not to foster our institutions on others. We ask only to be left alone in peace with our traditions—traditions which we may chose to change over the years." Central to their arguments, as in all previous civil rights battles, remained their conviction that, on the whole, segregation fostered amicable race relations. Allen Ellender contended that, although outside agitators had succeeded in spoiling some of the racial accord in the region, social intercourse between blacks and whites, if no longer disturbed, would soon revert to its idyllic form. Indeed, racial separation, the Louisianan claimed, was "99 percent by choice." Blacks and whites would separate themselves just as "oil and water" divide when mixed, regardless of efforts to integrate them. In a sense, therefore, the legal apparatus of Jim Crow only codified a situation that would naturally occur, as illustrated by residentially segregated northern communities. At the same time they uttered such claims, southerners also forwarded contradictory contentions. Ensuring that "whites . . . marry whites and Negroes marry Negroes" also represented one of the major reasons they desired to maintain segregation. If, as they argued, the races would naturally separate as oil does from water, then how could they explain their fear of miscegenation? Speech after southern speech contained this dichotomy, balancing one part natural separation with an equal part coerced segregation. No theory ultimately emerged that unified these conflicting outlooks, a fact that highlights a significant internal flaw in segregationist logic. As on previous occasions, caucus members did a far better job enunciating the legal foundation of Jim Crow than they did the social, cultural, and biological premises that allegedly necessitated segregation.[34]

34. For examples of the southern use of race and their justifications for Jim Crow, see *CR*, 26 February 1964, 3714 (Ervin); *CR*, 19 March 1964, 5691 (Holland); *CR*, 13 March 1964, 5239 (Long); *CR*, 3 April 1964, 6820 (Long); *CR*, 13 April 1964, 7749 (Holland); *CR*, 18 April 1964, 8350 (Eastland); *CR*, 28 April 1964, 9283 (Thurmond); *CR*, 1 May 1964, 9824–9825 (Byrd of W.Va.); *CR*, 16 May 1964, 11102–11103 (Ellender); *CR*, 3 June 1964, 12555 (Ellender). For cita-

That their arguments often lacked a solid logical foundation made little difference to caucus participants because they remained focused on a more important objective. Throughout much of the legislative battle over civil rights, southern senators played to northern prejudices, hoping to rally those above the Mason-Dixon line to their cause. Political events occurring contemporaneously with the southern filibuster only reinforced their preconceived view of the northern populace. Former Alabama governor and staunch segregationist George Wallace's strong showing in the Wisconsin and Maryland Democratic primaries revealed to caucus members what they had always suspected—northern whites did not hold African Americans in high regard either. As Wallace's sizable electoral returns illustrated, many northerners did indeed find the violence that often followed civil rights protests disturbing, just as they placed much of the blame for the unrest on the black community that, in their eyes, never seemed satisfied. Following this line of reasoning, southerners claimed that wherever a large black population lived in close proximity to a white one racial unrest would ensue, resulting first in violence, then in the exodus of both the "Anglo-Saxon type of citizen" and "even the liberals." Southerners thus continually echoed the refrain that "the racial problem" was "no longer only a southern problem" as evidence of racial discord began emerging in the North. Resurrecting an old argument, caucus members held that race relations could only change slowly over time, while a radical alteration in the social configuration as proposed in the president's bill would unleash a wave of violence across the nation, even in northern communities. Attempting to capitalize on what some caucus participants perceived as a shift in public opinion in favor of the southern position, Richard Russell proposed holding a national plebiscite to decide the fate of the pending civil rights bill since the Georgian had little doubt that his countrymen would reject the legislation by a convincing margin.[35]

Russell's referendum drive further underscores the caucus's confidence

---

tions, see CR, Johnston, 15 April 1964, 8053 ("we southerners seek . . ."); CR, Sparkman, 10 March 1964, 4855 ("99 percent by . . ."); CR, Holland, 13 April 1964, 7749 ("oil and water"); CR, Long, 13 March 1964, 5239 ("whites . . . marry . . .").

35. CR, Long, 10 April 1964, 7563 ("Anglo-Saxon type . . ."); CR, Hill, 23 March 1964, 5694 ("no longer only . . ."). For other examples of southerners attempting to nationalize the race question, see CR, 18 March 1964, 5636 (Fulbright); CR, 18 April 1964, 18354 (Eastland); CR, 20 May 1964, 11490 (Long). For national plebiscite discussion, see CR, 26 February 1964, 3696 (Russell); CR, 4 June 1964, 12640–12641 (Russell).

in the existence of widespread northern prejudice. As racial disturbances spread, the charge of "racism" utilized to denigrate the South would increasingly become applicable to many northern districts. Although that day had yet to arrive, senators such as Richard Russell assured all who would listen that it inevitably would. At the time of the 1964 filibuster, a group of civil rights demonstrators in New York City, for example, attempted to disrupt the World's Fair. For southerners, the protest and the resultant heavy-handed response of the New York City Police Department provided grist for their speeches. Strom Thurmond, for one, pointedly observed that the state of New York had every conceivable civil rights bill in its law books, including all of the proposals encapsulated in House Resolution 7152. Despite this, the Empire State still experienced racial turmoil, a fact that southerners felt underscored their argument that nothing would satisfy black leaders. Responding to such evidence of northern racism, southern senators pointed out that the bill would open the way for efforts to push the civil rights question in northern blue collar communities, not particularly known for their tolerance, by way of forced racial balances in their public school systems. This line of reasoning proved very influential. For a brief period, it looked as if the southern caucus might again sway enough senators to prevent the invocation of cloture. As the frantic efforts of the bill's supporters to mitigate the apprehensions of their Senate colleagues illustrated, southern senators had hit on a fundamental reality—that an element of hypocrisy existed in the northern push for civil rights: If de facto segregation fell under attack, many of those supporting the demise of Jim Crow would alter their position on the civil rights measure.[36]

After unveiling their central arguments against the proposal, the southern forces conceded on 26 March to a vote on the motion to consider the bill. It passed easily, sixty-seven to seventeen. Oregon's Wayne Morse, who supported the measure but believed in orderly Senate procedure, moved to send the bill to the Judiciary with instructions to report back no later than 8 April. This maneuver, as on previous occasions, failed, fifty to thirty-four. After the vote, a defiant Richard Russell addressed the chamber. Regarding the recent roll call decisions, he commented, "a battle has been lost. We shall now begin

36. CR, 16 March 1964, 5338–5342 (Russell); CR, 14 April 1964, 7878–7879 (Russell), 7899 (Thurmond); CR, 21 April 1964, 8616 (Sparkman); CR, 26 May 1964, 11920 (Russell).

to fight the war." Later, he touted the strength of southern resolve, observing "despite overwhelming odds, those of us who are opposed to the bill are neither frightened nor dismayed. We shall renew the contest next week with a firm conviction that we are fighting the good fight for constitutional government." Russell's private musings from the same period further revealed his determination, although not his optimism. To one Georgian he wrote that he would spare nothing in the civil rights fight and that "if I am overwhelmed, it will be in the last ditch." The national media, Russell claimed, made the task of the southern caucus more difficult by repeatedly depicting the civil rights battle as "a fight between the South and the rest of the nation," a contention that he believed alienated "some of our friends from the West who have helped us in the past." One of the more persistent constituent queries to the Georgian centered on whether his friendship with Lyndon Johnson influenced his own actions and conversely whether he could use that relationship to dissuade the president from his unbending civil rights stance. Concerning the commander in chief, he observed, "he knows my views but I cannot force him to accept my advice," before adding, "my friendship with President Johnson will in no way deter me from my all-out battle against the misnamed and misbegotten civil rights bill."[37]

Like Russell, most southerners labeled their undertaking an "educational campaign," not a filibuster. Of course, as time went on and southerners ran through their primary arguments, they merely recycled old ones, until very little "education" was taking place. They were wasting time. At least in the early stages of the "debate," southern senators still remained hopeful that tangible good could come from their discussions. So convinced did many of them remain that once the American people became fully aware of the bill's provisions, once they recognized the measure's fundamentally un-American objectives, the proposal would "never be enacted into law." At least in public, many southern senators maintained a brave front. Sam Ervin, for example, believed the caucus had made progress, noting, "I trust that we will win this fight notwithstanding the great odds against us." Summarizing the overall

37. CR, 26 March 1964, 6455 (vote on the motion) and ("a battle has . . ."), 6456 ("despite overwhelming odds . . ."); RR to J. R. Allen, 25 March 1964, Box 3, Folder 1, Russell MSS ("if I am . . ."); RR to Chester Hayne, 31 March 1964, Box 44, Folder 4, Russell MSS ("a fight between . . ."); RR to John S. Whaley, 30 March 1964, Box 44, Folder 5, Russell MSS ("he knows my . . ."); RR to Ernest D. Key, 30 March 1964, Box 44, Folder 6, Russell MSS ("my friendship with . . .").

perception among caucus members as March turned to April, Spessard Holland of Florida remarked, "I wish that every American would inform himself completely on the provisions of this bill. If they did, public sentiment against it would be overwhelming." Southern senators remained confident that their arguments were not falling on deaf ears, that they were indeed making a difference. South Carolina's Olin Johnston proclaimed, "I sincerely believe that we are breaking through the paper curtain that has been surrounding the southern viewpoint on this issue for so long." Johnston maintained his conviction that "resentment" against the bill would grow as northerners digested southern claims. Joining Johnston in his optimism, John Sparkman observed, "we are making some headway against the bill," while also noting the potential for positive action on amendments to remove "the harsher aspects" of the proposal. A major reason for the Alabaman's sanguine assessment was his belief that not all northerners were "committed" to the legislation. In addition, he held that senators from beyond the Mason-Dixon line "must be impressed by some arguments which we have offered against the bill." Russell Long, too, succinctly stated, "we are going to continue this fight all the way and I think we are going to win." The conviction that a white backlash would emerge due to the increasingly aggressive civil rights protest movement that now spilled beyond Dixie's borders remained strong. In previous civil rights battles, they banked on popular indifference to the plight of southern blacks and found their convictions well placed. As the 1964 debate continued, the confidence of many southern senators grew.[38]

Not all members of the caucus shared the assessment of the southern fight held by Sparkman, Johnston, and Long. Some, most notably Strom Thurmond, saw not a southern renaissance in 1964 but a further surge in the forces favoring black equality. "It looks like the Negroes have our country

38. SE to Robert T. Kimzey, 4 March 1964, Box 98, Folder 4370, Ervin MSS ("never be enacted . . ."); SE to Charles J. Bloch, 11 March 1964, Box 98, Folder 4375, Ervin MSS ("I trust that . . ."); SH to T. E. Williams, 1 April 1964, Box 808, Folder 28, Holland MSS ("I wish that . . ."); OJ, 16 April 1964, Cox 128, "Media Script, 1964" Folder, Johnston MSS ("I sincerely believe . . ."); JS to Billie E. Black, 9 April 1964, 18-E-9, Box 25 (there are no folders in this box), Sparkman MSS ("we are making . . ."); JS to E. M. Goodgame, 20 April 1964, 18-E-9, Box 25, no folder, Sparkman MSS ("the harsher aspects . . ."); JS to Rhett Payne Jr., 23 April 1964, 18-E-9, Box 25, no folder, Sparkman MSS ("committed") and ("must be impressed . . ."); R L to Florence P. Hanisch, 10 April 1964, Box 598, Folder 85, Long MSS ("we are going . . ."); see also transcript, radio address, 13 March 1964, Box 598, Folder 78, Long MSS.

by the throat today," the South Carolinian observed. Nonetheless, like Johnston and Sparkman, Thurmond did sense that many white Americans had begun opposing the granting of "preferential rights for Negroes." He, however, lacked total faith that this "sentiment can be coalesced soon enough to prevent a complete take over in this country." True enough, white opinion throughout the nation rose against the lawlessness that often accompanied civil rights demonstrations, unrest that many above the Mason Dixon line attributed to what they considered the exorbitant demands of the black community, but that tide might reach its height only after the bill's passage—too late to save Jim Crow. Evidence did suggest that the tide might be turning. Gallup poll figures indicate that 65 percent of nonsouthern whites thought that mass demonstrations would "likely hurt the Negro's cause for racial equality." And that slim hope further diminished on 13 May 1964, when the much maligned civil rights advocate Hubert Humphrey warned that "the hour for cloture on the bill is fast approaching." Humphrey's threat came at a time when the repetitive nature of southern arguments had become painfully evident. In past years, many nonsoutherners accepted various caucus claims regarding the deleterious consequences of civil rights legislation. Caucus members returned to these same contentions in 1964, making only subtle changes in their traditional arguments. As the filibuster dragged on and southerners began repeating themselves, the redundancy, and oftentimes illogic, of the points raised by caucus members grew readily apparent. It became clear to some that southern senators had said just about all they could on the subject. The actions of some caucus members indicated that they too sensed the end approaching. Clarence Mitchell, the Washington director of the NAACP, observed much of the civil rights debate from his seat in the Senate gallery. Describing an Olin Johnston speech, Mitchell observed, "At the time he was giving it he was joking with a lot of people, although he would say a fierce thing in a monotone. He would smile and it was evident that this was just something being done for home consumption." With the filibuster thus shifting from an "educational campaign" to mere obstructionism, the time for a vote grew near.[39]

<hr />

39. At one point, Thurmond contended that if the South lost the fight in 1964 it would not be the result of fierce external pressure, but from internal apathy in the southern ranks. ST to J. R. McVicker, 8 March 1964, Box 3, "Civil Rights 1, Folder V" Folder, Thurmond MSS; ST to Hugh Grant, 10 March 1964, Box 3, "Civil Rights 1, Folder V" Folder, Thurmond MSS;

As the battle reached a crescendo, some caucus members looked to the heavens for solace. In April 1964, President Johnson caused a furor among animal lovers when he lifted his canine companion off of the ground by his ears, causing a yelp from the dog. Some journalists who witnessed the spectacle thought that the animal cried out in pain, but Johnson, a self-proclaimed outdoorsman, assured onlookers that such was the practice with hunting dogs. Regardless of the pros and cons of Johnson's actions, a constituent alerted Virginia's A. Willis Robertson of a scriptural passage, Proverbs 26:17, with direct relevance to the president's treatment of his dog and his handling of the civil rights controversy. It read, "He that passeth by, and meddleth with strife belonging not to him, is like one that taketh a dog by his ears." In between bouts of chiding the president for supporting the type of legislation he once opposed as a senator, the seventy-seven-year-old Virginian prepared a memo to his caucus mates that directed their attention to the biblical reference that he considered so relevant to their struggle. Along with Robertson's scriptural encouragement, some southerners, at least in the first half of May, still found reason for confidence. Russell Long, for example, observed that the "longer we fight it the more strength I think we are picking up. I am encouraged about that matter." John Sparkman also believed that they could "hold out indefinitely if Republicans and northern Democrats did not join together in a cloture bid."[40]

Before advancing a cloture petition, supporters of the administration's bill unveiled their final initiative to procure the necessary votes to shut off debate. Senate Minority Leader Everett Dirksen of Illinois demanded certain changes in the legislation before he would put his support behind the measure. Satisfying Dirksen became a central objective of the bill's floor managers. Indeed, before the debate began, President Johnson alerted Hubert

---

ST to Shirley Ann Willis, 27 April 1964, Box 4, "Civil Rights 1, Folder XV," Thurmond MSS ("It looks like . . .") ("preferential . . ."), and ("sentiment can be . . ."); George Gallup, *The Gallup Poll: Public Opinion, 1935–1971*, vol. 3, *1959–1971* (New York: Random House, 1972), 1829; *CR*, Humphrey, 13 May 1964, 10765 ("the hour for . . ."); transcript, Clarence Mitchell Oral History 1, 30 April 1969, by Thomas H. Baker, ACC#73–21, p. 20, LBJL ("at the time . . .").

40. Memo, A Willis Robertson to southern senators, 12 May 1964, Series 39:2, Box 11, Folder 5, Fulbright MSS; transcript, *Face the Nation*, 3 May 1964, Box 598, Folder 96, Long MSS ("longer we fight . . ."); JS to Joseph T. Conwell, 15 May 1964, 18-E-10, "States, Human Rights" Folder, Sparkman MSS ("hold out indefinitely . . .").

Humphrey "that the bill can't pass unless you get Ev Dirksen." After all, he controlled the pivotal swing votes needed to carry a cloture petition. Once assured that Dirksen's requests would not undermine the proposal, Johnson, along with the leaders of the civil rights coalition, Hubert Humphrey and Tom Kuchel, agreed to cooperate with the Minority Leader. A product of countless hours of conferences between Republican and Democratic Senate leaders as well as members of the Johnson administration, the so-called Dirksen substitute added over forty pages of mostly technical amendments to the president's fifty-five-page bill. Southerners found two aspects of the substitute unacceptable. It granted states with fair employment and public accommodations laws the opportunity to adjudicate discrimination complaints on the local level before the federal government intervened. Below the Mason-Dixon line no such legislation existed, a fact that ensured that federal officials would handle all discrimination suits in the region. In the North, federal control would only become an issue if local authorities refused to rectify the situation on their own or if local laws did not adequately protect an individual's civil rights. Another facet of the Dirksen substitute made the bill even more contemptible to white southerners. It amended the public education portion of the measure to prevent federal courts from ordering the transportation of pupils to correct racial imbalances in state-run schools located in residentially segregated neighborhoods. The antibusing provision prompted southern charges of northern hypocrisy concerning civil rights. After examining the substitute, Richard Russell immediately announced his displeasure over what he labeled the blatant sectionalism of the bill. Not since William Dieterich's 1938 rider to the Wagner–Van Nuys antilynching proposal that exempted mob and labor related murders from that legislation did such an unabashed example of sectionalism make its way into a civil rights proposal. "The bill has now been stripped of pretense and that it stands as a purely sectional bill; that in order to get votes, as the proponents conceive it, to impose a gag rule in the Senate, provisions have been written into the bill which would draw a monumental wall—a wall that would make the Wall of China look like a toadstool—around all the States that are North of the Mason-Dixon line, and which could not possibly be scaled by the best engineer." From the beginning of the debate, southerners considered the bill a sectional measure; now they believed they had undeniable proof for their claim. On this occasion, Russell and his forces had a good point. Only after moderate and conservative politicians above the Mason-Dixon line received a clear assurance that the residentially segregated areas they represented would not fall under the aegis of the bill could cloture succeed. In 1964, something less than pure idealism led to the final passage of the civil rights proposal.[41]

On 26 May, the day Dirksen announced his substitute bill, the mood of the caucus dramatically changed. Where once Richard Russell thought Everett Dirksen "friendly to our view," he grew more critical of the Republican leader after it became apparent that the Illinoisan would play a key role in passing a civil rights bill that year. By mid-May, Russell observed, "Senator Dirksen cannot resist the chance to get in the limelight—stage center." For the southern leader, the likelihood of a civil rights bill in 1964 seemed inevitable; however, he still recognized "a considerable difference of opinion as to the nature of the bill" individual senators would support. "This difference of opinion is our only hope to get enough votes to defeat cloture." As June approached, J. William Fulbright joined Russell in expressing the urgency of the situation. Two days after public announcement of the Dirksen substitute, Fulbright wrote, "Frankly, it appears that in the end those in favor of this legislation will muster sufficient votes to invoke cloture" against the southern filibuster. But caucus members decided they would not relent. If defeat were to meet their efforts, it would have to come in the last ditch. Nothing short of the imposition of cloture would serve as a fitting end to their campaign in defense of "the southern way of life." The notion of a last-ditch fight against integration surfaced in the correspondence of all southern senators. Harry Byrd, for example, noted regarding the civil rights proposals, "I intend to fight them to the bitter end." Summarizing the viewpoint of his southern colleagues, Russell Long stated, "we will fight right on to the bitter end. We feel that our people expect us to fight it to the utmost of our ability with all the power at our command." And, so they did.[42]

41. Transcript, Hubert H. Humphrey Oral History 3, 21 June 1977, by Michael L. Gillette, ACC#79–43, p. 6, LBJL ("that the bill . . ."); Dirksen substitute: CR, 26 May 1964, 11926–11935; Time, 29 May 1964, 22–23; CR, Russell, 26 May 1964, 11943 ("The bill has . . ."); see also CR, 17 June 1964, 14238 (Russell). For earlier southern claims of sectionalism, see CR, 17 March 1964, 5433 (Thurmond); CR, 24 March 1964, 6078 (Long); CR, 13 April 1964, 7783 (Tower); CR, 16 April 1964, 8184–8185 (Robertson).

42. RR to Jack McKinley, 31 March 1964, Box 44, Folder 4, Russell MSS ("friendly to our . . ."); RR to E. J. Hammond, 19 May 1964, Box 40, Folder 7, Russell MSS ("Senator Dirksen cannot . . ."); RR to D. R. Bryan, 28 May 1964, Box 40, Folder 1, Russell MSS ("a considerable

On Monday, 1 June 1964, Majority Leader Mike Mansfield announced his intention of laying a cloture petition before the chamber on Saturday with a vote on it scheduled for Tuesday, 9 June 1964. In a final effort to forestall imposition of the "gag rule," Richard Russell tried to force votes on the nearly four hundred amendments to the bill offered by southerners and nonsoutherners alike. The caucus did win a delay, but only for one day, as the Senate leadership opted to withhold filing the cloture petition to ensure they had the requisite sixty-seven votes to win. Proponents of the legislation faced one final obstacle. As the media heaped praise on Everett Dirksen for his part in the civil rights fight, some of his Republican colleagues headed by Bourke Hickenlooper of Indiana wished to steal his limelight by demanding action on a series of perfecting amendments favored by this small group of conservative midwestern Republicans. The Senate responded by passing a jury trial amendment advocated by the Hickenlooper faction that quieted the revolt and that all but ensured southern defeat. Jury trials were now guaranteed in all criminal contempt cases resulting from the bill except for litigation emerging from the measure's suffrage title which remained subject to the jury trial provision of the 1957 Civil Rights Act. With the dissension thus stilled, the leaders of the civil rights forces had all of the support they needed.[43]

Decades of resistance came down to this moment. Southern senators had long hidden behind chamber rules, using them for protection whenever regional racial customs came under attack. For years, Rule 22 in particular served as the white South's ultimate weapon. A filibuster, or even the threat of one, caused opponents to lose faith in their legislative position and give ground rather than fight. In previous battles, such caviling in the face of a southern shows of force had some merit. Many civil rights bills,

---

difference . . .") and ("This difference is . . ."); JF to Wiford R. Pruett, 26 May 1964, Series 39:2, Box 12, Folder 1, Fulbright MSS ("frankly, it . . ."); HB to Benjamin B. Borroughs, 1 April 1964, Box 277, "First District—Virginia Beach" Folder, Byrd MSS ("I intend to . . ."); transcript, *Face the Nation*, 3 May 1964, Box 598, Folder 96, Long MSS ("will fight right . . .").

43. Mansfield comments: *CR*, 1 June 1964, 12274; RR wants votes on amendments: *CR*, 4 June 1964, 12642–12643. Loevy, *Civil Rights Act of 1964*, 294; Mann, *Walls of Jericho*, 423–424; Whalen and Whalen, *Longest Debate*, 191–195. The vote on the jury trial provision narrowly passed, 51 to 48. For a breakdown, see *CR*, 9 June 1964, 13051. As a result, a Title XI was added to the civil rights bill to encompass the new jury trial provision that set the maximum possible reproof under the legislation at six months imprisonment or a $1,000 fine. Cloture filed: *CR*, 8 June 1963, 12922.

such as antilynching and anti-poll-tax proposals, were barely constitutional, if constitutional at all. Securing votes for cloture on such measures proved formidable and to many seemingly impossible. Legal concerns undermined them, as did the absence of a groundswell of moral outrage surrounding the issue. Important too, the American people as a whole exhibited little enlightenment on racial matters during much of the first half of the twentieth century. Discrimination was a national problem. These attitudes changed in response to a variety of factors, including World War II, anthropological challenges to traditional definitions of race, the *Brown* ruling, and the heroism of the grass-roots protests. Racism still persisted outside the South, but the strain of it found in Dixie fell out of favor. Excesses committed in its defense seemed increasingly pointless, brutal, and, to a growing number of people, immoral. America had, just as it still has, a long way to go regarding race relations, but it was moving in the right direction. Jim Crow, a remnant of nineteenth-century southern desires to find stability after emancipation, simply could not long survive in such a changing world. For segregationists, Rule 22 thus had worked when support for civil rights was limited, as well as when it was mounting, but once a critical mass was reached, its protective cloak was blown off. An absence of drama in many ways marked the 1964 vote on cloture. This time Lyndon Johnson ensured that Hubert Humphrey had properly counted noses, and if necessary, he had a few reserve votes in his back pocket. If Johnson had any doubts, no cloture petition would have been advanced. By June of 1964, the last doubts were erased. On 10 June 1964, the Senate easily voted cloture for the first time during a civil rights debate, seventy-one to twenty-nine. Only one senator representing a state from the former Confederacy, Ralph Yarborough of Texas, voted for the bill. Five Republicans, headed by Barry Goldwater, along with Democrats Carl Hayden of Arizona, who would have voted for cloture if needed, Alan Bible of Nevada, and Robert Byrd of West Virginia, who aided the caucus in the filibuster, sided with the South. After the successful cloture bid, each member of the Senate had only one hour apiece to voice his or her opinion on the legislation and no amendments could be considered during this time except for those already on the table.[44]

44. Cloture vote: *CR*, 10 June 1964, 13327. In addition to Goldwater, Republicans Edwin Mechem of New Mexico, Milton Young of North Dakota, Wallace Bennett of Utah, and Alan Simpson of Wyoming voted against the petition.

Following imposition of the "gag rule," many southerners took the opportunity to call up the amendments they introduced earlier, forcing roll-call votes on over one hundred items. Most civil rights advocates questioned the southern approach. It appeared to them that the caucus had prepared no strategy for postcloture action, resulting in what many considered the loss of a golden opportunity. Had southern senators methodically advanced some of their more reasonable perfecting amendments immediately after the cloture vote, they might have wrested at least some concessions from the chamber. Since only those amendments already on the table were admissible during postcloture debate, civil rights advocates would have been unable to modify the impact of successful southern additions to the proposal. Rather than capitalize on the situation, individual caucus members haphazardly introduced amendments many of which had no chance of success. According to some observers, southern leader Richard Russell, along with John Stennis, Lister Hill, and others, simply wanted to hasten the final vote on the bill, seeing no opportunity for any change in the measure. Sam Ervin, Russell Long, and Strom Thurmond, however, wanted to keep the battle going until they exhausted either their amendments or their allotted time. The debate thus sputtered on for several more days. During the last phase of the battle, southern senators described their amendments for approximately thirty seconds before requesting a vote with the time needed to call the roll not counted against the individual. Not surprisingly, lopsided margins defeated practically all of these efforts that ranged from an amendment by Florida's George Smathers to add age discrimination to the EEOC's purview, to John Stennis's so-called Freedom Rider amendment making it a federal crime to cross state lines for the purpose of violating state law, to Richard Russell's effort to place House Resolution 7152 before the American people in a national plebiscite.[45]

By a margin of seventy-six to eighteen, the Senate voted on 17 June in favor of the Mansfield-Dirksen substitute to the administration bill. On this occasion, Al Gore of Tennessee and Ralph Yarborough of Texas voted against their southern colleagues. John Tower of Texas and A. Willis Robertson of Virginia did not participate in the roll call, but both were paired against the substitute. With that vote, the end was in sight. Lest observers missed the sectional nature of the fight, Richard Russell pushed an amendment that

45. Smathers amendment: *CR*, 11 June 1964, 13492 (28 to 63); Stennis amendment: *CR*, 12 June 1964, 13663 (22 to 67); Russell plebiscite vote: *CR*, 12 June 1964, 13663 (22 to 67).

would have permitted the attorney general to attack de facto segregation. It too fell to defeat, eighteen to seventy-one. Thus in the end it appeared that an overwhelming majority of the Senate favored a civil rights bill in 1964, but it became equally plain that nonsouthern legislators were not prepared to face racial discrimination above the Mason-Dixon line. They supported the principle of integration so long as it remained confined to the South. So much for the legislative path of the bill that largely ended de jure segregation, a bill that, according to Everett Dirksen, represented "an idea whose time has come."[46]

With the outcome effectively decided, southerners used their remaining time to denounce the bill. Allen Ellender, for one, then seventy-three years old, reverted to his 1938 form by vehemently denouncing the black race. African Americans would never gain acceptance, the Louisianan contended, until they attained "the moral, intellectual, and cultural standards of the white race." No longer feeling the need to hide his racism, Ellender forged ahead, "one need only to look to Ethiopia, Liberia, or Haiti to put an end to the charge that the white man has kept the Negro from improving himself." At least for Ellender, the time to mask his prejudices behind a constitutional veneer had ended. Texan John Tower, the only Republican actively participating in the caucus, counterbalanced the unabashed white supremacy of Ellender by observing, "I hasten to say that as a native southerner I am deeply ashamed of the way that we have treated our Negro citizens in the South." However, enactment of the civil rights bill did not represent the best way of solving the problem. In his eyes, it would only exacerbate existing tension, a claim that South Carolina's Olin Johnston fully supported as he felt the proposal would "never be enforced without the cost of bloodshed and violence."[47]

As the hour allotted to the leader of the southern caucus ticked toward an end, he addressed the chamber one last time. After years of success in defeating civil rights legislation, observers noted tears forming in the eyes of the proud and defiant Richard Russell. He did not dwell on the alleged inadequacies of the black race like Ellender and until the end claimed "the

46. Dirksen substitute vote: *CR*, 17 June 1964, 14239; Russell amendment: *CR*, 15 June 1964, 13822. All caucus members either voted for or were paired for the amendment. Republican Milton Young of North Dakota was the only nonsoutherner to vote for it.

47. *CR*, Ellender, 18 June 1964, 14277 ("the moral, . . .") and ("one need not . . ."); *CR*, Tower, 19 June 1964, 14503 ("I hasten to . . ."); *CR*, Johnston, 19 June 1964, 14457 ("never be enforced . . .").

central issue at stake in this debate has been the preservation of the dual
system of divided powers that has been the hallmark of the genius of the
Founding Fathers." For his southern colleagues, the Georgian had nothing
but praise. "No group of men could have worked harder in a nobler cause.
Undismayed and unintimidated . . . we have fought the good fight until we
were overwhelmed and gagged," Russell tearfully observed. With only seconds of his time remaining, he concluded, "I salute each and all of the 19
stalwarts with whom I have been associated in this fight with the assurance
that I count it as one of the proudest experiences of my life to be numbered
among their ranks." After this final statement of regional fealty, the time of
the Georgian as well as the hopes of many white southerners expired. On 19
June the Senate voted, seventy-three to twenty-seven, in favor of the Civil
Rights Act of 1964. Except for Ralph Yarborough, Dixie's entire Senate delegation stood as one. As during the cloture vote, southern senators received
the support of five Republicans. Only one "northern" Democrat, Robert Byrd
of West Virginia, sided with the caucus. For decades the chamber served as
a stumbling block in the struggle for black equality. Despite the best effort
of the southern caucus, the Senate finally lived up, at least in part, to the nation's highest ideals. De jure segregation came to an end.[48]

Southern senators responded to defeat in a manner reminiscent of how
their forebears, who fought for the Confederacy during the Civil War confronted their own loss. "We were simply faced with overwhelming numerical
odds," contended Lister Hill. Virginian Harry Byrd adopted a similar tone, observing that "the odds were against us from the beginning." Others made the
analogy between their fight and that of a previous generation of southerners
more explicit. Describing the outcome of the civil rights battle, Louisiana's
Russell Long commented that "perhaps we could describe it as a second Appomattox." Pointing to a later but equally salient chapter in southern history,
Sam Ervin noted, "We have faced dark days before. During Reconstruction
somewhat similar bills were passed."[49]

48. CR, Russell, 18 June 1964, 14299 ("the central issue . . ."), 14302 ("No group of . . .")
and ("I salute each . . ."). For the final vote, see CR, 19 June 1964, 14511. Republicans Barry
Goldwater of Arizona, Bourke Hickenlooper of Iowa, Norris Cotton of New Hampshire, Edwin
Mechem of New Mexico, and Alan Simpson of Wyoming all voted against the bill.
49. LH to William I. Byrd, 23 June 1964, Box 496, Folder 162, Hill MSS ("We were simply . . .");
HB to W. F. Barclay, 14 July 1964, Box 347, "July 1964 Constituent Correspondence" Folder,

The emphasis of southern senators on the overwhelming odds that they had confronted played an important role in blunting the worst possible scenario following the passage of the bill—widespread racial violence. Long before 1964, they warned their constituents that defending segregation grew increasingly difficult with each succeeding Congress. White southerners got the message. Polling data reveals the growing awareness throughout the region that segregation would not continue forever. In 1957, when questioned whether the races would one day share public accommodations, only 43 percent of southerners responded in the affirmative. By 1963, when asked the same question, 83 percent of southerners believed that day would come—almost 49 percent of whom thought it would take place within five years. Throughout their battle in defense of "the southern way of life," caucus members no doubt had at times magnified the difficulty of the struggle they faced in Washington to make their actions appear all the more heroic. As such, the routine southern emphasis on diminishing prospects for success from the 1930s through the 1960s, in part, served callous political ends. Appearing to snatch victory from the jaws of defeat, certainly, would not hurt their standing in the eyes of their constituents. But in a larger sense, their rhetoric reflected the concept of strategic delay that labeled seemingly innocuous civil rights bills not for what they would in fact accomplish if enacted, but for what precedents they might set if passed. Each year support for black equality did, in fact, increase among Washington politicians. Caucus members expected this and foresaw that the trend would continue. In response to this frightening prospect, they repeatedly offered their constituents a worst case scenario regarding the final outcome of individual civil rights battles, emphasizing always the smallness of their ranks. Following the last battle in that war, they mythologized their service to the South by attempting to make their now defunct battle akin to a Second Lost Cause. They had fought valiantly but were defeated. The day they all dreaded had arrived, yet in many ways it did not come unexpectedly.[50]

Byrd MSS ("the odds were . . ."); *Washington Newsletter,* 20 June 1964, Box 599, Folder 8, Long MSS ("perhaps we could . . ."); SE to C. L. Miller 23 June 1954, Box 100, Folder 4438, Ervin MSS ("we have faced . . .").

50. For the 1957 statistics, see Gallup, *Gallup Poll* 3:1507; for the 1963 statistics, see Gallup, *Gallup Poll* 3:1829.

Although some caucus members blustered that they would continue the fight by seeking to repeal the bill through a national referendum or through litigation, these efforts went nowhere. Just as southerners in the nineteenth century accepted the end of slavery, most of Dixie's twentieth-century denizens accommodated themselves, however reluctantly, to the demise of their racial order. The relative peace that followed the bill's passage indicated that the campaign of massive resistance always had a smaller number of faithful adherents than many realized. Had the majority of white southerners favored defiance against federal efforts to compel integration, then surely the 1964 Civil Rights Act would have resulted in unparalleled turmoil. Richard Russell, perhaps more than any other member of the southern caucus, assisted in preventing the collapse of Jim Crow from culminating in widespread bloodshed. Rather than command southern whites to resist the legislation, he adopted the ideal of his boyhood hero Robert E. Lee by urging them to accept defeat. Like his caucus mates, he noted, "Our ranks were too thin and our resources too scanty." And like them, he too requested that southerners comply with the verdict. "All that we can do now is swallow hard and hold our heads high, knowing that we did everything humanly possible to further the cause of constitutional government," he declared. He encouraged his fellow Georgians "to refrain from violence in dealing with this act." "The die is cast now and there is nothing that can be done about it." No fire and brimstone vow to continue the battle for white supremacy, the South's premier national spokesman for segregation preached restraint and for the most part the southern populace honored his request. Russell fully believed that Hubert Humphrey's handling of the civil rights fight ultimately played the largest role in limiting southern violence. By allowing the caucus considerable time to debate the measure, the Minnesotan helped white southerners to recognize that their region had been accorded the necessary freedom to state its case in the court of public opinion. As a result, the defenders of segregation could not claim that the measure was railroaded through the Senate. Being an honorable people, the region's white citizenry, Russell believed, would accept the chamber's verdict because it resulted from a fair fight in which their intrepid senators had an unfettered forum to defend segregation. The southern senators, however, still had work to do. As implementation of the legislation began, a sizable roadblock to black equality became evident.

Title I of the 1964 Civil Rights Act proved inadequate in breaking through the impediments placed before African Americans in the voter registration process. One last fight remained for the southern caucus.[51]

51. For examples of southern bluster, see ST to R. L. Prince, 24 June 1964, Box 6, Folder XXIII, Thurmond MSS and *Washington Newsletter,* 20 June 1964, Box 599, Folder 8, Long MSS; RR to May Gee, 23 June 1964, Box 8, Folder 3, Russell MSS ("our ranks were . . ."); RR to George R. Hill, 19 June 1964, Box 38, Folder 4, Russell MSS ("All that we . . ."); RR to Guy Hornsny, 25 July 1964, Box 36, Folder 1, Russell MSS ("to refrain from . . ."); RR to D. R. Bryan, 19 June 1964, Box 38, Folder 4, Russell MSS ("The die is . . ."); Whalen and Whalen, *Longest Debate,* 204–205.

7. Inevitable Defeat

RICHARD RUSSELL'S HEALTH had steadily declined after he developed emphysema-like symptoms in 1958. Although he quit smoking after experiencing difficulty breathing, his respiratory system progressively worsened. On 2 February 1965, less than a year after the climactic civil rights fight, the sixty-eight-year-old southern leader suffered a severe case of pulmonary edema. The affliction filled the senator's lungs with fluid and constricted his breathing until an emergency tracheotomy reopened his airways. Following the surgery, the Georgian spent a lengthy convalescence at the U.S. Army's Walter Reed Medical Center. His illness left a gap in the leadership of the southern caucus, a role filled by the region's most healthy senior senator, Allen Ellender of Louisiana. As southern senators prepared for the next civil rights battle, they did so without the assistance of the Georgia Giant, who had led them for the previous seventeen years.[1]

Russell's illness coincided with the early stages of another civil rights protest organized by Martin Luther King Jr., this one addressing the problem of black disfranchisement. Less than 44 percent of the South's eligible black voters were registered in 1964, ranging from a high of 69.4 percent in Tennessee to a low of 6.7 percent in Mississippi. By comparison, approximately 73 percent of the region's eligible white voters were registered. King selected Selma, Alabama, in early January 1965 as the focal point of his voter registration drive for obvious reasons. A mere 1 percent of the city's 15,100 African American residents had access to the ballot. After several weeks, King's

1. Fite, *Richard B. Russell, Jr.*, 371, 426; Mann, *Walls of Jericho*, 463; *Harper's Magazine*, September 1966, 101.

efforts provoked many arrests but did little to expand the franchise. More important, Selma police refrained from the use of excessive force. Without clear evidence of white brutality, such as occurred at Birmingham in 1963, the civil rights leader knew he would not inspire the moral outrage that hastened the legal end of Jim Crow the year before. Two months later, King settled on a more provocative strategy. He planned a march from Selma to the state capital of Montgomery, which Governor George Wallace strictly forbade on the grounds that he could not guarantee the safety of the protestors. Despite Wallace's warning, the march went on as scheduled. Before the demonstrators left Selma's city limits, they fell victim to a savage police attack. King finally had the spur for federal intervention he had sought from the outset of his campaign. President Lyndon Johnson responded by calling on the Justice Department to draft legislation that would ensure free and fair access to the electoral system. Another civil rights showdown loomed.[2]

Before the protest, many senators mistakenly believed that the Civil Rights Act of 1964 provided sufficient suffrage protections. That legislation required in all counties uniform registration procedures for the right to vote in federal elections. Also, it presumed any person with a sixth grade education was literate, and in states requiring a literacy test to vote, an applicant had the right to request a certified copy of his or her exam. Loopholes abounded in the provision, though none proved so glaring as the absence of a suitable mechanism to ensure that requirements such as literacy tests were, in fact, equitably administered. As in 1964, President Johnson placed the full weight of his administration behind legislation to correct the shortcomings in existing civil rights laws. On 15 March 1965, he addressed a joint session of Congress, demanding enactment of the newly minted voting rights

2. The percentage of eligible blacks registered in the South for the 1964 election were as follows: Alabama, 23 percent; Arkansas, 54.4 percent; Florida, 63.7 percent; Georgia, 44 percent; Louisiana, 32 percent; Mississippi, 6.7 percent; North Carolina, 46.8 percent; South Carolina, 38.8 percent; Tennessee, 69.4 percent; Texas, 57.7 percent; and Virginia, 45.7 percent. *Congressional Quarterly Almanac: 89th Congress, 1st Session, 1965* (Washington, D.C.: Congressional Quarterly, 1966), 537. Blumberg, *Civil Rights*, 128–133; Branch, *Pillar of Fire*, 552–570, 575–588, 591–600; Carter, *Politics of Rage*, 226–263; Garrow, *Bearing the Cross*, 368–409; Johnson, *Vantage Point*, 161–164; J. Morgan Kousser, *Colorblind Injustice: Minority Voting Rights and the Undoing of the Second Reconstruction* (Chapel Hill: University of North Carolina Press, 1999),12–68; Mann, *Walls of Jericho*, 444–457; Miller, *Lyndon*, 521–529; Oates, *Let the Trumpet Sound*, 325–346; *Time*, 29 January 1965, 20–21; *Time*, 5 February 1965, 24; *Time*, 19 March 1965, 22–28.

bill. As Johnson delivered his nationally televised remarks, he stood before his countrymen as a truly national leader, a man who had broken from the crippling shackles imposed by his southern heritage, a president of all of the people. That night he spoke of American heroes from generations past, he reminisced about the impoverished Mexican students he had taught as a young educator, and he praised the perseverance and patience of America's black population. Johnson outlined the roadblocks to suffrage before adding a phrase employed by civil rights demonstrators—"We shall overcome"—a statement that elicited thunderous applause. Every negative historical assessment of Johnson that exists, and there are scores of them, must at some point confront this Lyndon Johnson, a man determined to do the right thing with an unshakable conviction. Few can deny Johnson was a man of great ambition and this ambition often compelled him to seek compromise rather than stand out on a limb. His was an ambition that some considered ruthless, even "amoral," in it application. Despite all of this, his ambition could on occasion serve the noblest of ends. In 1964 he became *the* civil rights president by supporting a no-quarter brawl with Richard Russell's forces over segregation. Less than a year later he was prepared to do the same thing with voting rights. Sure Johnson had his eyes on the history books that night in 1965, but he also had his eyes on simple fairness. His ambition had linked with the march of history; nothing now could stand in the way.[3]

The legislation that emerged from his Justice Department would permit federal registrars to enroll voters in counties where less than 50 percent of the people of voting age were either registered for or participated in the 1964 presidential election. Only those states that required literacy tests fell under the jurisdiction of the bill's "triggering" mechanism. Therefore the legislation applied almost exclusively to the southern states of Alabama, Virginia, Georgia, Louisiana, Mississippi, and South Carolina since less than 50 percent of eligible voters there participated in the 1964 presidential election. It also covered thirty-four counties in North Carolina because, although more than 50 percent of the eligible voters cast ballots statewide, less than half of the potential electorate in these specific locales had exercised the franchise. Although fewer than half of its voters participated in 1964, Texas fell beyond the aegis of the bill's punishment clauses since the legislation applied only

3. Mann, *Walls of Jericho*, 459–463.

to states that employed literacy tests. Not surprisingly, veteran opponents of civil rights noted the "coincidence" that the legislation conveniently excluded the president's home state. But as in the past, they recognized that the drive for black equality often came linked with the interests of individual politicians. In their minds political expediency still determined the type of civil rights legislation favored by Washington statesmen. Lyndon Johnson was no different, they claimed. The president knew he would get little support from deep southern states in future elections because of his civil rights activism. He could not, however, risk alienating Johnson-friendly districts by subjecting them to punitive legislation. At least according to southern senators, his voting rights proposal reflected these concerns since it so clearly focused on states that supported Goldwater in 1964.[4]

As a result of the president's actions, a new civil rights battle approached—only this one lacked much of the suspense of previous efforts. The standoff between King's protestors and Selma's police officers at the Edmund Pettus Bridge represented yet another heroic episode in the struggle for racial equality. The legislative fight over what became the Voting Rights Act of 1965, which the protest precipitated, proved somewhat less dramatic. Even with significant support behind the bill, a number of caucus participants planned on airing their grievances against the proposal, all the while knowing that they could no longer succeed. The feared southern caucus, whose string of legislative successes once prompted civil rights advocates to dub it the "battalion of death," was fighting against the stream of history and most of its members knew it.[5]

In 1965, pessimism filled the thoughts of southern senators as they followed the course of the Selma protest and awaited the Johnson administration's voting rights proposal. Aware of the daunting legislative situation before them, some caucus members still put up a bold front by raising arguments similar to those they employed when confronting previous civil rights initiatives. Their fidelity to such rhetoric illustrates that they had not completely

4. Johnson, *Vantage Point,* 164–166. Aside from the southern states, the bill's triggering mechanisms also ensnared the entire state of Alaska, along with the counties of Aroostook in Maine, Elmore in Idaho, and Apache in Arizona. Counties could avoid federal intervention if they provided suitable evidence that something other than deliberate discrimination accounted for their low voter turnouts.

5. Douglas, *In the Fullness of Time,* 217 ("battalion of death").

abandoned the principles that informed their defense of the now defunct Jim Crow system. Indeed, as many of them viewed it, theirs remained primarily a battle over constitutional principles, not a fight for white supremacy, or at least that is how they chose to portray it. At the same time, southerners wondered when the spate of legislation designed to quiet black demands would cease. As early as the 1930s, southern senators considered civil rights activists nothing more than aggressive lobbyists who needed to continually broaden their agenda in order to remain in power. The yearly increase in demands only hardened their faith in the existence of what they considered a never-ending civil rights crusade with an open-ended agenda. Pointing to the 1957, 1960, and 1964 Civil Rights Acts, Herman Talmadge of Georgia, for one, debated the necessity of further suffrage legislation since the right to vote "is probably the most protected right we have." Why, if not for scarcely concealed political opportunism, he wondered, should Congress consider another suffrage bill? The climate of opinion in the country, Talmadge argued, was such that anyone critical of the pending voting rights legislation immediately received the label, "racist demagogue." Objectivity "seems to have been absorbed by the overwhelming desire to take punitive action against the South." As usual, South Carolina's J. Strom Thurmond, who joined the Republican Party in September 1964, outdistanced others in his portrayal of the political situation in early 1965, facetiously claiming that "King Martin Luther" held absolute "control of this country." Even worse, the South Carolinian feared that, if the inflammatory actions of the protest movement continued, the South would face "another Reconstruction era all over again."[6]

Alabama's Senate contingent had a direct personal connection to the suffrage controversy once Martin Luther King chose their state as the setting for his protest against voter discrimination. As events there spiraled out of control, Hill and Sparkman met personally with the president, who informed them that administration aides had "strongly" urged King to cease the demonstrations. Echoing a common complaint, John Sparkman reaffirmed to the president his belief in the inherent lawlessness of the grass-roots campaign

6. Press release, 10 February 1965, Talmadge Series II, Sub-Series P, Box 277, Folder 6, Talmadge MSS ("is probably the. . ."); press release, 31 March 1965, Box 277, Folder 13, Talmadge MSS ("seems to have . . ."); Cohodas, *Strom Thurmond*, 359; ST to Telmer P. Vaughan, 10 March 1965, Box 2, "Civil Rights 3, Folder I," Thurmond MSS ("King Martin Luther") ("control of this . . ."), and ("another Reconstruction era . . .").

by observing, "King apparently feels himself bound only by laws with which he agrees." Although Johnson took a conciliatory approach with the Alabamians, he had no control over King's actions. The president in part pushed for a voting rights bill in 1965 under the assumption that he could corral King's activism. Johnson and his advisors hoped that the expansion of the electorate would terminate the protests. When a wave of riots swept the country after the bill's passage, Johnson discovered that his pedestrian view of the nation's racial problems proved hopelessly inadequate. Legislation alone could not cure the ills created by decades of racial oppression. Before then, he thought another bill would end the civil rights controversy. Sixty-six senators from both parties, one short of the number necessary to invoke cloture if all of the Senate's members voted, joined him by pledging in advance for the voting rights measure. Based on initial polls of chamber opinion, John Sparkman saw little chance for a southern victory. "It looks as if a great part of the country will be lined up solidly against us."[7]

While some caucus members girded themselves for a quixotic final fight, other longtime opponents of civil rights questioned the value of engaging in another filibuster to defend a dying racial order. In January 1965, Louisiana's Russell Long became the Democratic Party's Senate whip, something that shocked many in light of his unblemished service on behalf of Jim Crow. Long, however, shifted with the times, claiming, "I've been able to recognize that things move, they change and to adjust myself to a changing world, and I think that all southerners will have to do that." He also announced his support for a voting rights proposal, a decision that enraged Louisiana's race-conscious white citizens. "The southern Senators," observed Long, "will not be able to defeat a voting rights bill by taking the attitude that nothing is wrong and that no action is needed." His new position as party whip undoubtedly curtailed Long's wilder statements regarding civil rights; nonetheless, his break from his previous unbroken record of opposition to black equality occurred in dramatic fashion. Less than a year before, few southerners, save for Thurmond and Ervin, proved as vocal as Long in the battle against the 1964 Civil Rights Act. With passage of a sweeping voting rights

7. JS to R. C. Bonds, 12 March 1965, 67-A-959, Box 1, Folder 13, Sparkman MSS ("strongly") and ("King apparently feels . . ."); JS to Cleveland C. Adams, 16 March 1965, 67 A 959, Box 1, Folder 1, Sparkman MSS ("It looks as . . ."); see also JS to S. O. Bynum, 20 March 1965, 67 A 959, Box 1, Folder 19, Sparkman MSS.

bill now all but assured, the Louisianan saw the handwriting on the wall. Still a young man, he had a lengthy political career ahead of him. Behind the scenes he began courting black support. Hubert Humphrey later related that Long asked him for assistance in opening a dialogue with Louisiana and national NAACP officials. Long informed Humphrey, "I would just kind of like to have a little better, closer contact with them." To remain in office after Louisiana's sizable black population began voting in large numbers, he recognized, he would have to adjust, if only slightly, his civil rights position to help bridge the gap that separated him from his growing African American constituency.[8]

Always more reserved than Russell Long when it came to civil rights, J. William Fulbright, although long a stalwart in the southern ranks, planned to abandon his former hardline stand by not actively participating in an organized filibuster. With segregation ended, the future of southern politics was uncertain, a fact that compelled some caucus members to undertake a skilled ideological balancing act between racial conservatism and racial moderation. On national television, the Arkansan noted regarding voting rights, "I am for it. I think they [blacks] should be allowed to vote." Concerning the remaining pockets of white resistance, he observed that "these are the last gasps . . . of the opposition. I think it is nearing an end of the very active opposition." Like Long and Florida's George Smathers, Fulbright indicated he would support a bill if punishing the South did not serve as its primary objective. Fulbright placed blame for the emergence of the bill on Alabama state troopers who used excessive force to dispel King's demonstrators. His decision to condemn white transgressors rather than black malcontents or outside agitators reveals a substantive change in the perspective of Fulbright as well as many white southerners. The Arkansan himself indicated that with the passage of the 1964 Civil Rights Act southerners needed to alter how they dealt with African Americans. Few believed that complete racial harmony would result, but most came to the realization that blacks and whites needed to configure a more egalitarian social order. The white South tried to resist, but failed. Now it had little recourse save for accepting its defeat. After almost

8. Transcript, *Face the Nation,* 3 January 1965, Box 599, Folder 75, Long MSS ("I've been able . . ."); *Washington Newsletter,* 23 March 1965, Box 600, Folder 12, Long MSS ("The southern Senators . . ."); transcript, Hubert H. Humphrey Oral History 3, 21 June 1977, by Michael L. Gillette, ACC 79–43, LBJL ("I would just . . .").

thirty years of silence, moderate southern senators finally spoke out against racial oppression, by urging, at least limited, changes in the status quo.[9]

With Jim Crow ended, the region's moderate leaders took tentative steps away from unabashed support for white supremacy. Their departure from their previous positions, however, remained minimal. Racial moderates, in effect, placed themselves in a no-lose situation. By claiming to support voting rights in theory, they made a limited good-faith effort to attract future black support. By stating in advance their opposition to punitive legislation aimed at the South, they preordained themselves to vote against the administration's bill. After all, southern states flagrantly transgressed the Fifteenth Amendment, a fact that guaranteed the region would bear the brunt of any legislation designed to increase voter participation. Regardless of their ulterior motives, racial moderates did take a bold step in challenging the principles of segregationist dogma by publically noting that peculiarities existed in the region's voter registration process. Times were changing and, however slowly, politicians young enough or liberal enough to do so were changing with it.

Albert Gore Sr. had a shorter ideological distance to travel than Long or Fulbright when he announced his support for the Voting Rights Act that aimed at protecting the franchise "so clearly guaranteed by the Constitution." Gore's seeming racial progressivism in 1965 must be viewed in relation to his actions the previous year. Of Gore, President Johnson once claimed that the "little son of a bitch never had anything but political thoughts in his life." Like any rational statesman, Gore rarely adopted policy preferences that outdistanced the ideological predisposition of his electorate, especially not concerning the hot-button civil rights issue. He knew Tennesseans would likely not resist protecting the franchise, but how his constituents would react to integration remained less clear. Therefore, when facing reelection in 1964, he opposed the Civil Rights Act on the grounds that he could not abide Title VI of the measure that withheld federal assistance from locales resisting integration. Gore allied himself with the southern caucus against House Resolution 7152, a decision that led to a comfortable electoral victory later that year. Speculation regarding his actions in 1964 is not surprising, considering his narrow reelection bid in 1958, which many pundits claimed resulted

9. Transcript, *Meet the Press*, 14 March 1965, Series 72, Box 24, Folder 21, Fulbright MSS ("I am for . . .") and ("these are the . . ."); JF to Clyde S. Andrews, 23 March 1965, Series, 39:2, Box 13, Folder 2, Fulbright MSS (Selma police blamed).

from his civil rights moderation. He did not make the same mistake in 1964, although he claimed, at least in theory, to oppose all forms of discrimination. After the imposition of cloture, Gore, like the rest of the southern senators, stressed that "all citizens should comply" with the 1964 legislation. The next year he again took a position designed to least displease his white constituents. "No Negroes are being systematically denied the right to vote in Tennessee and we do not have discriminatory procedures," he wrote, as if to assure Volunteer State denizens that the bill and his support for it would not bring fundamental changes to the state. Gore clearly learned a valuable lesson; even with the demise of Jim Crow he would address the question of civil rights with caution. Still, the southern caucus would receive only limited assistance from the Tennessean.[10]

Despite defections, the remainder of the southern bloc planned another all-or-nothing battle. Unlike in 1964 when a chance for victory still existed, no prospect for success remained. Although southern senators had long anticipated failure, they took the fall of segregation hard largely because it happened during their watch. In 1965, a serious morale problem infected the caucus. Reflecting southern pessimism, Allen Ellender lamented the loss of Fulbright, Long, and Smathers almost as much as the absence of Richard Russell to illness. This was surely not the ebullient, cocksure Ellender of old. The "Minotaur" of 1938 fame had given way to a despondent leader of a shrinking southern caucus with little reasonable chance for victory. Dejection marked the Louisianan's forecast of the pending fight's ultimate outcome. "Frankly," he wrote, "we who are opposing this bill are greatly outnumbered and even a filibuster to prevent action on the legislation stands little chance" in light of the precedent setting cloture verdict the year before that all but assured a repeat performance in 1965. Even the combative Strom Thurmond realized that time had run out on the reign of white supremacy.

10. AG form letter, 25 March 1965, Issue Mail, A 37, "Voting Rights 1965, 1 of 5" Folder, Gore MSS ("so clearly guaranteed . . ."); Mooney, *LBJ*, 45 ("little son of . . ."). For Gore's perspective of Title VI of the 1964 bill, see AG to Robert Kennedy, 5 June 1964, C-15, "Judiciary—Civil Rights—1964" Folder, Gore MSS; AG to Charles H. Anderson, 27 April 1964, C-15, "Judiciary—April 1964" Folder, Gore MSS; AG to Louise Vincent, 10 June 1964, C-15, "Judiciary—June 1–10" Folder, Gore MSS; newsletter, June edition, C 44, Folder 14—Newsletters, Gore MSS; AG to Jennie A. Ashworth, 11 February 1965, Legislation C-21, "Judiciary—Civil Rights—1965" Folder, Gore MSS ("that all citizens . . ."); AG to Shirley Ann Pope, 23 March 1965, Legislation C-21, "Judiciary—Civil Rights—1965" Folder, Gore MSS ("No Negroes are . . .").

"It does appear," he noted, "that Congress will follow the President's request and pass" the bill. Alabama's Lister Hill joined the chorus of nay-sayers when he observed that "our fight will be a tough one and perhaps the toughest we have ever had on civil rights legislation." Although not as candid as Ellender and Thurmond, Hill's comments made clear that he, one of the South's veteran fighters, expected defeat. After all, if 1965 represented the toughest civil rights battle ever, then certainly the outcome would prove equally as disastrous as the "easier" fight the previous year. On the Senate floor, John McClellan of Arkansas announced the southern view of the political landscape. "I am a realist, and I know the proponents of this proposed legislation have the votes to pass practically any version of a voting rights bill they choose to pass, unconstitutional or otherwise."[11]

Even with the knowledge that they would lose, caucus members steadfastly depicted their forthcoming battle as one in defense of constitutional government. In their minds, they did not oppose the bill because they supported voter discrimination; they believed that the exercise of the franchise should occur within the parameters established by the Constitution. Sam Ervin, for one, proclaimed that he fought the bill because "I am impelled by my oath as a Senator to uphold the Constitution to oppose any legislation which I believe would dilute the authority of the Constitution." Should the Senate pass it, Herman Talmadge added, discrimination would still exist in the voter registration process "as long as our laws are executed by human beings rather than angels." Joining the remaining southern holdouts, Harry Byrd noted that "the emotion of domestic hysteria" had unduly influenced the Johnson administration, and in the process of trying to still racial discord with legislation, the president only exacerbated tensions by "inflaming so-called civil rights issues." On the eve of the voting rights debate, the Virginian informed *Newsweek* columnist Sam Shaffer that he would resist the measure, before adding, "But you know you can't stop this bill. We can't deny the Negroes a basic constitutional right." With Jim Crow destroyed, the mythological view of southern race

11. AE to William Colmer, 21 April 1965, Box 872, "Legislation—Civil Rights—1965—January thru [sic] April" Folder, Ellender MSS ("Frankly, we . . ."); see also AE to David Bernhardt Jr., 21 April 1965, Box 872, "Legislation—Civil Rights—1965—January thru [sic] April 1965" Folder, Ellender MSS; ST to Allen W. Hester, 5 April 1965, Box 2, "Civil Rights 1, Folder 1," Thurmond MSS ("It does appear . . ."); LH to J. G. Adams III, 15 April 1965, Box 498, Folder 259, Hill MSS ("our fight will . . ."); CR, McClellan, 89th Cong., 1st sess. (all subsequent CR citations from same session and Congress until otherwise noted), 28 April 1965, 8839 ("I am a . . .").

relations collapsed with it. As Byrd's comments reveal, even the stalwart defenders of white hegemony hinted at the presence of the pervasive racial injustices that they long claimed did not exist. At the same time, his statement intimates southern recognition of the hypocrisy of employing constitutional arguments to defend the unconstitutional practice of voter discrimination. Most caucus participants prided themselves on their faithful adherence to the letter of the Constitution. Although knowing that irregularities existed in the electoral system that they defended, these senators, nonetheless, claimed that practically all qualified African Americans had access to the franchise. The self-proclaimed protectors of the Constitution as wrought by the founders apparently had few compulsions about subjectively interpreting the document to suit their own needs.[12]

Those southern senators still inclined to fight advanced arguments against the bill that they utilized during previous battles over voting rights. What separated the filibuster in 1965 was the near total absence of references to the Jim Crow system. For years, caucus members tied their defense of the southern electoral system to the hegemonic white social order spawned by segregation. Now, discussions of race proved more limited than ever as southerners attempted to blunt claims made by the bill's advocates that discrimination existed in the region's voter registration process. Even without Jim Crow, they still fought for the preservation of states' rights and, as in the past, race no doubt undergirded their fears of expanding the electorate, although the latter concern remained largely unstated. Their trepidation concerning the legislation was not without foundation. Many caucus members recognized the revolutionary potential of the president's suffrage proposal. In states with sizable black populations, such as South Carolina and Mississippi, a political upheaval would result if all qualified African Americans gained access to the ballot. Southern stalwarts could not sit idly by while civil rights advocates dismantled overnight a political system eighty years in the making.

Absent too from southern rhetoric in 1965 was any reference to preserving "the southern way of life," the catch phrase long employed by caucus members to illustrate the influence of segregation and its code of racial etiquette in shap-

12. SE to Walton N. Bass, 9 April 1965, Box 114, Folder 5032, Ervin MSS ("I am impelled . . ."); newsletter, "Reports from the United States Senate," 2 April 1965, Box 277, Folder 44, Talmadge MSS ("as long as . . ."); press release, 2 April 1965, Additional Papers, Box 2, "Civil Rights Legislation (Voting)" Folder, Byrd MSS ("the emotion of . . ."); Miller, *Lyndon*, 528–529 ("but you know . . .").

ing society and culture in the region. With social equality, at least in theory, a reality, the need to keep blacks off the voter rolls to preserve the Jim Crow edifice lost much of its salience. Mass black disfranchisement, which had once served as the linchpin of Jim Crow, could no longer outlast the destruction of its raison d'être. Like segregation, it too was on the way out. No matter how much the remaining southern stalwarts might have wished to sound off regarding the futility of granting the franchise to a race they considered unprepared for full citizenship, they, with few exceptions, kept such sentiments private. Perhaps they too wondered what the future would bring in the wake of the bill's passage. Or maybe deep down they held out hope that their colleagues would see the unconstitutionality of the bill and, at the last minute, regain their reason and rise above the political passions of the hour. Whatever the case, they would fight this bill in the last ditch as they had its predecessor.

Before long the caucus commenced the symbolic battle hinted at by Harry Byrd. After Lyndon Johnson's appearance before the joint session of Congress on 15 March in which he urged prompt passage of the voting rights bill, interim southern leader Allen Ellender leveled the first broadsides against the proposal. Since his appointment to the Senate in 1937, Ellender had rivaled the most reactionary caucus members in his opposition to black equality. Unlike fellow Louisianan Russell Long, he refused to change with the times. An ideological conservative on most policy issues, his voting record appealed to like-minded Louisianans, a group that comprised the majority of the state's electorate. This core constituency would surely not rebuke his opposition to the suffrage bill. Looking to the future, he had no expectations that Louisiana's black citizenry would rally to his banner if they received unfettered access to the ballot box. Advancing in years, Ellender would likely never see the day when African Americans had a significant impact in Louisiana elections, so he trifled not with concerns over alienating future members of the electorate. In the opening guns of the 1965 fight, therefore, he employed similar rhetoric to that which he utilized when Jim Crow still existed. Political pressure, Ellender contended, served as the prime catalyst behind the legislation. Agitators such as Martin Luther King would not cease their demands, the Louisianan postulated, until Washington politicians stood firm by denying the extortionist requests of the protestors. Should Congress pass the law and permit the overwhelming majority of the populace to vote, he feared that many communities would fall under the leadership of "incompetents." The demonstrators should first attempt to overcome "their ignorance, disease, and crime," and then "they will overcome the franchise." His racially charged rhetoric proved the exception rather than the rule in this fight, but his determination to conduct a spirited opposition, if only for show, did not. "It is my intention," the diminutive southerner concluded, "to filibuster against it and talk against it as long as God gives me breath."[13]

Two days after Ellender's oration, Majority Leader Mike Mansfied of Montana motioned for the Senate to send the recently drafted voting rights legislation to the Judiciary Committee with instructions to report it out in fifteen days. On 9 April 1965, the committee responded as directed, a development that prompted John Sparkman to warn his Senate colleagues that "hasty legislation based on the racial emotionalism of the hour is not a sensible or advisable course to follow." The Alabaman, like Herman Talmadge before him, urged senators to postpone consideration of the bill until after sufficient tests of the existing voting rights laws. If the extant legislation failed to increase the black electorate, then he held that the Senate could legitimately consider the more drastic proposals contained in the administration's bill. Not all southerners made such moderate appeals. Florida's Spessard Holland, for example, claimed that civil rights advocates mistakenly believed that they could overcome the "inertia" in the black community created by a century of political inactivity. In his mind, blacks failed to vote out of apathy, not because of white transgressions. Low African American participation in the political process remained a vestigial remnant of slavery, a cultural legacy that the Floridian assured his colleagues would gradually diminish as the black community reconciled itself to the responsibilities of citizenship. His, of course, was an old argument rooted in the traditional caucus claim that no discrimination existed under Jim Crow. Southern senators such as Holland had once swayed their colleagues by deceiving them with this mythological portrait of the southern racial order. But in 1965, few senators believed such claims.[14]

Evidence of the hopelessness of the caucus fight came early. With the precedent-setting cloture vote the previous year, civil rights advocates had

13. CR, Ellender, 16 March 1965, 5163 ("their ignorance, . . ."), 5164 ("It is my . . .").

14. CR, 18 March 1965, 5387 (Mansfield's motion); CR, 9 April 1965, 7758 (bill reported); CR, Sparkman, 9 April 1965, 7758 ("hasty legislation based . . ."); CR, Holland, 22 April 1965, 8309 ("inertia").

confidence in again securing the same result. Four days after the measure's release from the Judiciary Committee, Mansfield's motion to consider the bill carried without southern dissent. In past years, such a motion would have touched off spirited southern resistance. In 1965, the caucus had little fight left. Under agreement, action on the bill was slated to begin on 21 April 1965. A battle over voting rights was little more than one week away. When that date arrived, the Senate adjourned early out of respect for Olin Johnston of South Carolina, who had succumbed to cancer that weekend. Another of the South's remaining stalwarts had fallen. Death or illness eliminated Russell and Johnston from the southern ranks; want of conviction robbed the caucus of Long, Fulbright, and Smathers. Others, such as Virginia's aging duo of Harry Byrd and A. Willis Robertson, both in their late seventies, could not be expected to contribute much. A dozen southern senators remained to man the ramparts. Of those left, few if any entered the battle with confidence. They would nonetheless put on a good show for constituent consumption and fulfill the region's historical legacy of fighting in the last ditch on behalf of white supremacy.[15]

When debate officially began, North Carolina's Sam Ervin led the way in establishing the caucus' legal grounds for combating the legislation. Like all of his regional colleagues, Ervin believed that any person meeting the requirements to vote in their respective states should have access to the franchise. Those who denied qualified citizens this right, the North Carolinian argued, "add immeasurably to the task of those of us who reverence the Constitution." With the exception of a few isolated precincts, most southern registrars, or so the senator claimed, conscientiously administered qualifications such as literacy tests without regard to race. The North Carolinian thus resorted to the well-worn southern argument that the Fifteenth Amendment, which prohibited states from withholding the franchise on account of race, color, or previous condition of servitude, provided only a "negative mandate." Based on Ervin's assessment, Article I, Section 2 of the Constitution granted each state the right to fix voter qualifications within its sovereign domain so long as those qualifications did not violate the Fifteenth Amendment. Any proposal, such as the president's bill, that threatened to do otherwise represented nothing more than a deliberate effort to undermine the intent of the framers. Caucus members thus, in this, their last major

15. *CR*, 13 April 1965, 7801 (motion to consider).

civil rights fight, returned to the contention that they sought only to defend the American political system as wrought by the founders. Race, they boldly exclaimed, had nothing to do with their opposition. Commenting on the difficulty they faced, Allen Ellender remarked, "The task of making it clear that one is not against voting rights, but only in favor of maintaining voting qualifications, is not always an easy one." Southern senators followed this line of reasoning first unveiled in the poll-tax battles of the 1940s until the end of the legislative fight against civil rights. They knew no other way, for in their minds their arguments remained rooted in immutable laws. "Time and circumstances" changed, they always held, "but principles" did not.[16]

More than the bill's legal shortfalls informed their rhetoric. During the half-hearted filibuster, Martin Luther King and the nonviolent protest movement, always the subject of caucus ridicule, attracted the full fury of southern discontent. Again, southern senators condemned the civil rights crusade as a fundamentally un-American movement bent on destroying the nation's political system. Longtime defender of segregation James Eastland praised those southerners who resisted "the forces of racial hatred and violence and civil disorders which have been unleashed in the name of civil rights but which serve effectively the purposes and the objectives of the world communist conspiracy." Eastland's comments reveal that many white southerners still refused to permit the collapse of the last bulwark of white supremacy without a fight. In an effort to revive the resistance movement, Eastland raised those who challenged the grass-roots protestors to a heroic status for their role in defending what the senator considered the highest of constitutional principles. Joining Eastland, Strom Thurmond argued that all Americans should recognize that the Voting Rights Act emerged from "one of the most successful, calculated propaganda operations ever undertaken." He added, "The movement is nothing more or less than a war against society and the existing political order—in short, an insurrection." King, according to Thurmond, would not cease his agitation for black equality until he succeeded in stripping all power from state governments. And yet, this same un-American movement, Thurmond opined, had such influence in Washington

16. CR, Ervin, 23 April 1965, 8352 ("add immeasurably to . . ."); CR, Ellender, 22 March 1965, 5554 ("the task of . . ."); CR, Byrd, 20 May 1964, 11522 ("Time and circumstances . . ."). See also CR, 18 March 1965, 5395 (Stennis); CR, 28 April 1965, 8826 (Robertson); CR, 3 May 1965, 9236 (Thurmond); CR, 4 May 1965, 9335 (Stennis); CR, 5 May 1965, 9484–9485 (Hill), 9488 (Sparkman).

that the Senate stood on the verge of passing legislation championed by this subversive element. Had something not gone wrong in America, the South Carolinian wondered, if the Constitution was flouted at the urging of violent agitators? Herman Talmadge best summarized the perception of his caucus mates regarding the civil rights demonstrations when he observed that "this bill was conceived by an unholy alliance of lawless mob action on the one hand and murder and mayhem on the other."[17]

Alabama's John Sparkman joined the southern stalwarts in denouncing the demonstration movement. He viewed the political situation in 1965 as akin to the difficulties faced by the Continental Congress. In 1783, that body moved the capital to Princeton to "maintain the dignity and authority" of its proceedings in the wake of unruliness in Philadelphia following the Revolution. Sparkman wondered why his colleagues in the twentieth century did not see it as their responsibility to safeguard American institutions against similar mob pressures. No, he did not expect the Senate to reconvene in some isolated outpost to carry on its work, but yes, he felt the chamber should at least follow the example of its Revolutionary predecessor and preserve the authority of the Senate by not capitulating to another of Martin Luther King's seemingly endless demands. Southern senators, of course, believed they knew why the Senate had conceded its role as a bulwark against the passions of the mob. A. Willis Robertson of Virginia, for one, rehashed the old caucus argument that northern politicians championed civil rights to ensure the support of black voters come election time. The bill emerged because "both major parties are engaged in a contest to see which can outbid the other for the support of the Negro vote." Adding to the chorus, Arkansan John McClellan claimed that the legislation "was prepared in haste, and it will be passed in the heat of passion. What a sad commentary on the state of the Great Society."[18]

Not surprisingly, Russell Long, who initially supported a voting rights bill, grew apprehensive upon examining the legislation proposed by the Justice Department. In a moment of unusual candor, Long conceded a point he had

17. CR, Eastland, 18 March 1965, 5452 ("the forces of . . ."); CR, Thurmond, 3 May 1965, 9236 ("one of the . . ."), 9327 ("The movement is . . ."); CR, Talmadge, 30 April 1965, 9082 ("this bill is . . ."); see also CR, 16 March 1965, 5163 (Ellender).

18. CR, Sparkman, 5 May 1965, 9488 ("maintain the dignity . . ."); CR, Robertson, 28 April 1965, 8818 ("both major parties . . ."); CR, McClellan, 28 April 1965, 8836 ("was prepared in . . ."); see also CR, 13 May 1965, 10448 (Thurmond); CR, 18 May 1965, 10856 (Eastland).

ignored on previous occasions, admitting that "in some of Louisiana discrimination had been practiced against the Negroes." Like Byrd earlier in the
year, the Louisianan finally admitted that racial injustice existed in the region.
Nonetheless, he found fault with the bill's triggering mechanism. In Louisiana,
he noted, less than 50 percent of eligible voters participated in the 1964 presidential election because everyone knew that Barry Goldwater would win
the state in light of Lyndon Johnson's civil rights policies. Many Louisianans
simply stayed home. Long observed that in the more competitive gubernato-
rial race earlier that year, more than half of the state's eligible citizens participated. From his perspective, therefore, "a bill ought to be passed, but not in
the form in which this one is drafted." Thus even those southerners who initially claimed to support voting rights legislation conveniently backpedaled
once they understood the scope of the president's proposal and its potential
to upset the established political order in their states. Racial moderates still
could not fully escape the powerful pressure exerted by white defenders of the
status quo on the grass-roots level. Like Albert Gore, they learned that they
could not too loudly support initiatives fundamentally out of step with the
ideological predisposition of their electorates. The future might bring changes
to the South, yet it still remained too soon to tell. Racial moderates such as
Long might not have joined their filibustering colleagues, but they also did
not support the president's proposal. After all, it struck most white southerners as a punitive measure designed to denigrate the region. Long's step away
from unequivocal support for caucus actions was a very short one indeed.[19]

Of all the questions surrounding the 1965 Voting Rights Act, few
prompted as much discussion as the poll tax, although, at the time, only
Alabama, Mississippi, Texas, and Virginia still imposed it. When originally
drafted by the staff of Attorney General Nicholas Katzenbach, the bill made
no mention of the poll tax. A major reason for its exclusion remained the
strength of the well-crafted and much-supported southern argument regarding the unconstitutionality of a legislative repeal. Based on the Fifteenth
Amendment, which served as the legal foundation for the proposal, a state
could not deny a citizen the right to vote because of race, color, or previous
condition of servitude. Unlike practices such as the literacy test in which
discrepancies in its implementation could result in discrimination, the poll

19. *CR*, Long, 23 April 1965, 8305 ("in some of . . ."), 8306 ("a bill ought . . .").

tax was levied equally on both blacks and whites. Unswayed by such constitutional claims, freshman senator Edward Kennedy of Massachusetts sought to inject a poll-tax provision into the bill that would abolish the requirement in state and local elections, as the Twenty-fourth Amendment did in federal contests, based on his belief that the tax placed a financial burden on the poor and thus led to economic discrimination. According to most Senate leaders as well as administration officials, Kennedy's amendment threatened to make the whole measure unconstitutional. Therefore, many staunch advocates of voting rights ironically fought efforts to inject a repeal of the poll tax into the legislation in order to protect the rest of the measure from judicial challenge. The bill's floor managers countered Kennedy with their own amendment that, if adopted, would place Congress on record against the poll tax. In turn, they hoped that the federal judiciary would uphold the position of the legislative branch by ruling the qualification unconstitutional. As in all previous poll-tax debates, the overwhelming majority of southern senators opposed the tax itself but continued to claim that a constitutional amendment represented the only legal means of repealing it. Spessard Holland, who almost singlehandedly brought about the Twenty-fourth Amendment after two decades of lobbying, observed regarding the Kennedy proposal, "I believe that the Constitution means the same thing now as it did in 1789. I deplore any philosophy which comes to the conclusion that we have a right to decide now that the framers of the Constitution did not mean what they obviously meant at the time they placed these words in the Constitution." In particular, he resorted to the well-worn theory employed by caucus members throughout the debate that Article I, Section 2 of the Constitution specifically granted individual states the right to prescribe voter qualifications. This interpretation of the Constitution, he theorized, received further support from the Tenth Amendment that enabled states to make laws in any field not specifically relegated to the federal government—in this case, establishing voter qualifications. Further validation for the southern contention emerged from their interpretation of the Nineteenth Amendment that, in the process of granting women's suffrage, also upheld a state's right to impose any voter requirement, excluding those involving race or gender, that it saw fit.[20]

20. CR, Holland, 7 May 1965, 9938 ("I believe that . . ."). For some of the southern arguments in defense of the poll tax, see CR, 7 May 1965, 9927 (Robertson); CR, 10 May 1965, 10032 (Eastland), 10050 (Tower); CR, 18 May 1965, 10849 (Eastland); CR, 19 May 1965, 11010 (Hill).

Enough senators still saw the validity of southern arguments concerning the poll tax. On 11 May 1965, the Senate defeated the Kennedy amendment, forty-five to forty-nine. Twenty-four Republicans, along with ten northern Democrats, sided with the southern caucus. Tennessee senators Al Gore Sr. and Ross Bass, Ralph Yarborough of Texas, and Louisiana's Russell Long voted yea. Long's vote in particular surprised many. The Louisianan argued that he supported the amendment because the poll tax discriminated against poor whites. He also observed that his late father Huey repealed the poll tax in Louisiana during the 1930s, a fact that encouraged the son, who often lionized the father, to belatedly follow in his footsteps. On previous occasions, Long believed that action by state legislatures or a constitutional amendment served as the only legal means of ending the poll tax. His vote for the failed amendment, however, was about as far as he was willing to go in support of voting rights. Long, who claimed to desire a voting rights bill at the start of 1965, clearly possessed a very narrow conception of adequate suffrage protections.[21]

As southern stalwarts droned on, others in the chamber planned to bring the debate to an end. In mid-May, Majority Leader Mansfield questioned southerners whether they planned another eighty-five-day debate as occurred in 1964. Caucus members assured him in no uncertain terms that they intended to fight the legislation to the bitter end. Following the poll-tax vote, North Carolina's Sam Ervin answered a question he frequently fielded. Why did he routinely offer amendments to civil rights bills that he, along with everyone else in the chamber, knew would not succeed? The North Carolinian replied with a biblical injunction from Exodus 32:2: "Thou shalt not follow a multitude to do evil." Ervin planned to fight until the invocation of cloture in defense of constitutional justice as he defined and interpreted it. Few of the southern amendments to modify the proposal mustered more than twenty-five votes, a fact that led the North Carolinian to speculate, "I don't think I could even get a denunciation of the Crucifixion in here." Outside of sporadic support from midwestern and western Republicans, along with Democrat Robert Byrd of West Virginia, the southern diehards, joined by self-declared voting rights advocates Fulbright, Long, and Smathers, stood alone. Even if the Senate approved their recommendations, caucus members observed that they would still vote against the bill. As John Sparkman noted,

21. *CR*, 11 May 1965, 10081 (vote). Long was the only usual caucus participant to vote for the amendment.

southerners introduced their amendments only "to soften the impact of this deplorable proposal and to bring it a little closer to constitutionality," not to create a measure that they could support. Nothing but the defeat of the bill would serve as a palatable outcome for the majority of southern senators. Allen Ellender did concede that his compatriots would allow a final vote on the legislation if the chamber adopted some of the amendments preferred by the caucus. This outcome would never result without cloture, largely because most of the southern proposals aimed primarily at emasculating the measure.[22]

Debate and lopsided votes against most amendments continued throughout May. The Senate did accept, sixty-nine to twenty, the limited poll-tax amendment that emerged in response to the broader Kennedy proposal. The same coalition that voted against the repeal of all poll taxes also opposed this milder amendment. Of the substantive southern requests only one received favorable attention. Reacting to caucus criticism of the mass disfranchisement of Puerto Ricans in New York on account of their inability to speak English, Jacob Javits and Edward Kennedy forwarded an amendment to abolish the English requirement in state election laws if the potential registrant attended an accredited school where English was not the primary language of instruction. Although several southern senators supported the amendment, many others, who often condemned northern hypocrisy in dealing with civil rights, opposed the initiative on the grounds that it was unconstitutional because it prevented a state, in this case New York, from exercising its right to fix voter qualifications. Their stand against the amendment indicated that their interpretation of the Constitution knew no sectional boundaries, that the caucus fight remained, at least in the minds of some of its participants, one of principle. Southern pleas aside, the Senate voted, forty-eight to nineteen, in favor of the initiative. Southern senators J. William Fulbright, Spessard Holland, Russell Long, John McClellan, and George Smathers joined the majority in supporting the amendment. Again a handful of conservative Republicans and West Virginia Democrat Robert Byrd sided with the majority of the southern bloc in opposition. With that decision, the chamber prepared to put the is-

22. *CR*, 12 May 1965, 10371 (Mansfield); *CR*, Ervin, 11 May 1965, 10102 ("thou shalt not . . ."); Time, 4 June 1965, 18–19 ("I don't think . . ."); *CR*, Sparkman, 13 May 1965, 10445 ("to soften the . . ."); *CR*, 17 May 1965, 10735, 10765 (Ellender).

sue to rest. On Friday, 21 May, Mansfield advanced a cloture petition. One of the final acts in the history of the southern caucus was about to unfold.[23]

The only bright spot for the southern forces during the debate occurred on the eve of the cloture vote. No, they did not win a major concession to weaken the bill or pick up a few recruits who finally saw the "rationality" of caucus arguments; instead, their intrepid leader through many a civil rights battle, Richard Russell, made his first appearance in the chamber since his emergency tracheotomy. Unscripted applause greeted his return, but the presence of the "Georgia Giant" did not change the legislative situation. Senators from beyond the Mason-Dixon line admired Russell for his devotion to the nation as chairman of the Armed Services Committee and for his thirty-year Senate career, not for his racial views. Had he led the caucus in 1965 instead of Ellender, the end result would have remained the same. And as expected, the Senate voted cloture on 25 May 1965, seventy to thirty, after a mere twenty-four days of debate—sixty-one days less than occurred in the 1964 fight. On this vote, the caucus lost the support of both Tennessee senators and the never reliable Ralph Yarborough of Texas. Arizona Democrat Carl Hayden, who prided himself on having never voted cloture, Robert Byrd, Nevada Democrats Alan Bible and Howard Cannon, and seven western Republicans joined the southerners.[24]

Hoping to pull the chamber back from what he considered the brink of chaos, Spessard Holland urged his colleagues to consider the lessons of the nineteenth century. After the Civil War, many a "well-intentioned" law aimed at changing the region met fierce resistance, he warned. "The fact remains," he observed regarding Reconstruction, "that it brought an unparalleled course of violence upon the whole country." Should the Congress proceed in 1965 to enact the "well-intentioned" legislation on top of the Civil Rights Act of 1964, it would precipitate similar domestic turmoil. But his colleagues by now had grown tired of the old caucus threats. By a margin of seventy-seven to nineteen, the Senate, one day after invoking cloture, enacted the voting rights bill. All senators from the eleven states of the former

23. CR, 19 May 1965, 11018 (poll-tax vote). Again, Russell Long was the only southern senator who traditionally worked with the caucus to vote in favor of the poll-tax repeal. CR, 20 May 1965, 11061–11074, 11074 (Kennedy-Javits); CR, 21 May 1965 (cloture advanced).

24. CR, 25 May 1965, 11466 (cloture vote).

Confederacy, except the Tennessee delegation and Ralph Yarborough, voted against the proposal. No one else in the chamber joined the southerners except Robert Byrd, who was paired against the bill. The South had taken its last stand and as in the 1860s it suffered total defeat. The fact that few southerners took advantage of the hour afforded them in postcloture debate underscores the resignation with which they viewed this battle.[25]

After the bill's passage, John Stennis of Mississippi thanked Allen Ellender for his leadership in the 1965 fight. "We had the points and the arguments and we had the Constitution. In fact we had everything except the votes," Stennis wrote the Louisianan. Indeed, their final battle proved the least offensive to twenty-first-century racial sensibilities. The caucus kept its arguments germane and largely free of slurs. Although southern senators fought the battle along constitutional lines, theirs remained a stagnant interpretation of the document that did not permit change in the face of the broader social reconfiguration that occurred in the North after World War II—the same change that propelled the Supreme Court to alter longstanding but allegedly outmoded judicial precedents that southerners tenaciously defended as immutable principles. Speaking of the southern fight, Ellender plaintively remarked, "We did our best, but we were unable to keep talking when the liberals" invoked cloture. John Sparkman echoed similar sentiments. We "fought the measure in every way that we could," he claimed, but "we were simply overwhelmed when nearly all of our colleagues from the North, the East, and the West voted" against us. Without bluster, Strom Thurmond also accepted the outcome of the battle. "I did all that I could to prevent its passage," the South Carolinian explained. Now, he believed, "the only thing that can be done at this point is for those of us who are concerned to voice our concern to all who will listen." Thurmond neither promised a final great southern counteroffensive, nor offered a ray of hope that a solution enabling the continuation of white dominance might still emerge. He too knew the battle had been lost. Following the caucus's defeat, Lister Hill promised, "I will continue to fight legislation aimed at the South and our people." Hill would

25. *CR*, Holland, 26 May 1965, 11720 ("well intentioned") and ("The fact remains . . ."); *CR*, 26 May 1965, 11752 (final vote), 11751–11752. The Voting Rights Act next went to a House-Senate Conference Committee to iron out differences in the language of the bills passed by each chamber. On 4 August, the Senate approved the committee report, seventy-nine to eighteen. *CR*, 4 August 1965, 19378.

have to pursue that fight in a different context. Little remained of the legal foundation of "the southern way of life" that he had defended since his 1938 arrival in the Senate. Over the years, he, along with his regional colleagues, had battled together against civil rights legislation. During the same period, Hill, unlike some southerners, also waged a war to ensure that the region received its fair share of federal funding for public works and social services. This latter battle he would continue. As for the former, it no longer commanded preeminent attention. The South he had known, a South of legally enforced racial discrimination and mass disfranchisement, was no more.[26]

Although absent for the majority of the 1965 debate, Richard Russell, the dean of southern senators, was not without opinion on the bill. Regarding its passage, he observed that "the country was worked into such an emotional state over this legislation that the voice of reason and logic had no effect." As for his old friend Lyndon Johnson, who helped to bring about the situation that Russell so lamented, he hoped the president would "shake off the extreme left-wingers who surround him," just as the Georgian wished that the administration would curtail granting "special privileges to a small group at the expense of the white people of the South." For years, Russell warned of the potential for anarchy if Washington politicians insisted on rewarding unlawful civil rights protests. The Watts Riot in Los Angeles after the passage of the Voting Rights Act surprised many Americans. But not Richard Russell. He had foreseen such a possibility all along. By repeatedly caving in to the demands of black activists, Russell theorized that civil rights advocates gave the more "ignorant" of the black community "a license to commit any offense they desire," a fact that could "only lead to the breakdown of all orderly society and usher in a period of anarchy." In his mind that was exactly what happened in Watts.[27]

26. John Stennis to AE, 4 June 1965, Box 873, "Civil Rights 1965—July thru [sic]–" Folder, Ellender MSS ("we had the . . ."); AE to W. M. Caskey, 8 June 1965, Box 873, "Legislation—Civil Rights—1965" Folder, Ellender MSS ("we did our . . ."); JS to Jeanette Campbell, 17 June 1965, ACC 67 A 959, Box 16, Folder 20, Sparkman MSS ("fought the measure . . ."); ST to J. E. Schroeder, 7 June 1965, Box 2, "Civil Rights 1, Folder II," Thurmond MSS ("I did all . . ."); ST to Charles Mack, 9 June 1965, Box 2, "Civil Rights 1, Folder II," Thurmond MSS ("the only thing . . ."); LH to R. H. Reed, 11 August 1965, Box 498, Folder 278, Hill MSS ("I will continue . . .").

27. RR to B. R. Snooks, 28 May 1965, Box 33, Folder 5, Russell MSS ("the country was . . ."); RR to Kames M. Aiken, 15 May 1965, Box 33, Folder 5, Russell MSS ("shake off the . . ."); see

The bill's passage also marked the closing of an important chapter in Richard Russell's career. With his health deteriorating, he began divesting himself of the powers that once led journalists to consider him the most powerful man in the Senate, a man who allegedly ran the chamber with a wink and a nod. It is clear that the defeats in 1964 and in 1965 challenged the Georgian's faith in the nation's future. As he saw it, if the processes of social anarchy and centralization of government power continued, "our civilization—the greatest that has ever existed under the canopy of heaven—is doomed." Although counseling white southerners to refrain from violence, Russell personally refused to make peace with the idea of black legal and political equality. He retained a visceral distrust of the South's largest minority group. More than a year after the passage of the 1964 Civil Rights Act, Russell still bitterly observed that "the Negro race is the only race that feels they are being downgraded by association with members of their own race." He would never lose his racial hostility, in part because it remained integrally attached with his entire conception of the American political system. Jim Crow's demise represented, in his eyes, just another example of the federal government's assault against state autonomy and individual liberty. Time would not alter this perception.[28]

For three decades southern senators had blocked all perceived assaults against the region's racial order. By 1965, their ability to defend the status quo in Dixie had disappeared, and all of them recognized it. During the fight against the Voting Rights Act, caucus hardliners engaged in one final battle in defense of white supremacy for constituent consumption. Their arguments, as in the past, downplayed the centrality of racism in their worldview. This time, as in 1964, the effects of the grass-roots protest movement on public opinion stripped the caucus of its ability to sway its Senate colleagues. In 1965, southern senators never had a chance. Even some caucus stalwarts chose to sit out the filibuster. For them, limited participation in the debate served as their first break from unabashed support for caucus actions. True,

---

also RR to Newton Wilcox, 22 June 1965, Box 32, Folder 3, Russell MSS; RR to John S. Buchanan, 7 September 1965, Box 32, Folder 6, Russell MSS ("ignorant") and ("a license to . . ."); RR to Mack W. Mayes. 26 October 1965, Box 32, Folder 5, Russell MSS ("only lead to . . .").

28. RR to W. M. Landrum Jr., 13 October 1965, Box 32, Folder 5, Russell MSS ("our civilization"); see also RR to R. G. Philbeck, 7 September 1965, Box 32, Folder 6, Russell MSS; RR to G. Cecil Jones, 11 October 1965, Box 32, Folder 4, Russell MSS ("the Negro race . . .").

their departure from regional norms remained confined to public recognition that voter discrimination existed in Dixie, but their decision signaled their readiness to come to terms with new political realities. Even if all of the southern senators had participated in the fight, the end result would not have changed. With the franchise, at least in theory, secured by the passage of the Voting Rights Act, African Americans in the South once again had access to the power that would enable them to have some control over their own destiny—free at least from the institutionalized racism that formerly impeded them.

Conclusion

WITH LEGAL AND political equality procured, at least in theory, with the landmark legislation of 1964 and 1965, the civil rights movement splintered as the focus of the crusade shifted northward to the economic injustices that impeded the advancement of the nation's black community. When the protest effort expanded, it fractured over its objectives and divided over the nonviolent philosophy that once proved so successful in the South. White opposition, as it developed in the U.S. Senate, also fragmented, albeit for different reasons. Born in the 1930s to stem the nascent civil rights crusade, the unified southern Senate bloc lost its focus once the reason for which it existed—maintaining white supremacy—collapsed under the weight of civil rights legislation in the 1960s. After the passage of the Housing Rights Act of 1968, Richard Russell officially relinquished his leadership role over what remained of the southern caucus. The group that staggered on as a mere shadow after 1965 no longer had the power or the troops it once had, or a clear set of "southern interests" to defend.

The demise of the caucus did not diminish the political strength of Dixie's senators. Many of them, including Richard Russell, John Stennis, James Eastland, Allen Ellender, John McClellan, and Herman Talmadge, still chaired important Senate committees and thus continued to dominate the legislative process in the chamber. A shift in national opinion toward greater conservatism, however, gradually eroded the size of the Democratic majority in the Senate. During the presidency of Ronald Reagan (1981–1989), Republicans regained control of the Senate for the first time since 1955, reducing southerners to minority status on the committees they once headed. When

Democrats recaptured the chamber following the 1986 election, eight of the Senate's fifteen standing committees again fell under southern control, but these leaders were "bona fide national Democrats" who, unlike their regional predecessors, consistently voted with the national party. When Richard Russell and Harry Byrd occupied the chamber, southern senators shared many of the ideological tendencies of chamber Republicans and often voted with the GOP in what observers called a "conservative coalition." This coalition, which emerged in response to President Franklin Roosevelt's attempt to pack the Supreme Court with more liberal justices, eroded over time, especially after the 1960s, when the national Democratic Party became more centrist. In the 1970s and 1980s, the conservatism that typified southern opposition to civil rights became a national characteristic, a development that eroded the alliance between Republicans and southern Democrats.[1]

Following their losses in the 1960s, southern senators adapted to post–Jim Crow politics. Although in the twilight of his career, Richard Russell, for one, still had some moments of personal triumph. The retirement of Arizona's Carl Hayden after forty-two years of Senate service finally opened the chairmanship of the Appropriations Committee, a position the Georgian had long coveted but thought he would never attain because of Hayden's seeming immortality. On 3 January 1969, Russell was elected president pro tempore of the Senate, an honor bestowed on the chamber's most senior man. In March 1969, physicians discovered a tumor on Russell's left lung. The Georgian's health steadily declined until his 21 January 1971 death from pulmonary emphysema. Richard Russell outlived his beloved "southern way of life," but his historical legacy would forever remain linked with the cause to which he devoted much of his Washington career.

1. Numan V. Bartley, *The New South, 1945–1980* (Baton Rouge: Louisiana State University Press, 1996); Charles S. Bullock III and David W. Brady, "Party, Constituency, and Roll-Call Voting in the U.S. Senate," *Legislative Studies Quarterly* 8 (February 1983): 29–43; *Congressional Quarterly Weekly Report*, 1 August 1987, 1699–1705; Richard Fleisher, "Explaining the Change in Roll-Call Voting Behavior of Southern Democrats," *Journal of Politics* 55 (May 1993): 327–341; M. V. Hood III, Quentin Kidd, and Irwin L. Morris, "Of Byrd[s] and Bumpers: Using Democratic Senators to Analyze Political Change in the South, 1960–1995," *American Journal of Political Science* 43 (April 1999): 465–487; Keith T. Poole and R. Steven Daniels, "Ideology, Party, and Voting in the U.S. Congress, 1959–1980," *American Political Science Review* 79 (June 1985): 373–399; Kenny J. Whitby and Franklin D. Gilliam Jr., "A Longitudinal Analysis of Competing Explanations for the Transformation of Southern Congressional Politics," *Journal of Politics* 53 (May 1991): 504–518.

Many other caucus crusaders would also not live to see the full changes wrought by the legislation they desperately tried to prevent. Seventy-eight years old at the time of the voting rights debate, Harry Byrd of Virginia scarcely outlived the political struggle over civil rights that spanned his entire Senate career. By 1965, Byrd's mental alacrity was clearly on the wane, at the same time the tide of Lyndon Johnson's Great Society programs subsumed his three-decades-long effort to control government spending. On 11 November 1965, Byrd announced his retirement owing to an inoperable brain tumor. Less than a year later he died. Byrd's Virginia colleague, A. Willis Robertson, ended his career in 1968 and died two years later. Only five days after Robertson's death, Floridian Spessard Holland also passed on. One year later, a major heart attack felled Allen Ellender of Louisiana.

Other southerners enjoyed greater longevity. North Carolina's Sam Ervin resigned in December 1974, John McClellan of Arkansas died in office in late 1977, and Alabama's John Sparkman remained a senator until his January 1979 retirement. In 1980, Herman Talmadge's political career culminated in electoral defeat following a damaging public Senate investigation into his campaign and office expenses. Russell Long, who balanced both liberal and conservative policy preferences, weathered the political storm created by the large influx of black voters and closed his career in 1987. Two years after the Louisianan's retirement, Mississippi's John Stennis ended his Senate tenure. For Strom Thurmond, the conservatism that marked his civil rights position endeared him to his constituents, who reelected him until his January 2003 Senate retirement at the age of one hundred. The combative South Carolinian died a few months later.

For other southern senators, too, civil rights played an important if somewhat different role in shaping their political futures. At age seventy-four, Alabama's Lister Hill opted against a reelection bid in 1968. His advancing years certainly played a role in his decision, but observers noted something deeper. In 1962, Hill barely pulled out a narrow reelection triumph, a crushing blow to a man who since 1938 had done so much to help his fellow Alabamians. His near-defeat sprang from one source—a perception that he was "soft" on civil rights. Hill, of course, participated in every organized southern filibuster and never voiced discontent with the nature of race relations produced by Jim Crow. Nonetheless, many in the electorate saw his liberal policy views, at a time of grave crisis in the South, as a dangerous liability. Alabamians nevertheless elected Hill, but he had received an important message that race mattered more than all of his efforts in procuring federal funding for his constituents. Bitter at the 1962 outcome, Hill refrained from seeking further elective office. He would spend the rest of his life, until his death in 1984, lobbying for medical research and affordable health care.[2]

Unlike Hill, who chose to end his own career, Arkansan J. William Fulbright lost his seat in a 1974 electoral thumping at the hands of Dale Bumpers. For Fulbright, the defeat proved devastating. All of his years at the forefront of U.S. diplomacy as chairman of the Senate Foreign Relations Committee mattered little to his constituents. Fulbright neglected his state that year, allowing Bumpers, who courted the black electorate, to capitalize on the sitting senator's close association with Jim Crow. Furthermore, Fulbright's opposition to the Vietnam War alienated scores of his conservative constituents. In an ironic twist, Fulbright, the southern senator Strom Thurmond considered the least devoted to white supremacy, fell by the wayside because he followed the lead of Richard Russell when his heart was elsewhere. Southern politics after the second Reconstruction was no longer predictable.

Despite their eventual defeat, southern senators profoundly influenced the course of the civil rights struggle. Caucus members carried on a successful rearguard battle that delayed the collapse of segregation far longer than anything that occurred on the state level. Their success resulted from the moderating influence of strategic delay. Before the 1950s, southern senators recognized that the emerging civil rights movement, then in its nascent stages, would one day culminate in an assault against Jim Crow. In order to slow the anticipated attack, they changed how they conceptualized and fought civil rights battles. Under the auspices of strategic delay, southern senators believed that civil rights activists sought the end of segregation no matter what their stated intentions, and that northern politicians would acquiesce to black demands, no matter how unreasonable, to remain in office. As a result southerners began viewing the civil rights fight in broader terms, analyzing, in particular, how their actions impacted opinion above the Mason-Dixon line. Strategic delay demanded more than tactical flexibility; it also required a shift in rhetoric that enabled the region's senators to counter

2. In 1956, Hill ran unopposed. Six years later he received 201,937 votes, 50.9 percent of the total, compared to his Republican challenger James D. Martin's tally of 195,134 votes or 49.1 percent of the total. *Congressional Quarterly's Guide to U.S. Elections,* 2nd ed., 609.

the influence of civil rights pressure groups. Caucus members offered their colleagues more nonracial arguments in behalf of segregation. In large part southern senators adopted strategic delay to mitigate perceptions that white southerners were recalcitrant, unreconstructed rebels. The ideology they espoused served as the public face of Jim Crow, a more moderate alternative to offset the negative perception of the region created by episodes such as the Emmett Till lynching, the Ole Miss riots, and the excesses at Birmingham perpetrated by Bull Connor's police force. The segregationist ideology enunciated in the Senate reflected the values and principles of white southerners, who found their racial order or "way of life" under attack. It thus served as the primary vehicle through which white southerners transmitted their views regarding Jim Crow to outsiders. At the heart of segregationist ideology stood an assurance that whites below the Mason-Dixon line believed in the American political system and, more important, scrupulously followed the rule of law by upholding the Constitution as they claimed the founders had intended.

Most accounts of the civil rights movement tend to underscore the entrenched nature of the white South's strength, particularly in the U.S. Senate. These studies create a perception that breaching the caucus's Senate "citadel" required a herculean effort. On the other hand, southern senators viewed themselves as an embattled minority who could only stem the tide of civil rights activism by utilizing all of the parliamentary and rhetorical tools at their disposal. Many southern caucus participants recognized the possibility of defeat long before the *Brown* decision or the proliferation of grassroots demonstrations. By the presidential administration of Harry Truman, the tenor of the speeches and correspondence of southern senators grew more pessimistic. Early in the civil rights battle, southerners painted a bleak picture of their diminishing prospects for victory, even when circumstances indicated otherwise. The historical legacy of the Lost Cause, to which caucus members often made reference, provided a perfect safety valve if and when defeat arrived. To a region whose seminal historical experience proved a military defeat and a subsequent armed occupation, the words of those in the front lines of the civil rights battle struck a resonant chord. Southerners were a proud people, but a people acutely aware of their own history. The frequent juxtaposition of the civil rights fight and the Confederate war effort deliberately undertaken by caucus members linked the two battles in the southern conscious, making the resultant defeat in the former struggle far less crushing than it was in the latter. With the Lost Cause providing a precedent for quixotic battles within the region's historical memory, it became possible for southern senators to soften the blow of their Washington failure by stressing their own valiant fight against overwhelming odds.

An analysis of southern resistance to civil rights in the Senate also reveals the interconnection between white opposition and black protest. On the one hand, the skillful manipulation of tactics and rhetoric undertaken by southern senators played a pivotal role in garnering the support of their northern colleagues. In turn, the goodwill they won became crucial in preventing the passage of substantive civil rights legislation for decades. Their success in putting a moderate face on southern resistance never carried over to the state level. Although they often privately criticized the negative impact of the demagogue on their fight in Washington, they publically remained silent or even praised southern race baiters. If they had brought their considerable influence to bear on the state level by encouraging minor electoral reforms and helping rectify the worst discrepancies in the "separate but equal" doctrine, they might have at least temporarily defused the focus of civil rights activists. Instead, they did little, which helped precipitate the conditions that exacerbated African American discontent. More important, caucus members could not break from the constraints imposed upon them by their birthright. They grew up in the Jim Crow South and accepted, often without question, the region's central myths, especially the contention that segregation produced racial tranquility. Even when they conceded the existence of disparities between the quality of life enjoyed by blacks and whites, they maintained that time would rectify the discrepancies they claimed were a vestigial remnant of slavery. For southern senators, the important issue proved not Jim Crow's shortfalls, but how much the region's black citizens had advanced since emancipation. African Americans, who had heard such claims before, were in no mood to wait. Taken together, the success of southern resistance in Washington and the racial discrimination that occurred below the Mason-Dixon line demonstrated to black activists that only an aggressive, grass-roots protest campaign could produce the necessary political pressure to right the wrongs of the Jim Crow South. To rally northern opinion to their side, African American leaders needed a new approach to counteract the strength of both southern resistance and northern indifference. The nation had to see the oppression of Jim Crow that all blacks living in the South experienced on a day-to-day level, not the mythological portrait of segregation as it existed in the minds of white southerners.

The grass-roots protest movement undermined the ability of southern senators to sell Jim Crow's central myths to outsiders. When that happened, they could no longer continue their defense of white southern interests. Throughout the civil rights fight, southern senators recognized that northerners shared the same racial sensitivities as they did, but those above the Mason-Dixon line had yet to fully understand the rationale behind southern animosity. When the Civil Rights Act and Voting Rights Act passed, many northerners believed that the southern black community had righteousness on its side. As David Garrow reveals in *Protest at Selma*, Martin Luther King recognized after the failure of the Albany, Georgia, demonstrations in 1961–62 that white violence against peaceful protestors was an essential ingredient for rallying northern opinion in favor of black equality. During the same period, King also discovered that protest efforts lost much of their effectiveness if they lacked a clear, easily articulated message and if black demonstrators themselves resorted to violence. When white officials acted with restraint, black demonstrators departed from nonviolence, or a protest effort lacked a clear agenda, Garrow contends, northern sentiment rarely rallied behind civil rights activists. Events after the Selma protest that led to the passage of the Voting Rights Act demonstrate the validity of Garrow's theory.[3]

From the Watts riot in 1965 through the end of the decade, a host of racial disturbances swept across northern cities, an event President Johnson had expected. In a 1965 telephone conversation with Arkansan John McClellan, Johnson warned that southern racial disturbances in Birmingham and Selma would pale in comparison to the one's he expected when "the rats get going in Harlem and Chicago." Black violence turned northern opinion against the black community as Dixie legislators had long predicted would occur once citizens above the Mason-Dixon line came face to face with the turmoil formerly relegated to the South. With their cities experiencing riots, looting, and property destruction, northerners reassessed their initial take on the nobility of the civil rights fight. The moral imperative of the black struggle formerly illustrated in the South, according to many, grew increas-

3. David J. Garrow, *Protest at Selma: Martin Luther King, Jr., and the Voting Rights Act of 1965* (New Haven, Conn.: Yale University Press, 1978).

ingly difficult to perceive after 1965. Protests against the country's involvement in Vietnam only exacerbated the perception held by the vast majority
of Americans that the nation was under siege by subversive elements. Civil
rights protests in the early 1960s exposed the myth at the heart of segregationist ideology. War protests, the decadence of the counterculture, and the
riots of the late 1960s threatened national tranquility and convinced many
Americans of the need to change the country's direction. In 1968 and again
in 1972, the nation demonstrated its dissatisfaction with the liberalism that
many thought responsible for the unraveling of America by electing Republican Richard Nixon to the presidency. Taking a page from southern senators,
Nixon won those elections on a message of law, order, and constitutionalism that sounded remarkably like the rhetoric employed by the caucus in
its thirty year fight against civil rights. The southern view of politics had
become the American view. Had southerners delayed the implementation of
substantive civil rights legislation a few years later, they might have fulfilled
the preeminent objective of strategic delay—extending the life of segregation. If the legislative fight over Jim Crow had taken place in the context of
black violence in 1968 or 1969, rather than of white violence in 1964, the
caucus would very likely have had much greater northern assistance after
citizens above the Mason-Dixon line stopped drawing distinctions between
nonviolent protests against legitimate evils and seemingly senseless riots that
lacked a clear agenda. African Americans no doubt would have achieved legal and political equality by the twenty-first century, but precisely when and
after how much further suffering remains far less certain. Fortunately for the
United States, the country was never required to find out.[4]

4. Michael R. Beschloss, *Reaching for Glory: Lyndon Johnson's Secret White House Tapes,
1964–1965* (New York: Simon and Schuster, 2001), 237 ("the rats get . . ."); Geoff Andrews, ed.,
New Left, New Right and Beyond: Taking the Sixties Seriously (New York: St. Martin's Press, 1999);
John M. Blum, *Years of Discord: American Politics and Society, 1961–1974* (New York: Norton,
1991); James W. Button, *Black Violence: The Political Impact of the 1960s Riots* (Princeton, N.J.:
Princeton University Press, 1978); Dan T. Carter, *George Wallace, Richard Nixon, and the Transformation of American Politics* (Waco, Tex.: Markham Press Fund, 1992); Todd Gitlin, *The Sixties:
Years of Hope, Days of Rage* (New York: Bantam Books, 1987); Allen J. Matusow, *The Unraveling
of America: A History of Liberalism in the 1960s* (New York: Harper and Row, 1984); David Obst,
Too Good to Be Forgotten: Changing America in the 60s and 70s (New York: J. Wiley and Sons,
1998); Rick Perlstein, *Before the Storm: Barry Goldwater and the Unmaking of the American Consensus* (New York: Hill and Wang, 2001); Adolph Reed Jr., ed., *Race, Politics, and Culture: Critical Essays on the Radicalism of the 1960s* (Westport, Conn.: Greenwood Press, 1986); Adolph L.

When one considers southern politics after the second Reconstruction, the results are not surprising. White southerners with conservative ideological tendencies gravitated to the Republican Party in a political realignment that would have appalled earlier generations of southerners. To them the GOP was the party of Lincoln, the party that freed the slaves and tried to put "black heels on white necks" during Reconstruction. By the twentieth century, the Republican Party took black voter loyalty for granted, making little effort to keep this constituent base satisfied. Over time, blacks transferred their allegiance from the Party of Lincoln to the Party of Roosevelt. The national Democratic Party moved to the left of its southern base and soon contested the Republican monopoly on civil rights. Seniority on Capitol Hill and the plum committee assignments it afforded, kept southerners from bolting sooner. But ideologically, on a host of issues, conservative southerners shared much more in common with Republicans than with nonsouthern Democrats. With the defense of segregation ended and the perks of seniority eroding under a wave of reform of the national legislature, little remained to keep the region solidly Democratic. What better sign that it was time to leave the party than when longtime civil rights crusader Hubert Humphrey won the 1968 Democratic nomination? The other candidates that year, George Wallace running for the American Independent Party and Richard Nixon the Republican challenger, stressed the same issues only differing in the degree of their intensity. They railed against the lawlessness associated with black and antiwar protests, the profligacy of welfare programs, and the unchecked growth of the federal government. Ideas such as these played well among white southerners long accustomed to hearing such rhetoric from the Democratic Party. Aside from Texas, which voted for Humphrey, the remainder of the South split its vote between Wallace and Nixon.

In 1972, the solid South, which was never wholly solid, was solid again—solidly Republican. It would remain that way until the rise of Bill Clinton in 1992. The Republican Party grew by leaps and bounds in the region, receiving an influx of disgruntled white Democrats who had grown disenchanted with the party of their forebears. Today the GOP has a powerful presence in the South, just as the region once again has a two-party system, which

Reed, *Stirrings in the Jug: Black Politics in the Post-Segregation Era* (Minneapolis: University of Minnesota Press, 1999); Tom Wells, *The War Within: America's Battle Over Vietnam* (Berkeley and Los Angeles: University of California Press, 1994).

had all but disappeared as a result of electoral reforms in the 1890s. White moderates now hold the balance of power in most southern states, voting either Democratic or Republican based on the issues and, more important, on the candidate. Following passage of the Voting Rights Act, black voters gravitated toward the Democratic Party, which was once committed to their oppression. But this was no longer the house of Vardaman, Tillman, Bilbo, or even Woodrow Wilson. It was a party that embraced an array of social issues of interest to African Americans. It was a party no longer committed to delaying the dream.

Note on Sources

CIVIL RIGHTS HISTORIOGRAPHY remains varied and ever changing. Based on the voluminous outpouring of work on the subject, any effort to organize the literature will surely neglect some seminal studies. The following is an effort to provide readers with a point of departure for their own research.

Many historians employ a biographical approach to civil rights by telling the story of the central actors in the struggle for equality. In many cases they attempt to use the life of one person to capture the essence of the movement. Examples of this approach include David J. Garrow, *Bearing the Cross: Martin Luther King, Jr. and the Southern Christian Leadership Conference* (New York: W. Morrow, 1986); Stephen B. Oates, *Let the Trumpet Sound: The Life of Martin Luther King, Jr.* (New York: Harper Perennial, 1982); Michael E. Dyson, *I May Not Get There from Here: The True Martin Luther King, Jr.* (New York: Free Press, 2000); Paula F. Pfeffer, *A Philip Randolph: Pioneer of the Civil Rights Movement* (Baton Rouge: Louisiana State University Press, 1990); and Denton L. Watson, *Lion in the Lobby: Clarence Mitchell, Jr.'s Struggle for the Passage of Civil Rights Laws* (New York: Morrow, 1990).

Borrowing the methodological framework of slave studies, several scholars have eschewed the biographical approach in an attempt to tell the story of rank-and-file protestors. These studies seek to animate a people who left little written record. For example, see Jack M. Bloom, *Class, Race, and the Civil Rights Movement* (Bloomington: Indiana University Press, 1987); James W. Button, *Blacks and Social Change: Influence of the Civil Rights Movement in Southern Communities* (Princeton: Princeton University Press, 1989); William Chafe, *Civilities and Civil Rights: Greensboro, North Carolina and the Black Strug-*

gle for Freedom (New York: Oxford University Press, 1980); Richard A. Couto, *Ain't Gonna Let Nobody Turn Me Round: The Pursuit of Racial Justice in the Rural South* (Philadelphia: Temple University Press, 1991); John Dittmer, *Local People: The Struggle for Civil Rights in Mississippi* (Urbana: University of Illinois Press, 1994); Sara Evans, *Personal Politics: The Roots of Women's Liberation in the Civil Rights Movement and the New Left* (New York: Knopf, 1979); Richard H. King, *Civil Rights and the Idea of Freedom* (Athens: University of Georgia Press, 1996); and Stephen F. Lawson, *In Pursuit of Power: Civil Rights and Black Politics in America Since 1941* (Philadelphia: Temple University Press, 1991).

Many historians avoid efforts to write a synthetic work on civil rights, choosing instead to focus on singular events, limited time periods, or any other smaller and more manageable aspect of the struggle. For works focusing on singular events, see Dan Carter, *Scottsboro: A Tragedy of the American South* (Baton Rouge: Louisiana State University Press, 1979); David R. Colburn, *Racial Change and Community Crisis: T. Augustine, Florida, 1877–1980* (New York: Columbia University Press, 1985); Robert J. Norrell, *Reaping the Whirlwind: The Civil Rights Movement in Tuskegee* (New York: Columbia University Press, 1985); Glenda A. Rabby, *The Pain and the Promise: The Struggle for Civil Rights in Tallahassee, Florida* (Athens: University of Georgia Press, 1984); Mary A. Rothschild, *A Case of Black and White: Northern Volunteers and the Southern Freedom Summers, 1964–1965* (Westport, Conn.: Greenwood Press, 1982); Howard Smead, *Blood Justice: The Lynching of Mack Charles Parker* (New York: Oxford University Press, 1986); and Stephen J. Whitfield, *A Death in the Delta: The Story of Emmett Till* (New York: Free Press, 1988).

For works that highlight legal developments, see Michael R. Belknap, *Federal Law and Southern Order: Racial Violence and Constitutional Conflict in the Post-Brown South* (Athens: University of Georgia Press, 1987); David Garrow, *Protest at Selma: Martin Luther King, Jr. and the Voting Rights Act of 1965* (New Haven: Yale University Press, 1978); Charles V. Hamilton, *The Bench and the Ballot: Southern Federal Judges and Black Voters* (New York: Oxford University Press, 1973); Richard Kluger, *Simple Justice: The History of Brown v. Board of Education and Black America's Struggle for Equality* (New York: Knopf, 1976); Steven F. Lawson, *Black Ballots: Voting Rights in the South, 1944–1969* (New York: Columbia University Press, 1976); Charles Whalen and Barbara Whalen, *The Longest Debate: A Legislative History of the 1964 Civil Rights Act* (Cabin John, Md.: Seven Locks Press, 1985); and J. Harvie Wilkinson III,

From Brown to Bakke: The Supreme Court and School Integration, 1954–1978 (New York: Oxford University Press, 1979).

For presidential handling of civil rights, see William C. Berman, *The Politics of Civil Rights in the Truman Administration* (Columbus: Ohio State University Press, 1970); Carl M. Brauer, *John F. Kennedy and the Second Reconstruction* (New York: Columbia University Press, 1977); Robert F. Burk, *The Eisenhower Administration and Black Civil Rights* (Knoxville: University of Tennessee Press, 1984); Donald McCoy and Richard Reutten *Quest and Response: Minority Rights and the Truman Administration* (Lawrence: University Press of Kansas, 1973); and Allan Wolk, *The Presidency and Black Civil Rights: Eisenhower to Nixon* (Rutherford, N.J.: Fairleigh Dickinson University Press, 1971).

Civil rights organizations are also a popular subject of historical monographs. Some of these works include Clayborne Carson, *In Struggle: SNCC and the Black Awakening of the 1960s* (Cambridge: Harvard University Press, 1981); Herbert H. Haines, *Black Radicals and the Civil Rights Mainstream, 1954–1970* (Knoxville: University of Tennessee Press, 1988); Thomas R. Peake, *Keeping the Dream Alive: A History of the Southern Christian Leadership Conference and Martin Luther King, Jr.* (Athens: University of Georgia Press, 1987); Mark V. Tushnet, *The NAACP's Legal Strategy Against Segregated Education, 1925–1950* (Chapel Hill: University of North Carolina Press, 1987); and Robert J. Zangrando, *The NAACP Crusade Against Lynching, 1909–1950* (Philadelphia: Temple University Press, 1980).

Several important studies of white resistance to civil rights have been written in the aftermath of the landmark civil rights bills of the 1960s. For examples of this approach, see Numan V. Bartley, *The Rise of Massive Resistance: Race and Politics in the South During the 1950s* (Baton Rouge: Louisiana State University Press, 1969); Numan V. Bartley and Hugh D. Graham, *Southern Politics and the Second Reconstruction* (Baltimore: Johns Hopkins University Press, 1975); Earl Black, *Southern Governors and Civil Rights: Racial Segregation as a Campaign Issue in the Second Reconstruction* (Cambridge: Harvard University Press, 1976); Dan Carter, *The Politics of Race: George Wallace, the Origins of the New Conservatism, and the Transformation of American Politics* (New York: Simon and Schuster, 1995); David Chappell, *Inside Agitators: White Southerners in the Civil Rights Movement* (Baltimore: Johns Hopkins University Press, 1994); James W. Ely Jr., *The Crisis of Conservative Virginia: The Byrd Organization and the Politics of Massive Resistance* (Knoxville: University of Tennessee Press, 1976); Stephan Lescher, *George Wallace: American Populist* (Reading: Perseus, 1994); Neil McMillen, *The Citizens' Council: Organized Resistance to the Second Reconstruction, 1954–1964* (Urbana: University of Illinois Press, 1971); I. A. Newby, *Challenge to the Court: Social Scientists and the Defense of Segregation, 1954–1966* (Baton Rouge: Louisiana State University Press, 1967); and Roy Reed, *Faubus: The Life and Times of an American Prodigal* (Fayetteville: University of Arkansas Press, 1997).

Selected Bibliography

GOVERNMENT PUBLICATIONS

U.S. Congress. House. Appendix to the *Congressional Record*. Radio address by Hon. Lyndon B. Johnson. 75th Cong., 3rd sess. *Congressional Record*, 5 January 1938, vol. 83, pt. 1.

———. House. Debate and Procedure on Anti-Lynching Legislation. H.R. 801. 76th Cong., 3rd sess. *Congressional Record*, 10 January 1940, vol. 86, pt. 1.

———. House. Debate and Procedure on the Civil Rights Act of 1957. H.R. 6127. 85th Cong., 1st sess. *Congressional Record*, 18 June 1957, vol. 103, pt. 7.

———. House. Motion to Adjourn rather than Discuss an FEPC measure. 79th Cong., 2nd sess. *Congressional Record*, 5 June 1946, vol. 92, pt. 5.

———. Senate. Debate and Procedure on the Civil Rights Act of 1957. H.R. 6127. 85th Cong., 1st sess. *Congressional Record*, 7 June–10 July 1957, vol. 103, pts. 7–8.

———. Senate. Debate on Alteration of Rule XXII. 81st Cong., 1st sess. *Congressional Record*, 3 March 1956, vol. 95, pt. 2.

———. Senate. Debate on Alteration of Rule XXII. 85th Cong., 1st sess. *Congressional Record*, 3 January–1 March 1957, vol. 103, pts. 1–2.

———. Senate. Debate on Civil Rights Act. H.R. 627. 84th Cong., 2nd sess. *Congressional Record*, 19–27 July 1956, vol. 102, pts. 10–11.

———. Senate. Debate and Procedure on the Civil Rights Act of 1957. H.R. 6127. 85th Cong., 1st sess. *Congressional Record*, 11 July 11–8 August 1957, vol. 103, pts. 9–10.

———. Senate. Debate and Procedure on the Civil Rights Act of 1957. H.R. 6127. 85th Cong., 1st sess. *Congressional Record*, 9–30 August 1957, vol. 103, pts. 11–12.

———. Senate. Declaration of Constitutional Principles. 84th Cong., 2nd sess. *Congressional Record*, 12 March 1956, vol. 102, pt. 4.

MANUSCRIPT COLLECTIONS

Albert Gore Center, Middle Tennessee Sate University, Murfeesboro
    Albert Gore Sr. Papers
Alderman Library, University of Virginia, Charlottesville
    Harry F. Byrd Papers
Allen J. Ellender Memorial Library, Nicholls State University, Thibodaux, La.
    Allen J. Ellender Papers
Center for Regional Studies, Archives, Southeastern Louisiana University, Hammond
    AFL-CIO Collection
    Hebert Collection
    James H. Morrison Collection
Claude Pepper Library, Florida State University, Tallahassee
    Claude D. Pepper Papers
    Spessard L. Holland Papers
Hill Memorial Library, Louisiana State University, Baton Rouge
    Overton Brooks Papers
    Russell B. Long Papers
    Robert Mann Collection
Library of Congress, Washington, D.C.
    Thomas Connally Papers
Lyndon Baines Johnson Library, Austin, Texas
    Lyndon Baines Johnson Papers
        House of Representatives Papers
        Lyndon Baines Johnson Archives
            Congressional Files
            Famous Names
            Selected Names
    Pre-Presidential Confidential Files
    Senate Papers: Oral History Collection
McCain Library, University of Southern Mississippi, Hattiesburg
    Theodore G. Bilbo Papers
Mullins Library, University of Arkansas, Fayetteville
    J. William Fulbright Papers
Richard B. Russell Library, University of Georgia, Athens
    Richard B. Russell Papers
    Herman E. Talmadge Papers
South Caroliniana Library, University of South Carolina, Columbia
    Olin Johnston Papers
Southern Historical Collection, University of North Carolina, Chapel Hill
    Sam J. Ervin Papers

Strom Thurmond Institute, Clemson University, Clemson, S.C.
James F. Byrnes Papers
J. Strom Thurmond Papers
W. S. Hoole Special Collections Library, University of Alabama, Tuscaloosa
Lister Hill Papers
John Sparkman Papers

NEWSPAPERS, PERIODICALS, AND ANNUALS

Atlanta Constitution
Baton Rouge States-Item
Dallas Morning News
Harper's Magazine
Kansas City Star
Life
Look
Memphis Commercial Appeal
Morning Advocate (Baton Rouge)
Nation
New Orleans Item
New Republic
Newsweek
New York Times
Saturday Evening Post
Shreveport Journal
Time
U.S. News and World Report
Washington Post.

ARTICLES

Alsop, Stewart. "Johnson Speaking." *Saturday Evening Post* 231 (24 January 1959): 13–15, 38–43.
Billington, Monroe. "Lyndon Johnson and Blacks: The Early Years." *Journal of Negro History* 62 (January 1977): 26–42.
Bullock III, Charles S., and David W. Brady. "Party, Constituency, and Roll-Call Voting in the U.S. Senate." *Legislative Studies Quarterly* 8 (February 1983): 29–43.
Congressional Digest. "The Committee System—Congress at Work." *Congressional Digest* 34 (February 1955): 47–49, 64.
Dalfiume, Richard M. "The 'Forgotten Years' of the Negro Revolution." *Journal of American History* 55 (June 1968): 90–106.

Davidson, Bill. "Lyndon Johnson: Can a Southerner Be Elected President?" *Look* 23 (August 1959): 63–71.

Divine, Robert A. "The Cold War and the Election of 1948." *Journal of American History* 59 (June 1972): 90–110.

Finkle, Lee. "The Conservative Aims of Militant Rhetoric: Black Protest During World War II." *Journal of American History* 60 (December 1973): 692–713.

Fleisher, Richard. "Explaining the Change in Roll-Call Voting Behavior of Southern Democrats." *Journal of Politics* 55 (May 1993): 327–341.

Gray, Charles H. "A Scale Analysis of the Voting Records of Senators Kennedy, Johnson, and Goldwater, 1957–1960." *American Political Science Review* 55 (September 1965): 615–621.

Hood, M. V., III, Quentin Kidd, and Irwin L. Morris. "Of Byrd[s] and Bumpers: Using Democratic Senators to Analyze Political Change in the South, 1960–1995." *American Journal of Political Science* 43 (April 1999): 465–487.

Huie, William B. "The Shocking Story of Approved Killing in Mississippi." *Look* 20 (24 January 1956): 44–50.

Huitt, Ralph K. "Democratic Leadership in the Senate." *American Political Science Review* 55 (June 1961): 333–344.

Klarman, Michael J. "How Brown Changed Race Relations: The Backlash Thesis." *Journal of American History* 81 (June 1994): 81–118.

Meier, August, and John H. Bracey Jr. "The NAACP as a Reform Movement, 1909–1965: To Reach the Conscience of America." *Journal of Southern History* 59 (February 1993): 3–30.

Poole, Keith T., and R. Steven Daniels. "Ideology, Party, and Voting in the U.S. Congress, 1959–1980." *American Political Science Review* 79 (June 1985): 373–399.

Rable, George C. "The South and the Politics of Anti-Lynching Legislation, 1920–1940." *Journal of Southern History* 51 (May 1985): 201–220.

Shuman, Howard E. "Senate Rules and the Civil Rights Bill: A Case Study." *American Political Science Review* 51 (December 1957): 955–977.

Sitkoff, Harvard. "Harry Truman and the Election of 1948: The Coming of Age of Civil Rights in American Politics." *Journal of Southern History* 37 (November 1971): 597–616.

Steele, John L. "A Kingmaker or a Darkhorse?" *Life* 40 (25 June 1956): 111–124.

Whitby, Kenny J., and Franklin D. Gilliam Jr. "A Longitudinal Analysis of Competing Explanations for the Transformation of Southern Congressional Politics." *Journal of Politics* 53 (May 1991): 504–518.

White, William S. "Two Texans Who Will Run the Congress." *New York Times Magazine*, 30 December 1956, 5, 17, 20.

———. "Men of More than Distinction: Who Really Runs the Senate?" *Harper's Magazine* 214 (January 1957): 73–79.

Williamson, Joel. "Wounds Not Scars: Lynching the National Conscience and the American Historian." *Journal of American History* 83 (March 1997): 1221–1253.

Wood, Randall B. "Dixie's Dove: J. William Fulbright, the Vietnam War, and the American South." *Journal of Southern History* 60 (August 1994): 533–52.

Wynn, Neil A. "The Impact of the Second World War on the American Negro." *Journal of Negro History* 6 (1971): 42–53.

BOOKS

Adams, Sherman. *Firsthand Report: The Story of the Eisenhower Administration.* New York: Harper and Brothers, 1961.

Ader, Emile B. *The Dixiecrat Movement: Its Role in Third Party Politics.* Washington, D.C.: Public Affairs Press, 1955.

Ambrose, Stephen. *Eisenhower: Soldier and President.* New York: Simon and Schuster, 1990.

Ashmore, Henry S. *Hearts and Minds: The Anatomy of Racism from Roosevelt to Reagan.* New York: McGraw-Hill, 1982.

Ayers, Edward L. *The Promise of the New South: Life After Reconstruction.* New York: Oxford University Press, 1992.

Badger, Anthony J. *The New Deal: The Depression Years, 1933–1940.* New York: Hill and Wang, 1988.

Baker, Robert, with Larry King. *Wheeling and Dealing: Confessions of a Capitol Hill Operator.* New York: Norton, 1978.

Barnard, William D. *Dixiecrats and Democrats: Alabama Politics, 1942–1950.* University: University of Alabama Press, 1974.

Beals, Melba. *White Is a State of Mind: A Memoir.* New York: G. P. Putnam's Sons, 1999.

Becnel, Thomas A. *Senator Allen Ellender of Louisiana: A Biography.* Baton Rouge: Louisiana State University Press, 1995.

Bell, Inge Powell. *CORE and the Strategy of Non-Violence.* New York: Random House, 1968.

Berman, Daniel M. *A Bill Becomes Law: Congress Enacts Civil Rights Legislation.* 2nd ed. New York: Macmillan, 1966.

Berman, William C. *The Politics of Civil Rights in the Truman Administration.* Columbus: Ohio State University Press, 1970.

Berry, Mary Frances. *Black Resistance/White Law: A History of Constitutional Racism in America.* New York: Appleton-Century-Crofts, 1971.

Beschloss, Michael R. *Taking Charge: The Johnson White House Tapes, 1963–1964.* New York: Simon and Schuster, 1997.

Bilbo, Theodore G. *Take Your Choice: Separation or Mongrelization.* Poplarville, Miss.: Dream House, 1947.

Blum, John Morton. *V Was for Victory: Politics and American Culture During World War II.* New York: Harcourt Brace Jovanovich, 1976.

Blumberg, Rhoda Lois. *Civil Rights: The 1960s Freedom Struggle.* Rev. ed. Boston: Twayne, 1991.

Bone, Hugh A. *Party Committees and National Politics.* Seattle: University of Washington Press, 1960.

Boulware, Marcus H. *The Oratory of Negro Leaders, 1900–1968.* Westport, Conn.: Negro Universities Press, 1969.

Brauer, Carl M. *John F. Kennedy and the Second Reconstruction.* New York: Columbia University Press, 1977.

Brinkley, Alan. *The End of Reform: New Deal Liberalism in Depression and War.* New York: Alfred A. Knopf, 1995.

Brown, Walter J. *James F. Byrnes of South Carolina: A Remembrance.* Macon, Ga.: Mercer University, 1992.

Burdette, Franklin L. *Filibustering in the Senate.* Princeton, N.J.: Princeton University Press, 1940.

Burk, Robert. *The Eisenhower Administration and Black Civil Rights.* Knoxville: University of Tennessee Press, 1984.

Byrd, Robert C. *The Senate, 1789–1989: Addresses on the History of the United States Senate.* Washington, D.C.: Government Printing Office, 1988.

Byrnes, James F. *All in One Lifetime.* New York: Harper, 1958.

Campbell, Ernest Q. *Christians in Racial Crisis: A Study of the Little Rock Ministry.* Washington, D.C.: Public Affairs Press, 1959.

Caro, Robert. *The Years of Lyndon Johnson: Master of the Senate.* New York: Knopf, 2002.

———. *The Years of Lyndon Johnson: Means of Ascent.* New York: Knopf, 1990.

———. *The Years of Lyndon Johnson: The Path To Power.* New York: Knopf, 1982.

Carter, Dan T. *The Politics of Rage: George Wallace, the Origins of the New Conservatism, and the Transformation of American Politics.* New York: Simon and Schuster, 1995.

Cashman, Sean Dennis. *African-Americans and the Quest for Civil Rights, 1900–1990.* New York: New York University Press, 1991.

Claney, Paul R. *Just a Country Lawyer: A Biography of Senator Sam Ervin.* Bloomington: Indiana University Press, 1974.

Cobb, James C., and Michael V. Namorato, eds. *The New Deal and the South: Essays.* Jackson: University Press of Mississippi, 1984.

Cohen, Lizabeth. *Making a New Deal: Industrial Workers in Chicago, 1919–1939.* New York: Cambridge University Press, 1990.

Conkin, Paul K. *Big Daddy from the Pedernales: Lyndon Baines Johnson.* Boston: Twayne, 1986.

Connally, Tom. *My Name Is Tom Connally.* New York: Thomas Y. Crowell, 1952.

Cook, Robert. *Sweet Land of Liberty? The African-American Struggle for Civil Rights in the Twentieth Century.* New York: Longman, 1998.

Dabney, Dick. *A Good Man: The Life of Senator Sam J. Ervin.* Boston: Houghton Mifflin, 1976.

Dallek, Robert. *Flawed Giant: Lyndon Johnson and His Times, 1961–1973.* New York: Oxford University Press, 1998.

———. *Lone Star Rising: Lyndon Johnson and His Times, 1908–1960.* New York: Oxford University Press, 1991.

Dawley, Alan. *Struggles for Justice: Moral Responsibility and the Liberal State.* Cambridge: Harvard University Press, 1991.

Diamond, Robert A., ed. *Congressional Quarterly's Guide to U.S. Elections.* Washington, D.C.: Congressional Quarterly, 1975.

Dierenfield, Bruce J. *Keeper of the Rules: Congressman Howard W. Smith of Virginia.* Charlottesville: University Press of Virginia, 1987.

Donaldson, Gary A. *Truman Defeats Dewey.* Lexington: University Press of Kentucky, 1999.

Dray, Philip. *At the Hands of Persons Unknown: The Lynching of Black America.* New York: Random House, 2002.

Drury, Allen. *A Senate Journal, 1943–1945.* New York: McGraw-Hill, 1963.

Dugger, Ronnie. *The Politician: The Drive for Power from the Frontier to Master of the Senate.* New York: Norton, 1982.

Dulles, Foster Rhea.. *The Civil Rights Commission, 1957–1965.* East Lansing: Michigan State University Press, 1968.

———. *Labor in America: A History.* New York: Thomas Y. Crowell, 1966.

Eisenhower, Dwight D. *The White House Years: Waging Peace, 1956–1961.* Garden City, N.Y.: Doubleday, 1956.

Evans, Rowland, and Robert Novak. *Lyndon Johnson: The Exercise of Power.* New York: New American Library, 1966.

Fairclough, Adam. *Better Day Coming: Blacks and Equality, 1890–2000.* New York: Viking, 2001.

Farmer, James. *An Autobiography of the Civil Rights Movement.* New York: Arbor Press, 1985.

Foster, Gaines M. *Ghosts of the Confederacy: Defeat the Lost Cause and the Emergence of the New South.* New York: Oxford University Press, 1987.

Frederickson, Kari A. *The Dixiecrat Revolt and the End of the Solid South, 1932–1968.* Chapel Hill: University of North Carolina Press, 2001.

Freidel, Frank. *F. D. R. and the South.* Baton Rouge: Louisiana State University Press, 1965.

———. *Franklin D. Roosevelt: A Rendezvous with Destiny.* Boston: Little, Brown, 1990.

Freyer, Tony Allen. *The Little Rock Crisis: A Constitutional Interpretation.* Westport, Conn.: Greenwood Press, 1984.

Garfinkel, Herbert. *When Negroes March: The March on Washington Movement in the Organizational Politics of the FEPC.* New York: Atheneum, 1969.

Garrettson, Charles Lloyd, III. *Hubert H. Humphrey: The Politics of Joy.* New Brunswick, N.J.: Transaction, 1993.

Garson, Robert A. *The Democratic Party and the Politics of Sectionalism, 1941–1948.* Baton Rouge: Louisiana State University Press, 1974.

Gaston, Paul. *The New South Creed: A Study in Southern Myth-making.* New York: Knopf, 1970.

Goldman, Eric F. *The Tragedy of Lyndon Johnson.* New York: Knopf, 1969.

Goldsmith, John A. *Colleagues: Richard B. Russell and His Apprentice, Lyndon B. Johnson.* Washington, D.C.: Seven Locks Press, 1993.

Goodwin, Doris Kearns. *No Ordinary Time: Franklin and Eleanor Roosevelt: The Home Front in World War II.* New York: Touchstone, 1995.

Gore, Albert. *Let the Glory Out: My South and Its Politics.* New York: Viking Press, 1972.

Gorman, Joseph B. *Kefauver: A Political Biography.* New York: Oxford University Press, 1971.

Green, A. Wigfall. *The Man: Bilbo.* Baton Rouge: Louisiana State University Press, 1963.

Grossman, James. *Land of Hope: Chicago, Black Southerners, and the Great Migration.* Chicago: University of Chicago Press, 1989.

Hall, Jacquelyn Dowd. *Revolt Against Chivalry: Jessie Daniel Ames and the Women's Campaign Against Lynching.* New York: Columbia University Press, 1979.

Hays, Brooks. *A Southern Moderate Speaks.* Chapel Hill: University of North Carolina Press, 1959.

Haynes, George H. *The Senate of the United States: Its History and Practice.* New York: Russell and Russell, 1960.

Huthmacher, J. Joseph. *Senator Robert F. Wagner and the Rise of Urban Liberalism.* Cambridge: Harvard University Press, 1968.

Johnson, Lyndon B. *The Vantage Point: Perspectives of the Presidency, 1963–1969.* New York: Holt, Rinehart, and Winston, 1971.

Johnson, Sam Houston. *My Brother Lyndon.* New York: Cowles, 1969.

Johnston, Erle. *I Rolled with Ross: A Political Portrait.* Baton Rouge: Moran, 1980.

Karabell, Zachary. *The Last Campaign: How Truman Won the 1948 Election.* New York: Knopf, 2000.

Kearns, Doris. *Lyndon Johnson and the American Dream.* New York: Harper and Row, 1968.

Key, V. O. *Southern Politics in State and Nation.* New York: Knopf, 1949.

Kirby, John B. *Black Americans in the Roosevelt Era: Liberalism and Race.* Knoxville: University of Tennessee Press, 1980.

Kirk, John A. *Redefining the Color Line: Black Activism in Little Rock Arkansas, 1940–1970.* Gainesville: University Press of Florida, 2002.

Kluger, Richard. *Simple Justice: The History of Brown v. Board of Education and Black America's Struggle for Equality.* New York: Knopf, 1976.

Laue, James H. *Direct Action and Desegregation, 1960–1962: Toward a Theory of the Rationalization of Protest.* New York: Carlson, 1989.

Lawson, Steven F. *Black Ballots: Voting Rights in the South, 1944–1969.* New York: Columbia University Press, 1976.

———. *In Pursuit of Power: Civil Rights and Black Politics in America Since 1941.* Philadelphia: Temple University Press, 1991.

———. *Running for Freedom: Civil Rights and Black Politics in America Since 1941.* 2nd ed. New York: McGraw-Hill, 1997.

Lemann, Nicholas. *The Promised Land: The Great Black Migration and How It Changed America.* New York: Knopf, 1991.

Leuchtenberg, William E. *Franklin D. Roosevelt and the New Deal, 1932–1940.* New York: Harper and Row, 1963.

Loevy, Robert D., ed. *The Civil Rights Act of 1964: The Passage of the Law that Ended Racial Segregation.* Albany: State University of New York Press, 1997.

Loveland, Anne C. *Southern Evangelicals and the Social Order, 1800–1860.* Baton Rouge: Louisiana State University Press, 1980.

Mann, Robert. *The Walls of Jericho: Lyndon Johnson, Hubert Humphrey, Richard Russell, and the Struggle for Civil Rights.* New York: Harcourt Brace, 1996.

Marable, Manning. *Race, Reform, and Rebellion: The Second Reconstruction in Black America, 1945–1990.* 2nd ed. Jackson: University Press of Mississippi, 1991.

Mathews, Donald G. *Religion in the Old South.* Chicago: University of Chicago Press, 1977.

Matthews, Donald R. *U.S. Senators and Their World.* New York: Knopf, 1960.

Matusow, Allen J. *The Unraveling of America: A History of Liberalism in the 1960s.* New York: Harper and Row, 1984.

McCollough, David. *Truman.* New York: Simon and Schuster, 1992.

McCoy, Donald R., and Richard T. Ruetten. *Quest and Response: Minority Rights and the Truman Administration.* Lawrence: University Press of Kansas, 1973.

McMillen, Neil R. *The Citizens' Councils: Organized Resistance to the Second Reconstruction, 1954–1964.* Champaign: University of Illinois Press, 1974.

Meier, August, and Elliott Rudwick. *CORE: A Study in the Civil Rights Movement, 1942–1968.* New York: Oxford University Press, 1973.

Metcalf, George R. *From Little Rock to Boston: The History of School Desegregation.* Westport, Conn.: Greenwood Press, 1983.

Miller, Merle. *Lyndon: An Oral Biography.* New York: G. P. Putnam's Sons, 1980.

Miller, William. *Fishbait: The Memoirs of the Congressional Doorkeeper.* Englewood Cliffs, N.J.: Prentice-Hall, 1977.

Mooney, Booth. *LBJ: An Irreverent Chronicle.* New York: Thomas Y. Cromwell, 1976.

———. *The Lyndon Johnson Story.* New York: Farrar, Straus, and Cudahy, 1956.

Moore, John R. *Senator Josiah Bailey of North Carolina: A Political Biography.* Durham, N.C.: Duke University Press, 1968.

Morgan, Chester M. *Redneck Liberal: Theodore G. Bilbo and the New Deal.* Baton Rouge: Louisiana State University Press, 1985.

Morgan, Ted. *FDR: A Biography.* New York: Simon and Schuster, 1985.

Newby, I.A. *Jim Crow's Defense: Anti-Negro Thought in America, 1900–1930.* Baton Rouge: Louisiana State University Press, 1965.

Oates, Stephen B. *Let the Trumpet Sound: A Life of Martin Luther King, Jr.* New York: Harper Collins, 1994.

Patterson, James T. *Congressional Conservatism and the New Deal: The Growth of the Conservative Coalition in Congress, 1933–1939.* Lexington: University Press of Kentucky, 1967.

Peck, James. *Freedom Ride.* New York: Simon and Schuster, 1962.

Pepper, Claude D. *Pepper: Eyewitness to a Century.* New York: Harcourt, Brace, Jovanovich, 1987.

Perman, Michael. *Struggle for Mastery: Disfranchisement in the South, 1888–1908.* Chapel Hill: University of North Carolina Press, 2001.

Phipps, Joe. *Summer Stock: Behind the Scenes with LBJ in '48: Recollections of a Political Drama.* Fort Worth: Texas Christian University Press, 1992.

Powledge, Fred. *Free at Last? The Civil Rights Movement and the People Who Made It.* Boston: Little, Brown, 1991.

Reed, Merl E. *Seedtime for the Modern Civil Rights Movement: The President's Committee on Fair Employment Practice, 1941–1946.* Baton Rouge: Louisiana State University Press, 1991.

Reed, Roy. *Faubus: The Life and Times of an American Prodigal.* Fayetteville: University of Arkansas Press, 1997.

Reedy, George. *Lyndon B. Johnson: A Memoir.* New York: Andrews and McNeel, 1982.

Riddick, Floyd M. *Senate Procedure: Precedents and Practices.* Washington, D.C.: Government Printing Office, 1981.

Rorabaugh, W. J. *Kennedy and the Promise of the Sixties.* New York: Cambridge University Press, 2002.

Ross, Irwin. *The Loneliest Campaign: The Truman Victory of 1948.* New York: New American Library, 1968.

Salmond, John A. *"My Mind Set on Freedom": A History of the Civil Rights Movement, 1954–1968.* Chicago: Ivan R. Dee, 1997.

Salter, J. T., ed. *Public Men: In and Out of Office.* Chapel Hill: University of North Carolina Press, 1946.

Sherrill, Robert. *Gothic Politics in the Deep South: Stars of the New Confederacy.* New York: Ballantine, 1968.

Sitkoff, Harvard. *A New Deal for Blacks: The Emergence of Civil Rights as a National Issue: The Depression Decade.* New York: Oxford University Press, 1978.

Smith, H. Shelton. *In His Image but . . . Racism in Southern Religion, 1780–1910.* Durham, N.C.: Duke University Press, 1972.

Spitzberg, Irving J., Jr. *Racial Politics in Little Rock, 1954–1964.* New York: Garland, 1987.

Steinberg, Alfred. *Sam Johnson's Boy: A Close-Up of the President from Texas.* New York: Macmillan, 1968.

Talmadge, Herman E. *Talmadge: A Political Legacy, a Politician's Life.* Atlanta: Peachtree, 1987.

Tindall, George B. *The Emergence of the New South, 1913–1945.* Vol. 10 of *A History of the South.* Baton Rouge: Louisiana State University Press, 1967.

Tower, John G. *Consequences: A Personal and Political Memoir.* Boston: Little, Brown, 1991.

Truman, Harry S. *Memoirs of Harry S. Truman: Years of Trial and Hope.* New York: Doubleday, 1956.

Unger, Irwin, and Debi. *LBJ: A Life.* New York: Wiley, 1999.

Weiss, Nancy J. *Farewell to the Party of Lincoln: Black Politics in the Age of FDR.* Princeton, N.J.: Princeton University Press, 1983.

Whalen, Charles, and Barbara. *The Longest Debate: A Legislative History of the 1964 Civil Rights Act.* Cabin John, Md.: Seven Locks Press, 1985.

White, William S. *Citadel: The Story of the United States Senate.* New York: Harper Collins, 1956.

Whitfield, Stephen J. *A Death in the Delta: The Story of Emmett Till.* New York: Free Press, 1961.

Wicker, Tom. *JFK and LBJ: The Influence of Personality Upon Politics.* Chicago: Ivan R. Dee, 1968.

Wilkinson, J. Harvie, III. *From Brown to Bakke: The Supreme Court and School Integration, 1954–1978.* New York: Oxford University Press, 1979.

Williams, Juan. *Eyes on the Prize: America's Civil Rights Years, 1954–1965.* New York: Viking Press, 1987.

Woodward, C. Vann. *Origins of the New South, 1877–1913.* Baton Rouge: Louisiana University Press, 1971.

———. *The Strange Career of Jim Crow.* 3rd ed. New York: Oxford University Press, 1974.

Wolters, Ronald. *The Burden of Brown: Thirty Years of School Desegregation.* Knoxville: University of Tennessee Press, 1984.

Work, Monroe N., ed. *Negro Year Book: An Annual Encyclopedia of the Negro, 1937–1938.* Tuskegee, Ala.: Negro Yearbook, 1937.

Yarnell, Allen. *Democrats and Progressives: The 1948 Presidential Election as a Test of Postwar Liberalism.* Berkeley and Los Angeles: University of California Press, 1974.

Zangrando, Robert L. *The NAACP Crusade Against Lynching, 1909–1950.* Philadelphia: Temple University Press, 1980.

THESES AND DISSERTATIONS

Dyer, Stanford P. "Lyndon B. Johnson and the Politics of Civil Rights, 1935–1960: The Art of Moderate Leadership." PhD. diss., Texas A&M University, 1978.

Schlundt, Ronald A. "Civil Rights Policies in the Eisenhower Years." PhD. diss., Rice University, 1973.

Index

www.ingramcontent.com/pod-product-compliance
Lightning Source LLC
Chambersburg PA
CBHW051950270326

41929CB00015B/2601